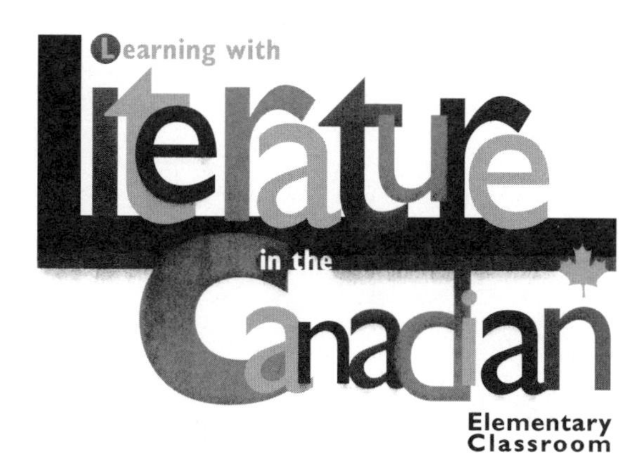
Learning with
Literature
in the
Canadian
Elementary
Classroom

To Paul, my husband and best friend.
– Love, S.P.

For Jordan Scott Levesque Edwards.
– J.B.

Learning with Literature in the Canadian Elementary Classroom

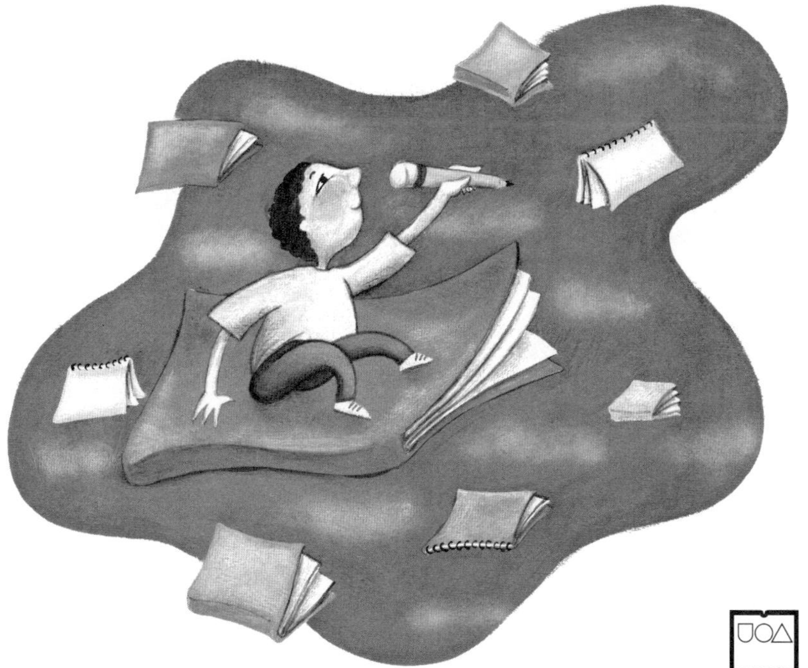

JOYCE BAINBRIDGE
& SYLVIA PANTALEO

The University of Alberta Press

DUVAL HOUSE PUBLISHING

Published by
The University of Alberta Press
Ring House 2
Edmonton, Alberta T6G 2E2
and
Duval House Publishing
18120 - 102 Avenue
Edmonton, Alberta T5S 1S7

Printed in Canada 5 4 3 2 1
ISBN 0-88864-330-6

Canadian Cataloguing in Publication Data
Bainbridge, Joyce, (date)
Learning with literature in the Canadian elementary classroom

Copublished by: Duval House Pub.
Includes bibliographical references and index.
ISBN 0-88864-330-6

1. Children's literature—Study and teaching (Elementary) 2. Language arts (Elementary) 3. Language arts—Correlation with content subjects. I. Pantaleo, Sylvia Joyce, (date) II. Title.
LB1575.5.C3B34 1999 372.64'044 C99-910720-8

∞ Printed on acid-free paper.
Printed and bound in Canada by Quality Color Press Inc.

The University of Alberta Press and Duval House Publishing acknowledge the financial support of the Government of Canada through the Book Publishing Industry Development Program for their publishing activities. The publishers also gratefully acknowledge the support received for their programs from the Canada Council for the Arts.

Canada

CONTENTS

PREFACE

Learning to read is one of the major educational challenges of childhood. We know a great deal about the process, but at its heart lies an ongoing mystery. Even readers themselves usually cannot describe what creates that moment when it all "clicks," when the marks on the page connect in the brain as words and then stories.

Reading involves decoding, but it also involves engaging, interpreting, enjoying. People who can only decode are a long way from developing the kinds of skills and strategies that will foster a lifelong connection to reading. And skills unused are apt to atrophy.

There is no instantaneous silver bullet that turns children into readers. At the heart of the process is the kind of daily, patient, consistent good practice that Joyce Bainbridge and Sylvia Pantaleo outline in this book. Making good books easily available, talking about selection strategies, reading books together, reading books privately, thinking and talking about the story, exploring some of the craft of writing and illustrating that makes a book successful: all of these activities are essential, irreplaceable, and profoundly time-consuming. At the same time, they lead to some of the most enjoyable moments in the classroom for both students and teachers.

In my view, working with readers revolves around two major premises. The first involves a bedrock of respect for the reader. You may not like what a child is reading, but if you do not respect the fact that the child is encountering the chosen text in a way that is meaningful to him or her, you may inadvertently undermine the child's whole relationship with the reading process. No matter what your own views of a particular title, it is possible, it is necessary, and it is usually highly instructive, to ask a question along the lines of, "What is it about this book that you like so much?" and to listen carefully to the answer. Aidan Chambers summed up the essence of this necessary question in two words: "Tell me." Listen to the young readers. Acknowledge what they have to say. Take them seriously as readers—a relationship that also involves proffering other titles and talking about the differences and similarities between stories.

The second principle is also a simple one: know the readers and know the books. Elementary school teachers are in a unique position to make links between particular individuals and particular books, but only if they pay serious attention to both. There is no substitute for reading children's books. This book offers a fine starting point with its lists of suggested titles.

There are two cautionary notes about reading books addressed to children. I have sometimes had to remind myself that only teachers read books to see how they can "use" them, and that this perspective is actually a very limiting one. In a related vein, I have sometimes registered that I needed to stop reading children's materials for a while and turn to some adult books, simply to keep my own reading muscles well exercised. If you want children to stretch themselves as readers, it is better not to forget what it feels like for yourself!

Books do many things for readers. They take them to new places or remind them of old places. They offer challenge or comfort, excitement or familiarity, surprise or recognition. In Canada, we have the advantage of access to books from many different countries and cultures. Our own home-grown children's literature is moving from strength to strength; at the same time we can also read books from many other countries— and do, and should. It is important for us to remember that students in many Canadian schools will have a definition of what is "familiar" that differs from that of their teacher and their classmates. Books that describe life in Canada are profoundly important, but for some readers such books can only ever describe a part of their own experiences. Books from other countries also provide a vantage point for understanding different perspectives. The experience of standing "inside" the skin of a fictional character, looking outwards into a culture that is familiar to the character but strange to the reader, is one of the ways that reading enriches our lives. For the duration of the book, we are not necessarily confined to looking at that culture only as an outsider; we can gain some sense of being an insider as well. A good example of how little we can take for granted about today's readers comes in the response of a Vietnamese-Canadian child to *My Kokum Called Today*, a picture book about a Cree grandmother: "I think this book is cool because it shows that Cree rule." The complexity of that culture-crossing response offers a window onto a new kind of world, one as close as the nearest classroom with a good stock of books.

Learning with Literature in the Canadian Elementary Classroom takes two premises very seriously. One is that it is highly important for Canadian children to have access to the many fine Canadian books now available to them. Anyone old enough to remember what it was like to grow up in a world so devoid of books related to your own experience that you assumed that books were always and automatically about *somewhere else* will appreciate this emphasis. Canadian children know their own world as real; they also need to know their own world as imagined and imaginable. At the same time, Bainbridge and Pantaleo remind us that the world of many Canadian children does not stop at the borders of this country, and that all our children also need to read about other places and other ideas. A good story is one of the best ways to move across borders and boundaries, and many examples of the importance of this experience are described within these pages. A great deal of hard work by a great number of highly committed people has transformed the Canadian children's publishing industry, and we all reap the benefits of that investment. But Bainbridge and Pantaleo never forget that true richness of reading involves stepping into many imaginary shoes, not just versions of the ones we wear every day.

The focus of this book is on fiction, and certainly all children need to explore the variety and excitement of fiction. There are those readers, even at a very young age, who will always be happier with some form of nonfiction, and their right to establish their own priorities should not be overlooked. Similarly, new and fascinating forms of text are being developed almost yearly, and today's young readers will encounter stories and information in a variety of media. However, the print-on-paper story, with or without accompanying illustrations, continues to be a vital part of our culture. The experience of reading, thinking about, discussing, and perhaps writing about print-on-paper stories enriches the mental and emotional lives of all children. To engage them in the lively process of making sense of meaningful and important stories is one of the privileges of teaching. This book offers a valuable toolkit for everyone involved.

Margaret Mackey
School of Library and Information Studies,
University of Alberta
Co-editor, North America,
Children's Literature in Education

ACKNOWLEDGEMENTS

We extend our sincere thanks to the University of Alberta Press and Duval House Publishing for preparing the manuscript for this book. We are especially grateful for the guidance of Leslie Vermeer, our editor, and we sincerely appreciate the expertise of Dr. Trevor Gambell of the University of Saskatchewan, who edited an earlier version of this manuscript. Thanks are also expressed to two friends and colleagues from "down under," Lyn Wilkinson of the Flinders University of South Australia, and Judy Thistleton-Martin of the University of Western Sydney, for their tremendous encouragement and help with aspects of literary theory and Australian children's literature.

Ingrid Johnson and Heather Blair, of the University of Alberta, and Frieda Maaskant, a teacher in Holman, Northwest Territories, provided invaluable expertise in assisting with the assembling of the multicultural materials. Additional thanks to Natalie Prytuluk for her help with picture song books; Karyn Cooper and Brenda Wolodko for their library searches; Shelley Peterson of the University of Toronto for her general help and encouragement; and Karen Day of the University College of the Cariboo for her support in this project. A very special thank-you to Jeffrey Canton, formerly at the Canadian Children's Book Centre in Toronto, who answered all of our inquiries! We extend our sincere thanks to Janet Fayjean and Marg Stephen of the Young Alberta Book Society, who assisted us in locating books and gathering information about authors and illustrators.

A very special acknowledgement is made to the detailed work of Paul Pantaleo, who was instrumental in preparing the appendix on children's literature websites and who helped with the proofreading of the children's literature references. His tireless support and patience are very much appreciated.

Finally, our thanks go to Mary Peace Effray, who worked diligently on formatting the manuscript. Her quiet attention to detail was invaluable.

INTRODUCTION

We approached the writing of a book on children's literature with very specific objectives. Having taught both undergraduate and graduate courses in children's literature in education, we were aware of the paucity of resource material that spoke directly to the Canadian educational and social context. We believed there was a need to write a book that would meet the requirements of undergraduate students (preservice teachers) and their instructors in teacher education programs across Canada. We also wanted to create a book that would be useful to teachers and graduate students studying the role of children's literature in the language arts.

It was important to us that we create a book that would explore children's literature, not as a subject unto itself, but as a vital and rich component of a balanced language arts program for Canadian elementary classrooms. We wanted the book to provide teachers with guidance in the design and implementation of learning strategies in reading, writing, and oral language. As a result, the activities suggested in this text address learning outcomes and expectations of Canadian elementary curriculum documents and programs of study in the language arts.

Our third consideration was that the book have a theoretically sound framework—a framework appropriate for a balanced language arts program. The book presents a reader-response orientation to the study of children's literature in Canadian elementary classrooms, and all our suggestions for learning activities derive from that philosophical stance. Reader-response is currently the most widely accepted theoretical framework for working with literature from kindergarten to college. A reader-response orientation acknowledges the *reciprocal* relationship between reader and text in the construction of meaning. Each reader brings a reservoir of life and literary experiences to the text and the literary work is brought into existence by the convergence of reader and text.

Finally, although international children's literature in the English language is discussed in the text, books by Canadian authors and illustrators are highlighted whenever appropriate. We have not attempted to recommend solely Canadian materials, fiction or nonfiction, for use in classrooms, as we do not believe that would serve the best interests of students or teachers. We have, however, deliberately suggested Canadian titles wherever possible because we strongly believe that Canadian children benefit from reading and studying high-quality Canadian literature. By reading Canadian literature, children can learn about and identify with their own cultural context, as well as with the cultures of those different from themselves.

This book contains resources (including Internet resources), criteria for selecting books, extensive book lists, and lists of award-winning Canadian books. Other features of the book include objectives for each chapter; profiles of Canadian authors and illustrators; reflection boxes that invite readers to think about their own reading experiences in light of the content of various chapters; vignettes of reading and response situations; and classroom scenarios that illustrate several instructional strategies. Further, the text promotes an understanding of the various genres of children's literature and their role in learning across the curriculum as well as in the language arts.

Chapter One establishes a context for the role of literature in the language arts program, exploring the relationship between the reading of good books and the process of learning to read (and becoming a reader). The chapter also looks at the selection of books for use in classrooms, and briefly examines censorship in the school context. In Chapter Two, we investigate the wide range of picture books available for children from preschool to the junior high grades. It includes a section on picture books for older readers and a section that highlights Canadian picture story books. We also discuss the contribution of illustrations to reading development, and the orchestration of illustrations and text to tell a story in picture books.

Chapter Three discusses the role of traditional literature and poetry in elementary classrooms, focussing on the importance of storytelling and the oral tradition. This chapter also presents ideas about sharing poetry and examines poetic devices and types of poetry. Chapter Four describes the various genres of fictional literature and the categories and topics within certain genres, as well as discussing the role of the classics in children's literature. The chapter includes a comprehensive discussion of both beginning novels and fictional literature appropriate for students in upper elementary grades.

Multicultural and transcultural literature, the focus for Chapter Five, includes materials by Aboriginal Canadians, books written in Aboriginal languages, and bilingual books. This chapter also presents criteria for examining the authenticity of multicultural and transcultural literature. Chapter Six describes various types of nonfiction, including narrative nonfiction, biographies, photodocumentaries, how-to books, experiment and activity books, question-and-answer formats, survey books, field guides, and picture song books. Criteria for selecting and assessing quality nonfiction books are also presented.

Chapter Seven provides an introduction to reader-response theories and encourages readers to consider the influence of various theoretical beliefs on the organization and implementation of literature- and response-based programs. In addition, this chapter examines the role of oral response in literature-based programs and presents a variety of activities that facilitate and encourage oral, visual, and dramatic responses to literature. Chapter Eight discusses the purposes of written responses in literature-based programs, including the organizational issues involved in working with written response and the many instructional issues related to the use of response journals. This chapter also examines the influential role of the teacher in structuring and implementing response-based programs.

The final chapter of the book, Chapter Nine, discusses organizing for instruction. We examine the issues involved in selecting literature for children, including children's reading interests and factors associated with reading motivation. Chapter Nine also describes various classroom organizational structures appropriate for literature- and response-based programs, such as novel studies, readers' workshops, individualized reading, thematic instruction, author studies, genre units, and topical units.

We hope you will find this book valuable to your work with children's literature in all curriculum areas, but especially in the language arts.

CHAPTER ONE

ESTABLISHING A CONTEXT FOR WORKING WITH LITERATURE

The objectives of this chapter are

- To establish a connection between reading literature (trade books) and learning how to read;
- To understand the importance of a reader's reading history;
- To make a connection between reading as a child and reading as an adult;
- To establish an awareness of the nature of selection and censorship issues in children's literature.

During shared reading time, two nine-year-old girls were reading *Very Last First Time* by Jan Andrews (1985). They were seated on the floor in a corner of the classroom. The quiet hum of their voices was suddenly disturbed by an exclamation and a rising intensity in their conversation.

"Her mom shouldn't have left her there. It's not right. It's too scary."

"No, it's not, look! She likes it there. She's exploring. Her mom will be back for her."

"What comes next? Turn the page."

The voices subsided, the hum resumed, and pages were flipped back and forth as the girls continued to explore the intricate story of *Very Last First Time.*

Probably the most exciting change in language arts instruction over the last twenty years has been the shift from a predominantly basal reader approach in teaching children how to read, to using children's literature and trade books on a daily basis in classrooms. The explosion of exciting literature written and illustrated for children, much of it Canadian, has contributed to this shift in instruction. It is clear to educators and researchers that children's literature is not a "frill," not something to be read when the "real" work is done. Researchers and scholars working with children and children's literature, along with many classroom teachers, have discovered that children's literature is an essential component of learning both how to read and how to appreciate reading as a pleasurable aesthetic experience.

A group of teachers working on a professional-development activity recently spent three hours poring over *Black and White* by David Macaulay (1990), *June 29th, 1999* by David Wiesner (1992), and *The Tunnel* by Anthony Browne (1989). The ensuing discussion focussed on postmodernism and metafiction, and included references to Italo Calvino's novel *If On a Winter's Night a Traveller* (1981) and Michael Ondaatje's novel *The English Patient* (1992). One might wonder what the relevance of these topics is to children learning to become readers and to love reading. What we have discovered is that it is not such a huge leap, after all, from books written for young readers to the work of authors such as Jane

Austen and the contemporary books that are becoming modern classics of adult literature. In *The English Patient*, Hana reads every night: "She entered the story knowing she would emerge from it feeling she had been immersed in the lives of others, in plots that stretched back twenty years, her body full of sentences and moments, as if awaking from sleep with a heaviness caused by unremembered dreams" (p.12). Most successful readers have similar experiences when they enter good books, and it is this experience that can be developed and nurtured through early interaction with books both in and out of school. The conversation about *Very Last First Time* reported at the beginning of this chapter is part of the meaning-making process that leads readers forward along this journey.

The Role of Literature in Language Arts

In the past, picture books were frequently viewed as books to be read to and with children *before* they could read competently for themselves. They were an entertainment for children, a reward for their efforts in attempting to read independently. Series books, such as *Goosebumps* and *The Baby-Sitters Club*, were regarded as largely undesirable in the school context, literature for the masses that had no role in helping youngsters to become literate and to develop as lifelong readers. Beginning novels (often called "chapter books" by children), such as *The Big Race* (McNicoll, 1996) and *Harold and Harold* (Wilson, 1995), were considered only as bridging materials designed to enable readers to make the transition from picture books to real novels. Nonfiction materials generally received little attention other than as information sources for written classroom reports. Fortunately, this discouraging picture of children's books has transformed radically in the last fifteen years.

Competent and avid adult readers often recollect fondly their visits to the bookmobile in the city, the arrival of the *Star Weekly* in the mailbox, the comics, their first library card, favourite books, and endless series books from *The Bobbsey Twins* and *Noddy* to *The Baby-Sitters Club*. From such recollections—and from all that has been written about teaching reading and the language arts—educators have come to embrace the concept of literature-based reading instruction, and many have created language arts programs based on trade books from many genres. The Children's Literature Round Table groups that meet across Canada and the excellent children's literature conferences, such as *Kaleidoscope* (held in Calgary every four years and sponsored by the Learning Resources Council of the Alberta Teachers' Association) and *Canadian Images Canadiens* (held in Winnipeg every four years and sponsored by the Manitoba School Libraries Association), underscore the recognition that children's literature receives in language arts education across all the grades from kindergarten onwards.

REFLECTION

Take a few moments to look back on your own reading history. Write a few paragraphs exploring your reading autobiography. Can you remember learning to read? Do you remember when you knew you could read? Did relatives or friends read to you? What are some of the earliest stories you remember? What were some of your favourite books?—favourite characters in books? Where and when did you read? Did you visit a library? Did your family subscribe to book clubs or to magazines? What do you read now? Do you have favourite authors and favourite books?

At this point, it is necessary to pause from a consideration of early reading experiences and favourite books to define what is meant by "children's literature." In this book, we use the term along with "trade books" and "literature written and illustrated for children." Today, these terms are used interchangeably. Not long ago, the term "children's literature" connoted an elite canon of "quality" books that largely included the classics, both old and contemporary, from *Anne of Green Gables* (Montgomery, 1908) to *Angel Square* (Doyle, 1984).

The term CHILDREN'S LITERATURE is used in this book to refer to those books, both fiction and nonfiction, that are acknowledged by critics to be of high quality, are well written, and provide children with pleasurable and challenging reading experiences. Reading good books connects us with the rest of the human race, letting us know that our feelings and experiences are not unique, but part of what makes us uniquely human. The term TRADE BOOKS has a broader definition, including all books published for pre-schoolers, young readers, and young adults that are not published as part of a basal reading series or as textbooks for use in schools; that is, they are published for the book trade. Trade books encompass many genres of literature including comics, series books, and magazines.

The term GENRE, a word borrowed from French, denotes a "literary species" or "literary form." Traditional genres include epics, tragedy, comedy, essays, biography, novels, and poetry. New forms have been added to this list, and the term genre is now used as a convenient (and somewhat arbitrary) way of classifying literary works, by describing a selection of literature which has certain common elements. The genres usually referred to in children's literature include picture books, classics, traditional literature (which may be subdivided into legends, myths, folktales, fairytales, and fables), historical fiction, contemporary realistic fiction, fantasy, science fiction, poetry, short stories, biography, and nonfiction. The latter may also be subdivided into a number of different categories or subgenres.

Angel Square by Brian Doyle

WHAT IS A GOOD BOOK?

If a book is regarded by critics, educators, and the public as "good," we must ask, what is it good for? Is it a challenging reading experience that will delight readers and help them become *better* readers by showing them something new? Is it suitable for taking on vacation and reading on the beach? Does it help to teach more about language arts skills or how to grow a beautiful garden on the prairies? Does it enable the reader to escape from real life and see it differently?

As a result of questions like these, teachers and librarians, as well as scholars of children's literature, understand that quality is not the same thing as popularity, and that describing the specific characteristics or features of "quality" literature is a complex undertaking. A book that demonstrates how to create a healthy tropical aquarium will differ enormously from a book of short stories. A book that is deemed to be so notable that one wants to keep a copy on one's bookshelf is likely to be very different from the paperback picked up as reading material prior to embarking on a long plane trip. The "quality" of each of these books varies according to the purpose of the author and to the purpose, interests, and reading experiences of the reader.

Over the years, children, parents, and, of course, teachers and librarians have decided what constitutes "quality" in a book produced for children. Many of the most prestigious awards for children's literature are awarded by library and other associations, with awards committees consisting solely of adults (such as the Amelia Frances Howard-Gibbon and Governor General's awards in Canada, the Caldecott and Newbery awards in the USA, and the Kate Greenaway and Carnegie medals in the UK). We know, however, that children's choices frequently vary from adult choices in terms of "good" literature. Children enjoy mystery, excitement, humour, and adventure. Teachers, on the other hand, often see these topical facets of a story as less important than the reader's ability to identify with and be interested in the characters. This latter element, not surprisingly, is not highly ranked by children. Because of this differential perception of quality, teachers often recommend books which may be good according to adult readers' tastes but which do not appeal to children's interests. As a result, children can learn to ignore teachers' suggestions for good books (Pantaleo, 1995).

In addition to the adult-determined awards for children's books, there are a number of Children's Choice Awards, usually at the regional level in Canada and at the state level in the USA. Voting for these awards is conducted through schools, and the awards are highly valued by authors and illustrators. Unfortunately, these awards are often not highly regarded by the critics, which raises questions about the perceived significance of children's interests and opinions about books, and also raises questions about the more prestigious awards and their intended purposes. There are many occasions, however, where both children's choices and adult choices of good books coincide. These books provide joyful meeting places where teachers, librarians, and children can share the excitement and pleasure of a good reading experience. The essential point in exploring what is meant by "good" or "quality" literature is an understanding that the definition changes with the audience and the context.

LITERATURE-BASED LANGUAGE ARTS

One major development largely responsible for spotlighting children's literature during the 1980s was the adoption of WHOLE LANGUAGE. Whole language, a term coined by Kenneth Goodman (1983), describes a philosophy about teaching reading, writing, and orality in a contextualized manner. One result of the acceptance of the principles of whole language has been a redefinition of reading. Where reading was at one time viewed mainly as "word-calling" (a child sounding out words), there is now a great deal more emphasis on the reader's construction of meaning from the words, symbols, and pictures on a page. A social constructivist perspective on learning has also reinforced the role of children's literature and reader response in language arts curriculum and instruction. Social constructivist theorists describe learning as being developmental, temporary (readily changing), internally constructed, and socially and culturally mediated (Fosnot, 1996). Hence, the meanings learners construct from their reading are mediated by the experiences of their lives, the specific situations in which they find themselves, and their discussions with teachers, family members, and peers.

Books written and published for children have, as a result of these and other developments, been accepted as the most appropriate vehicle for teaching children how to read, rather than using stories written specifically for basal reading series to teach reading. Basal reading series that are collections of excerpts from previously published works by well-known authors and illustrators have also been developed. Some of these works are modified for the basal series, but an attempt is usually made to retain as much as possible of the authentic voice and style of the author and illustrator. These basal series have now replaced the older ones, with their often didactic stories, restricted vocabulary, and simplistic plots. However, many teachers and schools have abandoned basal reading series entirely, realizing that, with a careful choice of books and appropriate instruction, children can learn to read from interesting and well-written, well-illustrated trade books.

Literature-based language arts instruction calls for increased knowledge and skill on the part of teachers. Not only are teachers called upon to know many children's books (including their titles, authors, themes, plots, characters, and structures), but they must also understand how books work and what the various literary techniques used in books teach to young readers. Literature-based instruction incorporates all the language arts and may involve such activities as novel studies, shared reading, drama work, art activities, puppetry, and journals and other kinds of writing, as well as book talks by children. As such, literature-based instruction requires a good deal of organization and knowledge of strategies such as literature circles and response groups. It also demands that teachers read the books their students are reading and be prepared to participate with children as they generate shared meanings from the works read.

What is the advantage of working with literature in the classroom? Even in the recent past, reading was often taught as if it were a set of discrete skills that readers learn in a sequential manner, eventually enabling them to become competent readers able to read at or above "grade level." Reading, however, is much more than the matching of written symbols with sounds, the acquisition of a reading vocabulary, and word meanings; reading ability is more than being able to answer someone else's questions about a text. Freebody and Luke (1990) describe four roles of a reader: code breaker, text participant, text user, and text analyst. They maintain that successful reading means being able to accomplish all four of these roles:

- *Being a code breaker involves understanding the sound-symbol relationship and the alphabetic principle.*
- *Being a text participant means developing the resources to engage the meaning systems of discourse: in their words, "the processes of comprehension call upon the reader to draw inferences connecting textual elements and background knowledge required to fill out the unexplicated aspects of text" (p.9).*
- *Being a text user means knowing how to use a variety of texts in real social contexts throughout daily life (i.e., knowing what to do with a text in a given social context; for example, reading a novel versus reading the instructions on a worksheet versus reading the label on a can or box).*
- *Being a text analyst means being a critical reader or having "conscious awareness of the language and idea systems that are brought into play when a text is used" (p.13). Here, Freebody and Luke are referring to the positioning of the reader with respect to the text: does the reader "buy into" the stance of the text or take a critical position in regard to the ideology of the text?*

We already know that many children learn to read from the reading materials they have in their homes long before they enter school. These often include trade books which, scholars, researchers, and teachers have learned, have a greater likelihood of teaching children to take on the four roles of the reader. The more contrived or artificial stories sometimes found in reading series are generally designed to encourage only code-breaking, while works of children's literature are more likely to challenge readers to make inferences, to analyze the text, and to predict events and outcomes. For example, in *Come Away from the Water, Shirley* (Burningham, 1977), the reader is encouraged not only to decode the text and read the words, but also to read the pictures which at first glance appear to have nothing at all to do with the words on the page. In order to construct a meaningful story, the reader must engage with the book as a text participant, text user, and text analyst. More than one story is being told in these pages; participating only as a code-breaker would create a limited story with little appeal to children.

Basal readers were developed at a time when teachers had very little professional training and few reading materials were available on a large scale for children. The basal reading series, along with the teachers' guides, were intended to be the basis of an instructional program in reading. They were to be "teacher-proof," meaning that any teacher could follow the directions in the teachers' guide and teach children to become competent readers. It was never intended that children do every exercise in the accompanying workbook or read every story in the basal reader. Nor was it intended that teachers *not* create alternatives to the activities suggested. Basal readers provided generations of children in North America with reading material where public and school libraries were not available. Basals were developed at a time when there was little material published for children, and many of the children's books that were in print were old and not necessarily of interest or relevance to contemporary readers. There are times even today when basal readers or specialized reading series can be very useful to teachers. If a large and varied collection of children's reading material is not available, or when a student has a particular learning need, a basal series may provide the resources necessary for instruction.

Children clearly need to learn code-breaking skills early in their lives, but they also need to learn to be text users, text analysts, and text participants if they are to become independent readers capable of constructing meaning from the texts they read. The nine-year-old girls described at the beginning of this chapter were using more than decoding skills to read *Very Last First Time*. They were also using more than the low-level comprehension strategies required in answering most comprehension questions found on worksheets. The girls were engaged in analyzing and inferencing, hypothesizing and reaching conclusions. They were responding to *Very Last First Time*, and, through their responses, they were at the same time understanding and creating the story that Andrews had begun for them. With the guidance of a competent teacher, children's literature provides the opportunity for students to learn both how to read and how to appreciate the ways in which texts work. The combination of the two creates rich possibilities for reading for pleasure and for information throughout life.

REFLECTION

What do you remember of your early reading instruction in school? Think back to your kindergarten or grade one classroom. Did your teacher group you for reading instruction? Did you read from a basal reader? Was there more than one series of books or more than one grade level of material used in your classroom? How did the teacher find out how well you could read? Did you engage in round-robin reading (taking turns to read a section of a story out loud)? Did you participate in response activities such as group discussions or journal writing about the books and stories you were reading? Did you visit the school library regularly and check out books to take home? Did you spend time in the library learning how to find the books you wanted and learning about the resource material that was available to help you in your school projects? Did your teacher talk with the class about well-known authors and illustrators and their work? Did your teacher introduce you to good books and encourage you to read them? Did published authors and illustrators visit your school to talk about their work?

Fifteen-month-old Oliver already enjoys books.

Literature and Literacy

Research in language learning and literacy development has consistently shown that one of the most important factors in a child's early literacy development is the amount a child is read to (and with) in the pre-school years. Gordon Wells' (1986) longitudinal study of language development, conducted in Britain during the 1970s, is one of the strongest pieces of evidence to support this claim. Early reading experiences also affect writing development and are influential in developing children's listening and comprehension skills. As we engage in what Yetta Goodman has described as "kid-watching" (Goodman, 1985), we see children who are less than a year old exploring books, sitting in a caregiver's lap, looking at the pages, and listening to the comforting and often musical and playful voice of the reader. Over a child's years in the elementary grades, reading and writing experiences play a huge role in learning across the curriculum. The more children read and are read to, and the more children talk about what they are reading and writing, the more successful they are likely to be in school and in their literacy endeavours.

THE EARLY YEARS

Oliver is fifteen months old. His mother has been reading to him and telling him stories since he was a tiny baby. Oliver will stop almost anything he is doing when he sees someone ready to read to him. He already has favourite books—Eric Carle's *The Very Busy Spider* (1984) and *The Very Hungry Caterpillar* (1968)—and he listens to stories with great interest. He watches the pictures and turns the pages. He watches his mother, often turning to look into her face as she reads. He reads along with her, matching his voice with her voice, mimicking the intonations of a story. Oliver is observant. He puts his fingers on parts of the picture that interest him.

He prevents his mother from turning the page if he is not yet ready to move on. Oliver cannot yet talk, but he certainly enjoys being read to.

Oliver is too young to read on his own, but he already knows what reading *is*, and he is learning that a book offers a pleasurable experience, that reading is a social activity, and that the contents of books and stories are interesting to him. These are all aspects of reading that are crucial in the later development of independent reading. The likelihood of Oliver's becoming a reader later in his life is increased with these early social experiences with books and his immediate family. These experiences with reading in his pre-school years will help him develop the sophisticated array of skills which Holdaway refers to as the "literacy set" (1979). From these experiences, and his later experiences with writing, Oliver will learn book-handling skills such as directionality—the front and back of a book, which way is the right way up and which way the story moves through the book. He will begin to develop decoding skills and recognize some of the basic patterns of stories, as well as many other necessary reading skills during this period of "emergent literacy." Oliver will learn mostly through experimentation and play, including activities such as the peek-a-boo games and nursery rhymes his family plays with him.

One of Oliver's favourite nursery rhymes is *Humpty Dumpty*. In this rhyme, as in many others, Oliver is exposed to the musical quality of a variety of language patterns: regular rhythm and rhyme; a definite sequence of events; a complete story with a beginning, a middle, and an end; a story that contains action, drama, and even tragedy (Humpty was doomed!). All this is achieved in four lines of verse—twenty-six words. Quite an accomplishment! The implications are profound. For Oliver, and most young children, nursery rhymes are appealing, can be committed to memory, and demonstrate that pictures help to tell a story (in the book versions). They introduce children to simple story structure, provide a vehicle with which to experiment with language, reflect children's interests, and can be a first introduction to the world of poetry and literature in general. Traditional literature, such as the nursery rhyme, provides a simply constructed pattern of narrative which helps the predictability of language and meaning. This pattern is apparently culturally universal. For example, researchers have concluded that there are over 1,000 different versions of Cinderella in existence, with 500 in Europe alone. Researchers such as Vladimir Propp (1968) have analyzed various folk tales, identified sequences of "functions" (or units), and generated models of story comprehension.

Each Peach Pear Plum by Janet and Allan Ahlberg (1978) is an extension of traditional literature. *Each Peach Pear Plum* contains illustrations rich in the detail of the nursery rhymes, folklore, legends, and fairy tales of western Europe. From books such as this one, children learn that reading is an active experience and that books are a way of obtaining pleasure and satisfaction. *Each Peach Pear Plum* can be used on a range of levels. The very young child, who is still unable to follow the plots of traditional stories, can enjoy the repetition of "each peach pear plum" and the rhyming patterns, as well as the predictability. Older children enjoy the humour derived from their prior knowledge of the fairy tales and nursery rhymes alluded to in the book.

The more experience with print that a child brings to the page, the greater the child's chance of reading success. That stored knowledge is vital, as there are numerous levels of information with print (Clay, 1985), just as there are a variety of roles for the illustrations in books. Illustrations can either support the text or tell their own story. Hence, the more children are immersed in print and in pictures, particularly in books, the greater their chances of becoming proficient readers. The language of books is generally different from the child's own oral language, although book language has changed in the last decade or so, with some books reflecting colloquial speech, as well as regional and cultural dialects. Familiarity with the sound of written language, however, remains an important factor in literacy development. This finding has powerful implications for children like Oliver, who are read to from birth. It also has powerful implications for those children who come from situations where reading is not common and is not regarded as a pleasurable and worthwhile endeavour.

READING REPERTOIRES

Margaret Meek (1988) is one of the scholars who has demonstrated how children come to understand *how texts work*, what constitutes a good book, how language can be used in different ways to create different meanings and effects, and how, in short, children become readers, not just people able to read. Young children first learn what reading is from picture books, and they learn how to read different kinds of books in different ways. For example, *Rosie's Walk* (Hutchins, 1969) contains thirty-two words, one sentence, and twenty-seven pages of pictures. It demands that more attention be paid to the pictures than to the text. If a reader reads only the text of this book, then only part of the story will be uncovered (a very small part!). *Granpa* (Burningham, 1984) requires that the reader read the text in two voices, as indicated by the regular typeface and the italics, one voice being Granpa's and the other voice being that of his granddaughter. *Rose Blanche* (Innocenti, 1985) requires a detailed and informed observation of the illustrations in order to comprehend the disturbing subtleties of the book. *The Disaster of the Hindenburg* (Tanaka, 1993) must be read with text, diagrams, photographs, maps, and charts integrated in order to facilitate understanding. Readers must move their eyes and mind from text to map to photograph and back again to comprehend the material. The strategies young readers learn and refine in these early experiences with books will assist them in reading more complex books later in their lives; this repertoire of strategies is continually built upon throughout a reader's life.

The reading of children's books such as *Each Peach Pear Plum* and *Granpa* is similar in many ways to reading such adult books as *The English Patient* or *The Englishman's Boy* (Vanderhaeghe, 1996). One of the similarities is in the role the reader must play. Readers of each of these books must be able to put together clues, question the text, and make inferences about the characters, setting and so forth in order to engage in a successful reading experience. Readers must risk being incorrect in their inferences and be willing to live with tentative "assumptions." In other words, the reading experience is active and fluid, and depends as much on the reader to create meaning as it does on the writer. Texts such as these are sometimes referred to as WRITERLY texts. In such texts, readers fill in gaps, draw inferences, make interpretations, generate hypotheses, and draw connections. Barthes (1970) states that writerly texts achieve plurality of meaning because different readers "write" them in different ways. He uses the term "scriptable" to describe such texts and the term "lisible" to describe what are now commonly called READERLY texts. In lisible texts, the writer has provided most of the information for the reader; the reader actually has to do very little work. Some texts even hint at what the reader should be feeling at certain points, and interpret settings and characters on the reader's behalf, rather than encouraging readers to make those interpretations and inferences for themselves. Children doubtlessly need both kinds of texts to become competent readers and writers, but they *must have* both kinds of texts if they are to grow as readers throughout their lives.

One characteristic of some writerly texts is that they contain gaps to be "filled in" by readers from their own experiences and imagination. The notion of textual gaps was first introduced by Wolfgang Iser (1978) and has since been developed by other notable scholars. Jack Thomson (1987, p.123) writes that "readers of literature use their experience of the world and their knowledge of the conventions of literature to fill in what the words of the text do not tell them." The more gaps the author leaves, the more demanding the book is for readers. Stephens and Watson (1994, p.10) point out that "there is some evidence to suggest that weak readers have failed to grasp the active nature of reading: they expect the text to do everything for them and therefore fail to fill in the gaps. It therefore seems important for students to realize quite explicitly that gap-filling is something all good readers do." In the image-saturated world of television and movies, there is little opportunity for the imagination to fill in gaps. Television shows, and most movies, are not constructed around gaps. Viewers generally expect the plot to unfold in a linear fashion and expect characters to be clearly established at the beginning of the show. Because there is so little opportunity for "gap filling" in the mass media, it is even more essential that youngsters be encouraged to attempt this activity in their reading and be presented with reading material which will enable it. It is this "gap filling" or inferencing that appears to be at the heart of reading, and readers of any age can only learn this art from reading books which leave gaps and challenge the readers' experience and imagination.

Burningham's *Granpa* and Alan Garner's *The Owl Service* (1967) can be described as writerly texts, books which seem to be created around gaps. The reader asks, how many stories are here? Times, places, and characters merge as the reader "bridges the gaps" and becomes a collaborator or co-author in the creation of meaning (Iser, 1978). These are not easy books to read, but they are well worth the time and effort required of them, and along the way, readers grow in their reading ability and in their understandings of the world.

Writerly texts engage the reader in other authoring strategies besides working with gaps. For example, there is the framed narrative, a strategy Janet and Allan Ahlberg use in *It Was a Dark and Stormy Night* (1993). The book begins:

> *It was a dark and stormy night, the rain came down in torrents, there were brigands on the mountains, and wolves, and the chief of the brigands said to Antonio, "I'm bored tell us a story!"*
> *Antonio was a small brave boy, eight years old, who had been kidnapped by the brigands and carried off to their secret cave. He scratched his curly head, puffed out his cheeks and said, "I don't know any stories."*
> *"Make one up," growled the chief.*
> *"Yeah," said the brigands. "Begin at the beginning."*
> *"Right-o!" Antonio said, and he paused for a moment—and began his story.*
> *"It was a dark and stormy night," said Antonio. (It was all he could think of).*

It Was a Dark and Stormy Night is a book of stories, of stories within stories, where it is left to the reader to work out which is which: who the narrator is (or are), whether it's the same narrator for each story, and where the stories begin and end. An adult example of this same technique is Henry James' *The Turn of the Screw* (1898), which opens with a group of house guests assembled on Christmas Eve around a large fire. Douglas, one of the guests, regales the others with a story, told over a number of evenings, about a governess and her two charges who were haunted by the ghosts of former employees of the family. James' story ends when the story told by Douglas ends. The reader must go back to the beginning of the story to find out, once again, how it all began, and ended.

A further authoring strategy in some writerly texts is the deliberate use of INTERTEXTUALITY (the ways in which a text relates to and depends upon the existence of other texts, both directly through reference and indirectly through allusion). The Ahlbergs make full use of intertextuality in *The Jolly Postman* (1986). They create a narrative for the book, but they situate within that narrative characters and events from other stories, such as *Goldilocks and the Three Bears* and *Robin Hood*. Anthony Browne does the same kind of thing in the illustrations in his books. *The Tunnel* (1989) features artifacts from traditional versions of *Little Red Riding Hood* and from Browne's own book *Gorilla* (1983), as well as from many other well-known stories.

Jon Scieszka's *The True Story of the Three Little Pigs* (1989) and Eugene Trivizas' *The Three Little Wolves and the Big Bad Pig* (1993) use parody as a way of creating writerly texts. These two texts rely on their readers' knowledge of the original story of the three little pigs to understand and appreciate the humour in the books. The reader must be "on the inside" or "in the know"—almost like belonging to a club with certain rules and rituals known only to members. Without the reader's prior knowledge, the humour of Scieszka's and Trivizas' books will not be fully appreciated, although the story can be accepted as a new story unto itself.

Black and White by David Macaulay (1990) is a picture book containing four stories (and potentially a fifth as the stories become one). On the title page, Macaulay presents the titles for the four stories in different quadrants of the page. Throughout the book, the four stories are told in the same quadrants of each page through illustrations and a small amount of text. This is an extremely sophisticated strategy which passive readers, expecting a simple narrative in a picture book, sometimes find frustrating. It is a book which must be approached as one approaches a game, as an interactive experience. Authors of books such as this one want the reader to maintain a certain distance from the text in order to think about what is happening in the stories. The book is constructed so that readers have to work at sense-making and cannot read the text as though the story is real. Thus, *Black and White* is an example of a metafiction.

METAFICTION is the deliberate attempt on the part of the author/illustrator to draw attention to a work of literature as a fictional construct. In most fiction, readers engage with the story and willingly suspend disbelief; in a good story, that disbelief is suspended indefinitely. A work of metafiction, however, deliberately makes the reader aware of the fictive nature of the work. The reader must examine his or her own role in creating the story and in engaging in the process of meaning-making. Thus bear, the central character in *Bear Hunt* (Browne, 1979), draws himself out of danger. The reader understands that this solution is a creation of the author, and the event underscores the nature of fiction itself. Macaulay takes this idea further in *Black and White* by telling a story in four separate narratives. The reader draws the connections among the stories and is thus reminded that storytelling is a fictional pursuit which can be accomplished in different ways by different people, each one creating a different story. In works of metafiction, "the words and concepts are linked through allusion, personal, often intimate reflections, asides, and rhythmic connectors—aligned nonsequentially" (Goldstone, 1998). Authors play with perception, representation, and interpretation, and usually refuse to provide closure or final, conclusive meaning. It is the metafictive, game-like feel of so many recent books for children and young adults that makes them intriguing—and challenging—for readers of all ages.

An innovative construction used successfully in some books for children and young adults is discontinuous narrative. Two especially powerful young-adult novels with this structure are by Australian writers: *Letters from the Inside* by John Marsden and *Strange Objects* by Gary Crew, both published in 1991. *Letters from the Inside* consists of a set of personal correspondence between two sixteen-year-old girls. Only the letters are provided for the reader; there is no connecting narrative text. It is up to the reader to construct the inferences necessary to fill in the gaps between the individual letters, thus creating a story. This book is shattering in its intensity. *Strange Objects* consists of a collection of documents relating to the disappearance of a sixteen-year-old boy. The documents are part of a "project book" which has been made public by a maritime archaeologist who provides a personal note at the beginning and end of the document set. The documents themselves are items from newspapers, the missing boy's journal entries, transcripts of audio-taped press conferences, archaeological reports, chapters from reference books, advertisements, and other artifacts. *Strange Objects* creates a memorable reading experience. Discontinuous narrative may be somewhat complex for children in the earlier grades, but the Ahlbergs use it successfully in *The Jolly Postman* (although they also provide a continuous narrative to accompany the various documents included inside the book). Discontinuous narrative is certainly a text structure to watch for in future literature for elementary children. The "trickle-down" effect of books written for adults and young adults is unmistakable, as can be seen in the picture books discussed in this chapter.

For example, in *Shortcut* (1995), David Macaulay explores cause-and-effect relationships. This sophisticated picture book consists of nine chapters and an epilogue. In the first chapter, Albert and his horse, June, take their weekly trek to town to sell their melons. Along the way, they take a shortcut and stop at the Railway Café for a rest. Two subsequent actions contribute to a dramatic chain of events, and the remainder of the book is devoted to a humorous string of seemingly unconnected occurrences: a missing pig, a hot-air balloon sailing out of control, a late train, a speeding driver, and a sinking boat. Each individual story within the book is connected to the other stories, but readers must examine the illustrations carefully in order to unravel and reconnect the multiple narratives.

One other text structure to be mentioned in this section is that of multiple narrators. Burningham used this structure in *Granpa*, where both Granpa and his granddaughter tell their stories on alternating pages of the book. Anthony Browne provides a further example in *Voices in the Park* (1998). Like Burningham, Browne uses different fonts to distinguish the four narrators, but he also devotes a "chapter" to each narrator/voice. The book moves from one voice (chapter) to another, sharing the individual perspectives of the characters as they describe their converging experiences in the park. In *Canyons* (1990), Gary Paulsen develops a story in which the first chapter is set in 1864. Here the reader meets Coyote Runs, a fourteen-year-old Apache boy about to participate in his first horse raid. The second chapter is set more than a hundred years later as readers are introduced to fourteen-year-old Brennan. Alternating chapters of the book continue their stories(set in two different fonts to represent the two boys). A tragedy befalls Coyote Runs during the horse raid, but more than a century later, Brennan is able to help in freeing Coyote Runs' spirit. The young-adult novel *Stone Cold* (Swindells, 1993) tells the story of a sixteen-year-old boy living on the streets of London, England. Between each of the chapters narrated in the voice of the boy are shorter inserts narrated by an unknown man. The identity of the man is not apparent until well into the book, when the paths of the two narrators cross. This technique creates tension in a most unusual way and adds to the intriguing nature of this Carnegie Medal-winning book.

Finally, some authors have created books about the act of storytelling—about the constructedness of texts (very much like *It Was a Dark and Stormy Night*). In *Aunt Isabel Tells a Good One* (Duke, 1992), Penelope asks her Aunt Isabel to tell her a story. When Aunt Isabel asks, "What kind of story?" Penelope answers, "A good story." Aunt Isabel tells Penelope that a good story is the hardest kind of story to tell because "We must put it together carefully, with just the right ingredients. When does the story begin?" Penelope says the story begins long, long ago. Aunt Isabel then asks where the story takes place, and asks Penelope to think of a place where exciting things can happen. Penelope decides the story must take place in a cave. At that point, Aunt Isabel begins her story. She continues to ask Penelope for input throughout the entire crafting of the story, but Penelope is not always satisfied and makes comments along the way. The cave is too scary. Certain problems should be left out. The result is a wonderful demonstration of how storytellers create their tales. *Aunt Isabel Tells a Good One* is strongly reminiscent of "William's Version" in Jan Mark's book of short stories, *Nothing To Be Afraid Of* (1981).

All of these strategies are part of the game a writer plays with the reader, and as with most games, they can be engaging. Such strategies draw the reader into the text, demanding that the reader be an active participant in the composition of the story. It is not possible to be a passive reader of these books. Sometimes the game appears to thwart the reader's best intentions. For example, John Fowles created a second epigraph or ending for his adult novel *The French Lieutenant's Woman* (1969). After completing the whole novel, the reader might expect an ending—the ending, not a choice from among the two provided by the author and the myriad possible others. In this instance, Fowles is reminding us that the book is a creation of both the author and the reader, and that it does not exist separate from either one of those: it is a fictive enterprise. Writerly texts are about readers "working" to understand a text and to engage with the writer in playing the game. Writerly texts are written by authors who are aware of their audience and of the fictive nature of their work. They are aware of the crucial constructive role the reader plays in the creation of a text.

BECOMING A READER

We now understand that reading is best taught in the context of "real" texts, but it is not until we look in detail at books like *Each Peach Pear Plum*, *Come Away from the Water, Shirley*, and *Rosie's Walk* that we fully understand the reading knowledge children garner from these books. Meek (1988) refers to these as "private lessons," the lessons good readers learn about reading without formal instruction. They are lessons young children frequently learn faster than their more "blinkered" adult companions, who have often become constrained by print and driven by plot. *Come Away from the Water, Shirley* tells one version of the story through the pictures (and through Shirley's eyes) and another version of the story through the text (through the parents' eyes). Some adults do not enjoy this structure, mainly because they don't "get it."

There is an important distinction to be made here between children learning *how to read* and children learning *how to become readers*. It is not a matter of one or the other, but of how children can effectively learn both at the same time. The distinction lies partly in how parents and teachers assist young readers in understanding how texts are structured. In novels from the eighteenth and nineteenth centuries, as well as in many novels from the beginning of the twentieth century, an authoritative orientation was provided by the author. The reader was left with few gaps to fill in. A moral stance was often provided, along with an explicit interpretation of the events, characters, and setting of the book. These books could be described as readerly texts. As Thomson (1987) points out, in contemporary works for adults and children, "there is no definitive frame of reference by which to judge the events of the narrative. There is an increasing complexity of narrative structures, with a range of perspectives, some or even all of which may be misleading or unreliable; there is an increase in the number of blanks; the logical, linear plot is a thing of the past" (p.125). One has only to read *Black and White* to understand fully what Thomson means. Today the moral is embedded in the text. We have moved from the didactic to the implied. This is a much more sophisticated enterprise, requiring a much more critical reading.

The complexity of many texts written for children, and how young readers respond to them, is more fully understood today than it was fifteen or twenty years ago. It would be extremely difficult to determine the "reading level," for example, of books such as *Black and White* and *June 29, 1999*. Comprehending these texts relies a great deal on understanding how texts work—that is, on the construction of the texts. Jonathan Culler has referred to the abilities involved in making meaning from texts as "literary competences" (1980). The more readers understand the options available to authors as they construct texts, the more they will "read" into the texts; as a result, their enjoyment of the texts will likely be heightened. It is also essential that young readers learn the "rules" of texts (Meek, 1988) through their reading and enjoyment of books. Authors play with these rules, creating new and fascinating challenges for readers, but if readers do not understand what is happening in the text, much of the pleasure in the book may be lost.

The narrative structure of textual material has changed enormously in recent years. It is no longer as predictable as it was in the days when the traditional tale ruled the world. The traditional structure then was "storytelling in print" (see Chapter 3 for a discussion of storytelling and oral literature). Although the art of storytelling is undergoing a revival, it has largely been a dying art, even among Aboriginal people. The lack of familiarity with storytelling is perhaps reflected in the changing structure of the written narrative. The structure of a traditional tale, such as *Goldilocks and the Three Bears*, is simple and linear. The narrative of a modern picture book, such as *Granpa*, is more complex, more sophisticated, and it uses such strategies as multiple narrators, framed narrative, and intertextuality, as well as illustrations in the telling of the story. It is very much a print form, for such structures are difficult to convey orally. However, such structures highlight the important role drama and theatre play in storytelling.

Although many children's books today demand more of their readers, presuming that readers already have the knowledge to engage with more sophisticated texts, some developing readers still need the predictability of the traditional tale. The greatly varying needs of readers make careful book choices a necessity, and early and continuous exposure to a wide range of reading materials is essential if children are to "fall in love" with reading and literature. Many children in Canadian classrooms today do not have rich and varied early literacy experiences; many do not have a western socio-cultural heritage and do not speak English as their first language. These social, political, and cultural aspects of literacy will not be addressed in this particular book, because many other books deal directly with these topics (Graff, 1987; Heath, 1983; Levine, 1986). However, access to books and multimedia, willing caregiver involvement, socio-economic considerations, and cultural background are all important factors in determining whether children will have successful experiences in early literacy, and must be considered when working with children and books in school.

Young readers, then, engage in a variety of different reading experiences depending on their cultural heritage, socio-economic background, and family support; and many engage in more sophisticated reading experiences than children of previous generations because they have access to more challenging, interactive, or writerly texts. These children are likely to grow up with different expectations of reading than children have done in the past, and they are also likely to have different reading skills. With informed and understanding guidance from their teachers, it should be possible for more of these children, as they mature as readers, to continue reading for pleasure as well as for information.

Selecting Literature for Children

Selecting appropriate literature for children is one of the major responsibilities of teachers in any school situation. Although there are many textbooks available for use in classrooms, most of the books used by children are trade books. Trade books can be used across the entire curriculum and are read for pleasure as well as for information. However, someone chooses the books that are on the school library shelves, and that person is also likely to be the person who decides what not to order for the collection. This is where a discussion of selection and censorship comes into play.

Many issues must be considered when selecting books for use in a school or classroom: the age and interests of the children, the curricular content being taught, the quality of available material, and the values we wish to present. Many Canadian books are available for elementary school children, but unless someone in the school makes a deliberate attempt to order Canadian materials and give them prominence in the reading and library programs, children are likely to miss much of this excellent literature.

CANADIAN LITERATURE FOR CANADIAN CHILDREN

Over the years, Canadians have become accustomed to receiving media largely from the United States and Britain; children's print materials are no exception. Most professional books currently available for teachers, especially those about multicultural literature, are from the United States, and they refer largely (and sometimes exclusively) to American books. The stories and experiences of Hispanic Americans, Afro-Americans, Chinese Americans, and other ethnic and cultural groups are not necessarily parallel to those of Canadian minority groups. Children need to see their own ethnic groups and their own cultures represented in the books they read. The Canadian Association of Children's Librarians was formed in 1932, establishing goals which include encouraging the writing and publishing of children's books in Canada. Yet until the 1980s, there were few Canadian publishers publishing children's materials, and Canadian authors and illustrators generally looked to the United States or Britain for publication of their work.

Canada's history in the creation of literature for children progressed slowly. It was not until 1945 that the first real picture book was published in Canada: *Ristonac* (Maillet, 1945), published by Éditions Lucien Parizeau in Montreal. The following year, the Canadian Library Association was formed, but it was not until 1967 that Tundra Books was established in Montreal, a publishing company devoted to the publication of Canadian materials. *The Republic of Childhood: A Critical Guide to Canadian Children's Literature* (Egoff) was also published in 1967 by Oxford University Press in Toronto. This was the first definitive guide to Canadian children's books in English and a turning point in the acceptance and promotion of Canadian children's books. The Amelia Frances Howard-Gibbon Award was first awarded by the Canadian Library Association in 1971, and the first Children's Literature Round Table was established (in Edmonton) in 1973. Following these events came Kids Can Press in 1973; the journal *Canadian Children's Literature* in 1975; the Canada Council Children's Literature Prizes in 1975; Annick Press in 1976; the Children's Book Centre (later the Canadian Children's Book Centre) in 1976; CANSCAIP (Canadian Society for Children's Authors, Illustrators and Performers) in 1977; Groundwood Books in 1977; the first Kaleidoscope Conference in Calgary in 1977; the first issue of *CM: Canadian Materials for Schools and Libraries* in 1980; and the first *Canadian Images Canadiens* conference in Winnipeg in 1986. In the 1980s, Canadian publishing companies began to produce Canadian basal reading series for schools rather than simply adding a few Canadian stories to American series. By the late 1980s, many strong Canadian publishing companies across the country were producing high-quality literature for children, changing the face of Canadian children's literature.

Today, a vast array of children's books is produced in Canada. The Canadian Children's Book Centre in Toronto (CCBC) publishes lists of books, information about authors, and a members' newsletter called *Children's Book News* (see sidebar).

CANADIAN CHILDREN'S BOOK CENTRE

The Canadian Children's Book Centre, located in Toronto, holds a collection of Canadian children's materials (available for browsing by members of the Centre) and extensive vertical files on Canadian authors, illustrators, and publishers. The Centre also produces a newsletter, *Children's Book News*, four times a year, which provides book reviews, information about authors and illustrators, lists of book awards and current winners, and information about author and illustrator visits to schools and libraries across Canada during Canadian Children's Book Week (held in November each year). The CCBC also annually publishes *Our Choice: Your Annual Guide to Canada's Best Children's Books and Videos*, an annotated list of books receiving the Our Choice Award. The newsletter and the *Our Choice* catalogue are available from CCBC at 35 Spadina Road, Toronto, Ontario, M5R 2S9. The e-mail address is ccbc@sympatico.ca; the website address is http://www3.sympatico.ca/ccbc/.

Why is it important to have Canadian materials in Canadian schools? It is generally believed that literature can be a powerful vehicle for the transmission of national culture anywhere in the world. For example, Jerry Diakiw writes that in "most culturally homogeneous countries, children grow up hearing and learning the stories that define their culture...and these shared stories lie at the heart of a culture's identity" (1997, p.37). Diakiw argues that there are powerful commonplaces in Canada's culture and identity—shared values that most Canadians can identify with—and that school is an important place to explore, discuss, and debate these commonplaces. One way to uncover them is through Canadian stories and literature. "Literature, arts and crafts, music, dance, film, and poetry blend together over time to crystallize an image that says, 'This is who we are'" (Diakiw, 1997, p.37).

Canada prides itself on its "cultural pluralism," where the importance of accepting different races, ethnicities, languages, and cultures is well recognized. Nieto describes this as "a model based on the premise that all newcomers have a right to maintain their languages and cultures while combining with others to form a new society reflective of all our differences" (1992, p.307). Yet Neil Bissoondath (1998) warns that Canada's policy of multiculturalism can lead to a reinforcement of stereotypes and a "gentle marginalization" of those who accept and display their ethnic heritage. He maintains that Canadian multiculturalism emphasizes difference and has retarded the integration of immigrants into the Canadian mainstream. A 1991 national survey found that, in general, "Canadians identify most strongly with being Canadian, rather than identifying with their ethnic origins" (Esses & Gardner, 1996, paragraph 21). Bissoondath comments that "we need to focus on programs that seek out and emphasize the experiences, values and dreams we all share as Canadians, whatever our colour, language, religion, ethnicity or historical grievance. And pursue acceptance of others—not merely tolerance of them" (1998, p.22).

Reading about Canadian people and Canadian places in the literature they encounter in their classrooms can enhance the possibilities that Canadian children will better know themselves and the country in which they live. Researchers understand that when children read aesthetically, they may identify with the characters, setting, or events of a story. However, until the last twenty years or so, Canadian children had little with which they could identify. Most Canadian children grew up with a canon of British literature, partly because Canada is a Commonwealth country but also because very little children's literature was published in Canada.

Today, a wide range of high-quality children's literature is published all across Canada, some of which is published by school districts and relatively small publishing houses. The increased publication of children's literature in Canada has had an impact on Canadian children's reading. Now, students can read about Canadian people and places from Peggy's Cove to Saskatoon, to Ungava Bay to Victoria. When they read Canadian materials, children can imagine the prairie, mountains, or seacoast, and they learn more about Canada and who they are as Canadians. It has been suggested by many scholars and writers (see Nodelman, 1997) that the land—the actual environment or physical landscape of Canada—characterizes the Canadian short story and perhaps even Canadian literature in general. *Mister Got To Go* by Lois Simmie (1995) is a charming picture book set at the Sylvia Hotel in Vancouver; *The Doll* by Cora Taylor (1987) is a time-slip novel set in Fort Carlton, Saskatchewan; and *Rebellion* by Marianne Brandis (1996) is a novel set in historical Toronto. Each of these books provides a different insight into Canada and what it means to be Canadian, and each relies profoundly upon the landscape in which it is set. Perhaps through reading Canadian literature, children can develop pride in being Canadian and an appreciation and understanding of Canada's role in the global community. Defining our identity as Canadians is a continuing process, one in which our students play an important role.

From Canadian books, children learn that Canadians can be authors and illustrators and that authors and illustrators live in places where the students might also live. Authors become real people, and writing and illustrating become possible professions. Well-known authors and illustrators now regularly visit schools, and some of the hard work and craft of writing and illustrating are demonstrated to children as they listen to artists read and speak about their published work. In addition to the Canadian Children's Book Centre, organizations across Canada—such as the various provincial arts councils and the Young Alberta Book Society—exist for the sole purpose of enhancing literacy development and introducing Canadian authors and illustrators to children in schools.

The Doll by Cora Taylor

It is particularly helpful to have good nonfiction books about Canada written and published by Canadians. *Buried in Ice* (Beatty & Geiger, 1992) is a book about the Franklin expedition that most children find intriguing. It tells a fascinating story, explores Canadian history, and displays what Canadian scientists and journalists do in their work. This story received international attention, allowing Canadians to take pride in their accomplishments and identify with their Canadian heritage.

SELECTION TOOLS

When selecting materials for inclusion in a classroom or school library, teachers and teacher-librarians make every effort to choose books that meet the needs of children as well as the needs of the curriculum. Knowledge of child development and the literary quality of books, as well as knowledge of the provincial programs of study or curriculum expectations, help teachers to make appropriate selections. Critics might say that book selection is simply a code for a librarian's own brand of censorship, but, as Roberts (1996) asserts, there are distinct differences between selection and censorship:

> *Selection is a positive process that supports intellectual freedom when the selector considers resources in a holistic manner with the intent of including as many as possible in the library collection. Resources are selected objectively, according to set criteria, without regard for a selector's personal biases. Conversely, censorship is a negative process in which the censor searches for reasons, either internal or external, to exclude a resource. (p.19)*

Sound selection decisions are guided by the quality of reading and learning, even when, as Booth (1992) says, "reading reveals unpleasant truths or viewpoints opposed to those of a particular parent or child, as long as the child is deemed capable of dealing with such ideas" (p.9).

The selection of print materials for use in schools is a complex issue, for it is difficult to say, in a public education system, who should decide what children should and should not read. The debate involves freedom of expression and touches beliefs about what is appropriate for children, what is moral and what is immoral, what is acceptable and what is not acceptable in society. It is highly likely that most children will confront difficult and disturbing ideas as they grow up. Reading and discussing a broad range of literature may contribute to children becoming critical thinkers and thoughtful human beings capable of making sound judgements, both as individuals and as members of society.

The Canadian Library Association issued a statement on intellectual freedom which was adopted by the Canadian School Library Association. Two parts of that statement are of particular relevance for educators. The first asserts that it is a person's fundamental right to have access to all expressions of knowledge, creativity, and intellectual activity, and to be able to express his or her thoughts publicly; the second states that libraries must guarantee and provide access to all expressions of knowledge and intellectual activity, including those elements that conventional society might deem unacceptable or unpopular (Canadian Library Association, 1974). Adults who endorse this statement, and who thereby advocate selection as opposed to censorship of materials, continue to have the right to object to books, but they do not insist on removing them from the library shelves so that others are denied access to them. Advocates of book selection also respect the child's intellectual freedom (and innate common sense) and believe that adults have an obligation to be honest with children. This approach to selection does not argue that all books for children are of equal quality and equal value, or even appropriate for children of all ages, but it does assert that children have the right of access to the best literature and learning resources available.

The most important thing teachers can do when engaged in the selection of materials is to be aware of their own biases and values, stay current with book publication and reviews, and maintain files of policy statements, useful resources, procedures for dealing with challenges to materials, and guidelines from recognized authorities. Teachers need to know whether or not their employing jurisdiction has a policy on challenges to books: they need to be familiar with any policy that is in place and follow it. There are many professional selection tools available to aid teachers and librarians in making book selections. Professional journals such as *Canadian Children's Literature*, *Resource Links*, *Language Arts*, *The Reading Teacher*, and *The Horn Book* provide assistance and support for teachers; they are by far the best resources for teachers to use in their quest to stay current with issues, themes, and individual book titles.

Canadian Children's Literature is published out of the University of Guelph, Ontario, and provides reviews of Canadian publications as well as articles about Canadian children's literature. It is by far the most prominent children's literature journal in Canada. The *Our Choice* catalogue, published annually by the Canadian Children's Book Centre in Toronto, is a categorized listing of the best materials published each year in Canada. It includes fiction and nonfiction books, as well as videos, CD-ROMs, audio cassettes, and CDs. *Children's Book News*, published four times each year by the Canadian Children's Book Centre, contains book reviews, articles, news, and information about children's literature events held across the country.

The *Canadian Book Review Annual* is an evaluative guide to Canadian-authored, English-language publications. It reviews the year's trade publications, scholarly materials, reference books, and children's publishing. The emphasis is on the analysis and evaluation of resources, with a description and brief information about the books' contents. Whole volumes are devoted specifically to children's literature. *Resource Links: Connecting Classrooms, Libraries & Canadian Learning Resources* is published five times each year for the Council for Canadian Learning Resources. It examines the availability and use of Canadian learning resources for K-12 (fiction and nonfiction), including print, electronic, or other media, in schools and libraries.

CM: Canadian Review of Materials is an electronic journal that reviews Canadian materials published for pre-kindergarten children to young adults (www.umanitoba.ca/cm/). Published by the Manitoba Library Association, the journal is designed for use by teacher-librarians, teachers, librarians, parents, and professionals working with young people. This impressive journal provides clear and interesting descriptions of books and profiles of authors and illustrators (including colour photographs). These detailed profiles include biographical sketches, the reasons why a person became an author or illustrator of children's books, what inspired the various publications, and the process the person went through when creating the book. A free trial offer of fourteen issues is available.

Language Arts (National Council of Teachers of English) contains a regular section of book reviews, both fiction and nonfiction. *Notable Children's Books*, produced by the American Library Association, is a list of books (not annotated) which have won awards in the United States in the preceding year; the list is published in the *School Library Journal*. *Children's Choices* is a list of newly published books that children themselves choose as outstanding; the list appears in *The Reading Teacher*. *The Horn Book Guide to Children's and Young Adult Books*, published twice a year in March and September, contains brief reviews of all hardcover children's trade books published in the United States in the previous six months. *The Horn Book Magazine* is published six times a year and includes detailed reviews of those books deemed the best in children's literature. It contains articles about and interviews with authors and illustrators, and it prints the acceptance speeches for the Caldecott and Newbery awards each summer. *School Library Journal* is published monthly by R.R. Bowker Publications and contains reviews written by librarians of most children's books published in the United States.

The publications listed above are but a few of the professional selection aids available for teachers. Professional librarians can provide further suggestions, and teacher-librarians will generally order these professional journals for school collections, if asked.

CENSORSHIP OF CHILDREN'S MATERIALS

As noted above, there is a clear difference between the selection of materials for use in schools and the censorship of these materials. Where book selection uses positive criteria to determine which books to place in a collection (Nodelman, 1992, calls this "books we approve of"), censorship seeks to remove, suppress, or restrict books *already present* in a collection. Censorship is unpredictable and can be extremely disruptive to the life of a school. School libraries and classrooms encounter far more challenges to books than do public libraries in North America (Schrader, 1996), which makes it imperative that teachers and librarians be informed about the issues and be prepared to debate the relative merits of materials selected for use in their schools. Educators have a responsibility to fulfill their professional obligations to learners by providing students with the very best in children's literature—material that challenges children to think critically and explore new ideas and perspectives. Teachers have a further role, however, as they can help their students to become more thoughtful and critical about their own choices of reading materials, further developing their abilities to think for themselves and make sound judgements.

Teachers are usually surprised to see the titles of some commonly challenged children's books and textbook series: *Bridge to Terabithia* by Katherine Paterson (1977), *The Paper Bag Princess* by Robert Munsch (1980), *Thomas's Snowsuit* by Robert Munsch (1985), *Who is Frances Rain?* by Margaret Buffie (1987), and the *Impressions Series* (Booth, Phenix, Pauli & Swartz, 1984-88). While teachers and librarians cannot predict what might cause offense—particularly because we know that individuals respond to literature in different ways depending on their experiences, values, culture, and background with reading literature—we do know that there are basically two directions from which challenges are made. One of these is from what has been termed the "conservative right," the other from the "liberal left" (Amey, 1988). The "conservative right" is generally concerned about issues of sexuality, obscenity, profanity, family values, secular humanism (though this is less of a concern in the late 1990s), witchcraft and the occult, new-age thought, and fantasy and mythology. The "liberal left" is more concerned about racism, gender issues, ageism, respect for the environment, violence, issues regarding the physically challenged, and multiculturalism—issues often linked with political correctness.

David Jenkinson at the University of Manitoba has conducted long-term research into the issue of censorship in Manitoba's public schools. His first study explored the censorship of materials in 1982-84; in 1993, he conducted a follow-up study. Jenkinson sought to identify who challenged what, why, and with what results. The 1993 study shows that challenges to books increased in the ten years since the first study, with a far greater increase in urban areas than rural areas of the province. Most significantly, materials were much more likely to be removed from libraries in rural areas, as a result of challenges, than in urban Manitoba (Jenkinson, 1994). Parents or guardians were the most prevalent initiators of challenges to books (about 50%), but in-school personnel also initiated a considerable proportion of challenges (about 39%, many from professionals wishing to avoid controversy and many from people who volunteer in the schools). The most challenged authors in Jenkinson's study were Robert Munsch (*Giant: or, Waiting for the Thursday Boat*, 1989; and *A Promise is a Promise*, 1988), Roald Dahl (*Revolting Rhymes*, 1982; and *The Witches*, 1983), Alvin Schwartz (*Scary Stories to Tell in the Dark*, 1981) and William Steig (*The Amazing Bone*, 1976). Jenkinson (1994, complied from various charts) also identified the top ten reasons for challenges to materials in school libraries from 1991 to 1993:

- witchcraft/supernatural (24%)
- violence (18%)
- immaturity of readers (12%)
- explicit sex (10%)
- morality (9%)
- nudity (9%)
- obscenity (8%)
- profanity (7%)
- sexism/role stereotypes (6%)
- religion (excluding evolution) (5%).

The outcome of challenges made in Manitoba's schools in 1993 was that 45% of challenged material was removed from the shelves, 16% was given restricted access, 36% was retained on the shelf (the challenge was overturned), and 3% was changed in some way (for example, a K-8 teacher who was upset by nudity drew a diaper on Mickey in *In the Night Kitchen* by Sendak (1970)). In addition to these challenges are the unreported challenges where books simply go missing, have pages removed, or are ripped up.

Schrader (1996) maintains that successful self-censorship by schools and individual teachers is an illusion, that challenges to materials in schools are inevitable. Every school library collection, over time, is vulnerable to criticism and challenge. It is important to note that only a very small proportion of the titles challenged are challenged more than once. One-time complaints are not at all unusual: they reflect the variety of responses individual readers will have to any text. Picture books depicting same-sex family relationships (that is, gay and lesbian parents), such as *Daddy's Roommate* (Willhoite, 1990) and *Heather Has Two Mommies* (Newman, 1989), appear to be creating the greatest flurry of censorship activities recently. The 1998 banning in Surrey, B.C. of books about same-sex parents (particularly *Asha's Mums* by Rosamund Elwin, 1990; *Belinda's Bouquet* by Leslea Newman, 1998; *One Dad, Two Dads, Brown Dads, Blue Dads* by Johnny Valentine, 1994) underscores the unpredictable nature of censorship. It is regrettable that children living in same-sex families are denied the right to read about children living in the same social contexts in which they themselves live. Perhaps teachers and community members need to consider that only fifteen to twenty years ago, books featuring single-parent families or divorced parents were considered unsuitable for young readers.

Censorship can also be an attempt by special-interest groups to protect themselves against ideas or beliefs that may threaten their status. *Maxine's Tree* by Diane Lager-Haskell (1990), for example, was challenged in 1992 by members of the IWA-Canada local on British Columbia's Sunshine Coast as being "emotional and an insult to loggers" (Nodelman, 1992, p.132). By purging libraries of controversial material or by circulating lists of titles that have been labelled "objectionable," censors hope to make decisions on behalf of others and limit access to materials. Advocates of selection, however, feel that this "purging" infringes on the individual's right to make book selections and limits the circulation of ideas to which learners are exposed.

We must not forget that materials that are clearly pornographic or racist are censored by law in Canada. The challenges that schools deal with are generally based on the beliefs of individuals or groups (although in Canada there are few formal groups) and their responses to materials. They do, however, cover the full spectrum of human ideals and values.

It is therefore crucial that school boards or individual schools establish guidelines for handling complaints about books, including explicit details as to how book complaints will be received and reviewed. Assistance and information about legal rulings, organizations behind challenges, and how to resist challenges to books can be received from organizations such as the Book and Periodical Council (Toronto), which produces a kit for use during *Freedom to Read Week*; the Canadian Library Association (Toronto); the National Council of Teachers of English (Urbana, Illinois); the International Reading Association (Newark, Delaware); the National Coalition Against Censorship (New York); the American Library Association (Chicago); and the Freedom To Read Committee (New York). In addition, the National Council of Teachers of English and the American Library Association have sample forms and guidelines available. *Censorship and Selection: Issues and Answers for Schools* (Reichman, 1993) is a joint publication by the American Association of School

Administrators and the American Library Association. The book includes sample forms for collecting a statement of concern from a complainant, a sample letter to a complainant, instructions for an evaluating committee, and guidelines for student publications. It is an excellent resource for any school establishing a materials-evaluation committee. Another extremely useful publication is *The Students' Right to Read*, published by the National Council of Teachers of English (1982).

The National Council of Teachers of English and the International Reading Association have recently developed a CD-ROM resource, *Rationales for Challenged Books* (NCTE, 1998), which includes more than 200 rationales for over 170 commonly challenged materials for kindergarten through to grade twelve (the emphasis is on publications for grades seven to twelve). Publications are listed both by title and author on this web-type resource, and information is provided about book challenges and what can be done by schools and libraries to counter them.

Very few books for elementary school-age children deal with the topic of book selection and censorship, but one is *Maudie and Me and the Dirty Book* by Betty Miles (1980). Kate and Maudie, students in grade six, volunteer to read to first-grade children in a nearby primary school. They make careful book selections with the help of their teacher and based on the interests of the children in the class. Unfortunately, Kate's selection causes a furor among the parents, even though the children enjoy it. The book she reads to the children is about a little boy waiting to receive a puppy for his birthday. The puppy is to come from the family next door, but the babies are not born by the date of Ben's birthday. When the puppies do arrive, Ben is thrilled to actually see his puppy being born. *Maudie and Me and the Dirty Book* tells the story of a school and a community caught up in censorship issues, much to the dismay and incomprehension of Maudie and Kate. The book presents the various concerns regarding book selection in a comprehensive manner, and demonstrates the emotional response that literature can evoke, particularly in a school setting with young children.

Teachers and teacher-librarians who select materials for classroom or school libraries make every effort to choose books that meet the needs of children as well as the needs of the curriculum. As children grow up, encountering new situations and meeting new people, they confront families and communities different from their own. Some of the ideas and values they come across will perhaps be disturbing. However, we think that reading and discussing a broad range of literature may help children to become critical thinkers and thoughtful human beings capable of making sound judgements, both as individuals and as members of society. They may also become thoughtful, life-long readers, capable of selecting quality literature that will satisfy, entertain, and challenge them.

References

Amey, L. 1988. Pryramid power: The teacher-librarian and censorship. *Emergency Librarian* 16(1), 15-20.

Barthes, R. 1970, translated 1974. *S/Z: An Essay*. New York: Hill & Wang.

Bissoondath, N. 1998. No place like home. *New Internationalist* September 1998, 20-22.

Booth, D. 1992. *Censorship Goes to School*. Markham, Ontario: Pembroke Publishers.

Booth, J., J. Phenix, W. Pauli, and L. Swartz. (1984-88). *Impressions, K-7* Toronto: Holt-Harcourt Brace Jovanovich.

Calvino, I. 1979, 1981. *If On a Winter's Night a Traveller*. New York: Harcourt Brace and Co.

Canadian Library Association. 1974. *Statement on Intellectual Freedom*. 29th Annual Conference, Winnipeg, Manitoba.

Clay, M. 1985. *The Early Detection of Reading Difficulties*. Portsmouth, New Hampshire: Heinemann.

Culler, J. 1980. Literary competence. In *Reader-response Criticism: From Formalism to Post-structuralism*. J. Tompkins, ed. Baltimore: The Johns Hopkins University Press.

Diakiw, J. 1997. Children's literature and Canadian national identity: A revisionist perspective. *Canadian Children's Literature* 23(3), 36-49.

Esses, V. and R. Gardner. 1996. Multiculturalism in Canada: Context and current status. *Canadian Journal of Behavioural Science* [online], 28(3), 35 paragraphs. Available: http:www.cpa.ca/cjbsnew/1996/ful_edito.html [1998, March 11].

Fosnot, C.T. 1996. *Constructivism: Theory, Perspectives and Practice*. New York: Teachers College Press.

Fowles, J. 1969. *The French Lieutenant's Woman*. Boston: Little, Brown & Co, Inc.

Freebody, P. and A. Luke. 1990. "Literacies" programs: Debates and demands in cultural contexts. *Prospects* 5(3), 7-16.

Goldstone, B. 1998. Ordering the chaos: Teaching metafictive characteristics of children's books. *Journal of Children's Literature* 24(2), 48-55.

Goodman, K. 1983. *What's Whole in Whole Language?* Richmond Hill, Ontario: Scholastic Canada.

Goodman, Y. 1985. Kidwatching: Observing children in the classroom. In *Observing the Language Learner*. Angela Jagger and M. Trika Smith-Burke, eds. Urbana, Illinois and Newark, Delaware: National Council of Teachers of English and International Reading Association.

Graff, H. 1987. *The Labyrinths of Literacy: Reflections on Literacy Past and Present*. London: Falmer.

Heath, S.B. 1983. *Ways with Words: Language, Life and Work in Communities and Classrooms*. Cambridge: Cambridge University Press.

Holdaway, D. 1979. *The Foundations of Literacy*. Gosford, N.S.W. Australia: Ashton Scholastic.

Iser, W. 1978. *The Act of Reading: A Theory of Aesthetic Response*. Baltimore: Johns Hopkins University Press.

James, H. 1981, 1898. *The Turn of the Screw And Other Short Fiction*. New York: Bantam Classics.

Jenkinson, D. 1994. The changing faces of censorship in Manitoba's public school libraries. *Emergency Librarian* 22(2), 15-21.

Levine, K. 1986. *The Social Context of Literacy*. London: Routledge and Kegan Paul.

Meek, M. 1988. *How Texts Teach What Readers Learn*. Stroud, Gloucestershire, U.K.: Thimble Press.

National Council of Teachers of English. 1982. *The Students' Right to Read*. Urbana, Illinois: National Council of Teachers of English.

———. 1998. *Rationales for Challenged Books*. Urbana, Illinois: National Council of Teachers of English.

Nodelman, P. 1992. We are all censors. *Canadian Children's Literature* 68, 121-133.

———. 1997. What's Canadian about Canadian children's literature? A compendium of answers to the question. *Canadian Children's Literature* 23(3), 15-35.

Ondaatje, M. 1992. *The English Patient*. Toronto: Vintage Books Canada.

Pantaleo, S. 1995. Students and teachers selecting literature: Whose choice? *Illinois English Bulletin* 82(2), 33-46.

Propp, V. 1968. *The Morphology of the Folktale*. Austin: University of Texas Press.

Reichman, H. 1993. *Censorship and Selection: Issues and Answers for Schools*. Chicago: American Library Association.

Roberts, E.A. 1996. *A Survey of Censorship Practices in Public School Libraries in Saskatchewan*. Master's Thesis, University of Alberta, Edmonton, Canada.

Schrader, A. 1996. Censorproofing school library collections: The fallacy and futilty. *School Libraries Worldwide* 2(1), 71-94.

Stephens, J. and K. Watson. 1994. *From Picture Book to Literary Theory*. Sydney, Australia: St Clair Press.

Thomson, J. 1987. *Understanding Teenagers Reading: Reading Processes and the Teaching of Literature*. Norwood, S.A., Australia: Australian Association for the Teaching of English Inc.

Vanderhaeghe, G. 1996. *The Englishman's Boy*. Toronto: McClelland & Stewart.

Wells, G. 1986. *The Meaning Makers*. Portsmouth, New Hampshire: Heinemann.

CHAPTER TWO

PICTURE BOOKS

The objectives of this chapter are

- To develop an understanding of the characteristics of picture books;
- To become aware of the range of picture books available for children from preschool to the junior high grades;
- To appreciate how illustrations and text work together in picture books.

What Is a Picture Book?

In a picture book, the illustrations and text work together to convey a message. Both text and illustrations are necessary to construct meaning. An illustrated book, on the other hand, is dominated by the text, with the illustrations simply demonstrating, or enriching, the text. (Coffee-table books for adults are an example of illustrated books.) The books explored in this chapter are specifically those in which the illustrations and the text are equally important in creating the message or story (or, in the case of wordless books, in which the message is created entirely by the illustrations).

In Anthony Browne's picture book *Bear Hunt* (1979), the text is simple, almost a parody of an old-style "Dick and Jane" basal reader, yet the illustrations tell a fascinating and innovative story. As bear goes for a walk, he encounters hunters. Each time bear is threatened by the hunters, he steps out of his role as a fictional character and becomes the author/illustrator, drawing himself out of the difficult situation and recreating his circumstances so that he can escape. Browne's stylized jungle plants and flowers have faces and ties, and are made of candy and various items of clothing. Children usually notice these aspects of the illustrations before adults do, because they have not yet become constrained by print and are sophisticated readers of images. As a result of this differing sensitivity, the authors and illustrators of picture books have the freedom to play with ideas and with children's imaginations in the most stimulating of ways. Children's fascination with picture books, with turning the page and unfolding the story, is kept alive by authors and illustrators who live up to the challenge of children's imaginations. The books presented in this chapter are those that we consider worthy of a child's time and interest, and that, at the same time, entertain and stimulate their adult readers.

Every genre of literature—including realistic fiction, historical fiction, fantasy, poetry, and traditional literature—is represented in picture books. The term "picture book" indicates a basic format and way of communicating a message within a book. In this chapter, we have attempted to highlight the most common types of picture books, including wordless books, concept books (such as counting and alphabet books), predictable books, easy-to-read books, and picture story books. It is important to remember that there is often overlap among the types.

Wordless Books

Wordless books are appropriate for and enjoyed by both emergent and older readers. Children learn many important reading lessons through interacting with wordless books, including the personal pleasure of reading. They can develop a concept of story (that a story is a logical narrative with a beginning, middle, and end) and gain an understanding of the literary elements of stories (such as characters, settings, problems, conflicts, and solutions). Children also develop vocabulary, book-handling knowledge (such as left-to-right page progression and front-to-back orientation), and comprehension skills (such as following a sequence, analyzing an author's intent, identifying main ideas, recognizing details, and making predictions). "Reading" wordless books requires careful observation and interpretation. Children are able to bring their own experiences and language to wordless books and are prompted to create, interpret, and tell their own stories from the illustrations in the books. Readers can express their own interpretations of the action in wordless books through a variety of written and oral language activities. "Encouraging children to talk about what they see and what they think it means lets them hear the thought processes of others and work together to construct meaning from the illustrations" (Glazer, 1997, p.217).

Mercer Mayer is credited with popularizing wordless books with his 1967 publication of *A Boy, a Dog, and a Frog*. Mayer is adept at creating characters and telling the story through illustrations. In his books, the "facial expressions speak with the power of words, visual actions foreshadow events, and the story line flows seamlessly" (Jacobs & Tunnell, 1996, p.147). *Frog Goes to Dinner* (1974) is a humorous story about the mischief Frog gets into when he secretly accompanies the family to dinner in an elegant restaurant. *One Frog Too Many* (Mayer & Mayer, 1975), *Frog, Where Are You?* (1969), and *Frog on His Own* (1973) are other books in this series.

David Wiesner's wordless book *Tuesday* (1991) won the 1992 American Library Association's Caldecott Medal. One Tuesday evening at 8:00 p.m., frogs at a pond become airborne when the lily pads on which they are sitting mysteriously become miniature flying carpets. The frogs' facial expressions in Wiesner's outstanding illustrations convey their individual personalities and depict their emotions as they soar over a nearby town on their lily pads. The flying amphibians cruise by a window as a man enjoys a late-night snack, become entangled in laundry, visit an elderly lady who has fallen asleep while watching television, and chase a dog. As dawn approaches, the lily pads lose their ability to fly, and the frogs fall to earth. The grounded amphibians hop back to the pond and sit wistfully on new lily pads, musing over their night's adventures. In the morning, perplexed police officers and detectives examine the evidence of the frogs' flight. The following Tuesday at 8:00 p.m., the sky is once again inhabited by flying creatures; but on this Tuesday evening, a different creature is airborne.

Three other delightful wordless books are *The Snowman* (Briggs, 1978), *Good Dog, Carl* (Day, 1985), and *Deep in the Forest* (Turkle, 1976). *The Snowman* is about a little boy who wakes up to see a heavy snowfall outside his house. The boy goes to play in the snow and makes a snowman. In the evening, he says goodnight to the snowman and retires to bed. During the night, the boy awakens, checks on his snowman, and discovers that the snowman has come to life. Boy and snowman explore the wonders of life in a modern home, then take a magical flight through the night to the north pole. The pair returns before daybreak, and the boy goes back to bed. When he awakens, the sun is shining and the snowman is melting; but in his pocket, the boy has a wonderful memento of the night's adventures. Briggs tells this story in comic-book style, and the pictures must be read in the order of a comic book. It is clearly a picture book for readers of all ages.

Good Dog, Carl is about a mother who goes out on an errand and leaves her baby in the care of Carl, the family dog. Carl is a most obedient and resourceful dog, and he entertains, feeds, and washes the baby while the mother is away. The adventures that Carl and the baby enjoy together remain undiscovered by the mother. There are several other wordless picture books that further chronicle the adventures of Carl (e.g., *Carl Goes Shopping*, 1992; *Carl Goes to Daycare*, 1995; *Carl's Birthday*, 1997).

Deep in the Forest is an alternative version of the story of Goldilocks and the Three Bears. In this book, the humans and the animals play reverse roles: the character of Goldilocks is a baby bear who wanders into a cabin in the woods. No one is at home when the bear arrives, so it samples the food in the bowls and tries out the chairs (breaking the smallest, of course) and beds. The humans return home, examine the damage, and discover the intruder in the daughter's bed. The cub flees and returns safely to the paws of its mother.

Fernando Krahn has created several wordless books. In *How Santa Claus Had a Long and Difficult Journey Delivering His Presents* (1970), Santa experiences difficulties after the sleigh reins break and his reindeer fly away. The toys try to help Santa fly the sleigh but he requires further assistance; luckily, some angels come to Santa's rescue. Some of Krahn's other wordless books include *The Secret in the Dungeon* (1983), *The Mystery of the Giant Footprints* (1977), *Arthur's Adventure in the Abandoned House* (1981), *Catch That Cat!* (1978), *Who's Seen the Scissors?* (1975), *Here Comes Alex Pumpernickel!* (1981), and *Amanda and the Mysterious Carpet* (1985). Other popular wordless books are listed at the end of the chapter.

Concept Books

Concept books (including alphabet and counting books, which are dealt with in a separate section of this chapter) attempt to make abstract and concrete ideas more understandable to readers by explaining or exploring an activity—for example, a given occupation (e.g., teaching, policing), a concept or idea (e.g., light, water), or an object (e.g., boats, machines), rather than telling a story. Concept books are generally children's first information books. Some concept books include the use of repeated elements in the text and/or illustrations. Concept books usually foster cognitive development and stimulate language development as children interact with them.

Concepts may be introduced and/or clarified through concept books. Glazer (1997) has generated four questions to consider as guidelines for evaluating concept books.

1. *Are the facts, descriptions and relationships accurate? Has omitted information resulted in a misrepresentation of the concept?*
2. *Is the information (i.e., text and illustrations) presented clearly? Are examples within children's range of experience and understanding?*
3. *Does the book have artistic merit?*
4. *Does the book extend children's thinking? (p.175)*

The topic of shapes is popular in concept books. In *Sea Shapes* (MacDonald, 1994), the author transforms distinct shapes on white pages to sea creatures in their underwater world. For example, a triangle becomes the teeth of a shark, a square becomes a ray, and a hexagon becomes the pattern on a turtle's shell. Other concept books about shapes include

Lynn and James selecting books in the library

Look Around! A Book About Shapes! (Fisher, 1987), *Shapes, Shapes, Shapes* (Hoban, 1986), *Let's Look for Shapes* (Gillham & Hulme, 1984), *Circles, Triangles and Squares* (Hoban, 1974), *All Shapes and Sizes* (Hughes, 1989), and *Shapes* (Kightley, 1986).

There are also books about the concept of transportation. *Trucks* (Barton, 1986) shows trucks in use and labels and identifies the uses of each truck. *Trains* (Barton, 1986), *Freight Train* (Crews, 1978), *Truck* (Crews, 1980), *Boats, Boats, Boats* (Ruane, 1990), and *The Big Concrete Lorry* (Hughes, 1990) are a few books that explore the topic of transportation.

Lists at the end of the chapter identify other examples of concept books, including books about the popular topics of colours, seasons, and opposites.

ALPHABET AND COUNTING BOOKS

There are many beautiful, and often humorous, alphabet and counting books. *The ABC of Things* by Helen Oxenbury (1983) is a long-lasting favourite with children, as is *John Burningham's ABC* (Burningham, 1967). Ted Harrison's *A Northern Alphabet* (1982) and Mary Beth Owen's *A Caribou Alphabet* (1990) are other high-quality alphabet books. Jacobs and Tunnel (1996) note that "most alphabet books are not well suited to teaching the ABC's along with their phonic generalizations, and they are not intended to serve such a purpose" (p.146). Rather, most alphabet books are intended to entertain and introduce new vocabulary and concepts. The alphabet is often used as a categorization scheme or as an organizational structure to present concepts and/or information.

An intriguing and engaging alphabet book is *Whatley's Quest: An Alphabet Adventure* (Whatley & Smith, 1994). In the beginning of this wordless alphabet book, the author extends several invitations to readers: to join the animals in the hunt for buried treasure, to find the hidden letters on each page, to identify all the objects and animals beginning with the same letter on each page, and to make up sentences and stories from the words they find (the objects and animals identified on each page). This book is enjoyable for readers of all ages as it can be read on many levels of sophistication, depending on which of the author's challenges readers wish to accept and pursue.

In *Illuminations* (Hunt, 1989), each letter of the alphabet introduces a term from the Middle Ages. An illustration and explanatory paragraph are provided for each term (e.g., falconry, joust, quintain, etc.). *A...B...Sea* (Kalman, 1995) follows a similar format, with a photograph and informative paragraph about each undersea creature featured in the book (e.g., king helmet shell, lionfish, etc.). *Geography from A to Z: A Picture Glossary* (Knowlton, 1988) has 63 entries from A to Z which describe the physical geography of the earth. An explanation and pictorial representation accompany each geographical feature (e.g., "palisade—a bold line of high, steep cliffs. A long palisade that joins two level areas of land is an escarpment" [p.34]).

Two other alphabet books with intriguing formats are *The ABC Mystery* (Cushman, 1993) and *Antics! An Alphabetical Anthology* (Hepworth, 1992). *The ABC Mystery* is a "whodunit" that must be solved by following the clues revealed by each letter of the alphabet. The text is written in rhyming verse. *Antics! An Alphabetical Anthology* is a clever and creative piece of work. Each word is represented by one or more human-like ants and has the word ant embedded in it. For example, for the letter O, Hepworth shows two ants, characterizing Sherlock Holmes and Watson, with a very observant Holmes peering through a magnifying glass.

Counting books assist children in learning basic numbers and provide practice with counting. Most counting books include the printed Arabic number and the accompanying number of like objects on each page. They often incorporate themes or devices to create textual interest and cohesion. *When We Went to the Park* (Hughes, 1985) and *Anno's Counting Book* (Anno, 1977) are examples that provide the young reader with many opportunities to count items as the pages are turned. Pat Hutchins has created a puzzle as well as a number story in *1 Hunter* (1982). Hutchins has thoughtfully used line and simple colour in this book in order to aid children in clearly picking out the number units. The story is cumulative in that all the animals reappear on various pages throughout the book and come together as the story progresses.

Alphabet and counting books are popular and plentiful, and many of these books are appropriate for older, as well as younger, students. A selection of alphabet and counting books is identified in the reference lists at the end of this chapter.

Predictable Books

Predictable books, sometimes called pattern books, include the repeated use of particular phrases, words, questions, sentences, refrains, or plot events. Often these texts have strong rhythm and rhyme, and these language features, in combination with the aforementioned elements of repetition, assist the emergent reader. Predictable books help children in learning language patterns and predicting forthcoming action due to the repetition in story patterns and the clues in the illustrations. Predictable books can also provide models for writing. For example, after reading *I Went Walking* (Williams, 1989), students can create their own books or a class book by using the same pattern of "I went walking. What did you see? I saw a brown horse looking at me." Topics such as the zoo, wild or domesticated animals, or people can be used as the basis for the students' pattern books.

It Looked Like Spilt Milk (Shaw, 1947) repeats the phrases "Sometimes it looked like ..." and "But it wasn't ..." when describing the white figures on the pages adjacent to the text. Readers discover the identity of the white figures on the final page of the book. *Is This a House for Hermit Crab?* (McDonald, 1990) contains repetition of action as the story describes Hermit Crab testing the suitability of various objects for his new house. The book also repeats words and phrases. With each new item, the question is asked, "Is this a house for Hermit Crab?", and when the object is inappropriate, the text reads, "So he stepped along the shore, by the sea, in the sand ... *scritch-scratch, scritch-scratch*." Don Wood's *King Bidgood's in the Bathtub* (1985), a 1986 Caldecott Honor book, also contains repetition in action and language. The king's page alerts everyone that "King Bidgood's in the bathtub, and he won't get out! Oh, who knows what to do?" A knight, the Queen, a duke, and the king's court attempt to get King Bidgood out of the tub but instead, these individuals end up in the tub with the king. Eventually, a practical solution suggested by the page resolves the problem!

Cumulative stories provide for even greater repetition as "each event builds on the previous one, and all are repeated each time a new event occurs" (Glazer, 1997, p.191). *The Napping House* (Wood, 1984) is a cumulative tale about a granny, a child, a dog, a cat, and a mouse napping in a house. A wakeful flea creates a tremendous disturbance when it bites the mouse! In *Too Much Noise* (McGovern, 1967), an elderly man named Peter believes that his house is too noisy. He visits the wise man of the village to seek advice, and the wise man instructs Peter to get a cow. However, the cow does not solve the noise problem. Peter returns to the wise man on several occasions and each time follows the wise man's instructions. After a number of tries, Peter has a quiet house. *The Big Sneeze* (Brown, 1985) is a cumulative story about the chain of events that happen when a fly lands on a sleeping farmer's nose. Other cumulative tales include *Drummer Hoff* (Emberley, 1967), *The Jacket I Wear in the Snow* (Neitzel, 1989), *Bringing the Rain to Kapiti Plain* (Aardema, 1981), *Jump, Frog, Jump!* (Kalan, 1981), *I Know an Old Lady Who Swallowed a Pie* (Jackson, 1997), *The Little Old Lady Who Was Not Afraid of Anything* (Williams, 1986), and *Mr. Gumpy's Outing* (Burningham, 1970).

Some books are predictable because they incorporate familiar sequences such as days of the week or numbers. *Busy Monday Morning* (Domanska, 1985) contains days of the week and a repetitive refrain. *The Very Hungry Caterpillar* (Carle, 1969) incorporates days of the week and numbers, and *The Grouchy Ladybug* (Carle, 1977) uses numbers (hours of the day) and repetition of language and events.

There are many predictable or pattern books for children. Additional titles are identified in a list at the end of this chapter.

Easy-to-Read Books

Easy-to-read books often "use larger print, more space between lines, limited vocabulary, as well as such devices as word patterns, repeated text, rhyming text, and illustration clues" (Tomlinson & Lynch-Brown, 1996, p.78). Although easy-to-read or beginning-to-read books are often limited in sentence and text length, it is important that these books have a strong story, engaging writing style, and appropriate vocabulary and syntax. "Beginning reader picture books that are stilted and contrived, that follow the unnatural language patterns of the old style Dick and Jane basal readers, are actually more difficult for young readers" (Jacobs & Tunnell, 1996, p.151).

The characteristics of easy-to-read or beginning-to-read books encourage emergent readers to read independently and foster a sense of accomplishment.

Easy-to-read books can be fictional or factual, and many of the counting and predictable books identified in this chapter are also easy-to-read books. The reading level of beginning-to-read books varies as these books may have very few words (e.g., *Rosie's Walk*, Hutchins, 1969) or they may include considerable text and be divided into short chapters (e.g., *Frog and Toad are Friends*, Lobel, 1970).

In 1957, the first beginning reader picture books—*Cat in the Hat* (Seuss) and *Little Bear* (Minarik)—were published. Minarik's *Little Bear* books became part of Harper's *I Can Read Book* series. This series includes high-quality work that represents all genres, and many well-known authors and illustrators are included in this well-respected collection. Arnold Lobel's *Frog and Toad are Friends* (1970), a 1971 Caldecott Honor book, *Frog and Toad Together* (1972), *Frog and Toad All Year* (1976), and *Days with Frog and Toad* (1979) are examples of books published in Harper's *I Can Read* series. Some teachers use the Frog and Toad books for class novel studies and Literature Workshops (see Chapter 9).

Other publishers have also developed beginning reading series: Dutton's *Easy Reader*, Puffin's *Hello Reading* and *Easy-to-Read*, Random House's *Stepping Stone*, Grosset & Dunlap's *All Aboard Reading*, Holiday House's *A First Mystery Book*, Macmillan's *Ready-to-Read*, Dell's *Young Yearling*, and Dutton's *Speedsters*. Marjorie Sharmat has an easy-to-read mystery series about the detective Nate the Great (e.g., *Nate the Great and the Stolen Base*, 1992), and Cynthia Rylant has an easy-to-read series about Henry and his dog Mudge (e.g., *Henry and Mudge and the Happy Cat*, 1990). Beginning reader series normally contain more vocabulary than other easy-to-read picture books, and some teachers classify them as beginning chapter books.

Easy-to-read books may have a considerable number of words, like the beginning reader series books noted above, or they may have very few words. One book with few words is *Where's My Teddy?* (Alborough, 1992). In this engaging story for young readers, Eddie sets out in the woods to find his lost teddy, but finds instead a gigantic teddy bear—as well as a real bear that has lost its teddy as well. In the end, Eddie and the bear both find their teddies. *The Knight and the Dragon* (dePaola, 1980) tells the tale of a dragon who is unskilled at fighting knights and a knight who is equally incompetent at fighting dragons. Although both the dragon and the knight have researched the art of fighting and practise the necessary skills, neither is successful in battle. In the end, they work cooperatively in their pursuit of new careers. *Moonbear's Books* (Asch, 1993) is about the different kinds of books that Moonbear loves, including tall and short, thin and thick, and old and new books. In *In the Tall, Tall Grass* (Fleming, 1991), the author uses rhyming text to describe the creatures a fuzzy caterpillar sees and hears as it crawls through the tall grass. *The Big Big Sea* (Waddell, 1994) tells the story of a young girl and her mother going to the sea on a moonlit night. They paddle and splash in the water and walk along the shore, alone and together. The story ends with the young girl at home reflecting how "I'll always remember just Mama and me and the night we walked by the big big sea" (unpaginated).

Such high-quality easy-to-read books meet the needs of beginning readers. Good books of this type do not sacrifice interest and entertainment for readability. In addition, children derive pleasure from reading these books aloud to an appreciative and encouraging audience.

A selection of additional easy-to-read books appears at the end of the chapter. It is important to remember that the many categories of picture books overlap. For example, an easy-to-read book can be a picture story book or a chapter book, and a counting book can be a predictable, easy-to-read, picture story book.

Picture Story Books

There is a wealth of high-quality picture story books available for children in the elementary grades today. Children in the preschool and kindergarten years enjoy sitting alone or in small groups reading many of these books. The work of Janet and Allan Ahlberg is especially well loved by children. Their books include *The Jolly Postman* (1986), *Each Peach Pear Plum* (1978), and *The Baby's Catalogue* (1982). Picture story books are an intricate blending of picture and text which enables the reader to create a many-layered story.

Picture story books are plentiful and, like all types of literature, vary in quality. A wide range of topics and themes is represented in picture story books. Some books deal with everyday experiences, while others deal with difficult subjects like divorce, death, war, and prejudice. Many picture story books deal with biographical and informational subjects (see Chapter 6). A growing trend in picture story books is to convey biographical and expository information through a narrative text structure, rather than through an expository style (e.g., Joanna Cole's *Magic School Bus* series).

The plot structures of picture story books range in complexity. The narratives may have a simple plot structure such as in *Who Is the Boss?* (Goffin, 1992). In this book, a duck and two toy-like men in a toy boat crash into a rock because the men are arguing about who is the boss. Goffin's book ends with the boat sinking, the men riding on the duck's back, and the question, "Now! Who is the boss?". Alternatively, the narratives of picture story books may be more complex. In *Miss Rumphius* (Cooney, 1982), Alice (the young Miss Rumphius) tells her grandfather that she wants to travel to faraway places and live beside the sea. Grandfather listens to Alice's desires and instructs her to do something to make the world more beautiful. When she is older, Miss Rumphius travels to faraway places and lives by the sea. However, she remembers there is one more thing she must do and so she thinks very hard about how she can make the world a more beautiful place. Eventually, she completes her task and the story ends with Miss Rumphius issuing the same challenge to her own great-niece.

Other picture story books are even more complex because they have parallel plots. David Macaulay's *Black and White* (1990), the 1991 American Library Association's Caldecott Medal winner, is a sophisticated picture book with at least four stories told simultaneously. This picture story book is indeed challenging, as readers must decide how to begin, how to put events and characters together, and how the multiple plots relate to each other. (See the discussion of *Black and White* in the section Picture Books for Older Children, later in this chapter.)

A classic picture story book is *Where the Wild Things Are* (Sendak, 1963), winner of the 1964 Caldecott Medal. This is a fantasy story about a young boy named Max who is very naughty and is sent to bed without any supper. A forest grows in Max's room and he magically sails to the land of the Wild Things, where he becomes king. Max enjoys being King of all the Wild Things and engages in a wild rumpus where no one tells him to behave. At the end of the day, however, the aroma of his waiting supper lures him back to his home again. Sendak uses the size of the pictures on the page to indicate the climaxing of the plot and the circular journey Max takes. As Max gets further away from home, further into the fantasy world of his imagination, and more involved with the Wild Things, the pictures get larger, finally taking up two entire double-page spreads with no text at all. As Max begins to think about home, beginning to retreat from the Land of the Wild Things, the illustrations take up less space on the page and become contained within a black border. When Max is finally in his own room again, the picture is small, and, on the very last page, there are no words at all, just one tiny picture—Max's hot meal on the table.

Family relationships is a popular theme in picture story books. As discussed in Chapter 1, *Granpa*

(Burningham, 1985) is a touching story about a loving relationship between a young girl and her grandfather. Cynthia Rylant's *The Relatives Came* (1985), a 1986 Caldecott Honor book, is a story about a family's wonderful summer when relatives from Virginia come for a visit. In *Grandfather's Journey* (1993), winner of the 1994 Caldecott Medal, Allen Say shares some of his grandfather's experiences in America and his grandfather's yearning for Japan. Although grandfather returns to Japan, where he meets his grandson for the first time, he misses America. Say's grandfather tells Say about California, and, although grandfather plans to return to America, he never makes that final trip. Say, like his grandfather, loves both countries and when in one, misses the other. The setting of *Smoky Night* (Bunting, 1994), winner of the 1995 Caldecott Medal, is the 1993 riots in Los Angeles. As Daniel and his mother look out into the smoky night, they see street looters and distant fires. When they are forced to leave their building, Daniel's cat cannot be found and neither can Mrs. Kim's, a local store-owner. The people from the apartment building go to a shelter; a firefighter later brings both cats to the shelter. The cats have become good friends during the ordeal and the humans learn an important lesson from the cats.

There are numerous picture books about animals, birds, and other creatures. *Stellaluna* (Cannon, 1993) is the story of a fruit bat named Stellaluna who is separated from her mother. Stellaluna falls into a bird's nest and learns to live like a bird. One night when she becomes separated from her bird siblings, Stellaluna meets some other fruit bats and is reunited with her mother. Stellaluna discovers who she is and learns that even though bats and birds are different, they can still be friends. In *Owl Moon* (Yolen, 1987), the 1988 Caldecott Medal winner, a young girl and her father go owling on a winter night. Although they walk quietly into the still woods, when father calls to the owls, there is no answer. They travel on, and the girl is quiet and does not ask questions for she understands, through her father, the etiquette of owling. Finally, in a clearing in the dark woods, the father's owl call is answered. In *North Country Night* (San Souci, 1990), the northern forest comes alive as its inhabitants move about during a snowy night. Facts about each creature are shared, and San Souci skillfully connects each creature to the next one in his story.

Mister Got To Go by Lois Simmie (1995), set at the Sylvia Hotel in Vancouver, British Columbia, tells the story of a stray cat who is allowed into the hotel one rainy night by Mr. Foster, the manager. Although Mr. Foster continually asserts that, once it stops raining, Mr. Got To Go must indeed leave the hotel, the feline remains.

> *And so, every time Mr. Foster put the cat out, the cat came back in and rode up the elevator. He played with the ball of wool at the end of Miss Pritchett's knitting, and she gave him tuna sandwiches from her lunch. Old Harry, the bellhop, saved him leftovers from the Room Service trays. And the cook gave him scraps from the kitchen. (unpaginated)*

The cat greatly enjoys his life at the hotel and shows his worth in several ways, including ridding the hotel of a raccoon. Mr. Got To Go continues to stay in the hotel, although not without causing some disturbance and becoming one of its most famous residents.

There are several picture story books about the environment. *Where the Forest Meets the Sea* (Baker, 1987) is about a boy's visit to the Daintree Rainforest in North Queensland, Australia. The boy walks among the ancient trees and wonders about the past, present, and future life and activity in the rain forest. *Here Is the Tropical Rain Forest* (Dunphy, 1994) and *Here Is the Arctic Winter* (Dunphy, 1993) are cumulative poems that present the interdependent life cycles of the rain forest and the far north. *The Great Kapok Tree* (Cherry, 1990) is another book which describes an interdependent community of creatures. In an Amazon rain forest, several creatures speak to a sleeping man who plans to cut down the kapok tree, explaining their dependence and interdependence on the tree. In *Squish! A Wetland Walk* (Luenn, 1994), a child explores the sights, sounds, smells, and uses of a wetland.

Other exemplary picture story books include *Come Away From the Water, Shirley* by John Burningham (1977), *The Very Hungry Caterpillar* by Eric Carle (1968), *Not Now Bernard* by David McKee (1980), and *John Brown, Rose and the Midnight Cat* by Jenny Wagner (1978).

Canadian Picture Story Books

Many outstanding Canadian picture books are available for young readers today. In addition to the Canadian selections already identified in this chapter, many other Canadian picture books are described and recommended in Chapters 3, 4, 5, and 6.

In many selections of Canadian children's literature, the experiences of the characters are essentially linked with the geographical region in which the story is set. *The Fishing Summer* (Jam, 1997) is set on the Atlantic coast; *At Grandpa's Sugar Bush* (Carney, 1997) and *The Sugaring-Off Party* (London, 1995) are set in eastern Canada; *Tiger's New Cowboys Boots* (Morck, 1996) and *Bibi and the Bull* (Vaage, 1995) are set on the prairies of central Alberta; *Rainbow Bay* (Hume, 1997) and *Driftwood Cove* (Lightburn, 1998) are set in British Columbia; and *Hold On McGinty!* (Harty, 1997) takes readers on a cross-Canada tour. Michael Arvaarluk Kusugak writes about his Inuit experiences and a selection of his books are discussed in Chapter 5 (e.g., *Northern Lights: The Soccer Trails*, 1993; *Hide and Sneak*, 1992; *My Arctic 1 2 3*, 1996; and *Arctic Stories*, 1998). *Very Last First Time* (Andrews, 1985), another book discussed in detail in Chapter 5, relates the story of an Inuit child living on Ungava Bay in the far north of Quebec. *Out on the Ice in the Middle of the Bay* (Cumming, 1993) is also set in northern Canada.

In *The Fishing Summer*, three brothers who live in a village on the Atlantic coast are visited by their sister and nephew each summer. The nephew longs to accompany his uncles on their daily fishing excursion, but his mother believes he is too young. One night, the nephew sneaks aboard the boat and when he awakens the next day, the boat is out at sea. On their return from a day of fishing, the nephew falls into the ocean but is easily rescued by his uncles. For the remainder of the summer, the boy and his mother spend every day on the fishing boat. At the end of the story, the boy sadly explains the many changes that have occurred in the village because of the depleted fish stocks.

At Grandpa's Sugar Bush tells the story of a boy's visit to his grandfather's farm during spring break. The boy helps his grandfather tap the sugar maples and collect and boil the sap. The boy explains the process of making maple syrup and his role in assisting his grandfather. In *The Sugaring-Off Party*, Paul, a young boy, is about to experience his first maple-sugaring party. At his request, Paul's grandmother tells the story of her first sugaring-off party, complete with feasting, dancing, and the tasting of maple syrup!

In *Tiger's New Cowboys Boots*, illustrated by Georgia Graham, Tiger is excited about participating in his Uncle Roy's annual cattle drive. This year, he has "real cowboy boots" to wear instead of running shoes, and he hopes his new boots will impress the cowboys and his cousin, Jessica. However, no one seems to notice his footwear. By the time the herd reaches the summer meadow, Tiger's cowboy boots are "broken in," and Jessica compliments him by remarking, "your boots are just like mine."

GEORGIA GRAHAM

Georgia Graham lives on a farm in central Alberta in the middle of a rolling prairie landscape. The artwork for her illustrations in children's books greatly reflects this locale. Georgia grew up in the city of Calgary and says that it took her a long time to see and appreciate the beauty of the countryside—the flowers along the fence lines and the changing sky. Georgia attended the Alberta College of Art in Calgary; it was here, she says, that she learned how to learn. Given time to focus on English, history, and drawing, she developed as an artist. She says she was fortunate that the school brought so many models into the studio, because this experience taught her to draw.

After college, Georgia fully intended to move to New York to pursue life as an artist. Instead, she married a farmer and moved to Lacombe. Georgia continued her artwork and began writing stories for children. She took her portfolio and ideas to Tree Frog Press in Edmonton, who eventually sent her a manuscript to illustrate. Her first book, *Comet's Tale* by Sue Ann Alderson, was published in 1983. Georgia recalls that after this initial success, she sent material to 30 or 40 publishers before she had any further professional work. Looking back on that period, Georgia says the work she submitted was bad—she just didn't realize how bad! She submitted stories as well as illustrations, and all were rejected. She finally illustrated *The Most Beautiful Kite in the World*, written by Andrea Spalding and published in 1988. This was the true beginning of her career as an illustrator.

Bibi and the Bull by Carol Vaage, illustrated by Georgia Graham

Bibi and the Bull, written by Carol Vaage, was not published until 1995. Georgia spent the intervening years caring for her two children. *Tiger's New Cowboy Boots* by Irene Morck quickly followed *Bibi* in 1996. This book proved to be back-breaking work for Georgia. To prepare for the book, Georgia took part in a cattle drive on her brother-in-law's ranch, where she shot 22 rolls of film. She spent 1,400 hours drawing the cows alone! Georgia often uses her own children and family members as models for her work, and bases her drawings on photographs. *The Strongest Man This Side of Cremona* (1998) was the first book Georgia both wrote and illustrated.

Georgia says she can feel herself growing as a writer and illustrator and she has learned that a good story is not enough to make a good book. There must be a story within a story—the real story. *The Strongest Man This Side of Cremona* is not about a tornado, but about a boy's faith in his father; *Tiger's New Cowboy Boots* is not about a cattle drive, but about a boy's need to be accepted. Georgia still has work rejected by publishers, but she now knows that each rejection is a point of growth for her. She respects her publisher's opinions and comments because she knows he will publish only the very best. Georgia loves her work as an illustrator and feels fortunate to have such a life: she finds it immensely satisfying.

Bibi and the Bull (Vaage, 1995) is a popular story with Canadian children in preschool and kindergarten. One summer, Bibi, the heroine of the story, goes to visit her grandfather's farm. Grandpa takes Bibi on a tour of the farm, pointing out the dangerous places and telling her not to go near them. One day, while Grandpa is in the barn, the bull escapes from his pen, and Bibi, through her fearless—and loud—yelling, manages to scare him back into his pen. The story is based on an event from Carol Vaage's own family life and is richly illustrated by Georgia Graham.

Rainbow Bay (Hume, 1997) is an island in the Pacific Northwest. The story follows a boy and his dog through a day in the spring as they explore the surrounding area.

> *It's morning and the earth is new. Scout yawns and scratches an ear. We look out the window at Rainbow Bay. Water is flowing out to the sea. The tide is getting low. Things the sea had hidden are coming into view. (unpaginated)*

They visit the beaches, examine the tide pools, pick juicy strawberries, walk through the cedar forest, listen to the croaking frogs, and appreciate the solitude of their island. In *Driftwood Cove* (Lightburn, 1998), Matthew and Kate are visiting their grandparents on the west coast. During their explorations on the beach, they meet Selena and learn that she and her family are squatters. Kate and Matthew learn how Selena and her family survive and develop an appreciation of their lifestyle.

Hold On McGinty! (Harty, 1997) takes readers on a cross-Canada tour. McGinty has lived in Newfoundland for over 60 years. When the fish stocks diminish, his granddaughter encourages him to move to Vancouver Island. After much consideration, McGinty decides to leave Newfoundland. He flies to Toronto but sends his beloved boat by train. Once aboard the train, McGinty sleeps in his boat, which is strapped to a freight car. McGinty and his boat travel through northern Ontario. "The moon was low in the sky, shining across the islands of Lake Superior. The Northern Lights shivered in the heavens and on the water" (unpaginated). Across the prairies, over the Alberta foothills, and through the Rocky Mountains the train travels to Vancouver. A short ferry ride to Vancouver Island reunites McGinty and his granddaughter, and McGinty is able to fish once again.

Out on the Ice in the Middle of the Bay (Cumming, 1993) tells the story of an encounter between humans and polar bears. Leah's father instructs her to stay inside due to the proximity of polar bears. Simultaneously, a mother polar bear warns her cub not to stray, as humans are nearby. Each child disregards the parental warning and begins to explore. Leah and the cub meet out on the ice in the middle of the bay. Confused, Baby Nanook innocently allows Leah to snuggle into his warm fur coat. In search of their children, Leah's father and the mother polar bear meet, and each tries to attack the other. The noise of their confrontation frightens Leah and Baby Nanook, and the parents are astonished by the sight of their children, together. The children take refuge with their parents, and Leah's father uses his rifle to frighten away the bears.

Several Canadian picture books focus on specific periods of Canadian history. *The Dust Bowl* (Booth, 1996), *Tess* (Hutchins, 1995), *Prairie Willow* (Trottier, 1998) and *Emma and the Silk Train* (Lawson, 1997) are four such books. In *The Dust Bowl*, 50 years have passed since the drought of the 1930s, and the prairies are once again bone-dry. Matthew's grandfather recounts the many hardships suffered during the Dust Bowl and explains that although many farmers left their land, he and Matthew's grandmother stayed. Matthew's father, although frustrated with the current conditions, agrees not to sell the land. *Tess* is set many years ago on the prairies. To save money, Tess and her brother gather *malongo* (cow manure) to burn as their family's summer fuel. Tess feels ashamed when an unfriendly neighbour laughs scornfully at her sack of *malongo*. That winter, Tess rescues the unfriendly neighbour's dog from a pack of coyotes; the neighbour shows his gratitude by gathering *malongo* for Tess and her family. *Prairie Willow* tells the story of a family homesteading on the prairies. The family is constantly challenged by the elements of nature as they build a sod house and sow and harvest their crops. One of the children longs for a tree and orders a sapling from a catalogue. The rest of the story observes the family's experiences over the years, the willow tree symbolizing their strength and love.

Emma and the Silk Train tells the story of Emma, who is fascinated by the speeding silk trains that roar past the station where her father works. She longs to have some silk of her own. A train derailment provides her with the opportunity to rescue some of the silk which is now floating down the river.

> *One afternoon, Emma's search took her farther than she was allowed to go. She was rounding the bend, promising herself she would head straight back, when she saw a splash of color a little ways from the shore. The current caught the color and unfolded it into one long rippling stream. It looked red, until the sunlight touched it. Then it shimmered gold. (unpaginated)*

Emma is swept away by the current while trying to retrieve a bolt of the precious material she has discovered and becomes stranded on an island in the middle of the river. But Emma uses the silk in a unique way and, with the assistance of the crew of a passing silk train, is rescued. In a historical note at the end of the book, Lawson explains that the story is based on an event that happened in 1927 about 170 km east of Vancouver, British Columbia.

Human relationships provide a major focus for many picture story books, including *The Moccasin Goalie* (Brownridge, 1995), *Jeremiah Learns to Read* (Bogart, 1997), *Waiting for the Whales* (McFarlane, 1991), and *Something From Nothing* (Gilman, 1992). *The Moccasin Goalie* is about Danny and his three friends who have "hockey on the brain." Danny, the goalie, wears moccasins rather than skates due to a physical impairment. When it is announced that a hockey team is going to be formed, Danny and his friends are thrilled.

> *Everyone was silent as Mr. Matteau began reading out the names for the new team. Marcel was first to be called. The rest of us anxiously held our breath as the other names were added. Finally Mr. Matteau put down his clipboard. Anita, Petou and I couldn't believe it. We were not on the team. (unpaginated)*

Danny and his friends are very disappointed but when the regular goalie is injured, Danny has an opportunity to demonstrate his abilities. In *The Final Game: The Further Adventures of the Moccasin Goalie* (Brownridge, 1997), Danny and his friends are once again faced with the challenge of proving their worth as members of the hockey team.

Emma and the Silk Train by Julie Lawson, illustrated by Paul Mombourquette

In *Jeremiah Learns to Read*, Jeremiah, an elderly man, is capable of doing many, many things, but he cannot read. Jeremiah decides to attend school with the children in the area and, as a result, learns how to read and write. Jeremiah shares his new gift with his wife and inspires her to learn to read as well.

At the beginning of *Waiting for the Whales*, winner of several Canadian awards, including the 1992 Governor General's Literary Award for Illustration, readers meet a lonely grandfather. He lives by himself by the ocean and each year he anticipates the return of the whales.

> *But it was the orcas he longed to see. They travelled up and down the strait in front of his home. Sometimes he caught sight of them blowing in the distance. They were so very far away that seeing them only made him lonelier. (unpaginated)*

His daughter and new granddaughter move in with him, and although he grumbles about being followed by the child, he cherishes her beyond words. The grandfather shares his knowledge and love of the whales with his granddaughter; in the end, it is the orcas who help the girl deal with her grandfather's death.

PHOEBE GILMAN

Phoebe Gilman was born in the Bronx, New York, where she studied at the High School of Art and Design and at the Art Students' League at Hunter College in Manhattan. She describes herself as a good student who did as she was told and was good at drawing, but she wasn't the best. She adds that no one inspired her in school. It was her mother who instilled a love of literature in Phoebe at a very early age. She read to Phoebe frequently and made sure that Phoebe had her own library card. Phoebe remembers loving fairy tales, and as an adolescent she read the Nancy Drew series because she wanted stories with female protagonists.

Phoebe went on to study art in Europe and in Israel, where she had a number of solo exhibitions of her work in Tel Aviv. Phoebe settled in Canada in 1972, where she still lives. She was an instructor at the Ontario College of Art for fifteen years before she began to write and illustrate children's books full-time. Phoebe works in a studio built over her garage.

Phoebe's first book, *The Balloon Tree* (1984), was inspired by an incident that happened while she was taking a walk with her daughter. After her daughter's balloon became entangled in tree branches and burst, Phoebe imagined a scenario where a magic tree blossomed with balloons. She says she received at least 50 rejection letters from companies, over a period of 15 years, before the book was accepted by Scholastic. Among Phoebe's best-loved books are her three stories about Jillian Jiggs: *Jillian Jiggs* (1985), *The Wonderful Pigs of Jillian Jiggs* (1988), and *Jillian Jiggs to the Rescue* (1994). The plots of the three books were inspired by events that happened to one of Phoebe's daughters.

Phoebe won the Ruth Schwartz Children's Book Award for her seventh book, *Something From Nothing* (1992), which she adapted from a Jewish folktale. Her illustrations depict two parallel stories taking place simultaneously: one about the human family living in the cottage, the other about the mouse family living below the floorboards. Phoebe's use of borders surrounding the illustrations adds to the magic of the central storyline. In 1993, Phoebe was awarded the Vicky Metcalf Award for a Body of Work. *Pirate Pearl* (1998) continues Phoebe's quest for stories with strong female protagonists.

Something From Nothing by Phoebe Gilman is a beautiful, gentle adaptation of a traditional Jewish tale about family life. The story begins when Joseph is a baby and his grandfather makes him a blanket. As Joseph grows up, the blanket wears out, and his mother decides it's time to throw it out. But Joseph refuses to part with the blanket and takes it to his grandfather, who makes the remaining fabric into a jacket. From there, it eventually becomes a vest, a tie, a handkerchief, and, finally, a button. One day, the button rolls between the wooden floorboards, and Joseph has to accept that even his grandfather cannot make something from nothing.

Throughout the book, Gilman's illustrations depict a mouse family living below the floor of grandfather's house. At times, these illustrations appear to be part of the border of the page, but close scrutiny reveals a second story parallelling Joseph's growth. Gilman's illustrations are oil and egg tempera paintings, built up in alternating layers on gessoed D'Arches satin finish watercolour paper.

We conclude our presentation of Canadian picture story books by mentioning three well-known fantasy books about an adventurous cat named Zoom. In Tim Wynne-Jones' *Zoom at Sea* (1983), illustrated by Eric Beddows, Zoom travels to an address his Uncle Roy has written in his diary; there, at Maria's unusual house, Zoom has an adventure at sea. In *Zoom Away* (1985), Zoom again goes to Maria's house, and together they travel to the North Pole in a quest to find Uncle Roy. In *Zoom Upstream* (1992), Zoom and Maria are once more in search of Uncle Roy. Through a bookcase in Maria's house, Zoom descends a flight of stairs to a dark river. Using a crate for a boat, Zoom travels down river until he reaches Egypt. At the end of this adventure, both Zoom and the reader finally meet Uncle Roy.

Selecting a small sample of Canadian picture story books from the many available is not an easy task. Additional picture story books are listed at the end of this chapter, and a list of professional resources is also provided to help you to locate further outstanding examples of picture story books to use in your classroom.

TIM WYNNE-JONES

Like many authors and illustrators, Tim Wynne-Jones came to the art of writing for children in a round-about way. In addition to his series of *Zoom* books, Tim is known for his young-adult work, *Some of the Kinder Planets* (1993), *The Maestro* (1995), and *Stephen Fair* (1998). Tim was born in Cheshire, England, but moved to British Columbia as a young child. From there, he moved to Ontario, where he still resides. He graduated with a Bachelor of Fine Arts degree from the University of Waterloo, followed by a Master of Fine Arts from York University in 1979. Interestingly, Tim's first career choice was architecture, a profession pursued by many other well-known authors and illustrators of children's books, including David Macaulay. Tim, however, did not find architecture satisfying, although he does find that visual images are important in his writing.

When Tim first turned to writing, he looked to adult fiction. His first novel, a suspense story entitled *Odd's End* (1980), won the Seal First Novel Award (with a prize of $50,000). Since then, he has produced numerous picture books and novels for children, an opera libretto, a children's musical, and more than a dozen plays for CBC. His first successful children's book was *Zoom at Sea* (1983), a picture book about a cat named Zoom. The book won the 1984 IODE Book Award and the 1984 Ruth Schwartz Children's Book Award, as well as the Amelia Frances Howard-Gibbon Award for illustrator Eric Beddows. *Some of the Kinder Planets*, a book of short stories, won the 1994 Governor General's Award, the 1994 Canadian Library Association Award for Children, and the 1995 Boston Globe-Horn Book Award for Fiction. "The Hope Bakery," one of the stories from *Some of the Kinder Planets*, won the 1994 Vicky Metcalf Short Story Award. The stories in this collection tell the individual tales of nine "average" Ontario children and the adventures they find themselves involved in. Tim's young-adult novel, *The Maestro*, earned him his second Governor General's Award in 1995 and met with high critical acclaim. Many consider *The Maestro* to mark Canada's "coming of age" in young-adult literature.

Tim notes that Canadian children's literature has made great strides since the publication of his first children's book in 1976. In that year, only 35 children's books were published in Canada; in 1996, more than 400 children's books were published, many of them selling overseas. Many quality publishing houses in Canada now produce books for children, among them Northern Lights, the children's arm of Red Deer Press, for whom Tim worked for a number of years as an editor. Under his guidance, many fine children's books were produced including *Mister Got to Go* by Lois Simmie (1995) and *Tiger's New Cowboy Boots*, written by Irene Morck and illustrated by Georgia Graham (1996).

Tim continues his writing for children, but he is very much an extrovert and his great passion is his music: writing, performing, and recording CDs with his rock group, an endeavour that brings a huge smile to Tim's face whenever he has an opportunity to talk about it!

Picture Books for Older Readers

Some older readers may at first feel puzzled at being invited to read a picture book, but picture books designed for older children are challenging in content and style. Sixth-grade children respond very powerfully to books such as *Black and White* (Macaulay, 1990), *The Tunnel* (Browne, 1989), and *June 29, 1999* (Wiesner, 1992). One sixth-grade class we know spent most of one noon hour looking at the pictures in *The Tunnel*, picking out the hidden characters and the references to fairy tales.

Black and White is an adventure in metafiction, a constant and deliberate reminder that a book is something an author and reader create together, something that is not real but fictional and that is open to many interpretations and structures. "By drawing attention to how texts are structured, metafictions can show readers how texts mean and, by analogy, how meanings are ascribed to everyday reality"

(Stephens & Watson, 1994, p.44). *Black and White* consists of four narrative strands, each making use of different narrative and pictorial techniques. Each double-page spread is divided into four sections so that the four narratives unfold at the same time. "Seeing Things," "Problem Parents," "A Waiting Game," and "Udder Chaos" become visually mixed in the later section of the text as the frames are broken by images that spill over into adjacent frames. On the title page the author warns readers: "This book appears to contain a number of stories that do not necessarily occur at the same time. Then again, it may contain only one story. In any event, careful inspection of both words and pictures is recommended."

The Tunnel by Anthony Browne begins like many traditional fairy stories: "Once upon a time there lived a sister and brother who were not at all alike" (unpaginated). Fairy stories provide the background and the symbolism for this book, which tells the story of a girl who is afraid of scary things and is tested to the limit when she has to rescue her brother from a desperate situation. Her brother is fearless and a risk-taker, but it is the sister's courage that creates the circumstances for the two to come to know each other and acknowledge their mutual love. Browne's illustrations depict the fear, and the bravery, of the characters through subtle allusion to well-known fairy stories, particularly *Hansel and Gretel* and *Little Red Riding Hood.* The double-page illustration in the centre of the book is one of the most powerful images in current picture books.

In a very different story, *June 29, 1999,* student Holly Evans develops an ambitious and innovative project for her science assignment. While her classmates are sprouting seeds in paper cups, Holly launches seedlings into the sky on tiny air balloons. Although her teacher and fellow students are skeptical, only five weeks later giant vegetables begin to fall from the sky, landing in various parts of the United States. Holly is elated as she tracks the landing of the vegetables. There is just one problem for her: arugula lands in Ashtabula. Holly did not launch arugula. "More curious than disappointed, Holly asks herself, "What happened to my vegetables? And whose broccoli is in my backyard?" (unpaginated). Her question is answered on the last page, although Holly is unlikely to discover that answer herself. The book displays Wiesner's unconventional artwork and the dry humour first encountered in *Free Fall* (1988) and *Tuesday* (1991). The pictures must be read carefully to appreciate the full impact of Wiesner's craft. On one page, the illustration depicts Holly watching the television news as more vegetables come to earth. A copy of the tabloid newspaper *Star* lies open on the floor with the headlines "4,000 lb. radish has face of Elvis" and "Man kidnapped by space aliens," possible clues in the unravelling of the mystery.

These picture books, and others created for older readers, are not necessarily easy-reading books. Many of them deal with mature themes and contain illustrations that provide powerful messages supporting and adding to the text. Two books set in Europe during World War Two are *Rose Blanche* (Innocenti, 1985) and *Let the Celebrations Begin!* (Wild, 1991). In *Rose Blanche,* the reader is told that Rose gradually sees her town change, food items become scarce, and troops arrive. One day Rose Blanche sees the mayor bullying a young boy (clearly labelled as a Jew in the illustrations). The boy is bundled into a military vehicle and is not seen again. Rose Blanche tries to follow the truck and, in doing so, discovers the concentration camp imprisoning the Jewish children outside the town. Rose Blanche attempts to help the children but eventually loses her life in the effort. Innocenti's illustrations provide almost all of the details, creating the emotional impact of the story. The text is written from the perspective of a naïve child during the first part of the book, and from a more distanced, third-person perspective in the second part of the book. The words *Nazi, Jew,* and *concentration camp* are not mentioned in the text. The illustrations, created in drab colors with much khaki and dull red, express a sombre mood of pain and desolation; they emphasize the story's message of the futility of armed hostility and the vulnerability of children in such circumstances.

Let the Celebrations Begin!, an Australian book, has been published in Canada as *A Time for Toys*; it is published in the United Kingdom and the United States under its original title. This publishing information is relevant to our discussion, since the book has generated some controversy. The story is one of hope, a gentle and beautiful retelling of a true story that happened in one Polish concentration camp towards the end of the World War Two. As news spreads through the camp that the allied army is on the brink of liberating the camp, the survivors begin to plan celebrations. The women, having decided they will make soft toys for the children, begin to beg odd scraps of fabric from each other in order to create toys for a generation of children who have never known freedom nor owned toys. When the liberation army enters the camp, encountering the women and children for the first time, the scene is one of great awe. The story is a tribute to the human spirit and to the survival of so many innocent people who lived for years in horrific conditions.

Julie Vivas' illustrations are in bright colors—red, blue, and yellow—and the faces of the women and children are animated and full of hope as well as sadness. When plans were being made to publish the book in Canada, many groups were invited to provide a response to the text. In response to this feedback, Wild changed the names of the characters to more common Jewish names instead of the Polish names she had originally chosen; some of the language in the text was also changed. However, since the book is an Australian publication, Wild refused to totally "Americanize" the book (although this was at the request of the Canadian publishers, not the American publishers). Consequently, a second version of the book was developed for the North American audience, but the title was changed for the Canadian edition only.

Canadian authors William Kaplan and Shelley Tanaka tell the true story of Kaplan's father's and grandparents' escape from the Holocaust in *One More Border: The True Story of One Family's Escape From War-Torn Europe* (1998). In 1939, Kaplan's grandparents leave their home in Memel, Lithuania for fear of being captured by Nazi soldiers. However, Lithuania is invaded by the Russians, who also dislike the Jewish people. A plan is made to travel to Canada where Kaplan's great-grandparents reside, but the family needs written permission to leave Lithuania. Kaplan's grandfather is able to obtain visas from the Japanese consul, Mr. Sugihara. However, Kaplan's grandmother is Russian and needs separate permission to leave the country. Minutes before their departure, she obtains permission to leave Lithuania but not Russia. The family travels on the Trans-Siberian Express from Moscow to Russia's far-eastern port, Vladivostok. At Vladivostok, Kaplan's grandmother must once again obtain a visa. Money and jewelry are exchanged for a visa, and the family is finally free to leave Russia. They travel by boat from Japan to Vancouver, where they board a train and travel across Canada to Cornwall, Ontario. The narrative is gripping, and Kaplan provides many interesting details about the family's dangerous journey. Sidebars, archival photographs, and maps assist the reader in understanding the geographical and historical context of the story. In *Passage to Freedom: The Sugihara Story* (Mochizuki, 1997), the son of consul Mr. Sugihara tells the story of his father's remarkable courage in helping Jewish people (like the Kaplans) in Lithuania.

There are also a number of powerful picture books about the dropping of the atomic bomb on Hiroshima on August 6, 1945, including *My Hiroshima* (Morimoto, 1987), *Sadako* (Coerr, 1993), *Hiroshima No Pika* (Maruki, 1980), and *Shin's Tricycle* (Kodama, 1995). In *My Hiroshima*, Junko Morimoto remembers her childhood, growing up in Hiroshima in a society at war. She was in high school when she witnessed the dropping of the atomic bomb and the remarkable survival of her family. Her story is vividly depicted in the illustrations, which manage to capture the devastation and suffering of the people in a sensitive, yet disturbing, way—a book that attempted to depict the atomic blast without also presenting the great suffering of the population would be unconscionable. The book is not for the faint-hearted, but it is a beautiful book that reminds us that we must learn from history. The back of the book contains a photograph of the Peace Memorial in Hiroshima and the words from the memorial: "Let all the souls here rest in peace, for we shall not repeat the evil." Morimoto graduated from Kyoto University in Fine Arts and taught in Japan for six years. She now lives in Australia and has published a number of award-winning children's books.

Sadako, Hiroshima No Pika, and *Shin's Tricycle* are also based on personal accounts of people who experienced the bombing of Hiroshima. Sadako was only a baby when the atomic bomb was dropped on Hiroshima, but she remembers the "Thunderbolt." One day, Sadako, now a nine-year-old who loves to run and who seems to be full of energy, faints in the school yard. Her condition is diagnosed as leukemia, and she is hospitalized. Sadako's friend, Chizuko, tells her the story of the crane: "It's supposed to live for a thousand years. If a sick person folds one thousand paper cranes, the gods will grant her wish and make her well again" (unpaginated). Sadako begins folding paper cranes, but dies on October 25, 1955 before completing the thousand. Her friends and classmates work together to fold the remaining 365 paper cranes so that Sadako is buried with 1,000 paper cranes. Sadako's friends envision a monument built in her honour, and people from all over Japan work together to collect money. In 1958, a statue of Sadako was erected in Hiroshima Peace Park, and every Peace Day, garlands of paper cranes are hung under the statue. At the base of Sadako's monument, the children's wish is engraved: "This is our cry, this is our prayer: Peace in the world" (unpaginated).

Eight years after the atomic bomb was dropped, Toshi Maruki was exhibiting pictures about the tragic event in a small town on the island of Hokkaido. A woman attending the exhibition recounted the story of how she "had tried to escape the Flash, carrying her wounded husband upon her back and leading her child by the hand" (unpaginated). Although *Hiroshima No Pika* is based on the woman's story, Maruki has also woven in other experiences she has collected about the dropping of the bomb.

Shin's Tricycle is a true story about four-year-old Shin, who desperately wanted a tricycle and was thrilled when he received one as an early birthday present from his uncle. On the morning the atomic bomb was dropped, Shin and his best friend were riding the tricycle outside Shin's house. After the explosion, his parents found Shin alive; their other children had perished in the fires. Shin later died as well, and his parents buried him in their backyard alongside his best friend. They buried the remains of Shin's beloved tricycle next to the children. Years later, Shin's parents decided to give their children a proper burial. When they uncovered the tricycle, Shin's father decided to donate it to the Peace Museum in Hiroshima. Although the tricycle serves as a reminder of the victims of Hiroshima, it also inspires humankind to strive for lasting peace.

Many books for older readers are entertaining, playful, and clever, stimulating the imagination and stretching our notions of reading. There are parodies of well-known tales, such as *The Three Little Pigs and the Big Bad Wolf*; these are discussed in the section on traditional literature in Chapter 3. Other picture story books aimed at older readers include *The Mummer's Song* (Davidge and Wallace, 1993), *Night in the Country* (Rylant, 1986), *Piggybook* (Browne, 1986), and *The Widow's Broom* (Van Allsburg, 1992). Each of these picture books creates a sense of wonder and provides challenging perspectives on the reading event and the nature of the picture book. Additional titles of picture books suitable for older readers are presented at the end of the chapter. In addition, *Worth a Thousand Words: An Annotated Guide to Picture Books for Older Readers* (Ammon &

Sherman, 1996) is a worthwhile professional resource for those individuals searching for picture books for older readers.

It is important to remember that the appropriateness of picture books for particular age levels is influenced by how teachers use the literature, by the theme or topic of the book, and by the language and text structures used in the book. Many picture books designed for young children can be used with children in the upper elementary grades if done with a specific and appropriate purpose in mind.

The Illustrations in Picture Books

As we browse the selection of picture books noted in this chapter, we are struck by the high quality of the artwork and the ingenuity of the storytelling involved in the interweaving of picture and text. Throughout this chapter we have focussed on the stories and visual art of authors and illustrators such as Janet and Allan Ahlberg, David Macaulay, David Wiesner, John Burningham, Anthony Browne, Georgia Graham, and Phoebe Gilman. Many of the artists who illustrate children's books, including Ken Nutt (Eric Beddows) and Harvey Chan, exhibit their work in galleries and shows, and all have been educated at highly regarded art colleges. Their work in creating illustrations for children's books is one aspect of their creative and artistic talents. When an artist can both illustrate and tell a story, it is a particularly powerful combination.

Judith Graham (1990) maintains that the contribution of illustrations to reading development has been seriously underestimated. In the last fifteen years or so, our understanding of the act of reading has developed considerably—it now includes such things as knowledge of narrative conventions and imaging (or interior visualization). Michael Benton and Geoff Fox (1985) conclude that "picturing is the most important element in the way in which a reader brings a story to imaginative life" (p.13) Graham (1990) adds that in many picture books, the images are so interwoven with the text "that to give the text alone would be like giving a performance of a concerto without an orchestra" (p.17). This is especially true in the work of author/illustrators like John Burningham and Anthony Browne. In Browne's *Piggybook* (1986), for example, the reader must move constantly between text and illustration "in a complex process of picturing the text and verbalizing pictures," allowing one to complement the other (Graham, 1990, p.83). The illustrations in *Piggybook* have their own way of ensuring the reader's involvement in the book and the creation of a story: each illustration is fed by an earlier and a later one. Graham says that the book, if we let it, teaches the reader how to bring meaning to reading. This is very much the point Margaret Meek makes in her wonderfully succinct book *How Texts Teach What Readers Learn* (1988). The most important aspect of the art in picture books, however, is that it must speak to children.

Perry Nodelman (1988) maintains that picture books are unlike any other form of verbal or visual art: the pictures in picture books are not meant primarily to excite our aesthetic sensibilities, but exist mainly to assist in the telling of stories. He speaks of the importance of the semiotic content of the artwork—that is, aspects of colour, tone, angle, view, the relations of visual objects to each other, the relative placement of text and pictures, and the graphic style. An illustration in a picture book must be evaluated very differently from a print hanging on a wall. The art in children's books must clarify or add information, expand upon or interpret the author's meaning, evoke mood, establish setting, and portray character; otherwise it is simply decorative. "Because the communication of narrative information and not aesthetic beauty for its own sake is their purpose, because they are more significantly meaningful than either accurate or beautiful, the pictures in picture books always have much more in common with cartoons. In an important sense, they almost always are cartoons" (Nodelman, 1988, p.98).

Many educators would disagree with Nodelman's point of view. Schwartz and Sommerfeld (1990) maintain that it is from the art in children's picture books that most children receive their formal visual-aesthetic education. Schwartz and Sommerfeld say that although few children will become professional artists or designers, most need to become aesthetically literate consumers of products and services, including magazines, movies, and the art in picture books. They have found that children's books can be highly suitable resources for teaching art in the elementary school, particularly books illustrated by artists such as George Littlechild, Barbara Reid, and Ted Harrison.

Judith Graham (1990) writes:

> *From the moment they are born, children in our culture are surrounded not only by reality in the form of people and objects and actions but also by a different sort of reality, representations of reality which issue from television screens and radio, posters, pictures and books. It may take the child some time to work out how this second order reality is related to and reflects upon the first, but there is no doubt that for many children the representation is as intriguing as the real thing. (p.7)*

It is certainly true, in the picture books highlighted in this chapter, that the artwork is as intriguing as the real world—possibly more so!

Zena Sutherland (1997) asserts that children begin their reading lives as strong literalists. They want the illustrations in a book to provide a truthful interpretation of the text, and they prefer colour to black and white. Thus they enjoy books such as *Can't You Sleep, Little Bear?*, written by Martin Waddell and illustrated by Barbara Firth (1992), and *Zoom Upstream*, written by Tim Wynne-Jones and illustrated by Eric Beddows (1992). Even very young children notice the detail in book illustrations and look for accuracy and consistency. Children are fascinated, for example, by the parallel story of the mice under the floorboards in Phoebe Gilman's *Something From Nothing*.

John Burningham has been creating books for young children since 1963, when his first book, *Borka, The Adventures of a Goose With No Feathers*, won the Kate Greenaway Medal in England. Burningham uses a wide range of materials and varies the style of his artwork to suit the subject of the book. Humour is present in almost all of his books, even in the cumulative tale *Mr Gumpy's Outing* (1970), for which he won his second Greenaway Medal. This simply written story, about a man who takes a group of animals and children for a boat ride followed by afternoon tea, has flowery pastel pictures that are very different from the bold alphabet illustrations of *John Burningham's ABC* (1967) or the vibrant colours of *Come Away from the Water, Shirley* (1977). In *Cloudland* (1996), Burningham uses completely different materials to depict the tale of a child who gets lost in his daydreams and finds himself living in the clouds. A combination of photographic collage and drawing provides the engaging visual narrative.

As readers mature, they look for something quite different in picture book illustrations. David Macaulay is one author/illustrator who has made a particularly strong contribution to the whole field of picture books. His first book, *Cathedral: The Story of Its Construction* (1973), developed from his earlier study of architecture, is a detailed description of the architectural advances of the times in which the great medieval cathedrals were built. Quite different is his artwork in the spoof *Motel of the Mysteries* (1979) and the hilariously funny *Shortcut* (1995). His work of metafiction, *Black and White* (1990), is different again, telling four or five stories in one. *The Way Things Work* (1988) has been acclaimed as his most outstanding book, combining informative drawing and visual beauty.

Ian Wallace has been illustrating books since 1974, but his first major success was *Chin Chiang and the Dragon's Dance* (1984), which he both wrote and illustrated. In preparation for the book, Wallace travelled to Vancouver, New York, and other major cities with Chinatowns of their own. Wallace wanted to create a story that would accurately represent the culture but that would also present a child with the kinds of problems and feelings that all other children at some time experience. The illustrations for *Chin Chiang and the Dragon's Dance* are vibrant, colourful, and energetic; they make a strong contrast with the delicate, muted pencil-crayon illustrations of *The Name of the Tree: A Bantu Tale* (Lottridge, 1989). Wallace received high praise for *A Winter's Tale* (1997) and is credited with an ever-expanding style, especially evident in his depiction of the sky, trees, shadows, and snow banks in this book. His bold illustrations in *Boy of the Deeps* (1999) continue to build Wallace's reputation as an illustrator and storyteller.

Without a doubt, most children's books, in both the text and illustrations, reflect a middle-class environment. Only recently have books sensitively portrayed such issues as poverty or authentically and respectfully depicted cultural and ethnic groups outside the mainstream of Canadian society. There is still much to be done in children's book illustration to reflect the heterogeneous nature of the Canadian audience. Authors and illustrators working together to create authentic representations of Canadian life and society are, however, slowly making a difference. The combined work of Paul Yee and Harvey Chan, and the illustrations of Rhian Brynjolson, George Littlechild, Leo Yerxa, and Annouchka Galouchko are beginning to reflect the multicultural nature of Canadian readers.

References

Ammon, B. and G. Sherman. 1996. *Worth a Thousand Words: An Annotated Guide to Picture Books for Older Readers*. Englewood, Colorado: Libraries Unlimited, Inc.

Benton, M. and G. Fox. 1985. *Teaching Literature 9-14*. Toronto: Oxford University Press.

Glazer, J. 1997. *Introduction to Children's Literature*. Second edition. Upper Saddle River, New Jersey: Prentice-Hall, Inc.

Graham, J. 1990. *Pictures on the Page*. Sheffield, England: National Association for the Teaching of English.

Jacobs, J. and M. Tunnell. 1996. *Children's Literature, Briefly*. Englewood Cliffs, New Jersey: Prentice-Hall, Inc.

Kiefer, B. 1995. *The Potential of Picturebooks*. Englewood Cliffs, New Jersey: Prentice-Hall, Inc.

Meek, M. 1988. *How Texts Teach What Readers Learn*. Stroud, England: Thimble Press.

Nodelman, P. 1988. *Words About Pictures: The Narrative Art of Children's Picture Books*. Athens: University of Georgia Press.

Schwartz, B. and J. Sommerfeld. 1990. Visual images in books, a neglected resource in children's aesthetic education. *Canadian Children's Literature* 60, 25-33.

Sutherland, Z. 1997. *Children and Books*. Ninth edition. New York: Longman.

Tomlinson, C. and C. Lynch-Brown. 1996. *Essentials of Children's Literature*. Second edition. Needham, Massachusetts: Allyn & Bacon.

Stephens, J. and K. Watson, eds. 1994. *From Picture Book to Literary Theory*. Sydney, Australia: St. Clair Press.

Wynne-Jones, T. 1980. *Odd's End*. Toronto: McClelland & Stewart.

Professional Resources

Ammon, B. and G. Sherman. 1996. *Worth a Thousand Words: An Annotated Guide to Picture Books for Older Readers*. Englewood, Colorado: Libraries Unlimited, Inc. • The book features 645 picture books, arranged alphabetically by author or editor's last name. Each entry gives a brief annotation, a subject list (e.g., theme, genre, topics) to enhance the book's potential classroom use, and suggestions for using the book in other curricular areas.

Glazer, J. 1997. *Introduction to Children's Literature.* Second edition. Upper Saddle River, New Jersey: Prentice-Hall, Inc. • Glazer's text focusses on children, from preschool through grade four, and their interactions with books. In the first six chapters, she defines literature for children, discusses the values of literature, classifies books according to format and genre, explores children's responses to literature, and discusses how literature can be used in all curricular areas. The remaining six chapters explore the various literary genres in depth and provide practical classroom examples for each genre.

Kiefer, B. 1995. *The Potential of Picturebooks: From Visual Literacy to Aesthetic Understanding.* Englewood Cliffs, New Jersey: Prentice-Hall. • This textbook is devoted to examining the many issues associated with picture books, including children's responses to picture books and the development of contexts that support and encourage children's responses to picture books. Keifer devotes the second section of her book to discussions of the history of picture books, the process of creating picture books, and the artistic styles of picture books. In the third section of the book, "Picturebooks in the Classroom," she explores the art of picture books, provides suggestions for studying an illustrator, and discusses book-making and publishing. Kiefer provides many classroom suggestions and identifies numerous picture book titles throughout her book.

Wordless Books

Amoss, B. 1987. *What Did You Lose, Santa?* New York: Harper & Row, Publishers.

Baker, J. 1991. *Window.* New York: Greenwillow Books.

Bang, M. 1980. *The Grey Lady and the Strawberry Snatcher.* New York: Crown. (1981 Caldecott Honor book)

Collington, P. 1990. *On Christmas Eve.* New York: Alfred A. Knopf, Inc.

Goodall, J. 1988. *Little Red Riding Hood.* New York: M. McElderry Books.

Hutchins, P. 1971. *Changes, Changes.* New York: Macmillan.

Mayer, M. 1967. *A Boy, a Dog, and a Frog.* New York: Dial Books for Young Readers.

McCully, E.A. 1984. *Picnic.* New York: Harper & Row, Publishers

————. 1987. *School.* New York: Harper & Row, Publishers.

————. 1988. *The Christmas Gift.* New York: Harper & Row, Publishers.

Ormerod, J. 1981. *Sunshine.* Harmondsworth, UK: Puffin Books.

————. 1982. *Moonlight.* Harmondsworth, UK: Puffin Books.

Rohmann, E. 1994. *Time Flies.* New York: Crown. (1995 Caldecott Honor book)

Spier, P. 1977. *Noah's Ark.* New York: Doubleday.

————. 1982. *Peter Spier's Rain.* New York: Doubleday.

Tafuri, N. 1988. *Junglewalk.* New York: Greenwillow Books.

Wiesner, D. 1988. *Free Fall.* New York: Lothrop.

Wouters, A. 1992. *This Book Is Too Small.* New York: Dutton Children's Books.

Concept Books

COLOUR

Ehlert, L. 1989. *Color Zoo.* New York: Lippincott. (1990 Caldecott Honor book)

Hoban, T. 1978. *Is It Red? Is It Yellow? Is It Blue?* New York: Greenwillow Books.

————. 1989. *Of Colors and Things.* New York: Greenwillow Books.

————. 1995. *Color Everywhere.* New York: Morrow.

Jonas, A. 1989. *Color Dance.* New York: Greenwillow Books.

Lynn, S. 1986. *Colors.* New York: Little, Brown and Company.

Serfozo, M. 1988. *Who Said Red?* New York: M. McElderry Books.

Walsh, E.S. 1989. *Mouse Paint.* New York: Harcourt Brace and Jovanovich.

SEASONS

Florian, D. 1987. *A Winter Day.* New York: Greenwillow Books.

————. 1988. *A Summer Day.* New York: Greenwillow Books.

Fowler, S.G. 1989. *When Summer Ends.* New York: Greenwillow Books.

Gibbons, G. 1995. *The Reasons for the Seasons*. New York: Holiday House.

Gomi, T. 1989. *Spring Is Here*. San Francisco: Chronicle Books.

McEvoy, G. 1995. *Alfie's Long Winter*. Toronto: Stoddart Publishing.

Wildsmith, B. 1980. *Animal Seasons*. New York: Oxford University Press.

OPPOSITES

Demi. 1987. *Demi's Opposites, An Animal Gamebook*. New York: Grosset & Dunlap.

Gillham, B. and S. Hulme. 1984. *Let's Look for Opposites*. New York: Coward.

Hoban, T. 1972. *Push Pull, Empty Full: A Book of Opposites*. New York: Macmillan.

Hoban, T. 1990. *Exactly the Opposite*. New York: Greenwillow Books.

Kightley, R. 1986. *Opposites*. New York: Little, Brown and Company.

Leedy, L. 1987. *Big, Small, Short, and Tall*. New York: Holiday House.

Spier, P. 1972. *Fast-Slow High-Low: A Book of Opposites*. New York: Doubleday.

Turner, G. 1993. *Opposites*. New York: Viking Press.

OTHER CONCEPT BOOKS

Aliki. 1990. *My Feet*. New York: Crowell.

———. 1990. *My Hands*. New York: Crowell.

Anholt, C. and L. Anholt. 1992. *Kids*. London: Candlewick Press.

Baer, G. 1989. *Thump, Thump, Rat-a-tat-tat*. New York: Harper & Row, Publishers.

Barton, B. 1987. *Machines at Work*. New York: Crowell.

———. 1989. *Dinosaurs, Dinosaurs*. New York: Crowell.

Browne, A. 1989. *I Like Books*. New York: Alfred A. Knopf.

Browne, P. 1996. *A Gaggle of Geese*. New York: Simon & Schuster.

Burton, K. 1995. *One Grey Mouse*. Toronto: Kids Can Press.

Collier, J. 1993. *The Backyard*. New York: Viking Press.

Crews, D. 1986. *Flying*. New York: Greenwillow Books.

Emberley, R. 1987. *Jungle Sounds*. New York: Little, Brown and Company.

Goennel, H. 1987. *When I Grow Up...* Boston: Little, Brown and Company.

Henkes, K. 1995. *The Biggest Boy*. New York: Morrow.

Kandoian, E. 1989. *Is Anybody Up?* New York: Putnam.

Koch, M. 1991. *Hoot, Howl, Hiss*. New York: Greenwillow Books.

Lember, B. 1994. *A Book of Fruit*. New York: Ticknor and Fields.

Marlette, D. 1994. *The Before and After*. Boston: Houghton Mifflin Company.

McMillan, B. 1989. *Super Super Superwords*. New York: Lothrop.

———. 1991. *Eating Fractions*. New York: Scholastic Inc.

Nolan, H. 1995. *How Much, How Many, How Far, How Heavy, How Long, How Tall Is 1,000?* Toronto: Kids Can Press.

Oppenheim, J. 1996. *Have You Seen Bugs?* Richmond Hill, Ontario: North Winds Press.

Siddals, M. 1997. *Tell Me a Season*. New York: Clarion Books

Tafuri, N. 1987. *In a Red House*. New York: Greenwillow Books.

———. 1987. *Where We Sleep*. New York: Greenwillow Books.

verDorn, B. 1990. *Moon Glows*. New York: Arcade.

Winthrop, E. 1986. *Shoes*. New York: Harper & Row, Publishers.

Alphabet Books

Anno, M. 1975. *Anno's Alphabet*. New York: Crowell.

Aylesworth, J. 1992. *Old Black Fly*. New York: Holt, Reinhart & Winston.

Base, G. 1986. *Animalia*. New York: Harry N. Abrams, Inc., Publishers.

Bowen, B. 1991. *Antler, Bar, Canoe—A Northwoods Alphabet Year*. Boston: Little, Brown and Company.

Bruna, D. 1987. *B is for Bear*. New York: Methuen.

Chin-Lee, C. 1997. *A is for Asia*. New York: Orchard Books.

Chwast, S. 1991. *The Alphabet Parade*. San Diego: Harcourt Brace and Jovanovich.

Dragonwagon, C. 1987. *Alligator Arrived with Apples: A Potluck Alphabet Feast*. New York: Macmillan.

Ehlert, L. 1987. *Growing Vegetable Soup*. New York: Harcourt Brace and Jovanovich.

————. 1989. *Eating the Alphabet: Fruits and Aegetables from A to Z*. New York: Harcourt Brace and Jovanovich.

Ellis, V.F. 1990. *Afro-bets First Book About Africa*. New York: Just Us Books.

Elting, M. and M. Folsom. 1980. *Q is for Duck: An Alphabet Guessing Game*. New York: Clarion Books.

Fisher, L.E. 1991. *The ABC Exhibit*. New York: Macmillan.

Geisert, A. 1986. *Pigs from A to Z*. New York: Houghton Mifflin Company.

Johnson, S.T. 1995. *Alphabet City*. New York: Viking.

Jonas, A. 1990. *Aardvarks, Disembark!* New York: Greenwillow Books.

Kitamura, S. 1992. *From Acorn to Zoo*. New York: Farrar, Straus & Giroux.

Kitchen, B. 1984. *Animal Alphabet*. New York: Dial Books.

Lear, E. 1992. *A Was Once an Apple Pie*. New York: The Dial Press.

Lobel, A. 1981. *On Market Street*. New York: Greenwillow Books.

————. 1990. *Allison's Zinnia*. New York: Greenwillow Books.

MacDonald, S. 1986. *Alphabatics*. New York: Bradbury Press.

Marshall, J. 1995. *Look Once, Look Twice*. New York: Ticknor & Fields.

Martin, C. 1992. *A Yellowstone ABC*. Niwot, Colorado: Roberts Rinehart Publishers.

Micklethwait, L. 1992. *I Spy an Alphabet in Art*. New York: Greenwillow Books.

Mullins, P. 1993. *V for Vanishing: An Alphabet of Endangered Animals*. New York: HarperCollins Publishers.

Musgrove, M. 1986. *Ashanti to Zulu: African Traditions*. New York: The Dial Press.

Neumeier, M. and B. Glaser. 1985. *Action Alphabet*. New York: Greenwillow Books.

Onyefulu, I. 1993. *A Is for Africa*. New York: Cobblehill Books.

Pallota, J. 1986. *The Ocean Alphabet Book*. Watertown, Massachusetts: Charlesbridge Publishing.

Paul, A. 1991. *Eight Hands Round: A Patchwork Alphabet*. New York: HarperCollins Publishers.

Pelletier, D. 1996. *The Graphic Alphabet*. New York: Orchard Books.

Powell, C. 1995. *A Bold Carnivore: An Alphabet of Predators*. Niwot, Colorado: Roberts Rinehart Publishers.

Reasoner, C. and V. Hardt. 1989. *Alphabite*. Los Angeles: Price.

Rutherford, E. 1994. *An Island Alphabet*. Charlottetown: Ragweed Press.

Ruurs, M. 1996. *A Mountain Alphabet*. Toronto: Tundra Books.

Ryden, H. 1988. *Wild Animals of America ABC*. New York: Lodestar/Dutton.

Shannon, G. 1996. *Tomorrow's Alphabet*. New York: Greenwillow Books.

Van Allsburg, C. 1987. *The Z Was Zapped: A Play in Twenty-six Acts*. New York: Houghton Mifflin Company.

Viorst, J. 1994. *The Alphabet from Z to A (With much confusion on the way)*. New York: Atheneum.

Wilks, M. 1987. *The Ultimate Alphabet*. New York: Holt, Rinehart and Winston.

Wilner, I. 1990. *B is for Bethlehem*. New York: Dutton Children's Books.

————. 1991. *A Garden Alphabet*. New York: Puffin Unicorn Books.

Counting Books

Aker, S. 1990. *What Comes in 2's, 3's and 4's?* New York: Simon & Schuster.

Anno, M. 1983. *Anno's Counting House*. New York: Thomas Y. Crowell.

Aylesworth, J. 1988. *One Crow: A Counting Rhyme*. New York: Lippincott.

Bang, M. 1983. *Ten, Nine, Eight*. New York: Mulberry.

Charles, F., comp. 1996. *A Caribbean Counting Book*. New York: Houghton Mifflin Company.

Dunrea, O. 1989. *Deep Down Underground*. New York: Macmillan.

Ehlert, L. 1990. *Fish Eyes: A Book You Can Count On*. New York: Harcourt, Brace and Jovanovich.

Ernst, L. 1986. *Up to Ten and Down Again*. New York: Lothrop.

Falwell, C. 1993. *Feast for 10*. New York: Clarion Books.

Feelings, M. 1971. *Moja Means One: Swaahili Counting Book*. New York: Dial Books.

Fleming, D. 1992. *Count!* New York: Holt.

French, V. 1991. *One Ballerina Two*. New York: Lothrop.

Gardner, G. 1987. *Can You Imagine...? A Counting Book*. New York: Dodd, Mead.

Geisert, A. 1992. *Pigs from 1 to 10*. New York: Houghton Mifflin Company.

Giganti, P. 1992. *Each Orange Had 8 Slices: A Counting Book*. New York: Greenwillow Books.

Grossman, V. 1991. *Ten Little Rabbits*. San Francisco: Chronicle Books.

Harshman, M. 1993. *Only One*. New York: Cobblehill Books.

Hoban, T. 1985. *Count and See*. New York: Greenwillow Books.

Hoban, T. 1985. *1, 2, 3*. New York: Greenwillow Books.

Hughes, S. 1985. *When We Went to the Park*. New York: Lothrop.

Hutchins, P. 1986. *The Doorbell Rang*. New York: Greenwillow Books.

Jonas, A. 1995. *Splash!* New York: Morrow.

Kitchen, B. 1987. *Animal Numbers*. New York: Dial Books.

Kusugak, M. 1996. *My Arctic 123*. Toronto: Annick Press

Lindbergh, R. 1987. *Midnight Farm*. New York: Dial Books.

Linden, A. 1992. *One Smiling Grandma: A Caribbean Counting Book*. New York: Dial Books.

MacDonald, S. and B. Oates. 1989. *Puzzlers*. New York: Dial Books.

McMillan, B. 1986. *Counting Wildflowers*. New York: Lothrop.

Pacovska, K. 1990. *One, Five, Many*. New York: Clarion Books.

Peek, M. 1987. *The Balancing Act: A Counting Book*. New York: Clarion Books.

Penny, D. 1988. *Ten in the Bed*. London: Walker Books, Ltd.

Scott, A. 1990. *One Good Horse: A Cowpuncher's Counting Book*. New York: Greenwillow Books.

Sheppard, J. 1990. *The Right Number of Elephants*. New York: HarperCollins Publishers.

Sis, P. 1988. *Waving: A Counting Book*. New York: Greenwillow Books.

Sloat, T. 1991. *From One to One Hundred*. New York: Dutton Children's Books.

Strickland, P. 1997. *Ten Terrible Dinosaurs*. New York: Dutton.

Tafuri, N. 1986. *Who's Counting?* New York: Greenwillow Books.

Trottier, M. 1999. *One Is Canada*. Toronto: HarperCollins Publishers Ltd.

Walsh, E. 1991. *Mouse Count*. New York: Harcourt Brace and Jovanovich.

Wildsmith, B. 1988. *Brian Wildsmith's 1, 2, 3's*. New York: Watts.

Wise, W. 1992. *Ten Sly Piranhas: A Counting Story in Reverse*. New York: Dial Books.

Predictable Books

Ahlberg, J. and A. Ahlberg. 1978. *Each Peach Pear Plum*. New York: Viking Kestrel.

Anholt, C. and L. Ahnholt. 1991. *What I Like*. New York: Putnam.

Burningham, J. 1970. *Mr. Gumpy's Outing*. New York: Henry Holt and Company.

Brown, M.W. 1947. *Goodnight Moon*. New York: Harper & Row, Publishers, Inc.

Brown, R. 1981. *A Dark, Dark Tale*. New York: Anderson Press Limited.

Carle, E. 1984. *The Very Busy Spider*. New York: Philomel.

———. 1990. *The Very Quiet Cricket*. New York: Philomel.

Carlstrom, N. 1986. *Jesse Bear, What Will You Wear?* New York: Macmillan.

Charlip, R. 1964. *Fortunately*. New York: Four Winds Press.

Cuyler, M. 1991. *That's Good, That's Bad*. New York: Holt.

Edwards, F. 1997. *The Zookeeper's Sleepers*. Illustrated by J. Bianchi. Kingston, Ontario: Bungalo Books.

———. 1998. *Is the Spaghetti Ready?* Illustrated by J. Bianchi. Kinston, Ontario: Bungalo Books.

Fox, M. 1987. *Hattie and the Fox*. New York: Macmillan.

————. 1990. *Shoes from Grandpa*. New York: Orchard Books.

Galdone, P. 1984. *The Teeny, Tiny Woman*. New York: Clarion Books.

Ginsburg, M. 1982. *Across the Stream*. New York: Greenwillow Books.

————. 1992. *Asleep, Asleep*. New York: Greenwillow Books.

Goennel, M. 1990. *My Dog*. New York: Orchard Books.

Greely, V. 1990. *White Is the Moon*. New York: Macmillan.

Guarino, D. 1989. *Is Your Mama a Llama?* New York: Scholastic Inc.

Hayes, S. 1990. *The Grampalump*. New York: Clarion Books.

Hellen, N. 1990. *The Bus Stop*. New York: Orchard Books.

Hennessy, B.G. 1990. *Jake Baked the Cake*. New York: Viking.

Hutchins, P. 1990. *What Shall We Play?* New York: Greenwillow Books.

Kraus, R. 1986. *Where Are You Going, Little Mouse?* New York: Greenwillow Books.

Lindbergh, R. 1990. *The Day the Goose Got Loose*. New York: Dial Books.

Littledale, F. 1966. *The Magic Fish*. New York: Scholastic, Inc.

Lyon, G.E. 1991. *The Outside Inn*. New York: Orchard Books.

Martin, B. 1967. *Brown Bear, Brown Bear, What Do You See?* New York: Henry Holt and Company.

————. 1991. *Polar Bear, Polar Bear, What Do You Hear?* New York: Henry Holt and Company.

Nerlove, M. 1988. *I Meant To Clean My Room*. New York: M. McElderry Books.

Numeroff, J. 1985. *If You Give a Mouse a Cookie*. New York: Harper & Row, Publishers.

Pizer, A. 1990. *It's a Perfect Day*. New York: Lippincott.

Roe, E. 1990. *All I Am*. New York: Bradbury Press.

Rosen, M., reteller. 1989. *We're Going on a Bear Hunt*. New York: M. McElderry Books.

Shannon, G. 1995. *April Showers*. New York: Greenwillow Books.

Shapiro, A. 1991. *Who Says That?* New York: Dutton Children's Books.

Shaw, N. 1986. *Sheep in a Jeep*. New York: Houghton Mifflin Company.

————. 1989. *Sheep in a Ship*. New York: Houghton Mifflin Company.

Sheppard, J. 1994. *Splash, Splash*. New York: Macmillan.

Slate, J. 1988. *Who Is Coming to Our House?* New York: Putnam.

Sundgaard, A. 1988. *The Lamb and the Butterfly*. New York: Orchard Books.

Tolstoy, A. 1968. *The Great Big Enormous Turnip*. New York: Watts.

Van Laan, N. 1990. *Possum Come A-knockin'*. New York: Alfred A. Knopf.

Viorst, J. 1972. *Alexander and the Terrrible, Horrible, No Good, Very Bad Day*. New York: Atheneum.

Weiss, N, 1989. *Where Does the Brown Bear Go?* New York: Greenwillow Books.

Easy-to-Read Books

Alder, D.A. 1984. *My Dog and the Birthday Mystery*. New York: Holiday House.

Appelt, K. 1993. *Elephants Aloft*. New York: Harcourt Brace and Company.

Apablasa, B. and L. Thiesing. 1992. *Rhymin' Simon and the Mystery of the Fake Snake*. New York: Dutton Books.

Baker, B. 1988. *Digby and Kate*. New York: Dutton Children's Books.

Bulla, C.R. 1987. *The Chalk Box Kid*. New York: Random House.

————. 1990. *The Christmas Coat*. New York: Alfred A. Knopf Inc.

Byars, B. 1990. *Hooray for the Golly Sisters!* New York: Harper & Row, Publishers.

Cazet, D. 1998. *Minnie and Moo Go the Moon*. Toronto: Stoddart Kids.

————. 1998. *Minnie and Moo Go Dancing*. Toronto: Stoddart Kids.

Cherry, L. 1988. *Who's Sick Today?* New York: Dutton Children's Books.

Coerr, E. 1986. *The Josefina Story Quilt*. New York: Harper & Row, Publishers.

———. 1988. *Chang's Paper Pony*. New York: Harper & Row, Publishers.

Cohen, M. 1988. *It's George!* New York: Greenwillow Books.

———. 1990. *First Grade Takes a Test*. New York: Greenwillow Books.

Fleming, D. 1993. *In the Small, Small Pond*. New York: Henry Holt and Company, Inc.

Gay, M.-L. 1999. *Stella, Star of the Sea*. Toronto: Groundwood Books.

Gelman, R. 1985. *Why Can't I Fly?* Richmond Hill, Ontario: Scholastic-TAB Publications Ltd.

George, L. 1995. *In the Woods*. New York: Morrow.

Hayes, S. 1986. *This Is the Bear*. New York: Harper & Row, Publishers.

Hoban, L. 1989. *Arthur's Great Big Valentine*. New York: Harper & Row, Publishers.

Hoban, L. 1990. *What Game Shall We Play?* New York: Greenwillow Books.

Kraus, R. 1970. *Whose Mouse Are You?* New York: Scholastic Book Services.

Little, J. 1998. *Emma's Magic Winter*. Toronto: HarperCollins Publishers Ltd.

Lobel, A. 1977. *Mouse Soup*. New York: Harper & Row, Publishers.

———. 1978. *Grasshopper on the Road*. New York: Harper & Row, Publishers.

———. 1981. *Uncle Elephant*. New York: Scholastic Book Services.

Moore, L. 1988. *I'll Meet You at the Cucumbers*. New York: Atheneum.

Porte, B. 1998. *Harry in Trouble*. New York: Greenwillow Books.

Rabin, S. 1994. *Casey Over There*. New York: Harcourt Brace and Company.

Rascha, C. 1993. *Yo! Yes?* New York: Orchard Books.

Rylant, C. 1994. *Mr. Putter and Tabby Pour the Tea*. New York: Harcourt Brace and Company.

Sendak, M. 1962. *Chicken Soup with Rice*. New York: Harper & Row, Publishers.

Shapiro, A. 1991. *Who Says That?* New York: Dutton Children's Books.

Van Leeuwen, J. 1990. *Oliver Pig at School*. New York: Dial Books for Young Readers.

———. 1991. *Amanda Pig on Her Own*. New York: Puffin Books.

Wellington, M. 1989. *All My Little Ducklings*. New York: Dutton Children's Books.

Wells, R. 1973. *Noisy Nora*. New York: Scholastic Book Services.

Wood, D. and A. Wood. 1991. *Piggies*. San Diego: Harcourt Brace and Company.

Picture Story Books

Aardema, V. 1975. *Why Mosquitoes Buzz in People's Ears*. New York: Dial Books.

Ackerman, K. 1988. *Song and Dance Man*. New York: Alfred A. Knopf.

Ahlberg, J. and A. Ahlberg. 1986. *The Jolly Postman*. London: Heinemann.

Alexander, L. 1992. *The Fortune-tellers*. New York: Dutton Children's Books.

Allard, H. 1977. *Miss Nelson Is Missing*. New York: Houghton Mifflin Company.

Aoki, H. and I. Gantschev. 1988. *Santa's Favorite Story*. New York: Scholastic Inc.

Babbitt, N. 1994. *Bub or the Very Best Thing*. New York: HarperCollins Publishers.

Barber, A. 1990. *The Mousehole Cat*. New York: Macmillan.

———. 1996. *Back to the Cabin*. Victoria: Orca Book Publishers.

Brett, J. 1989. *The Mitten*. New York: Scholastic Inc.

Browne, A. 1983. *Gorilla*. New York: Alfred A. Knopf.

Bruchac, J. 1993. *Fox Song*. Toronto: Oxford University Press.

Bunting, E. 1989. *The Wednesday Surprise*. New York: Clarion Books.

———. 1990. *The Wall*. New York: Clarion Books.

———. 1994. *A Day's Work*. New York: Clarion Books.

———. 1996. *Train to Somewhere*. New York: Clarion Books.

Cole, J. 1990. *The Magic School Bus Lost in the Solar System*. New York: Scholastic Inc.

Crowe, R. 1976. *Clyde Monster*. New York: Dutton Children's Books.

Denton, K.M. 1995. *Would They Love a Lion?* New York: Kingfisher Books.

dePaola, T. 1975. *Strega Nona*. New York: Prentice-Hall.

Dorros, A. 1991. *Abuela*. New York: Dutton Children's Books.

Eyvindson, P. 1993. *The Missing Sun*. Winnipeg: Pemmican Publications.

Ferber, E. 1995. *The Squeeze-More-Inn*. Richmond Hill, Ontario: Scholastic Canada.

Fox, M. 1990. *Possum Magic*. New York: Harcourt Brace and Company.

Gill, S. 1990. *Alaska's Three Bears*. Homer, Alaska: Paws IV Publishing Company.

Gilmore, R. 1998. *A Gift for Gita*. Toronto: Second Story Press.

Graham, G. 1998. *The Strongest Man This Side of Cremona*. Red Deer, Alberta: Red Deer College Press.

Gregory, N. 1995. *How Smudge Came*. Red Deer, Alberta: Red Deer College Press.

Harrison, T. 1997. *Don't Dig So Deep, Nicholas*. Toronto: Owl Books.

Henkes, K. 1996. *Lilly's Purple Plastic Purse*. New York: Greenwillow Books.

Hissey, J. 1986. *Old Bear*. New York: G.P. Putnam's Sons Ltd.

Hodges, M., reteller. 1984. *Saint George and the Dragon*. Boston: Little, Brown & Company.

James, B. 1994. *The Mud Family*. Toronto: Stoddart Publishing.

Johnson, T. 1985. *The Quilt Story*. New York: Greenwillow Books.

Jukes, M. 1993. *I'll See You in My Dreams*. New York: Alfred A. Knopf.

Keats, E. 1964. *The Snowy Day*. New York: Viking.

————. 1967. *Peter's Chair*. New York: Harper Collins Publishers.

Kellogg, S. 1979. *Pinkerton, Behave!* New York: Dial Books.

Khalsa, D.K. 1986. *Tales of a Gambling Grandma*. Montreal: Tundra Books.

Little, J. 1991. *Once Upon a Golden Apple*. Markham, Ontario: Viking.

Lionni, L. 1963. *Swimmy*. New York: Pantheon.

Lobel, A. 1982. *Ming Lo Moves the Mountain*. New York: Scholastic Inc.

Lyon, G. 1990. *Come a Tide*. New York: Orchard Books.

Martin, R. (1992). *The Rough-faced Girl*. New York: G.P. Putnam's Sons.

Mayer, M. 1987. *There's an Alligator Under My Bed*. New York: Dial Books for Young Readers.

McCloskey, R. 1941. *Make Way for Ducklings*. New York: Viking.

MacDonald, A. 1998. *The Memory Stone*. Illustrated by Joanne Ouellet. Charlottetown: Ragweed Press.

McFarlane, S. 1994. *Moonsnail Song*. Victoria: Orca Book Publishers.

McGugan, J. 1994. *Josepha: A Prairie Boy's Story*. Red Deer, Alberta: Red Deer College Press.

Mollel, T. 1991. *The Orphan Boy*. Toronto: Oxford University Press.

Muller, R., reteller. 1982. *Mollie Whuppie and the Giant*. Richmond Hill, Ontario: Scholastic-TAB Publications Ltd.

Munsch, R. 1983. *David's Father*. Toronto: Annick Press.

Nichol, B. 1997. *Dippers*. Toronto: Tundra Books.

Ottley, M. 1995. *What Faust Saw*. New York: Dutton Books.

Pfister, M. 1992. *The Rainbow Fish*. New York: North-South Books.

————. 1995. *Rainbow Fish to the Rescue*. New York: North-South Books.

Polacco, P. 1988. *The Keeping Quilt*. New York: Simon & Schuster.

————. 1990. *Thundercake*. New York: G.P. Putnam's Sons Ltd.

————. 1996. *Aunt Chip and the Great Triple Creek Dam Affair*. New York: Philomel.

Ringgold, F. 1991. *Tar Beach*. New York: Crown.

Romanova, N. 1985. *Once There Was a Tree*. New York: Dial Books.

Ryder, J. 1995. *Bears Out There*. New York: Atheneum.

Rylant, C. 1982. *When I Was Young in the Mountains*. New York: Dutton Books.

Schwartz, A. 1988. *Annabelle Swift, Kindergartner*. New York: Orchard Books.

Scieszka, J. 1989. *The True Story of the Three Little Pigs*. New York: Scholastic Inc.

Slyder, I. 1995. *The Fabulous Flying Fandinis*. New York: Cobblehill Books.

Smucker, B. 1995. *Selina and the Bear Paw Quilt*. Toronto: Lester Publishing.

Snihura, U. 1998. *I Miss Franklin P. Shuckles*. Illustrated by Leanne Franson. Toronto: Annick Press.

Steig, W. 1969. *Sylvester and the Magic Pebble*. New York: Simon and Schuster.

Steig, W. 1982. *Doctor DeSoto*. New York: Farrar, Straus & Giroux.

Steptoe, J. 1987. *Mufaro's Beautiful Daughters*. New York: Lothrop.

Thompson, R. 1993. *Who*. Victoria: Orca Book Publishers.

Tibo, G. 1988. *Simon and the Snowflakes*. Montreal: Tundra Books.

Tibo, G. 1990. *Simon Welcomes Spring*. Montreal: Tundra Books.

Tunnell, M. 1997. *Mailing May*. New York: Greenwillow Books.

Valgardson, W.D. 1995. *Winter Rescue*. New York. M. McElderry Books.

Van Allsburg, C. 1981. *Jumanji*. Boston: Houghton Mifflin Company.

———. 1984. *The Mysteries of Harris Burdick*. Boston: Houghton Mifflin Company.

———. 1985. *Just a Dream*. Boston: Houghton Mifflin Company.

———. 1985. *The Polar Express*. Boston: Houghton Mifflin Company.

Waber, B. 1972. *Ira Sleeps Over*. New York: Houghton Mifflin Company.

Wallace, I. 1997. *A Winter's Tale*. Illustrated by I. Wallace. Toronto: Groundwood Books.

Waterton, B. 1978. *A Salmon for Simon*. Richmond Hill, Ontario: Scholastic-TAB Publications Ltd.

Wiesner, D. 1990. *Hurricane*. New York: Clarion Books.

Wild, M. 1990. *The Very Best of Friends*. New York: Harcourt Brace and Company.

Willams, V. 1990. *More, More, More, Said the Baby*. New York: Greenwillow Books.

Wood, A. 1987. *Heckedy Peg*. New York: Harcourt Brace and Company.

Zolotow, C. 1992. *The Seashore Book*. New York: HarperCollins Publishers.

Picture Story Books For Older Readers

Bedard, M. 1992. *Emily*. New York: Doubleday.

Bowen, G. 1994. *Stranded at Plimoth Plantation 1626*. New York: HarperCollins Publishers.

Browne, A. 1998. *Voices in the Park*. New York: DK Publishing, Inc.

Butler, G. 1998. *The Hangashore*. Toronto: Tundra Books.

Carrier, R. 1985. *The Hockey Sweater*. Montreal: Tundra Books.

———. *The Longest Home Run*. Montreal: Tundra Books.

Cherry, L. 1992. *A River Ran Wild*. New York: The Trumpet Club, Inc.

Cowcher, H. 1991. *Tigress*. New York: Farrar, Straus & Giroux.

Demi. 1990. *The Empty Pot*. New York: Henry Holt and Company, Inc.

———. 1992. *Chingis Khan*. New York: Holt.

Dugan, B. 1992. *Loop the Loop*. New York: Greenwillow Books.

Eyvindson, P. 1994. *The Night Rebecca Stayed Too Late*. Winnipeg: Pemmican Publications.

Feiffer, J. 1997. *Meanwhile....* New York: HarperCollins Press.

Gerstein, M. 1987. *The Mountains of Tibet*. New York: HarperCollins Publishers.

Goble, P. 1989. *Beyond the Ridge*. New York: Bradbury Press.

Johnson, T. 1996. *The Wagon*. New York: Tambourine.

Joyce, W. 1993. *Santa Calls*. New York: HarperCollins Publishers.

Lewis, J. 1993. *How I Got My Dog Sled*. Waterloo, Ontario: Penumbra Press.

Macaulay, D. 1995. *Shortcut*. Boston: Houghton Mifflin Company.

Oberman, S. 1993. *The Always Prayer Shawl*. Honesdale, Pennsylvania: Boyd Mills Press.

Polacco, P. 1988. *The Keeping Quilt*. New York: Simon & Schuster.

———. 1994. *Pink and Say*. New York: Philomel Books.

Reynolds, M. 1993. *Belle's Journey*. Illustrated by Stephen McCallum. Victoria: Orca Book Publishers.

Rylant, C. 1992. *An Angel for Solomon Singer*. New York: Orchard Books.

San Souci, R. 1992. *Feathertop*. New York: Doubleday.

———. 1993. *The Snow Wife*. New York: Dial Books.

Scieszka, J. 1995. *Math Curse*. New York: Viking.

Sewell, M. 1986. *The Pilgrims of Plimoth*. New York: Atheneum.

Shaw-MacKinnon, M. 1996. *Tiktala*. Toronto: Stoddart Publishing.

Shulevitz, U. 1990. *Toddlecreek for Post Office*. New York: Farrar, Straus & Giroux.

Skrypuch, M. 1996. *Silver Threads*. Toronto: Viking.

Smucker, B. 1995. *Selina and the Bear Paw Quilt*. Illustrated by Janet Wilson. Toronto: Lester Publishing.

Spalding, A. 1998. *Sarah May and the New Red Dress*. Illustrated by Janet Wilson. Victoria: Orca Book Publishers.

Stanley, D. and P. Vennema. 1988. *Shaka: King of the Zulus*. New York: Morrow.

Stirling, L. 1993. *The Flying Fish Kite*. Dartmouth, Nova Scotia: Piper Press.

Thurman, M. 1993. *One Too Many*. Toronto: Viking Kestrel.

Turner, A. 1989. *Heron Street*. New York: HarperCollins Publishers.

Valgardson, W.D. 1996. *Sarah and the People of Sand River*. Toronto: Groundwood Books.

Van Allsburg, C. 1986. *The Stranger*. Boston: Houghton Mifflin Company.

———. 1991. *The Wretched Stone*. Boston: Houghton Mifflin Company.

———. 1993. *The Sweetest Fig*. Boston: Houghton Mifflin Company.

Yee, P. 1989. *Tales from Gold Mountain*. Toronto: Groundwood Books.

Yolen, J. 1992. *Encounter*. San Diego: Harcourt Brace and Company.

Zhang, S.N. 1993. *A Little Tiger in the Chinese Night*. Montreal: Tundra Books.

CHAPTER THREE

TRADITIONAL STORIES AND POETRY

The objectives of this chapter are

- To understand the role of traditional literature in the elementary school;
- To appreciate the importance of storytelling and the oral tradition;
- To become familiar with several poetic devices;
- To become familiar with the types of poetry that children appreciate and enjoy;
- To become familiar with a number of poetry books, specialized collections of poetry, and poetry anthologies.

Traditional Literature

The genre of traditional literature (which is sometimes referred to as folk literature) includes fairy tales, folk tales, Mother Goose rhymes, legends, myths, proverbs, epics, fables, and more. These forms are mostly short stories, reflecting the values and dreams of a society, and through which societies and their cultures come alive. Traditional literature in general represents a body of work originally passed orally from generation to generation, although it is believed that travelling poets and musicians did record some of it in writing, as they composed narratives and poems for use on their travels. What is interesting is that similar tales, poems, and songs appeared all over the world. It was not until the seventeenth century, however, that much of this genre was transcribed into printed form and made available to the reading public. Even now these stories continue to change as authors demonstrate their sensitivity to their audience of children and to current notions of what is appropriate content for them.

There are many educational issues surrounding traditional literature, especially since animated film versions have been marketed widely to a preschool audience. Children are often unaware of the original versions of traditional stories, and many of the new versions present distorted characters, settings, and plots (for example, *Beauty and the Beast*). Many traditional pieces of literature have been rewritten and illustrated by such author/illustrators as Ian Wallace (*Hansel and Gretel*, 1994), Stephen Kellogg (*The Three Little Pigs*, 1997), Jan Brett (*Goldilocks and The Three Bears*, 1987), and Anthony Browne (*Hansel and Gretel*, 1981). Children may therefore come to their reading of traditional tales with different ideas about them and sometimes *without* the traditional structure of, for example, a fairy story in their minds. The matter is not which is better, but that they are different and this difference has implications for children's development in writing as well as in reading.

Traditional literature is generally agreed to be an important genre for children, and it is frequently the first genre with which children become truly familiar. Young children all over the western world associate the phrase "Once upon a time" with the beginning of a good story: it signals the beginning of a fantasy narrative, taking the child into the world of imagination. The structure of the classic fairy tale has become ingrained in the western psyche. Jean Little's *Once Upon a Golden Apple* (1991) plays with children's internalization of this structure, and the humour in the book is based on children understanding the "rules" and knowing they are being manipulated.

Many college-level textbooks about children's literature provide detailed information on the subgenres of traditional literature, and may contain lists of appropriate versions of these stories for children in the elementary school. The works of Norton (1999) and Sutherland (1997) are especially helpful. These books are listed at the end of the chapter under Professional Resources.

FOLK TALES

Scholars of traditional literature categorize folk tales in a variety of ways. Categories may include cumulative tales, talking-beast tales, realistic tales, trickster tales, pourquoi tales, humorous tales, and magical tales. Cumulative tales are exemplified by stories such as "The Gingerbread Man," "The Three Little Pigs," "Henny Penny," and "The House That Jack Built." They contain sequentially repeated characters, actions, or speeches (e.g., "Run, run as fast as you can. You can't catch me, I'm the Gingerbread Man"). The structure of cumulative tales encourages children to participate in the reading or oral storytelling experience by joining in with the repeated sections, like a chorus to a song.

Folk tales that contain talking beasts (e.g., "The Three Billy Goats Gruff") are found in most cultures around the world, and they generally teach a lesson, although not as directly as do fables. Trickster tales involve characters who try to outwit others through cunning and deception (e.g., "Anansi the Spider"); pourquoi tales explain phenomena (e.g., why the spider has eight legs); humourous tales, sometimes known as drolls, noodles, dillies, or numbskull tales, are stories of fools and idiots (e.g., the Grimm brothers' telling of "Hans in Luck"). Folk tales that include magical possibilities are usually called wonder tales or, more commonly, fairy tales. Such stories include "Cinderella," "The Elves and the Shoemaker," and "Snow White."

Several common motifs or recurring elements found in folk tales include the presence of supernatural helpers (e.g., fairies); supernatural adversaries (e.g., ogres, giants, witches, dragons, trolls); magical objects (e.g., a cloak or a ring); deceitful or ferocious beasts (e.g., a wolf or dragon); magical powers (e.g., the granting of a wish); and magical transformations (e.g., a prince into a bear). Few folk tales can be described as realistic. The story of "Dick Whittington and His Cat," about a man who may have become the Lord Mayor of London, is one of the few well-known "realistic" tales. Most tales that have their origin with a real person or experience are so embroidered by retelling that they bear little resemblance to historical fact. Those that do retain a vestige of reality are more commonly referred to as legends rather than folk tales.

Many traditional versions of folk stories are available today. Some authors/illustrators—such as Laszlo Gal, Leo and Diane Dillon, Jan Brett, Trina Schart Hyman, Jane Yolen, Robert San Souci, and John Steptoe—have become well known for their renditions of these stories. Many of their books combine genres, usually picture book and fairy tale. Jan Brett's version of *Beauty and the Beast* (1989) is modelled on the classic work of Walter Crane. Paul Galdone's version of *Little Red Riding Hood* (1974) is particularly appropriate for young children, while Trina Schart Hyman's rendition of *Little Red Riding*

Hood (1983) is more appropriate for older readers. *The Twelve Dancing Princesses* has been retold by Janet Lunn and illustrated by Laszlo Gal (1979), by Marianna Mayer and illustrated by Kinuko Craft (1990), and by Ruth Sanderson (1990). Jan Ormerod and David Lloyd have retold *The Frog Prince* (1990), and Glen Rounds has produced a version of *The Three Billy Goats Gruff* (1993). A seemingly infinite number of retellings of folk stories are available to children in book, video, and game format (including colouring books).

Canadian author and illustrator Robin Muller has created a number of retellings of traditional folk tales. His best-known and best-loved book is probably *Mollie Whuppie and the Giant* (1982, 1995), which tells the story of Mollie and her three sisters, who are abandoned in the forest by their parents. The girls find an old house where they receive rest and food, but they learn that the house is inhabited by a giant. Mollie manages to outwit the giant, and she and her sisters flee the house and escape from the forest by crossing a bridge made from one hair. The girls then find themselves in a beautiful land ruled by an unhappy king. The king is unhappy because for years the giant has been robbing travellers of their gold and stealing little children to cook for his breakfast. When the king hears how Mollie has outwitted the giant, he is amazed: Mollie has done what his knights have been unable to do. The king asks Mollie to complete three daring tasks in exchange for rewards. Mollie fulfills the king's requests, and the story ends happily. Muller's other books include *The Sorcerer's Apprentice* (1985), *The Magic Paintbrush* (1989, winner of the Governor General's Award for illustration), and *Little Wonder* (1994).

Parodies of well-known tales include books such as *The Three Little Wolves and the Big Bad Pig* (Trivizas, 1993) and *The True Story of the Three Little Pigs* (Scieszka, 1989). Both of these books are based on the traditional story *The Three Little Pigs* and depend on intertextual connections for their humour and impact. Trivizas tells the story of three cuddly little wolves whose mother tells them it is time to go out and make their way in the world. As we might guess, a big bad pig arrives on the scene, intent on taking the little wolves' lovely brick house for his own. The wolves build a house of concrete, but it is not strong enough to withstand the destructive efforts of the pig. Barbed wire, iron bars, armour plating, plexiglass, and padlocks cannot keep the pig away. Finally, the wolves build a house of flowers. When the pig arrives to blow it down, he inhales the perfume of the blossoms and his heart becomes tender as he sees and smells the beauty before him. A reading of Trivizas' version of the story will forever change the way in which the traditional story is perceived. Scieszka works the story in a different way, telling the tale of *The Three Little Pigs* from the wolf's perspective as an innocent victim. However, since most readers will already know the traditional version of the tale, the wolf is immediately cast as an unreliable narrator, and readers know not to trust the wolf's point of view. This book is a huge success with children and teachers, and makes a perfect springboard for many activities in reading, writing, art, and drama.

There are a number of clever retellings of fairy tales where the texts deviate little from the original version, but the illustrations create a powerfully different meaning to the story. *Hansel and Gretel*, retold by Anthony Browne (1981), is one such book. "Browne's choice of a modern setting for the story enables him to make powerful comments on modern materialism (the family starving but there is a television set in the living room, and in the bedroom there are cosmetics on the dressing table and nylons hanging from the drawer), but some readers will find the stepmother/witch fusion disturbing. There is no doubt that students will find much to discuss..." (Stephens & Watson, 1994, p.12). This book highlights the difference between story (events, characters, and setting) and discourse (the language with which the story is told). In picture books, the illustrations are an integral part of the discourse, and in Browne's book, the illustrations play a crucial role in the meanings created—meanings that cause the reader to reflect on contemporary values. The illustrations remove the story from the "once upon a time" setting of the traditional version and place it squarely in the realm of contemporary realistic fiction.

Ian Wallace's (1994) rendition of *Hansel and Gretel* also places the story in a contemporary setting, this time in Atlantic Canada. The text opens with, "In a house by the sea on the edge of a large forest lived a poor fisherman with his wife and two children" (unpaginated). The fisherman can no longer earn a living from his trade, and so, in desperation, complies with his wife's wishes to get rid of the children. From this point on, the text deviates little from the original Grimm's version. It is the illustrations that clearly evoke life in a run-down 1960s or 1970s-era house situated in the middle of a forest from which major stretches have already been chopped for firewood. Wallace created the illustrations in pastel pencil on black Lana Balkis paper. The result is a book with a dark and disturbing tone from the very first page.

Modern fairy tales, such as *The Tough Princess* by Martin Waddell (1986), and *The King's Equal* by Katherine Paterson (1992), play with readers' expectations and knowledge of the fairy tale genre. These books raise questions about traditional gender roles and the messages implicit in most fairy stories (for example that women must be rescued by a man and are then dependent on him for living happily ever after). *The Tough Princess* manages to do this in a humorous way that questions traditional expectations from the first page: "Once upon a time there lived a King and a Queen who weren't very good at it. They kept losing wars and mucking things up" (p.1). Patrick Benson's illustrations can be clearly interpreted by all young readers, and the use of colloquial expressions and the presence of an independent,

IAN WALLACE

Ian Wallace is probably best known for *Chin Chiang and the Dragon's Dance* (1984) and *Very Last First Time* (Andrews, 1985), but he has written and/or illustrated more than fifteen books for children. Ian was born in Niagara Falls, Ontario, and completed a degree at the Ontario College of Art before obtaining a staff position with Kids Can Press in Toronto. He quickly realized that he wanted to create books for children and began working as a freelance artist and illustrator in 1974.

Ian recalls that his first exposure to art came not from museums and galleries but from the pictures in the books he read—books such as Kenneth Graham's *The Wind in the Willows* and Helen Bannerman's *Little Black Sambo*. These books allowed Ian to emulate the art work, eventually inspiring him to look at his own world and describe it through his own eyes and talent. His first book, *Chin Chiang and the Dragon's Dance*, won the Amelia Frances Howard-Gibbon Illustrator's Award in 1985. Now his books sell all over the world as well as in Canada.

Ian is aware that the challenge of writing about a different culture, whether it be of the Arctic, Chinatown, or Newfoundland (as in *The Mummer's Song* published in 1993 with Bud Davidge), is in "getting under the skin" of the characters in the story. He works at getting the details correct and is committed to working through the many pages of revisions that books such as these demand.

Hansel and Gretel (1994) is one of Ian's most challenging books. It is a dark retelling of an already dark fairy tale. *A Winter's Tale* (1997) is just the opposite—heavy symbolism is absent and instead this book is filled with beauty and freshness. *A Winter's Tale* is the story of Abigail, a nine-year-old city girl who is finally deemed old enough to accompany her father and brother on their annual winter camping expedition into the bush. *Boy of the Deeps* (1999) tells a story of the coal mines of Cape Breton and of the men and boys who worked in them. The book recounts James' first day working in the "deeps." James knows it is dangerous, but it is also exhilarating for him to work beside his father. This story hearkens back to Ian's own roots and the stories he heard as a child about his grandfather, a coal miner in Gloucestershire, England.

self-reliant princess who fights her own battles and eventually meets her own prince make this a book that children enjoy and can readily identify with. Paterson's book, *The King's Equal,* illustrated by Vladimir Vagin, raises the same questions as *The Tough Princess* but in a different manner: the book accomplishes much more than a reversal of traditional gender roles. Paterson has created a story in which all the participants learn from their actions, and the presence of the mysterious wolf adds a mystical element. Vagin's illustrations, done in the traditional style of fairy stories, add a rich serenity to an already compelling text. This modern fairy story is likely to become a classic.

MYTHS AND LEGENDS

Myths and legends are literary genres that children frequently do not encounter these days outside of school. However, many phrases in our language refer to myths, especially Greek myths: *the Midas touch, Pandora's box, Herculean effort,* and *Trojan horse,* to list but a few. Many novels for children and young adults—such as *The Owl Service* by Alan Garner (1967) and *The Golden Compass* by Philip Pullman (1995)—are based on the patterns, characters, and plots of the best-known myths and legends, and certain recurring themes in literature can be traced back to mythology. Thus, it is helpful for young readers to be introduced to myths and legends as part of the repertoire of elementary school reading—in addition, of course, to reading them for the sheer pleasure of a good story.

Myths are defined by Norton (1995) as stories that contain "fanciful or supernatural incidents intended to explain nature or tell about the gods and demons of early peoples. In the distant past, as in some traditional cultures today, the stories were taken as fact made sacred by religious belief" (p.300). Greek, Roman, Celtic, and Norse myths are well known in North America, but there are also many good books of Asian myths, South American myths, and Aboriginal myths, such as *Coyote Sings to the Moon* (King, 1998) and *The Fish Skin* (Oliviero, 1993). Joseph Campbell (1988) argues that myths are powerful literature and should be read by everyone if we want to understand ourselves as human beings and as social and spiritual creatures. Myths are statements about existence, models for belief.

In *The Fish Skin,* Jamie Oliviero retells a Cree myth about Grandfather Sun, who is distracted from his journey across the sky one day by his reflection in a large and beautiful lake. The day gets hotter and hotter as Grandfather Sun ceases to move. The Cree people living by the lake grow weary, the wolves are unable to howl, the turtle's shell cracks, and a young boy's grandmother becomes weaker and weaker. The boy decides that he must ask help from the Great Spirit, Wìsahkecàhk, who lives in the forest across the lake. The Great Spirit reads the boy's dreams and leaves him a magic fish skin. When the boy slides into the fish skin, he becomes a giant fish and is able to dive into the lake and swallow sufficient water to spit out as a cloud. This cloud provides rain for the earth, refreshing the people and animals. The turtle, however, remains to this day with a cracked shell. This beautiful traditional story is enhanced by Brent Morrisseau's vivid illustrations. The red, orange, purple, and blue hues spread across facing pages, creating a feeling of heat and awe.

The Dragon's Pearl is a retelling of an Asian myth with a theme similar to *The Fish Skin*. Written by Julie Lawson (1992) and beautifully illustrated by Paul Morin, *The Dragon's Pearl* won the Amelia Frances Howard-Gibbon Award for illustration in 1993. Xiao Sheng, a poor boy in China, spends his days cutting grass and selling it for fuel or fodder. When a drought comes to the land, Xiao Sheng must travel further and further from home to find grass to cut. One day, he finds a patch of beautiful green grass, which he returns to cut many times. Eventually, he decides to dig up the lush grass and move it to the land beside his house. While he is digging, he discovers a beautiful pearl, which he immediately gives to his mother. The pearl is stored

The Dragon's Pearl by Julie Lawson

carefully in the family's rice jar. The next day, the transplanted grass has withered and died, and Xiao Sheng is distraught. The rice jar, however, is full of rice. When a gold coin is placed in the jar, the jar overflows with gold coins. One night, robbers break in to the house and try to steal the pearl. As Xiao Sheng struggles with the robbers, he swallows the pearl, immediately feeling a searing heat tearing through his body. In search of relief, he runs to the river and drinks it dry. At once, a fierce storm breaks, and Xiao Sheng begins to change into a dragon, breathing clouds into the sky. The clouds bring much-needed rain to the land, and Xiao Sheng disappears into the river forever.

Priscilla Galloway has retold a number of Greek myths, including *Aleta and the Queen: A Tale of Ancient Greece* (1995), *Atlanta: The Fastest Runner in the World* (1995), *Daedalus and the Minotaur* (1997), and *My Hero Hercules* (1999). All are illustrated by Normand Cousineau and are part of the "Tales of Ancient Lands" series. *Daedalus and the Minotaur* is the story of Daedalus, an inventor, architect, and builder who is wrongfully accused of the murder of his nephew in Athens. Fearing unjust punishment, he flees from Athens with his young son Icarus, and makes a new home on the island of Crete. Once there, however, Daedalus becomes involved in the dangerous intrigues of the royal court and is commanded by the king to build a labyrinth. This maze of tunnels will house the child of the king and queen—a monster child with the head of a bull. When Daedalus meets the child, Minotaur, he feels sorry for him and builds a cart so that Minotaur can move around more easily. Daedalus' son, Icarus, befriends Minotaur, and

Daedalus and the Minotaur by Priscilla Galloway

Daedalus begins to dread the day when the huge labyrinth will be completed and Minotaur imprisoned in it. When the queen decrees that Icarus shall live in the labyrinth with Minotaur, as company for him, Daedalus begins planning for their escape from Crete. He invents a man-kite for himself and his son, designed to fly them from the clifftops and away from the island. Events overtake them, however, and Daedalus' plans are thwarted, giving rise to further mythic adventures for both Daedalus and his son.

The *Mabinogian* is a collection of Welsh myths dating back many hundreds of years. There are a number of adult translations available, the two most common being a facsimile edition (1977) of a translation by Lady Charlotte Guest (1877), and a modern translation by Jones and Jones (1949). *Tales from the Mabinogian* is a modern children's version of a selection of these myths, retold by Gwynn Thomas and Kevin Crossley-Holland (1985). The book is attractively illustrated by Margaret Jones and makes a wonderful addition to any classroom library. A further selection of children's versions of myths can be found at the end of the chapter.

Legends are stories told about real people and their feats or accomplishments. The narratives are usually mixed with superstition, and they expand and enhance the actual doings of their heroes. Legends are closely related to myths, but they do not contain supernatural deities, as myths do. The stories of Beowulf, King Arthur, Robin Hood, William Tell, Davy Crockett, and Johnny Appleseed are legends. A selection of retellings of legends can be found at the end of the chapter.

FABLES

The origin of the fable is thought to reside with a Greek slave named Aesop, who supposedly lived in the sixth century B.C. Experts, however, believe there were many sources of the fable, since they are found worldwide. Fables are brief fictional tales which are meant to entertain but also contain a moral. They usually have only two or three characters, frequently talking animals who possess human-like characteristics. Fables were among the first texts printed by William Caxton in the fifteenth century (Lenaghan, 1967) and have been popular with storytellers all over the world. Lenaghan maintains that their popularity is largely due to the fact that they could reach people of various degrees of intelligence, and that storytellers could emphasize whatever functions they chose. They are popular with young children today because of their humorous elements and the presence of talking animals. Fables such as *The Town Mouse and the Country Mouse* and *The Tortoise and the Hare* remain particular favourites with children. A selection of fables is presented at the end of this chapter.

Storytelling and Oral Literature

Many storytellers today retell stories that are already in print in a picture book format. True storytelling, however, calls upon stories that are part of the tradition of oral literature, stories that have many versions and can be modified to suit audience and purpose. These stories are handed down within families or cultural groups. The Aboriginal peoples of Canada, the US, Australia, and New Zealand have a rich store of tales, some of which are ritual stories which may not be shared with the general public. Families also have their stories and storytellers: stories of early settlement in homesteads on the prairie, of great-grandfathers who worked on the trans-Canada railway, of great hardship, illnesses, long journeys at sea, family treasures, and great adventures. These stories, which cannot easily be written down and neatly illustrated, have a special significance to the listener and frequently appeal to a small audience. This specificity marks the difference between storytelling and "performing" a text.

In the Canadian Aboriginal culture, history, legends, and ways of believing were passed orally from one generation to another. The storytellers in a community were the teachers and historians, and they spent many years perfecting their craft. They apprenticed under an old storyteller, spending many hours alone in the sacred places thinking, creating, and finding new ways to tell old stories (Campbell, 1985). They memorized and understood the old traditional stories so that these tales could be passed on to future generations. Current Aboriginal storytellers have a tremendous challenge: they must learn the traditional stories and pass them on in English as well as in their Aboriginal language. They must be able to translate not only the story but also the old ways of knowing and living. Aboriginal stories are not intended only for adults or only for children, but for everyone, and each listener takes from the story the meaning that is relevant for him or her.

Joe McLellan is a Winnipeg storyteller who has written almost a dozen books for children. All his stories are retellings of traditional Aboriginal myths. Before McLellan began writing the stories, he consulted with many elders, as he was concerned about putting oral stories into print. He says, "Sometimes, some stories have a great spiritual significance. For instance, the story may be very important for a ceremony, but, if you're not doing a ceremony, then you don't really need to know it. There's some stories where, culturally to Indian people, it would be appropriate, but it wouldn't be appropriate to people that didn't have a keen understanding of aboriginal culture" (Jenkinson, 1999). The elders whom McLellan consulted told him they believed writing the stories would be a positive thing to do. As one of them said, since one can no longer gather all one's grandchildren in a single room (because they no longer live in the same community), we have to tell our stories in a new way (McLellan, 1998). McLellan believes these tellings might help Aboriginal children learn who they are. He maintains that stories show how the spiritual and the earthly fit together, and it is the task of the storyteller to weave this body of knowledge into the lives of listeners. In his view, life is made up of both reality and mystery, and learning takes place in the mind and in the heart. McLellan says that stories speak to the whole of our being—our physical, emotional, intellectual, and spiritual selves. We are challenged and confronted by the meanings of life, death, nature, and relationships, and stories can help us to gain understanding.

JOE McLELLAN

Joe McLellan was born in California but grew up in the Warm Springs area of Oregon, close to his grandparents. His grandparents and father frequently told him stories—family stories as well as the more traditional tales. After his great-grandmother died, his family moved first to Wyoming and then, when Joe was six years old, to Fargo, North Dakota, where his father taught at North Dakota State University. Joe stayed in Fargo until the Vietnam War, at which point he moved to Winnipeg and began teaching. Joe describes himself as being of Aboriginal heritage (his grandmother was Nez Percé), but he is also proud of his Irish, French, and Scottish ancestry.

Joe has taught all grades from kindergarten to grade twelve, including six years working with children who are emotionally disturbed. He has taught university courses and workshops in Aboriginal Studies for the Faculty of Education at the University of Manitoba. In 1992, he was awarded the Hilroy Fellowship for Excellence and Innovation in Education by the Canadian Teachers' Federation. Joe currently teaches at the Winnipeg Education Centre at the University of Winnipeg. This is a program designed to meet the needs of Aboriginal people, recent immigrants, and others who require educational upgrading and access to university programs. Joe finds himself working as teacher, counsellor, and seminar leader, and spends much of his time focussing on the spiritual aspects of learning and human growth.

Joe first began to write books for children when the Manitoba Department of Education approached him to prepare a series of twelve books in collaboration with Pemmican Press. The books are about Nanabosho, a mythic figure who is "part spirit, part Manitou, part man, and he was sent to teach the people. Early on he found out that you can't tell people anything. They don't listen"

(Jenkinson, 1999, paragraph 17). The first two books, *The Birth of Nanabosho* and *Nanabosho Steals Fire*, are chronologically the first stories, when Nanabosho is still a child; in the rest of the books, he is a grown man. Joe maintains that chronology is essentially unimportant in the stories because they form a circle, and readers can enter the circle anywhere they want as long as they enter it with respect. Joe says that traditional stories are still best when told orally, because there is such a strong bond between the teller and the listener. People respond to stories differently, but they are affected as much by the storyteller as by the story itself. Many traditional stories are being lost to history, but by writing books he can "make the fire of the stories burn brighter."

When Joe visits schools, he tells a mixture of traditional and modern stories. Many of the story ideas come from the children as he asks them what they would like to hear. He then creates stories and weaves the children's ideas into them. Joe says that when we tell stories, every listener becomes a child once again, because the first stories we hear come from people who love and care for us. Our bodies slip into "listening-to-story" mode, whether we are two or eighty-two.

Children in the elementary grades enjoy a good storyteller, whether it is a professional storyteller such as Joe McLellan or Tololwa Mollel, or a senior citizen speaking of times past. The children of Lunenburg County, Nova Scotia, have been involved in oral history projects in their school for a number of years (Petite Riviere, 1993). The children have written and illustrated the collected stories, which they have then published within the community.

True storytelling demands discipline, so that a story is captured and shaped to suit the audience and the purpose for its telling. A rambling recollection of an event that occurred a number of years ago is not the same as a story. Thus storytellers today work at their craft and perfect the nuances of chosen vocabulary, intonation, facial expressions, and hand gestures, ensuring that their stories have cohesion, development, and appropriate closure, just as a good writer does.

Teachers can make full use of storytelling in their classrooms by involving children in storytelling and by reading many different versions of a traditional story themselves and retelling it in their own ways. This strategy can also be used across the curriculum as teachers retell well-known stories from history or relate aspects of a famous person's biography. Children frequently find the teacher's own rendition of such stories more interesting than printed versions taken directly from a book, because details can be added and relevant pauses included as the teacher responds to the audience's reaction to the story. Oral stories are invested with the thoughts and feelings of the teller. The storyteller thus becomes an integral part of the story experience; story and storyteller become one.

Two excellent storytelling resource books for teachers are *And None of It Was Nonsense* by Betty Rosen (1988) and *Tell Me Another* by Bob Barton (1986). Rosen describes her thinking, preparation, follow-up work, and the lessons themselves. She explains why she selects her stories (ones she likes "massively"), and instructs her readers to trust their instincts in choosing stories for telling. The book also includes selections of her students' work. Barton has put together a set of resource materials for storytelling, drawing on his experiences as a Canadian storyteller, teacher, and writer. He encourages teachers to tell their own stories, including the songs, rhymes, jingles, chants, and sayings they remember. These fragments trigger memories that he believes will, in turn, give rise to a wealth of stories. Barton takes the reader through a step-by-step process in working with stories and poems, playing with the sounds of words. He connects the worlds of storytelling, drama, games, movement, and role play in the creation of new stories, reminding us that stories can be revisited and remade again and again. In *Stories in the Classroom*, Bob Barton and David Booth (1990) collaborated to further their work on storytelling, drama, and response to literature. This volume proves to be an equally valuable resource for teachers.

Poetry

Poetry communicates experience by appealing to both the thoughts and the feelings of the reader; each word is carefully chosen for the nuances and emotive meanings it conveys. Poetry takes the sound of language and arranges it in beautiful forms. Cullinan and Galda (1994) tell us that "poetry is a poet's intuition of truth ... the essence of life and experience" (p.127). Learning to understand and appreciate poetry is an ongoing process, as with other forms of literature. Children are more likely to enjoy poetry if they have experienced it from their earliest days, through nursery rhymes, jingles, and songs. Nursery rhymes and skipping rhymes cannot be considered true poetry, but they do set the foundation for later journeys into poetic language.

Defining poetry is a challenge because many contemporary poets are breaking the traditional expectations of poetry, both in form and content. Words are placed across the page, at angles, and in bunches. Contemporary poetry deals with unconventional subjects (taking out the garbage, watching father eat mashed potatoes at dinner time, listening to a fight between parents). However, poems continue to make children laugh, ponder, imagine, remember, and see the world in new ways; indeed, poetry helps to develop insights and new understandings.

Children are naturally rhythmical and musical; they are generally intrigued by the sound of language as they play with it and learn its melody. Poetry for children should include both those rhymes and jingles intended for young children, which play with language, and more serious and reflective poems, which provide new perspectives on various aspects of life.

REFLECTION

Reflect upon your experiences with poetry in elementary school. Did your teachers read poetry aloud? If so, what kinds of poetry did they read? Were you asked to read aloud or memorize poetry? Were you given opportunities to select poetry and share it with your classmates in some manner? Did you study particular poets? Did you learn about particular types of poetry? Were you asked to generate poems of your own, emulating the styles you had studied? Did you like writing poetry? Why or why not?

Poetry for children must appeal to *children's* experiences and interests. It is not important who authored a poem, whether it be Tennyson, Farjeon, Ciardi, or Lee; what matters is that a poem speaks to children in the language of poetry *at their point in time* (Huck, Hepler & Hickman, 1993). As Booth and Moore note (1988), "Children's poetry has a special appeal: the form and language of poetry speaks directly to the child, to their senses, their imaginations, their emotions, their feelings, their experiences of childhood" (p.22). Poems of action, rhythm, rhyme, and energy invite young children to participate.

SHARING POETRY

If children are to be readers of poetry, they need to *experience* poetry; they need to interact with adults who enjoy poetry, who read poetry, and who share poetry with them. Hearing the skillfully crafted arrangement of sounds of a poem read aloud is one of the primary pleasures of poetry. Although enunciation is a fundamental component of any kind of oral sharing of poetry, it is also vital that poetry be read expressively! Readers of poetry, whether adults or children, need to consider the mood they wish to set when reading a poem aloud. The interpretation of a poem is greatly influenced by how readers use each of the following elements: tempo, volume, rhythm, pitch, and juncture. (TEMPO refers to how slowly or how quickly words or lines are read; VOLUME refers to

Stuart and Kim share a book in the library

loudness; RHYTHM describes emphasis or stress; PITCH refers to the lowering or raising of the voice; and JUNCTURE describes the location and length of pauses.) Teachers and students can vary these elements when reading poetry and then discuss if and how the changes affected their interpretations of the poems.

CHORAL READING is one way for students to share poetry. In choral reading, students either read together or take turns reading a poem or text selection. Multiple copies of the selection are required for choral reading; alternatively, the poem can be displayed on a chart or transparency.

There are several ways to complete a choral reading. The poem can be read by everyone in unison, or a leader can read a line and wait for the group to repeat the line, then read the next line, and so on. Another way to complete a choral reading is for a few children to be assigned the main part of the poem while the remainder of the class reads the chorus or refrain in unison. In some classrooms, the class is divided into groups, and each group is assigned particular lines or stanzas. Sylvia's preferred method is to use VOICE COLOUR (high, medium, and low-pitched voices) as the criterion of group allocation and then assign lines and/or phrases of the poem to particular voice-colour groups. The wording of particular lines often makes them more appropriate for a specific voice colour. The voice-colour grouping method is effective for either choral reading or choral speech.

CHORAL SPEECH differs from choral reading in that in choral speech, the poem or text selection is memorized by the individual(s) performing it. As in choral reading, the elements of tempo, volume, rhythm, pitch, and juncture can be used to enhance the effectiveness of the oral delivery of the choral speech selection. Two books of poems written specifically for choral reading are *I Am Phoenix: Poems for Two Voices* (Fleischman, 1985) and *Joyful Noise: Poems for Two Voices* (Fleischman, 1988).

Some people use drama techniques and activities when working with poetry. These activities may be informal and relatively unstructured, or they may be more formal and require polishing and refinement. Regardless, it is fundamental that students are aware of the expectations for the activities. One technique to enhance the oral presentation of poetry is the use of sound effects. The sound effects may be generated by the children, or sound tracks may be used to create a particular atmosphere or effect. Mime can also be used with poetry. The teacher can read a poem and the students can mime the action, their movements expressing their interpretations of the words. Alternatively, students can be assigned to small groups and each group can present its poem(s), with some members reading and others miming. Choral dramatization of poetic selections can be another useful technique in classrooms. To enhance their dramatizations, students may don attire appropriate for their poetry selections or use props and special effects. Puppets, shadow-plays, and role-playing are other dramatic techniques that can be used when presenting poetry.

POETIC DEVICES

To facilitate students' appreciation of the craft of writing poetry, and to assist them in their own poetry writing, it is important for students to develop an awareness of the devices that poets use. RHYME is a very common element of poetry; indeed, some children believe rhyme to be the sole feature of poetry! The poems of Michael Rosen, Dennis Lee, Jack Prelutsky, and Shel Silverstein, contemporary works frequently enjoyed by children, employ rhyme, rhythm, and playfulness as part of their appeal. Although rhyme is a popular poetic device, it is one expectation of poetry from which children need to be freed if they are to enjoy more sophisticated poems in later years.

Comparison is another common technique used by poets. SIMILES (explicitly comparing one thing to another using the words "like" or "as") and METAPHORS (comparing two things by implying that one is like the other) are two common comparison techniques used by poets. One beautifully illustrated picture book of similes is *As Quick as a Cricket* (Woods, 1982); a tongue-in-cheek collection of similes for older readers is *As: A Surfeit of Similes* (Juster, 1989).

Another poetic device used by writers is ALLITERATION, the repeated use of the same initial consonants in consecutive or proximate words that produces a pattern of the same or similar sounds. Chris Van Allsburg uses alliteration in his alphabet book *The Z was Zapped* (1987). The book is a play in 26 acts. Each right-hand page (recto) contains an illustration of a letter and an action; on the reverse page (verso) is a descriptive, alliterative text that embellishes the illustration. For example, on one page, water is being poured over an uppercase S on stage; on the following page, the text reads, "The S was simply soaked." The pattern of the book invites readers to generate predictions for subsequent letters, and the structure is an easy one for students to imitate in generating their own alliterations or alphabet books. Another book that uses alliteration to tell a tale is *Some Smug Slug* (Edwards, 1996). Edwards writes, "Slowly the slug started up the steep surface, stringing behind it scribble sparkling like silk. 'Stop!' screamed a sparrow, shattering the silence. 'Save him!' shrieked a spider, scurrying down its strand" (unpaginated). ASSONANCE (a run of similar vowel sounds) and CONSONANCE (a run of similar consonant sounds) are two other literary devices that can enhance the sounds of language in a poem.

ONOMATOPOEIA is a device in which a writer creates words (e.g., splash, slurp, boing) to sound like their meanings. The elements of tempo, volume, stress, and pitch can then be manipulated to assist in conveying the meaning and imagery of sound words. Onomatopoeia makes writing more vivid and more sensory. *Machine Poems* (Bennett, 1993), *Noisy Poems* (Bennett, 1987), and *Click, Rumble, Roar: Poems About Machines* (Hopkins, 1987) are three collections of poems that contain examples of onomatopoeia.

The repetition of words and phrases is another device used by many poets. For example, in *A Dark Dark Tale* (Brown, 1981), the author repeats the words "dark, dark." As the poem continues, each location described as "dark, dark" progressively decreases in size. The poem begins, "Once upon a time there was a dark, dark moor"; the next location is a dark, dark wood; then a house, then a door, and so on. Brown's pattern is an easy one for children to emulate and compose their own "dark, dark" poetry.

IMAGERY and FIGURATIVE LANGUAGE are other important poetic elements that play a major role in poetry for children. Langston Hughes' poem *City* (1958) creates the image of the city as a bird, while Carl Sandburg (1944) likens the fog descending on a city to a cat in his poem *Fog*. The language, imagery, and rhythm of a poem interact to create its emotional force. Hughes' poem entitled *Poem* (1960) evokes a powerful emotional response in most readers, as does *Listening to Grownups Quarrelling* by Ruth Whitman (1968):

standing in the hall against the
wall with my little brother, blown
like leaves against the wall by their
voices, my head like a pingpong ball
between the paddles of their anger:
I knew what it meant
to tremble like a leaf.
Cold with their wrath, I heard
the claws of the rain
pounce. Floods
poured through the city,
skies clapped over me,
and I was shaken, shaken,
like a mouse
between their jaws.

FORMS OF POETRY

It is important for children to be familiar with a repertoire of poetic forms in order to facilitate their development of a schema for poetry. As with all kinds of literature, this repertoire should represent a continuum with regards to types and quality. Children generally like limericks and narrative poetry, as well as poems that are humorous, and poems about animals and familiar experiences. Rhyme, rhythm, and sound are other important poetic elements that influence students' opinions of poems (Tompkins & Hoskisson, 1995).

Although there are many different kinds of poems for children to read and share, rhymed verse is the most common type of poetry. Ruth Heller has written and illustrated several rhyming picture books that focus on parts of speech. These books generate interest in language and serve as models for children to write their own books. Some of Heller's books include *A Cache of Jewels and Other Collective Nouns* (1987), *Kites Sail High: A Book About Verbs* (1988), *Many Luscious Lollipops: A Book About Adjectives* (1989), *Merry-go-round: A Book About Nouns* (1990), *Up, Up and Away: A Book About Adverbs* (1991), and *Behind the Mask: A Book About Prepositions* (1995). Sylvia Cassedy uses rhymed verse in many of her poems in *Zoomrimes* (1993). Using the alphabet as a framework, she has written 26 poems about things that "go." For the letter A, Cassedy's poem is called "Ark" and begins as follows:

Packed
back to back
on rack after rack,
stacked nose to nose,
there they all are,
in series and rows,
all praying for drought.
And there's no going out:

NARRATIVE POETRY tells a story. Two narrative poems that have been reproduced in picture-book format are *The Cremation of Sam McGee,* written by

Robert Service and illustrated by Ted Harrison (1987), and *Paul Revere's Ride,* written by Henry Wadsworth Longfellow and illustrated by Ted Rand (1990). Two types of narrative poems are epics and ballads. Epics are tales having "a human hero as the focus of the action and embodying the ideals of a culture" (Sutherland, 1997, p.215). Goforth (1998) describes ballads as "narrative poems, written in the language of the ordinary people to describe a dramatic situation....Typically the ballad includes a refrain. The ballad tells of an incident in the life of a real or fanciful subject" (p.215). Canadian poet Robert Priest has written *The Ballad of the Blue Bonnet* (1994), a humorous ballad about recycling. "Casey Jones," "John Henry," "Robin Hood," and "Yankee Doodle" are other examples of well-known ballads.

Two other forms of poetry are LYRIC and FREE VERSE. "Lyric poetry is melodic or song-like. Generally, it is descriptive, focusing on personal moments, feelings, or image-laden scenes" (Jacobs & Tunnell, 1996, p.170). Lyric poetry often describes a mood or feeling and elicits strong emotions about the subject of the poem. There are no required rhyming patterns or schemes for lyric poetry, and hence poets can sculpture their work to best express their subjects. Although free verse generally lacks rhyme, this type of poetry allows poets great freedom in creating their own rules of rhythm. Emotional language and imagery are especially important elements of free verse, and the topics of free verse are often abstract or philosophical.

HAIKU and CINQUAIN are forms of poetry that have prescribed structures. Haiku, a form of poetry originating in Japan, is a three-line poem whose first and last lines each have five syllables and whose middle line has seven syllables. Haiku traditionally dealt with topics associated with nature or the seasons, but modern haiku is written about a much broader range of subjects. At one time, cinquain, a five-line stanza, seemed to have included any five-line poem. However, Adelaide Crapsey created more explicit rules for this form of poetry, specifying that there be 22 syllables in a cinquain in a 2-4-6-8-2 syllable pattern.

Edward Lear popularized LIMERICKS. In this five-rhymed verse format, the first and second lines rhyme with the fifth line, and the shorter third and fourth lines rhyme with each other. The fifth line is often a repetition of the first line. Limericks are usually humorous or silly. Four books on limericks are *The Book of Pigericks* (Lobel, 1983) (limericks about pigs), *Lots of Limericks* (Livingston, 1991), *There Was an Old Man ... A Collection of Limericks* (Lear, 1994), and *The Hopeful Trout and Other Limericks* (Ciardi, 1989). Here is an example of a limerick from Edward Lear's *The Complete Nonsense Book* (1946, 1846):

There once was an old person of Dover
Who rushed through a field of blue clover.
But some very large bees,
Stung his nose and his knees,
So he very soon went back to Dover.

CONCRETE POEMS are arranged in a particular manner on a page to create an image or visual shape related to the poem's subject. For example, in *A Hippopotamusn't,* a book of poetry about animals, (Lewis, 1990), Lewis has written a concrete poem about the flamingo and has cleverly arranged the words in the shape of a flamingo. Concrete poetry is meant to be *seen* even more than heard, and often this form of poetry lacks a particular rhythm or rhyming pattern (although the most accomplished works in this form exploit sound as much as sight). *Seeing Things: A Book of Poems* (Froman, 1974), *Street Poems* (Froman, 1971), and *Concrete is Not Always Hard* (Pilon, 1972) are collections of concrete poetry. *Splish Splash,* a collection of poetry by Joan Bransfield Graham (1994), also includes concrete poetry. David Florian (1994, 1996, 1997) is another poet whose collections include concrete poetry.

PICTURE-BOOK VERSIONS OF POEMS

There are many picture-book versions of single poems, including Robert Frost's *Stopping by Woods on a Snowy Evening* (1978), illustrated by Susan Jeffers; Eugene Field's *Wynken, Blynken & Nod* (1982), also illustrated by Susan Jeffers; *The Lady With the Alligator Purse* (Westcott, 1988); and Dylan Thomas' *Fern Hill* (1997), illustrated by Murray Kimber. Sheree Fitch has published several single poems in picture-book format, including *There Were Monkeys in My Kitchen* (1992), *Mable Murple* (1995), and *There's a Mouse in My House* (1998). Jan Brett has illustrated a picture-book version of *The Owl and the Pussy Cat* by Edward Lear (1991), and Ed Young has illustrated Robert Frost's poem *Birches* (1988). Ted Rand has illustrated *My Shadow* by Robert Louis Stevenson (1990) and *Arithmetic* by Carl Sandburg (1993). Rand uses anamorphic techniques of drawing in *Arithmetic* as he skillfully stretches his drawings into distorted optical images. Rand has also illustrated *Storm on the Desert*, a poem by Carolyn Lesser (1997) that describes the changes to a desert landscape during a storm. *The Highwayman* by Alfred Noyes (1983) has been illustrated by Charles Mikolaycak. On one side of each double-page spread, readers view Mikolaycak's theatrical illustrations, framed drawings completed in shades of black and white. Neil Waldman has illustrated William Blake's poem *The Tyger* (1993). Waldman uses black-and-white illustrations as the background on each double page spread; on the right-hand page, he frames part of the illustration like a picture, and inside the frame, he uses colour.

In her picture book *In Flanders Fields: The Story of the Poem by John McCrae* (1995), Linda Granfield not only presents the poem "In Flanders Fields" but also provides contextual information about McCrae's actual writing of the poem. At the end of each stanza, Granfield shares information about the poet and his experiences working in a war field hospital, the living conditions and daily routines of the soldiers,

In Flanders Fields: The Story of the Poem by John McCrae by Linda Granfield, illustrated by Janet Wilson

facts about World War One, and the origin of the symbolic gesture of wearing a poppy. Janet Wilson, the illustrator, was concerned about the accuracy of her paintings, and travelled to Flanders as part of her research for the book.

Canadian poet sean o huigin has written many poems for children. Much of o huigin's work is traditional, humorous light verse. But he has written two serious picture books: *Atmosfear* (1985), an anti-pollution poem with a cautionary message, and *The Ghost Horse of the Mounties* (1983), a poem based on an event in 1874, when a violent thunderstorm caused the horses of the first Mounties in Manitoba to stampede. In 1983, *The Ghost Horse of the Mounties* became the first children's poetry book ever to win the Canada Council Children's Literature Prize (precursor to the Governor General's Literary Award).

SEAN O HUIGIN

sean o huigin was born in Brampton, Ontario as John Higgins. After his first visit to Ireland, he changed his name to sean o huigin in memory of Canadian poet Padraig O Broin. He dislikes using the shift key, hence the lower case on his name.

sean was a pioneer in bringing creative artists into Canadian schools. In 1969, sean was the first individual to be commissioned by the Ontario Arts Council's Artists in the Schools Program. At this time, he was involved in a program to promote author readings in inner-city public schools. Although he worked with children in schools for many years, sean did not write his first children's poetry until 1978. He claims that many of his ideas come from the insight he gains from working with young people in schools. His writing is also influenced by the information he discovers visiting prehistoric sites and Native settlements around the world. He is interested in such places and enjoys spending time in libraries and museums researching the sites and settlements he visits.

sean's other works include *Monsters, He Mumbled* (1989), *King of the Birds* (1991), and *A Dozen Million Spills (and Other Disasters)* (1993).

POETRY COLLECTIONS

Many books of poetry are collections of a single individual's work. *Demi's Secret Garden* (Demi, 1993), *Where the Sidewalk Ends* (Silverstein, 1974), *A Light in the Attic* (Silverstein, 1981), *The New Kid on the Block* (Prelutsky, 1984), *Zoomrimes* (Cassedy, 1987), *Dogs and Dragons, Trees and Dreams* (Kuskin, 1980), *Day Songs, Night Songs* (Priest, 1993), and *A Terrible Case of the Stars* (Priest, 1994) are examples. Arnold Adoff, Byrd Baylor, X.J. Kennedy, David McCord, Lilian Moore, John Ciardi, Jack Prelutsky, Eve Merriam, and Myra Cohn Livingston are just a few of the many poets who write poetry for children and who have published collected editions of their work.

The NCTE Award for Excellence in Poetry for Children, established in 1977 by the National Council of Teachers of English, is presented every three years to a living American poet for an aggregate body of work for children ages three to thirteen. Information about poets is available in *Speaking of Poets: Interviews With Poets Who Write for Children and Young Adults* (Copeland, 1993), *Speaking of Poets 2: More Interviews With Poets Who Write for Children and Young Adults* (Copeland & Copeland, 1994), and *A Jar of Tiny Stars: Poems by NCTE Award-Winning Poets* (Cullinan, 1996). In addition, there are professional articles, audiovisual materials, and websites that profile various poets.

DENNIS LEE

Dennis Lee was born in Toronto, Ontario, and saw his first poem published in a children's magazine when he was only seven years old. Dennis was an avid reader as a child and says that when he liked a book, he would "live inside it" until he was finished reading it. Dennis graduated with BA and MA degrees in English Literature from the University of Toronto and considered many careers before teaching at the university level for eight years. Dennis' collection of adult poetry, *Civil Elegies and Other Poems* (1972), won the Governor General's Award for Poetry in 1973. When Dennis' children were young, he began composing chants and rhymes for children; he especially included Canadian content. He felt it was important that Canadian children develop a sense of their Canadian identity, and he wanted to share his excitement over the huge shifts in the ethnic diversity of the Canadian population. Eventually this poetry was published in two books: *Alligator Pie* (1974), winner of the 1974 IODE Book Award – Toronto Chapter and the 1975 Canadian Library Association Book of the Year Award for Children, and *Nicholas Knock and Other People* (1974). Dennis' volume *Garbage Delight* (1977) won the 1978 Canadian Library Association Book of the Year Award for Children and the 1978 Ruth Schwartz Children's Book Award.

After the publication of *Jelly Belly* in 1983, Dennis decided he would not continue his writing for children. The poems just kept coming, however, and he finally accepted that he had a continuing role as a children's author. Dennis explains that when he writes poetry, he awakens the child in himself, and it is this aspect of himself that generates his subjects. In 1986, Dennis received the Vicky Metcalf Award for a Body of Work, and in 1992 he received the Mr. Christie's Book Award for *The Ice Cream Store* (1991). In 1994, Dennis was awarded the Order of Canada. In addition to writing poetry for children, Dennis wrote the book *Lizzie's Lion*, illustrated by Marie-Louise Gay (1984). He has also written song lyrics and continues to publish poetry for an adult audience.

SHEREE FITCH

Among other things, Sheree Fitch is an author, poet, storyteller, playwright, performer, and educator. She was born in Ottawa but her roots and upbringing were in the Maritimes. Sheree currently resides in Halifax, Nova Scotia, but she spent her early childhood in Moncton, New Brunswick; her teenage years and much of her adult life were spent in Fredericton, New Brunswick. Although as a child Sheree dreamed of becoming a writer, she originally planned on pursuing a career in nursing. However, marriage and young motherhood altered her plans.

Sheree began attending St. Thomas University in 1981 as a part-time student and graduated with an honours degree in English in 1987. During her undergraduate years, she became co-founder and member of the Enterprise Theatre, an alternative theatre troupe based in Fredericton. As well as performing her own poetry throughout New Brunswick, Sheree acted in a play and did some film work. She also did radio and television commercials.

Her first book of poetry for children, *Toes in My Nose and Other Poems* (1987), continues to be a Canadian bestseller. As well as writing other collections of poetry, *If You Could Wear My Sneakers!* (1997) and *Sleeping Dragons All Around* (1989), Sheree has published single poems in picture-book format. *There Were Monkeys in My Kitchen!* (1992), winner of the 1993 Mr. Christie Book Award; *Mable Murple* (1995), winner of the Nova Scotia Library Association's 1996 Ann Connor Brimer Award for Children's Literature; and *There's a Mouse in my House* (1998) are three such picture books. As well as writing poetry and books for children, Sheree has written poetry, plays, and satirical cartoons for adults.

Many poetry books are specialized collections of poems related to a single theme or topic, such as snow, dinosaurs, monsters, dragons, magic, festivals, machines, Hallowe'en, nightmares, or other subjects. For example, Canadian poet Sheree Fitch has written *Toes in My Nose and Other Poems* (1987), a collection of nonsense poems, and *If You Could Wear My Sneakers!* (1997), a collection of poems interpreting 15 of the 54 articles of the United Nations' Convention on the Rights of the Child. A list of specialized collections of poems, as well as a list of general poetry anthologies, can be found at the end of this chapter.

Anthologies of poems are useful for teachers to have at hand. Notable anthologies include the *Oxford Book of Poetry for Children,* compiled by Edward Blishen (1963), *The Random House Book of Poetry,* compiled by Jack Prelutsky (1983), *The New Wind Has Wings* compiled by Mary Alice Downie and Barbara Robertson (1987), and *'Til All the Stars Have Fallen,* compiled by David Booth (1989).

Booth and Moore write (1988), "Children come to poetry naturally, and then something happens to that linguistic emotional relationship. Is it the formality of teaching that takes away the appreciation? Is it the teacher's own attitudes that alter the child's enjoyment of this particular kind of print? For certain, something happens to many children, and the love of poetry as part of their life experience begins to wane" (p.23). Educators have the responsibility of cultivating and extending children's linguistic-emotional relationship with poetry. As teachers, we need to come to know the world of children's poetry. Poets use their great talents thoughtfully, their words creating vivid pictorial and emotional images. We need to share and enjoy these literary artworks with our students and increasingly read poetry for the pleasure of both children and ourselves.

References

Barton, B. 1986. *Tell Me Another*. Markham, Ontario: Pembroke Publishers Limited.

Barton, B. and D. Booth. 1990. *Stories in the Classroom: Storytelling, Reading Aloud and Roleplaying with Children*. Markham, Ontario: Pembroke Publishers Limited.

———. 1988. *Poems Please! Sharing Poetry with Children*. Markham, Ontario: Pembroke Publishers Limited.

Copeland, J. 1993. *Speaking of Poets: Interviews with Poets Who Write for Children and Young Adults.* Urbana, Illinois: National Council of Teachers of English.

Copeland, J. and V. Copeland. 1994. *Speaking of Poets 2: Interviews with Poets Who Write for Children and Young Adults.* Urbana, Illinois: National Council of Teachers of English.

Campbell, J. 1988. *The Power of Myth*. New York: Doubleday.

Campbell, M. 1985. *Achimoona.* Saskatoon: Fifth House Publishing.

Cullinan, B., ed. 1996. *A Jar of Tiny Stars: Poems by NCTE Award-winning Poets*. Honesdale, Pennsylvania: Boyds Mill Press.

Cullinan, B. and L. Galda. 1994. *Literature and the Child.* Third edition. New York: Harcourt Brace Jovanovich.

Goforth, F. 1998. *Literature and the Learner*. Belmont, California: Wadsworth Publishing Company.

Guest, J. 1977. *The Mabinogian* (facsimile edition). Cardiff: John Jones Cardiff Ltd.

Huck, J., S. Hepler, and J. Hickman. 1993. *Children's Literature in the Elementary School.* Fifth edition. New York: Harcourt Brace Jovanovich College Publishers.

Hughes, L. 1950. City. In *The Langston Hughes Reader*. New York: Harold Ober Associates Inc.

———. 1960. Poem. In *Don't You Turn Back: Poems by Langston Hughes*. Lee Bennett Hopkins, ed. New York: Knopf.

Jacobs, J. and M. Tunnel. 1996. *Children's Literature, Briefly*. Englewood, New Jersey: Prentice- Hall, Inc.

Jenkinson, D. 1999. Joe McLellan: A profile. *CM: Canadian Review of Materials* 5(12). Available: http://www.umanitoba.ca/cm/ [1999, February 12]

Jones, G. and T. Jones. 1949. *The Mabinogian*. London: J.M. Dent.

Lee, D. 1972. *Civil Elegies and Other Poems*. Toronto: Anansi.

Lenaghan, R. T., ed. 1967. *Caxton's Aesop*. Cambridge: Harvard University Press.

McLellan, J. 1998. Nanabosho: Weaving the dream into the classroom. *Issues in the North* 3, 107-110.

Norton, D. 1999. *Through the Eyes of a Child: An Introduction to Children's Literature*. Fifth edition. Upper Saddle River, New Jersey: Prentice-Hall, Inc.

Petite Riviere Elementary School. 1993. *History of Crousetown*. Lunenburg County, Nova Scotia: Petite Riviére Publishing.

Rosen, B. 1988. *And None of It Was Nonesense: The Power of Storytelling in the Classroom*. Richmond Hill, Ontario: Scholastic-TAB.

Sandburg, C. 1944. Fog. In *Chicago Poems*. New York: Harcourt Brace and Co.

Stephens, J. and K. Watson., eds. 1994. *From Picture Book to Literary Theory*. Sydney, Australia: St Clair Press.

Tompkins, G. and K. Hoskisson. 1995. *Language Arts: Content and Teaching Strategies.* Third edition. Englewood, New Jersey: Prentice-Hall, Inc.

Whitman, R. 1968. Listening to Grownups Quarrelling. In *The Marriage Wig and Other Poems*. New York: Harcourt Brace and Co.

Professional Resources

Barton, B. and D. Booth. 1990. *Stories in the Classroom: Storytelling, Reading Aloud and Roleplaying with Children*. Markham, Ontario: Pembroke Publishers Limited. • Bob Barton and David Booth draw on their 30 years of experience working as teachers, consultants, storytellers, and authors as they demonstrate how to find, choose, and use specific stories in classroom contexts. Based on the theoretical perspectives of Harold Rosen, Margaret Meek, Wolfgang Iser, Dorothy Heathcote, and others, this text develops a host of response activities ranging from story retellings, conversation, and dialogue to dramatization, thematic arts projects, and numerous writing activities.

Booth, D. and B. Moore. 1988. *Poems Please! Sharing Poetry with Children*. Markham, Ontario: Pembroke Publishers Limited. • This text includes a rationale, techniques, and strategies for sharing poetry with children.

The authors examine the evolution of poetry for children and the reasons for sharing poetry with children. They discuss how to select poetry for children and explore how poems work; they also offer many suggestions for reading, listening to, and writing poetry. The text includes an annotated list of over 200 poetry anthologies.

Norton, D. 1999. *Through the Eyes of a Child: An Introduction to Children's Literature*. Fifth edition. Upper Saddle River, New Jersey: Prentice-Hall, Inc. • The text is intended for anyone interested in evaluating, selecting, and sharing children's literature. Approximately twenty-five percent of the titles in the book were published within two years of publication of the fifth edition of the text. There is an excellent chapter on artists and their illustrations, and a thorough chapter on traditional literature. The book comes with a CD-ROM disk that contains all the children's literature titles referenced in the book along with their respective bibliographic citations.

Sutherland, Z. 1997. *Children and Books*. Ninth edition. New York: Longman. • Sutherland's remains one of the most comprehensive texts on children's literature. Now in its ninth edition, the book contains a chapter on poetry and two chapters on folk tales, fables, myths, and epics. The tales are arranged according to their country of origin. There is a detailed exploration of the history of children's literature and the classics, from *Aesop's Fables* (1484) to the Newbery Medal winners in the 1990s. Discussions of the various genres of literature and detailed descriptions of the books cited are extremely useful. The book is illustrated and well laid out.

Myths

Barth, E. 1976. *Cupid and Psyche*. New York: Seabury (Clarion).

Evslin, B. 1984. *Hercules*. New York: Morrow.

Fisher, L.E. 1984. *The Olympians: Great Gods and Goddesses of Ancient Greece*. New York: Holiday.

Hamilton, V. 1988. *In the Beginning: Creation Stories from Around the World*. New York: Harcourt, Brace, Jovanovich.

Harrison, M. 1987. *The Curse of the Ring*. London: Oxford University Press.

Hutton, W. 1994. *Persephone*. New York: Macmillan.

Mastin, C. 1998. *The Magic of Mythical Creatures*. Calgary: Grasshopper Books.

McDermott, G. 1984. *Daughter of the Earth: A Roman Myth*. New York: Delacorte.

McLellen, J. 1991. *Nanabosho Dances*. Winnipeg: Pemmican Publications.

Zeman, L. 1995. *The Last Quest of Gilgamesh*. Montreal: Tundra Books.

Legends

Crossley-Holland, K. 1982. *Beowulf*. London: Oxford.

dePaola, T. 1993. *The Legend of the Persian Carpet*. New York: Putnam.

Early, M. 1991. *William Tell*. New York: Abrams.

Hastings, S. 1981. *Sir Gawain and the Green Knight*. New York: Lothrop, Lee & Shepard.

Hodges, M. 1984. *St. George and the Dragon*. Boston: Little, Brown.

Lagerlof, S. 1990. *The Legend of the Christmas Rose*. Retold by Ellin Greene. New York: Holiday.

Leeson, R. 1994. *The Story of Robin Hood*. New York: Kingfisher.

Lemieux, M. 1993. *The Pied Piper of Hamelin*. New York: Morrow.

McKibbon, H. 1996. *The Token Gift*. Toronto: Annick Press.

Riordan, J. 1982. *Tales of King Arthur*. New York: Rand McNally.

San Souci, R. 1993. *Young Guinevere*. New York: Doubleday.

Fables

Bierhorst, J. 1987. *Doctor Coyote: A Native American Aesop's Fable*. New York: Macmillan.

Caldecott, R. 1978. *The Caldecott Aesop: A Facsimile of the 1883 Edition*. New York: Doubleday.

Carle, E. 1980. *Twelve Tales from Aesop*. New York: Putnam.

Craig, H. 1992. *The Town Mouse and the Country Mouse*. Cambridge, Massachusetts: Candlewick.

Kherdian, D. 1992. *Feathers and Tails: Animal Fables From Around the World*. New York: Philomel.

Lionni, L. 1967. *Frederick*. New York: Pantheon.

Paxton, T. 1991. *Androcles and the Lion and Other Aesop's Fables*. New York: Morrow.

Steig, W. 1971. *Amos and Boris*. New York: Farrar, Strauss & Giroux.

Stevens, J. 1984. *The Tortoise and the Hare*. New York: Holiday House.

Yolen, J. 1995. *A Sip of Aesop*. New York: Scholastic.

Young, E. 1992. *Seven Blind Mice*. New York: Philomel.

Specialized Collections of Poems

Carle, E. 1989. *Animals, Animals*. New York: Philomel.

Esbensen, B. 1992. *Who Shrank My Grandmother's House?* New York: Harper & Row, Publishers.

Florian, D. 1994. *Beast Feast*. New York: Harcourt Brace.

————. 1996. *On the Wing*. New York: Harcourt Brace.

————. 1997. *In the Swim*. New York: Harcourt Brace.

Foster, J. 1990. *Let's Celebrate: Festival Poems*. Don Mills, Ontario: Oxford University Press.

Foster, J., comp. 1992. *Egg Poems*. Don Mills, Ontario: Oxford University Press.

————. 1992. *Seed Poems*. Don Mills, Ontario: Oxford University Press.

————. 1997. *Magic Poems*. Don Mills, Ontario: Oxford University Press.

————. 1997. *Dragon Poems*. Don Mills, Ontario: Oxford University Press.

Foster, J. and K. Paul. 1997. *Dinosaur Poems*. Don Mills, Ontario: Oxford University Press.

————. 1997. *Monster Poems*. Don Mills, Ontario: Oxford University Press.

Harrison, M. and C. Stuart-Clark, eds. 1991. *A Year Full of Poems*. Don Mills, Ontario: Oxford University Press.

————. 1992. *The Oxford Book of Animal Poems*. Don Mills, Ontario: Oxford University Press.

Hopkins, L. 1996. *Opening Days: Sports Poems*. San Diego: Harcourt Brace.

————. 1997. *Song and Dance*. New York: Simon and Schuster.

Livingston, M.C. 1993. *Roll Along: Poems on Wheels*. New York: Macmillan.

Merriam, E. 1987. *Halloween ABC*. New York: Macmillan Publishing Company.

Morrison, L., comp. 1992. *At the Crack of the Bat: Baseball Poems*. New York: Hyperion Books.

o huigin, s. 1982. *Scary Poems for Rotten Kids*. Windsor, Ontario: Black Moss Press.

Prelutsky, J. 1976. *Nightmares: Poems to Trouble Your Sleep*. New York: Greenwillow Books.

————. 1984. *It's Snowing! It's Snowing!* New York: Greenwillow Books.

————. 1990. *Something Big Has Been Here*. New York: Greenwillow Books.

Rosen, M. 1996. *Food Fight*. New York: Harcourt.

Schertle, A. 1995. *Advice for a Frog*. New York: Lothrop/Morrow.

————. 1996. *Keepers*. New York: Lothrop/Morrow.

Schnur, S. 1997. *Autumn: An Alphabet Acrostic*. New York: Clarion.

Yolen, J. 1990. *Bird Watch: A Book of Poetry*. New York: Philomel.

Poetry Anthologies

Balaam, J. and B. Merrick. 1989. *Exploring Poetry: 5–8*. Sheffield, U.K.: National Association for the Teaching of English.

Blishen, E., comp. 1963. *The Oxford Book of Poetry for Children*. London: Oxford University Press.

Booth, D. 1989. *'Til All the Stars Have Fallen*. Toronto: Kids Can Press.

Bouchard, D. 1993. *If You're Not from the Prairie*. Vancouver: Raincoast Books.

Chandra, D. 1990. *Balloons and Other Poems*. New York: Farrar, Straus, & Giroux.

de Paola, T., ed. 1988. *Tomie de Paola's Book of Poems*. New York: Putnam's.

de Regniers, B.S., E. Moore, M.M. White, and J. Carr., comps. 1988. *Sing a Song of Popcorn: Every Child's Book of Poems*. New York: Lothrop, Lee & Shepard.

Downie, D. and B. Robertson, comp. 1987. *The New Wind Has Wings: Poems from Canada*. New York: Oxford.

Goldstein, B., ed. 1993. *Birthday Rhymes, Special Times*. New York: Delacorte.

Harrison, M. and C. Stuart-Clark, comps. 1988. *The Oxford Treasury of Children's Poems*. Toronto: Oxford University Press.

————. 1995. *The New Oxford Treasury of Children's Poems*. Toronto: Oxford University Press.

Kennedy, X.J., comp. 1985. *The Forgetful Wishing Well: Poems for Young People*. New York: M.K. McElderry Books.

Lansky, B., comp. 1991. *Kids Pick the Funniest Poems: Poems That Make Kids Laugh*. New York: Meadowbrook Press.

Larrick, N., ed. 1991. *To the Moon and Back*. New York: Delacorte.

Lesynski, L. 1999. *Dirty Dog Boogie*. Willowdale, Ontario: Annick Press.

Lee, D. 1977. *Garbage Delight*. Toronto: Macmillan Canada.

Merrick, B. 1991. *Exploring Poetry: 8–13*. Sheffield, U.K.: National Association for the Teaching of English.

Prelutsky, J. 1993. *The Dragons Are Singing Tonight*. New York: Greenwillow Press.

————. 1996. *A Pizza the Size of the Sun*. New York: William Morrow.

————, comp. 1983. *The Random House Book of Poetry*. New York: Random House.

————, comp. 1991. *For Laughing Out Loud: Poems to Tickle Your Funnybone*. New York: Alfred A. Knopf.

Rosen, M. 1984. *Quick, Let's Get Out of Here*. New York: Dutton.

Steig, J. 1988. *Consider the Lemming*. New York: Farrar, Straus, and Giroux.

Willard, N. 1981. *A Visit to William Blake's Inn*. San Diego: Harcourt, Brace, Jovanovich.

Wood, N. 1993. *Spirit Walker*. New York: Doubleday.

Worth, V. 1987. *All the Small Poems*. New York: Farrar, Straus, & Giroux.

CHAPTER FOUR

NOVELS FOR THE ELEMENTARY CLASSROOM

The objectives of this chapter are

- To develop an understanding of the role of the classics in children's literature;
- To develop an understanding of the role of beginning novels in the growth of readers;
- To develop an awareness of the many beginning novels appropriate for classroom use;
- To develop an understanding of the various genres of fictional literature and the categories and/or topics within certain genres;
- To develop an awareness of the many works of fictional literature appropriate for upper elementary grade readers.

The Classics

Over the years, many books have become firm favourites among elementary readers. *Little Women* (Alcott, 1867), *Black Beauty* (Sewell, 1877), and *Treasure Island* (Stevenson, 1883) have provided children with reading enjoyment for over a century. Such books are now referred to as classics.

Classics are books that have attracted readers from one generation to the next. They cross all genre lines; even picture books have classics among them, such as *Where the Wild Things Are* (Sendak, 1963), *Make Way for Ducklings* (McCloskey, 1941), and *Goodnight Moon* (Brown, 1947). Lawrence Sipe writes that, "All literate people probably have a mental list of the literary texts they consider classics; inclusion in this mental list is apt to be largely determined by the importance of the book to a person's own life" (1996, p.31). Sipe maintains that most people would be hard pressed to justify their choices for inclusion, however. Generally, a book is regarded as a classic when it has stood the test of time—when it has been read and enjoyed by generations of readers. Many of the books regarded as classics have been kept in the public mind through their presence on reading lists in schools or in university courses; as a result, they have been kept in print and widely available. Sipe questions whether the concept of a classic may itself be outmoded. He writes, "With the proliferation of so many contestatory discourses in literary criticism, so many contradictory critical viewpoints, how could we ever agree that a particular text fulfilled anyone's definition of a classic? Perhaps it was the relative homogeneity of Western culture until the first World War that enabled the socio-cultural construction of the very idea of 'classic' literature" (1996, p.33).

Many of the books deemed as classics were written at a time when there were few publications intended specifically for children. As a result, these books were revered by their owners and often passed from one generation to another within a family. As families owned few books, these volumes were treated with great respect. *The History of Little Goody Two-Shoes* (Goldsmith, 1765), one of the first children's books published by John Newbery in London, is of historical relevance to children's literature, but it has little appeal to readers in the 1990s. Other books, such as *Black Beauty*, which was originally published in protest against cruelty to animals, retain their appeal and continue to be reprinted.

Lukens writes that "The classics of one generation may be supplanted by later books but the appeals of other books may remain for a surprisingly long time" (1999, p.36). *Heidi* (Spyri, 1884), *Anne of Green Gables* (Montgomery, 1908), and *The Five Little Peppers and How They Grew* (Sidney, 1881) are still enduring favourites today. These books remain relevant to readers because they deal with issues that confront children growing up throughout the generations. Although the language and settings may be uncommon, the characters and the human situations depicted in many of these books are as believable today as they were when they were first written.

Although many classics continue to have wide appeal, we must remember that these books are not for all of today's children. Books written 80 or more years ago reflect a very different set of values and attitudes. Racism, sexism, and didacticism were especially rampant in many of these books—even the apparently innocuous *Bobbsey Twins* (Hope, 1904) were not immune. To be added to the list of "older" classics are the "new classics," contemporary books that enjoy continuing popularity. This list might include *Angel Square* (Doyle, 1984), *Underground to Canada* (Smucker, 1977), *The Keeper of the Isis Light* (Hughes, 1980), and *The Olden Days Coat* (Laurence, 1979), as well as *Charlotte's Web* (White, 1952), *The Lion, the Witch and the Wardrobe* (Lewis, 1950), *Bridge to Terabithia* (Paterson, 1977), *Winnie the Pooh* (Milne, 1926), and the Little House series by Laura Ingalls Wilder, among many others.

Lukens maintains that "What seems to keep classics in continuous circulation may be the significance of theme, the credibility of character, the continuing reality of the conflict or the engaging quality of the style" (1999, p.30)—characteristics that contemporary authors also strive to include in their work. In the remainder of this chapter, we highlight contemporary literature for elementary students that attempts to meet the qualities suggested by Lukens.

Beginning Novels

There are numerous novels appropriate for children in grades two and three, and many students in these grades express interest in reading "chapter books." The movement from reading exclusively picture books to reading books with chapters seems to denote a transition in an individual's growth as a reader. That is not to suggest that children are no longer interested in reading picture books; as discussed in Chapter 2, there are numerous picture books appropriate for older readers. And as noted earlier, a picture book, like all works of literature, can be read on many levels, and, hence, a book that is deemed appropriate for younger children can also be used with older readers.

The reading level (i.e., a level calculated by the application of a readability formula) of many beginning novels ranges from grades two to four. Several beginning novels contain illustrations to assist readers in the transition from picture books to novels. The content and writing style of most beginning novels are also appropriate for older elementary students whose reading levels are below grade level or for those who simply wish to read a "good" (albeit easier) book.

The number of beginning novels published each year seems to be growing. Some books are written

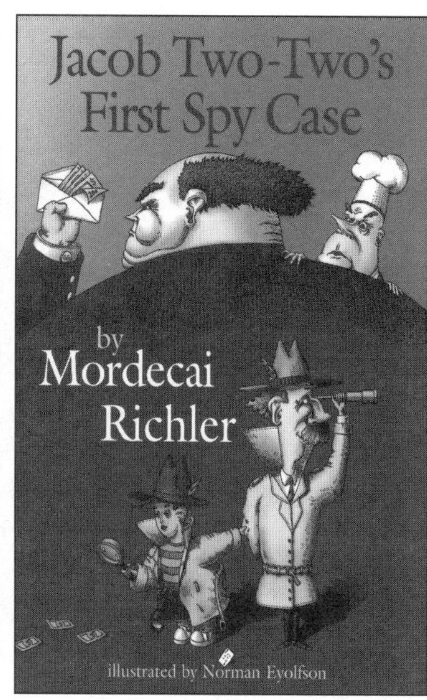

Jacob Two-Two Meets the Hooded Fang, *Jacob Two-Two and the Dinosaur*, and *Jacob Two-Two's First Spy Case*, all by Mordecai Richler

deliberately as beginning novels (e.g., the Magic Tree House series), but many others are not. Like all types of literature discussed in this book, it is vital for teachers to read the beginning novels they use in their language arts programs because the books vary in literary quality and reading levels.

THE BOOKS

The many beginning novels for students, like novels for older elementary readers, represent various genres of literature, with some chapter books combining genres. The various genres of fictional literature and the categories and/or topics within certain genres are discussed in detail later in this chapter.

Canadian author Mordecai Richler's three novels about Jacob Two-Two—*Jacob Two-Two Meets the Hooded Fang* (1975), *Jacob Two-Two and the Dinosaur* (1987), and *Jacob Two-Two's First Spy Case* (1995)—combine fantasy and realistic fiction. In *Jacob Two-Two Meets the Hooded Fang*, six-year-old Jacob, who says everything two times in order to be noticed, is convicted of insulting an adult and sent to a children's prison. However, the Hooded Fang, the dreadful warden, is not all he seems. With the assistance of Jacob's brother and sister, the duo known as CHILD POWER, Jacob Two-Two is successful in escaping from his imprisonment. In *Jacob Two-Two and the Dinosaur*, Jacob's birthday present, a tiny green lizard, continues to grow until it is evident that Dippy the lizard is really Dippy the diplodocus. Dippy attracts the attention of many individuals, some with unscrupulous motives, and Jacob and Dippy flee to British Columbia. In *Jacob Two-Two's First Spy Case*, the new Headmaster of Jacob's private school hires Perfectly Loathsome Leo Louse and his exceedingly miserly mother to prepare disgusting, tasteless, and dreadful food for the boys. Not only are the boys terrified to complain, lest they be punished mercilessly by the Headmaster, Mr. Greedyguts, but they must watch the gluttonous Mr. Greedyguts dine on scrumptious feasts as they are served their horrible meals. Luckily for Jacob, his new neighbour, Mr. X. Barnaby Dinglebat, Master Spy, wants to assist him in solving the problem of the disgusting school lunches. Jacob becomes Mr. Dinglebat's "apprentice spy," and with the help of

CHILD POWER, and some other friends at school, the treacherous and deceitful acts of Mr. Greedyguts and Leo Louse become known to all.

Ursula Le Guin's *Catwings* (1988), *Catwings Return* (1989), *Wonderful Alexander and the Catwings* (1994), and *Jane on Her Own: A Catwings Tale* (1999) are four beginning animal-fantasy novels about the adventures of cats with wings. Roald Dahl's *Fantastic Mr. Fox* (1970) is another animal fantasy. This humorous novel tells the story of Fantastic Mr. Fox's schemes to outwit three feeble-minded farmers. *The Magician's Trap* (Piper, 1976) is a fantasy about an evil magician who devises a treacherous plan to take over King Justin's kingdom by luring his son, Prince Harold the Daring, to partake in an adventure under the sea. The Magic Tree House series (Random House) is a time-travel fantasy series written by Mary Pope Osborne. In each book the main characters travel from the magic tree house to an extraordinary destination (e.g., the middle ages, the prehistoric period, an Amazon rain forest). Another fantasy, *The Chocolate Touch* (Catling, 1952), is an amusing story about the problems that unfold when John, a lover of chocolate, develops the "chocolate touch."

Two beginning chapter books which contain elements of truth are *The Whipping Boy* (Fleischman, 1986) and *Stone Fox* (Gardiner, 1980). *The Whipping Boy*, winner of the 1987 Newbery Medal, is based on the fact that many centuries ago some royal families kept a whipping boy to receive the prince's punishment. In Fleischman's book, Jemmy, the whipping boy, suffers the punishments owed to Prince Brat. Jemmy decides to run away (and who could blame him?), but Prince Brat joins him. The boys learn about themselves and each other through their many adventures. John Reynolds Gardiner explains that *Stone Fox* came from a Rocky Mountain legend. Although the characters in the book are fictitious, Gardiner writes that the tragic ending "belongs to the legend and is reported to have actually happened" (*Stone Fox*, p.83). The novel is about the participation of ten-year-old Willy and his dog, Searchlight, in a dog-sled race to keep the family farm. The race attracts the best sled racers in the country, one of whom is a legendary Native man, Stone Fox, who is also determined to win the prize money.

In *Tornado* (Byars, 1996), a family seeking refuge in the storm cellar during a tornado listens while Pete, a farmhand, recounts the story of how he came to own a dog named Tornado. When Pete was a boy, a tornado blew a doghouse, complete with a dog inside, into his yard! Pete shares many stories about Tornado's antics, passing the time while the storm rages above.

There are several other excellent realistic fiction beginning novels, including volumes written by Canadian authors Ken Roberts, Budge Wilson, Jean Little, Gisela Sherman, and Sylvia McNicoll. Two novels by Roberts, *Hiccup Champion of the World* (1988) and *Pop Bottles* (1987), each tell the story of a twelve-year-old boy with a problem. In *Hiccup Champion of the World*, Maynard Chan gets the hiccups but none of the cures generated by his family, friends, and peers are successful. Just before Maynard is about to appear on a television show, his hiccups cease—temporarily. The setting for *Pop Bottles* is Depression-era Vancouver. Will McCleary discovers that the walkway of his new house is made from thousands of buried pop bottles which could be returned for their deposit. Will must deal with many unusual situations and characters in his attempts to excavate his buried treasure. Wilson's *Harold and Harold* (1995) tells the story of a boy named Harold whose friendship with a beautiful blue heron helps him to be accepted by his coastal community. Confusion involving the heron changes the way everyone views Harold—and the way Harold views himself. In Jean Little's *Lost and Found* (1985), Lucy moves to a new town and is concerned about making friends when school begins. Lucy finds a dog, whom she names Trouble, and the dog helps to ease Lucy's loneliness. She hopes that no one will claim Trouble, but in the end, Lucy must make decisions that affect not only the welfare of Trouble, but of another dog as well.

King of the Class by Gisela T. Sherman

Two books that involve an element of peer pressure are *King of the Class* (Sherman, 1994) and *The Big Race* (McNicoll, 1996). *King of the Class* is part of the Shooting Star series of beginning chapter books; contributors to this series include Brenda Bellingham, Sylvia McNicoll, Martyn Godfrey, and Carol Matas. *King of the Class* is about Jonah, who desperately wants to be the "best" at something, to gain admiration and attention from his classmates. Another boy in the class, René, always brings the best of everything to school, so Jonah devises a plan. Although Jonah runs into problems, he does get to be the best at something—and King of the Class. *The Big Race* tells the story of a grade three boy's constant competition with a female classmate, who excels at everything she does. Readers learn about the consequences of the boy's jealousy, and discover how various events, including a broken nose, bring the characters together in the end.

SYLVIA McNICOLL

Sylvia McNicoll was born in Ajax, Ontario in 1954 and grew up in Montreal, Quebec. She loved writing from the time she wrote her first composition in grade four; but she thought that only dead American or British people were successful at writing! Sylvia worked as a clerk in a paper company during the day while earning a Bachelor of Arts from Concordia University at night. Once she left the corporate world to have her three children, Sylvia began to reflect and write again, something she had not done since school. She initially wrote some short stories, then a few household hints for magazines and freelance articles for a local paper.

Sylvia moved to Burlington, Ontario and took a children's writing course from Paul Kropp at Sheridan College. As a class project, she wrote *Blueberries and Whipped Cream* (1988). Since that time she has written several other books, including *Project Disaster* (1990), *Bringing up Beauty* (1995), and *Walking a Thin Line* (1997). *Bringing up Beauty* was winner of two children's choice awards, the 1996 Silver Birch Award and the 1997 Manitoba Young Readers' Association Award. Sylvia explains how the inspiration for the story came at a time in her life when several of her books had been rejected. Sylvia's friend, who was a contributing editor of *Owl* magazine at the time, asked her to write an amusing environmental story for the magazine. At the same time, another friend told Sylvia about fostering guide dogs for Canine Vision Canada; coincidentally, Sylvia's husband worked with an individual whose family had raised three dogs for the organization. Sylvia listened in awe to the stories about the emotional upheaval experienced by families who raise the puppies and then give them up to Canine Vision Canada after one year. In order to meet the environmental criterion, Sylvia included a compost heap at the beginning and the end of the short story for *Owl*. However, she had to substantially reduce the story in length for *Owl* and when it was finished, Sylvia knew she had to write the "full story."

Sylvia writes under a pseudonym in England; as Geena Dare, she has contributed several books to the "Stage School Series." As well as writing and travelling to schools and libraries to meet and talk with students, Sylvia has taught creative writing at Sheridan College. She has also been involved with the Writers in Electronic Residence Programme and has connected through the Internet with many young writers across Canada. She enjoys being a mentor to students who post their poems and short stories, and notes how she can do this work in the middle of the night if she wishes!

Sylvia loves to swim, throw a basketball or baseball around, and roller blade. While conducting research for a couple of her books, she attained a blue belt in judo!

Three compelling realistic fiction novels that address some aspect of survival include *A Taste of Blackberries* (Smith, 1973), *Snowshoe Trek to Otter River* (Budbill, 1976), and *Where's Buddy?* (Roy, 1982). *A Taste of Blackberries* is a tragic story about a boy, Jamie, who always teases and jokes with his friends. One day while picking blackberries with his friends, Jamie disturbs some bees and has a fatal allergic reaction to a sting. The narrator of the story must deal with the loss of his friend. *Snowshoe Trek to Otter River* contains three short stories about two boys who hike, canoe, and camp in the wilderness. Each story deals with one or both of the boys surviving in some manner on a wilderness adventure. In *Where's Buddy?*, Buddy, who is a diabetic, and his friend become trapped in a cave by the changing tides. Buddy's older brother searches frantically for Buddy to ensure that he is safe and has taken his desperately needed insulin shot.

The *First Novel* series offers contemporary beginning novels by Canadian authors. These novels vary in quality: some are well written while others are rather generic. The print is large and there are illustrations throughout each book. *Arthur's Dad* (Anfousse, 1989) is about Arthur, a very naughty boy, whose antics cause his father great difficulties in securing a babysitter. However, Arthur's dad does find a match—for Arthur and for himself. In *Fred's Dream Cat* (Croteau, 1994), Fred comes up with many schemes in order to get a cat. His parents, who own a fish store, are unreceptive to Fred's wishes, but he is persistent. *Go For It, Carrie* (Choyce, 1997) tells the story of ten-year-old Carrie, who is determined to learn how to rollerblade despite teasing from her brother Ernie and his friend. Carrie's friend Gregory, who has Down's Syndrome, is very supportive of her efforts, however, and both Carrie and Gregory learn the importance of persevering in order to achieve one's goals.

As discussed later in this chapter, mystery is often considered a subgenre or category within the realistic fiction genre. *Who Stole the Wizard of Oz?* (Avi, 1981) is a mystery about the disappearance of valuable children's books. Becky is accused of stealing a rare book, and she and her twin brother, Toby, investigate the thefts in order to prove her innocence.

Some series mystery books are beginning novels as well. David Adler has written several books about young detective Jennifer Jansen. Jennifer is called Cam (for "Camera") because of her amazing photographic memory. Cam closes her eyes, says "click," and visualizes scenes at various times. By comparing the changes in the scenes, Cam is able to deduce what has happened and is able to solve the mystery. Some of the titles in this series include *Cam Jansen and the Mystery of the Stolen Diamonds* (1980), *Cam Jansen and the Mystery of Flight 54* (1989), *Cam Jansen and the Triceratops Pops Mystery* (1995), and *Cam Jansen and the Ghostly Mystery* (1996). Two other mystery series include the *Nate the Great* books by Marjorie Sharmat and the *Something Queer* books by Elizabeth Levy. A few titles in Sharmat's series include *Nate the Great and the Sticky Case* (1978), *Nate the Great and the Fishy Prize* (1985), *Nate the Great and the Stolen Base* (1992), and *Nate the Great and the Tardy Tortoise* (1995). Some of the titles in Levy's series include *Something Queer on Vacation* (1980), *Something Queer at the Birthday Party* (1989), *Something Queer in Outer Space* (1993), *Something Queer at the Library: A Mystery* (1997), and *Something Queer in the Wild West* (1997). Although the quality of the literature in these series books is not as high (in our opinion) as the other books described in this section, these books do interest some readers and can serve as transition material. The rather formulaic writing, predictable format, and patterned plot development appeal to certain readers.

Matt Christopher, a prolific writer of sports stories (see the section on Sports later in the chapter), has written the Peach Street Mudders series. *The Hit-Away Kid* (1988), *Man Out at First* (1993), *Shadow Over Second* (1996), and *The Catcher's Mask* (1998) are some of the titles in Christopher's series about the Peach Street Mudders, a baseball team. The books range in length from 60 to 70 pages, and each book contains black-and-white illustrations.

We have identified a brief selection of the many beginning novels available for elementary students. A list at the end of the chapter contains additional book titles.

Novels for Upper Elementary Readers

Thousands of new books are published each year for children in the upper elementary grades. Although remaining current with new publications may seem like an overwhelming task for teachers, there are many professional resources to assist you in your book selections. (See discussions on this topic in Chapters 1 and 9.) A list at the end of the chapter includes many titles in addition to those discussed below.

Novels for upper elementary students, like beginning novels, can be categorized into various literary genres, with many books combining or crossing over genres. Moss further complicates the categorization of literature by genre by stating that "many genres, or types of children's literature, are hybrids (i.e., they contain elements of several genres)" (1996, p.35).

CONTEMPORARY REALISTIC FICTION

There is a multitude of high-quality contemporary realistic fiction novels available for elementary readers. This genre is popular with students and is the most widely read genre in the upper elementary grades (see the discussion on reading interests in Chapter 9). Contemporary realistic fiction provides readers with a way of knowing about the world beyond their own experiences and allows for further exploration of issues with which readers may have had some personal contact. Readers may also "come to feel that they are not alone...may learn to reflect on the choices in their own lives...[and] may learn empathy for other people" (Temple, Martinez, Yokota & Naylor, 1998, p.266). "Realistic fiction is derived from actual circumstances, with realistic settings and characters who face problems and possibilities that are within the range of what is possible in real life" (Temple, Martinez, Yokota & Naylor, 1998, p.265).

The subject matter of realistic fiction includes a child's whole world of relationships with self and others. Some aspects of human life treated in realistic fiction include families (nuclear, extended, alternative), peers, adolescent issues (e.g., self-discovery and independence, maturation, facing and overcoming fears), survival and adventure, persons with disabilities, and cultural diversity; in most, if not all, realistic fiction books, authors address more than one of the aforementioned issues. For example, *Shabash!* by Ann Walsh (1994) deals with families, peers, adolescent issues, and cultural diversity. Some popular topics in realistic fiction include sports, mysteries, animals, humour, and formula fiction (i.e., series books). There is again often an overlap of topics; for example, Roy MacGregor's Screech Owls books include elements of sports, mystery, adventure, and humour.

FAMILY

The family is an important subject in many realistic fiction novels. Indeed, most of the books mentioned in this chapter include one or more family-related issues. Betsy Byars, a popular author with upper elementary readers, has written numerous books addressing various family issues. One exceptional novel by Byars is *Cracker Jackson* (1985), in which eleven-year-old Cracker discovers that his former babysitter, Alma, is being physically abused by her husband. Cracker wants to help Alma, but Alma warns him to stay away to prevent the situation from escalating. Cracker chooses to become involved and discovers the pain and frustration that can occur in abusive family situations. Byars has also written several books about the Blossom family; each novel tells the story of the adventures and problems of at least one Blossom family member. (Several Blossom family books are included in the novel list at the end of the chapter.) *The Pinballs* (1977), *The Cartoonist* (1978), and *The Summer of the Swans* (1970), the 1971 Newbery Medal winner, are other books by Byars that focus on families.

The Grizzly (Johnson & Johnson, 1964) tells the story of David's fear of his father. David's father has taken David on a weekend camping expedition. David feels apprehensive about the weekend adventure and believes his father is constantly testing his capabilities. An attack by a grizzly bear tests all dimensions of David's strength, as he is forced to take charge. *The War with Grandpa* (Smith, 1984) also explores family tension. Peter loves his Grandpa, but because Grandpa is moving in with Peter's family, Peter must vacate his room. Unhappy about the situation, Peter—with some assistance from his friends—formulates some humorous plans to make Grandpa surrender the room. Grandpa retaliates with his own schemes, but Peter goes too far and one of his plans humiliates his grandfather. Through his experiences, Peter learns several lessons.

Three Canadian books that deal with family issues are *Jasmin* (Truss, 1982), *Exit Barney McGee* (Mackay, 1987), and *One Year Commencing* (Stinson, 1997). In *Jasmin*, Jasmin's parents seem unaware of the burden their twelve-year-old daughter shoulders in helping to raise a family of six children, or of the effects of those responsibilities. Jasmin, who is struggling with school, decides to run away from the possibility of repeating grade six and from the responsibilities of being the oldest in a large family. Spending time alone in the wilderness and meeting some new friends helps Jasmin in her search for independence and also brings assistance to her dysfunctional family. Barney, the main character in *Exit Barney McGee*, also runs away from home. Barney's mother has married Barney's grade six teacher, and they have had a baby. Barney's antagonism towards his stepfather and his dislike of the new family structure cause Barney to run away to find his birth father. Not only does Barney encounter dangers on his hitchhiking adventure to Toronto, but his hopes and expectations for his father are unfulfilled when he reaches his destination. *One Year Commencing* tells the story of the changes in twelve-year-old Al's life when a court order requires Al to leave her small Alberta community and spend a year living with her father in Toronto. Al experiences a wealth of emotions and faces many challenges as she adjusts to her new life.

PEERS

Peer relationships are a common component of realistic novels. Books dealing with peer relationships frequently address other issues associated with growing up as well (e.g., characters facing and overcoming fears, maturing, searching for identity).

Two Canadian novels in which characters learn to accept their peers as individuals are *Finders Keepers* (Spalding, 1995) and *The Onlyhouse* (Toten, 1995). *Finders Keepers* tells the story of two boys in Fort Macleod, Alberta. Danny, who has a learning disability, befriends Joshua, a Peigan native, after discovering an 8,000-year-old arrowhead. They share adventures uncovering the origin of the arrowhead, and together they deal with obstacles such as learning disabilities and racism. In *The Onlyhouse*, set in the 1960s, Lucija, a recent Croatian immigrant, moves to a new neighbourhood and tries to make friends. She discovers the joys of true friendship but also experiences the neediness of another peer, Jackie, and the problems of Jackie's mixed-up family.

Hey, Chicken Man (Brown, 1978), another Canadian novel, is a story about both positive and negative peer relationships. Tom's claustrophobia prevents him from successfully completing the initiation task to be a member of the Cobras. The Cobras taunt Tom and his new friend Andrew, who is extremely intelligent and knows a great deal about rocks and fossils. One day while hunting for fossils, Tom and Andrew are confronted by the Cobras, and Tom must face his fear in order to save his friend's life. In this novel, Tom experiences both the pain associated with being ostracized from a group of peers and the joys associated with true friendship.

Readers meet Bradley Chalkers in *There's a Boy in the Girls' Bathroom* (Sachar, 1987). He is the oldest student in grade five, is viewed as a behaviour problem by his teachers, tells incredible lies, picks fights with girls, has no friends, and has conversations with a collection of tiny animal figurines. Carla, the new school counsellor, assists Bradley in changing his attitude and behaviour. Bradley makes some friends and even receives his first invitation to a birthday party. Through some rather humorous, yet touching, events, Bradley learns how to interact successfully with his peers. When Carla is forced to leave the school, Bradley is angry because he believes he will regress to his previous self without her.

The Daring Game (Pearson, 1986), *Philip Hall Likes Me. I Reckon Maybe* (Greene, 1974), a 1975 Newbery Honor book, and *Maniac Magee* (Spinelli, 1990), the 1991 Newbery Medal winner, are three other novels that focus on peer relationships.

ADOLESCENT ISSUES

As mentioned previously, the content of many realistic fiction books generally focusses on more than one aspect of life. Issues such as self-discovery and independence, maturation, and facing and overcoming fears are often referred to as adolescent issues. Many of the books identified in this chapter include one or more issue associated with adolescence.

In *Different Dragons* (Little, 1986), Ben faces and learns to overcome many of his fears, including thunderstorms, dogs, new places, and new people. Ben's father decides that Ben should go somewhere without the rest of the family. Ben is nervous about being by himself and staying with his Aunt Rose. Aunt Rose surprises Ben with a golden Labrador retriever as a birthday present, but Ben is frightened of dogs and does not want to tell his aunt or his new friend. As the story progresses, Ben confronts his fears and learns that others, including dogs, have fears too.

Although more demanding in reading level and content than *Different Dragons*, *The Crossing* (Paulsen, 1987) also deals with adolescent issues. Manny is a fourteen-year-old Mexican orphan who faces many dangers living on the streets of Juarez, Mexico. He begs and steals to survive, and dreams of crossing the border to a better life. One night, Manny encounters Sergeant Locke, a Vietnam veteran who is drowning himself in alcohol to forget his war experiences. Manny and the Sergeant meet on several occasions, and on the night that Manny dares the crossing, the two characters meet for a final time.

When Paula and her mother move to Edmonton, in *My Name is Paula Popowich!* (Hughes, 1983), Paula becomes determined to uncover the mystery of her past and discover the truth about her father. Paula learns that her mother has lied to her about her father, and she decides to run away. She quickly realizes the danger of hitchhiking and returns home to continue her search. By discovering the truth about her father, Paula meets her grandmother and learns about her cultural heritage and herself.

Two other books that deal with adolescent issues are *Night of the Twisters* (Ruckman, 1984) and *Canyon Winter* (Morey, 1972). *Night of the Twisters* is based on an actual event, when a town in Nebraska was devastated by a series of tornadoes. Since the birth of Dan's baby brother, things have changed at the Hatch house and twelve-year-old Dan is not pleased with the changes. Dan is home alone with his best friend, Arthur, when a tornado strikes. With barely enough time to rescue the baby, Dan and Arthur take refuge in a basement shower and experience absolute terror as several tornadoes devastate the town. Dan then searches for his parents and assists others in the town. The natural disaster helps Dan to learn many lessons about the importance of family and helping others. *Canyon Winter* tells the story of Peter, who, after being stranded in the wilderness in a plane crash, meets Omar Pickett, a recluse who lives in the mountains. During their isolated winter, Peter learns about Omar's reasons for choosing a solitary life and develops an understanding of and an appreciation for living in the wilderness. Through his experiences and interactions with Omar, Peter experiences significant self-growth and maturation.

Marilyn Halvorson, an Alberta author, has written several engaging novels that simultaneously address adolescent issues and family and peer relationships. A few of Halvorson's books include *Cowboys Don't Cry* (1984), *Cowboys Don't Quit* (1994) (a sequel to the former), *Let It Go* (1985), *Nobody Said It Would Be Easy* (1987), *Dare* (1988), *Stranger on the Line* (1997), *But Cows Can't Fly (and Other Stories)* (1993), and *Bull Rider* (1989).

MARILYN HALVORSON

Marilyn Halvorson was born in Alberta and still lives on the farm she grew up on near Sundre, Alberta. As a child, Marilyn loved horses and the rodeo. She became a teacher and was teaching grade seven in Sundre when she wrote *Cowboys Don't Cry*, a book that won the 1983 Clarke Irwin/Alberta Culture Writing for Youth Competition award. Marilyn explains that she wrote the book about and for her students.

Marilyn believes that teaching, her rural life style, and her concern for the environment have influenced her writing. Many of the ideas for her books come from adventures and animals on her farm, from students she has taught, from local and regional events, and, of course, from her imagination. Marilyn says that stories are always developing in her mind, and when she writes, the first draft is always handwritten. In 1987, she won the R. Ross Annett Award for Children's Literature for *Nobody Said It Would Be Easy* (1987). Marilyn was also awarded the Canadian Children's Book Centre Our Choice award for *Stranger on the Run* (1992).

Death: One event in realistic fiction that often combines the subject matter of family, peers, and adolescent issues is the loss of a friend or family member. Such books can provide insight into how individuals cope with death and the grieving process. In *Bridge to Terabithia* (Paterson, 1977), the 1978 Newbery Medal winner, Jess must deal with the sudden death of his best friend, Leslie. Readers witness Jess' journey through the stages of death: denial, anger, bargaining, depression and guilt, and acceptance. In Jean Little's *Mama's Going to Buy You a Mockingbird* (1984), the 1985 Canadian Children's Book of the Year Award winner, the children's father dies of cancer and the surviving family members must cope with the loss. In *On My Honor* (Bauer, 1986), a 1987 Newbery Honor book, two boys lie about their afternoon plans and a dare results in the drowning of one of the characters. *Missing May* (Rylant, 1992), the 1993 Newbery Medal winner, *Tuck Everlasting* (Babbit, 1975), and *Walk Two Moons* (Creech, 1994), the 1995 Newbery Medal winner, are other books that deal with death in a realistic manner within the contexts of strong stories with believable characters and other important implicit themes.

SURVIVAL AND ADVENTURE

Survival and adventure are other popular issues addressed in realistic fiction. Indeed, many of the animal books mentioned later in this chapter include these elements. One popular dimension of survival is that of a character surviving adversity in the wilderness. In some books, the character chooses to venture into the wilderness and then must survive the often-harsh elements of nature. In *My Side of the Mountain* (George, 1959), a 1960 Newbery Honor book, and its sequel, *On the Far Side of the Mountain* (George, 1990), the characters elect to live off the land. In the first book, Sam Gribley runs away to live alone in the woods. Surviving off the land does not seem difficult for Sam as he has access to a town, trains a falcon, meets some people in the woods, and has generally prepared himself for this endeavour. Sam's family knows of his location, and in the end, they come to visit him. In the sequel, two years have passed since Sam first decided to live off the land. Now Alice, Sam's younger sister, also lives in the woods. Life becomes complicated for Sam when his falcon, Frightful, is confiscated by a conservation officer and Alice disappears. Sam must track Alice on the far side of the mountain and make a difficult decision about Frightful's future.

In other survival books, characters somehow become stranded in the wilderness. The element of adventure is a vital and inherent component of these stories. Although their planes crash in very different ecological environments—one on an island in the Pacific and one in the woods in northern Canada—the main characters in *Pilot Down, Presumed Dead* (Phleger, 1963) and *Hatchet* (Paulsen, 1987) must both be extremely resourceful in order to endure their isolated conditions. *The River* (Paulsen, 1991), another survival tale, is the sequel to Paulsen's 1988 Newbery Honor book, *Hatchet*. In *The River*, government officials wish to learn about Brian's knowledge of surviving in the wilderness by replicating his isolated circumstances. Although precautions are taken to guarantee the safety of all participants, an accident challenges Brian's endurance and resourcefulness once again. Interestingly, Paulsen has written another book called *Brian's Winter* (1996), imagining that Brian, the main character in *Hatchet*, is not rescued and is forced to endure a winter in the wilderness. Paulsen wrote *Brian's Winter* due to the incessant questioning by readers of *Hatchet* who wondered what would have happened if Brian had to remain in the wilderness for the winter. *Brian's Return* (1999) chronicles Brian's return to the northern wilderness where he was stranded two years earlier. The 54-day ordeal of surviving in the north has forever changed Brian, and he needs to revisit the solitude of the wilderness to discover where he belongs.

American author Gary Paulsen is a prolific writer of contemporary realistic fiction and is an extremely popular author with elementary and middle-grade students. Many of Paulsen's novels contain the elements of survival—physical, psychological, emotional, or social—and adventure, and he often uses the coming-of-age theme in his writing. Paulsen says he experienced little academic success in school and credits his interest in books to a librarian in a small town in northern Minnesota. One night while Paulsen was seeking warmth in the local library, the librarian offered him a library card. Paulsen's home life was miserable, so to be given something was a rare experience. He not only took the card but began making weekly treks to the library. From the age of fifteen, Paulsen worked at various jobs (including soldier, migrant worker, field engineer, truck driver, and magazine editor) to support himself. He draws on his varied background in his writing. Paulsen was awarded the 1997 Margaret A. Edwards Award for lifetime achievement in writing books for young adults. Several of Paulsen's books have already been mentioned in this chapter; others are noted in the list for upper elementary readers at the end of the chapter.

Paul and Heather enjoy reading together

PERSONS WITH DISABILITIES

Many selections of realistic fiction include characters with some type of disability. In *The Summer of the Swans* (Byars, 1970), fourteen-year-old Sara is experiencing a frustrating summer. She wants to escape from her bossy aunt, her beautiful older sister, her distant father, and most of all, from herself. Then there is Joe Melby, a boy that she thinks she dislikes. When Sara's brain-damaged brother, Charlie, becomes lost, she realizes the great love she feels for her brother.

Crazy Lady! (Conly, 1993), a 1994 Newbery Honor book, tells the story of twelve-year-old Vernon, whose mother is dead and whose father is trying to be two parents. Other characters include Maxine, a single-parent alcoholic who roams the streets, and her son, Ronald, who is cognitively impaired. Vernon and his father talk about Maxine and Ronald, about Vernon's mother, and about his older, brighter brother. Vernon learns much throughout the story, growing, maturing, and proving to be both a friend and a leader.

In *The Man Who Loved Clowns* (Wood, 1992), readers meet thirteen-year-old Delrita, who loves her Uncle Punky but sometimes feels ashamed of his behaviour because he has Down's Syndrome. The sudden death of Delrita's parents brings Delrita and Punky to live with Aunt Queenie. For 35 years, Punky has been sheltered from the public; now Aunt Queenie suggests Punky work at the Sheltered Workshop. Delrita must confront her own feelings, learn to let go, and let new friends in to both her own life and her uncle's life.

Tru Confessions (Tashjian, 1997) is about twelve-year-old Trudy and her developmentally delayed twin brother, Eddie, and *The Wild Kid* (Mazer, 1998) is about a boy who has Down's Syndrome. Three other

Canadian books about people with disabilities are *From Anna* (Little, 1972), a story about a girl with a visual impairment; *Mine for Keeps* (Little, 1962), a novel about a girl with cerebral palsy; and *A Friend Like Zilla* (Gilmore, 1995), a story about a friendship between two girls, one of whom is much older and has a developmental impairment. A website that identifies books written about or including characters with disabilities is listed in Appendix B.

CULTURAL DIVERSITY

The Watsons Go to Birmingham—1963 by Christopher Paul Curtis (1995) was the 1996 Coretta Scott King Award winner and a 1996 Newbery Honor book. Curtis writes about an African-American family living in Michigan in 1963. The parents decide to take their three children, thirteen-year-old Byron, ten-year-old Kenny, and five-year-old Joetta, on a summer trip to Birmingham, Alabama. The parents hope that the children's grandmother (Momma's mother) will have a positive influence on Byron's behaviour and attitude. The children have never been to the South before, and once in Birmingham, the family enjoys reunions with friends, makes new friends, has adventures, and experiences the racial unrest and church bombings endemic in the South in 1963. The Watsons return to Michigan much changed—and more aware of the problems of racial discrimination and the differences between the North and the South. This is not only a story of racial tensions but also a beautifully written tale of a family's growing up and growing together.

All It Takes Is Practice (Miles, 1976) and *Shabash!* (Walsh, 1994) are two other novels that focus on race. In *All It Takes Is Practice*, Stuart makes friends with Peter, a new boy in town. Unfortunately, some people in the town disagree with Peter's parents' interracial marriage. Stuart becomes involved in a racial incident and learns about race issues and true friendship. *Shabash!* tells the story of a Canadian Sikh boy, Rana, who is the first individual of an ethnic minority ever to play hockey in a small town in central British Columbia. Rana matures through his experiences and learns to deal with his own prejudices, as well as the prejudices of others.

Journey to Jo'burg (Naidoo, 1986), *The Gift* (Kertes, 1995), and *Skateway to Freedom* (Alma, 1993) are three other books about cultural diversity. In *Journey to Jo'Burg*, 13-year-old Naledi and her younger brother, Tiro, must travel 300 kilometres to Johannesburg, South Africa to bring their mother back to their village to tend to their ill baby sister. As a result of the journey to the city and the experiences and interactions with others in the city, Naledi understands the dangers, injustices, and conflicts in her country. She also realizes the sacrifices people are making as they struggle for freedom, equality, and self-respect. *The Gift*, written by Canadian author Joseph Kertes, is about community, cultural, and religious differences and the feeling of belonging. A young Jewish boy, Jacob, is intrigued with the delights of the Christmas season, pleasures in which he cannot partake. Through an unexpected discovery, Jacob comes to terms with his own heritage. In *Skateway to Freedom*, Canadian author Ann Alma tells the story of family members fleeing their country for Canada. In 1989, Josie and her family escape East Germany and, with the assistance of others, make their way to Calgary, Alberta. The family experiences difficulties and frustrations as they adjust to life in a new country.

Roll of Thunder, Hear My Cry (Taylor, 1976), the 1977 Newbery Medal award winner, and several of the other books listed in the historical fiction section, including *Journey Home* (Uchida, 1978), *Number the Stars* (Lowry, 1990), *The Upstairs Room* (Reiss, 1972), *Letters From Rifka* (Hesse, 1992), *Underground to Canada* (1977), and *Zlata's Diary: A Child's Life in Sarajevo* (Filipovic, 1994), depict stories of people from diverse cultures.

POPULAR TOPICS

Sports: Sports is a popular topic of realistic fiction. Matt Christopher is a prolific writer of sports

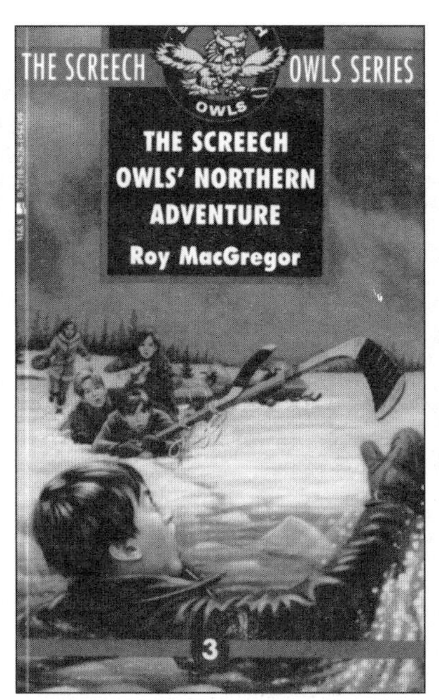

Mystery at Lake Placid, The Screech Owls' Northern Adventure, and *The Quebec Crisis,* all by Roy MacGregor

stories; his books generally follow a predictable plot pattern, with the story developing around some type of sport. *Dirt Bike Racer* (1979) is about twelve-year-old Ron who finds a dirt bike at the bottom of a lake while scuba diving. In order to help pay for the bike repairs, Ron works for an elderly man whose nephew also races dirt bikes. The nephew is jealous of Ron, and when Ron enters racing competitions, he experiences some unsporting conduct. *Dirt Bike Runaway* (1983), *Undercover Tailback* (1992), *Face Off* (1972), *Return of the Home Run Kid* (1992), *Ice Magic* (1973), and *Skateboard Tough* (1991) are a few of Christopher's many books.

Various sports, including gymnastics, basketball, figure skating, hockey, and competitive horse-jumping, are featured in the Sports Stories novels published by Canadian publishing company James Lorimer & Company. *The Perfect Gymnast* (Bossley, 1996), *Riding Scared* (Crook, 1996), *Fast Break* (Coldwell, 1995), *Roller Hockey Blues* (Barwin & Tick, 1997), and *Slam Dunk* (Bawin & Tick, 1998) are just some of the books in the Sports Stories collection.

Alfred Slote, Marion Renick, and Sigmund Brouwer are three other authors of sports stories who keep action levels high and provide explanations of games and their rules (which assist readers in understanding the contexts of the stories). In *Winter Hawk Star* (Brouwer, 1996), two stories occur concurrently, but neither story dominates the other. Riley, the star of the Portland Winter Hawks, a junior hockey team, has an ego problem; Tyler, another player on the team, is in danger of being released from the Hawks. When Riley and Tyler discover that a drug company is illegally testing drugs on children with ADD at the youth centre where they work, the hockey players get involved and try to stop the criminal activity. Then Tyler and Riley must not only worry about surviving on the ice, but off the ice as well. Another book by Brouwer, *Thunderbird Spirit* (1996), is about a seventeen-year-old hockey player named Mike who has a troubled background. Mike is traded to the Seattle Thunderbirds, where he makes friends with Dakota, a Native American player. When Dakota is being threatened, Mike gets involved and helps his friend. Mike learns how to control his temper both on and off the ice, and in the end, the truth becomes known about a theft for which Mike had accepted the blame. The hockey context provides a compelling background for the real story, and there is realistic character development in the novel as the characters deal with personal, emotional, and social issues.

ROY MACGREGOR

Roy MacGregor has been involved in hockey all his life. When his family moved from Whitney to Huntsville, Ontario, Roy had the opportunity to play minor hockey against a boy named Bobby Orr. Orr was a member of the Parry Sound hockey team, the bitter rivals of Huntsville. Roy also played lacrosse and baseball as a child.

As well as aspiring to play in the NHL, Roy considered being a mathematician and a bus driver. While working in a lumber mill with his dad, Roy began listening to pop music and because, as he says, he "couldn't sing," he began writing songs. Song lyrics sparked his interest in writing. Roy studied political science at university and subsequently travelled in Europe for a year. He then returned to university to study journalism, and as he says, "It has become my life."

Roy wrote two novels early in his career, but it was not until he co-authored *Home Game* with Ken Dryden in 1989 that his writing career began to flourish. Roy has written several well-respected adult books about hockey, including *The Home Team: Fathers, Sons & Hockey* (1995) and *The Seven A.M. Practice: Stories of Family Life* (1996). He has also written books about Native leaders and the Ottawa Valley.

Roy explains that Douglas Gibson, publisher at McClelland & Stewart, suggested he write books for young readers. Roy believed the books had to include more than hockey because "the stories would be too much the same," so he decided to include mystery and suspense elements as well. And thus the Screech Owls were born!

Roy now lives in Kanata, Ontario and writes for the *Ottawa Citizen* as well as working on his own books.

Canadian author Roy MacGregor writes the Screech Owls series, a collection of books about Travis Lindsay, his best friend Nish, and the rest of the Screech Owls coed peewee hockey team. In *Mystery at Lake Placid* (1995), the team travels to Lake Placid, New York to participate in an international peewee hockey tournament. There is much excitement on the team van during the trip, including the entertaining antics of the trainer, the prospect of playing on an Olympic rink, and the knowledge that hockey scouts will be in the crowd. However, once in Lake Placid, several incidents occur which lead the team to believe that someone is trying to sabotage the Screech Owls. Sarah, the star centre, seems to be the target of the undermining acts. The Screech Owls devise plans to discover who is trying to sabotage the team—one scheme requires claustrophobic Travis to spend a night in a dark, cramped locker. In the second book in the series, *The Night They Stole the Stanley Cup* (1995), the team is thrilled about participating in a huge hockey tournament in Toronto. However, several events—including Nish spraining his ankle, team members being caught shoplifting, and Travis overhearing two men plotting to steal the Stanley Cup—detract from the team's initial excitement about the tournament. The Screech Owls must save the priceless trophy *and* rise to the challenge of playing their best hockey ever. MacGregor's Screech Owls books combine elements of hockey, humour, and mystery. Some of the other titles in the series are included in the list of novels for upper elementary readers at the end of the chapter. Readers who wish to know more about MacGregor and the Screech Owls series can search the website at http://www.screechowls.com/.

Mysteries: Mysteries are often classified as a subgenre of contemporary realistic fiction. Children are intrigued by the problem-solving nature of mystery stories. They enjoy piecing the puzzle together, hypothesizing, and making inferences as they act as detectives in solving a mystery. Mysteries can range from simple, formulaic plot structures to more complex character stories. Suspense is a strong part of the appeal of mysteries.

Donald Sobol has written many books about child detective Encyclopedia Brown. The format of Sobol's books encourages readers to become actively involved in the sleuthing, as at the end of each case, Sobol asks readers how Encyclopedia solved the mystery. Readers can ponder the question and then find the solution for the case in the back of the book. Another series of mystery books about the T*A*C*K Team, consisting of four children, follows a similar pattern to Sobol's books: there are several cases in each book, and a solution follows each case. *T*A*C*K Into Danger* (Miller & Robinson, 1983) contains seven mysteries, including "The Great Blueberry Pie Robbery" and "The Comic Book Caper."

Betsy Byars has written a series of mystery books about a character named Herculeah Jones. *Death's Door* (1997), *Dead Letter* (1996), and *Tarot Says Beware* (1995) are three titles in the Herculeah Jones series. There are also mystery stories among Martin's *Baby-Sitters Club* books (e.g., *Kristy and the Mystery Train*, 1997). Canadian author Linda Bailey has written a mystery series about an eleven-year-old detective named Stevie Diamond. In the first book in the series, *How Come the Best Clues Are Always in the Garbage?* (1992), Stevie begins her detective career trying to solve a case that involves stolen money, an environmentally unfriendly restaurant, and mysterious phone calls. Some of the other books in the Stevie Diamond series are listed in the bibliography of books at the end of the chapter; a few other mystery series are listed in the beginning novels section. Many students continue to enjoy the Nancy Drew and the Hardy Boys series. When readers discover a series of books, they often want to read all of the books in the series as they become familiar with the characters and plot patterns.

There are several well-written mysteries for older readers. In *Is Anybody There?* (Bunting, 1988), thirteen-year-old Marcus is certain that someone is coming into their house. Marcus has evidence to support his belief: the key to the house that he hides in the oak tree is missing, food is disappearing, and other items are vanishing from the house. Marcus believes that Nick, the man who lives upstairs, is coming into the house, but Marcus needs proof to confirm his suspicions. In *Secrets in the Attic* (York, 1986), Jodie must unravel a mystery to prove her father's innocence. Jodie's father was killed in a car accident but rumours circulating in the town implicate him in the theft of some money. Jodie, her mother, and her brother move away from the town but return at Christmas. Some people continue to believe that Jodie's father is guilty, but through her explorations in her Aunt Winifred's attic, Jodie is able to expose the real thief. In *The Dragon Children* (Buchan, 1975) two mysteries occur concurrently. One involves the identity of Steven, a mysterious boy who appears and disappears suddenly. One day, while John is in the woods near his house, Steven appears and informs John about a crook in town who is swindling elderly people. Steven helps John to solve the second mystery in the book, namely, catching the criminal. At the end of the novel, readers learn the identities of both Steven and the criminal. In *Lucy Forever & Miss Rosetree, Shrinks* (Shreve, 1987), Lucy's father is a well-known child psychiatrist. Lucy is in grade six when she and her friend, Rosie, decide they will also be psychiatrists. Their pretend practice includes a number of interesting clients, but when they meet a young girl named Cinder, who does not speak and has a red scar across her neck, Lucy and Rosie become involved in a real-life case. In order to assist Cinder, the girls must unravel a mystery that involves child abuse.

Canadian author Eric Wilson has written many mystery stories. Wilson's appreciation for the vastness of Canadian geography and the variety in its culture derives from his childhood experiences living in different parts of Canada. Readers follow the escapades of Tom and Liz Austen through many parts of Canada in *The Kootenay Kidnapper* (Wilson, 1983), *Cold Midnight in Vieux Quebec* (1996), *The Inuk Mountie* (1995), and *Lost Treasure of Casa Loma* (1992)—just a few of Wilson's books.

Other well-written mysteries include *The Treasure of Alpheus Winterborn* (Bellairs, 1978), *Megan's Island* (Roberts, 1988), *The Mystery at Wolf River* (Shura, 1989), *Anywhere But Here* (Dueck, 1996), and *The Chinese Puzzle* (Brouillet, 1996).

Animals: Many realistic fiction books about animals include an adventure element. *Yuit* (1993), by Yvette Edmunds, tells the story of an Inuit girl and her adopted pet seal in the far north of Canada. Another Canadian book about animals is *Owls in the Family* (Mowat, 1961). In this book, readers discover how Billy acquires his two pet owls, Wol and Weeps, and follow the many adventures of Billy and his owl friends. In *Incident at Hawk's Hill* (Eckert, 1971), six-year-old Ben MacDonald communicates better with animals than with humans. One day, Ben wanders off from the farm and becomes lost. A female badger adopts him and teaches him how to survive like a badger. When Ben is found, both his family and the badger surrogate-mother must learn to accommodate each other. Ben is devastated when a violent act by George Burton, an evil trapper, threatens the life of the female badger. In *Return to Hawk's Hill* (Eckert, 1998), the sequel to *Incident at Hawk's Hill*, seven-year-old Ben runs away from George Burton and is whisked down the Red River in a rowboat. Ben is rescued by a Metis youth but is initially very frightened, as he has been taught to fear this group of Aboriginal people. Ben's parents embark on a desperate search for him and, along the way, encounter their own adventures.

Walt Morey's classic tale of *Gentle Ben* (1965) tells the story of Mark and his Alaskan brown bear friend, Ben. A special bond exists between Mark and Ben, and they have complete trust and faith in each other. However, some people do not believe that Ben should live in town and are determined to get rid of the bear. In his attempts to save Ben, Mark must face many challenges. Morey's *Gloomy Gus* (1976) is another story about a teenage boy and his love for a bear. Morey has also written *Runaway Stallion* (1973) and *Year of the Black Pony* (1976). Each book tells an exciting story about the relationship and adventures of a boy and a horse.

Many excellent books have been written about dogs. In the 1992 Newbery Medal-winning *Shiloh* (1991), Naylor shares the story of eleven-year-old Marty and his determination to save Shiloh, a young beagle, from an abusive owner. Naylor has written two other books about Shiloh: *Shiloh Season* (1996) and *Saving Shiloh* (1997). Theodore Taylor has written two books, *The Trouble with Tuck* (1981) and *Tuck Triumphant* (1991), about a disabled golden Labrador named Tuck. *Bringing Up Beauty* (McNicoll, 1994), winner of 1996 Ontario Silver Birch Award and of the 1997 Manitoba Young Readers' Choice Award, tells the story of Elizabeth, who is responsible for Beauty, a black Labrador that her family is raising for Canine Vision Canada. Jim Kjelgaard has written numerous books about dogs. *Big Red*, first published in 1945 and reprinted many times since, is a wilderness adventure about Danny and his loyal and courageous Irish Setter, Big Red. *Irish Red* (1951) and *Outlaw Red* (1953) each tell an adventurous story about one of Big Red's sons. Other books about dogs are included in the list of novels for upper elementary readers at the end of the chapter.

Humour: Humour is a common element in fiction, found in many of the books discussed in this chapter. Two Canadian authors who have written specifically humorous books are Gordon Korman and Martyn Godfrey.

Korman wrote *This Can't Be Happening at Macdonald Hall* (1978) when he was twelve years of age; he had published five other books by the time he graduated from high school. In Korman's first book, readers meet Bruno and Boots, two boys who attend a private school and who room together. We also meet the Fish (Mr. Sturgeon, headmaster of the school) and the girls from Miss Scrimmage's Finishing School. The Headmaster separates Bruno and Boots because they are constantly getting in trouble, but the boys are determined to be roommates again and devise several plans to accomplish their goal. Korman has written several other novels about the escapades of Bruno and Boots at Macdonald Hall. In *Go Jump in the Pool!* (1979), Bruno and Boots engage in some rather enterprising fund-raising efforts in order to finance a pool for Macdonald Hall. In *Beware the Fish!* (1980), Bruno and Boots, discovering that Macdonald Hall is in financial difficulties, believe that attracting attention to the school will help save it. In *The War With Mr. Wizzle* (1982), the Macdonald Hall boys and the girls from Miss Scrimmage's declare war on Mr. Wizzle, a teacher who is making the boys wear ties, assigning detentions, and computerizing the school. Three other books about Boots, Bruno, and Macdonald Hall are *The Zucchini Warriors* (1988), *Macdonald Hall Goes Hollywood* (1991), and *Something Fishy at Macdonald Hall* (1995). Korman has written many humorous books about characters other than Bruno and Boots; some of these selections are included in the list of novels for upper elementary readers at the end of the chapter.

Martyn Godfrey has written three books about Ms Teeny-Wonderful. In *Here She is, Ms Teeny-Wonderful* (1984), Carol's mother enters her in a beauty contest. Carol is "tomboyish" and resists her mother's encouragement until she learns of the contest's prize. Carol's unique talent is jumping over garbage cans on her BMX bike. She experiences some unsporting conduct from other competitors at the contest, but in the end, she is proud of her accomplishments. *It Isn't Easy Being Ms Teeny-Wonderful* (1987) and *Send in Ms Teeny-Wonderful* (1988) tell the further adventures of Carol and her friend Wally. Godfrey has written a fourth novel about Carol and Wally, *Wally Stutzgummer, Super Bad Dude* (1992), but this book focusses on Wally's adventures competing in a mountain-bike race and catching thieves. Godfrey's *It Seemed Like a Good Idea at the Time* (1987) is a highly amusing story about a twelve-year-old boy who, due to peer pressure, dresses up as a girl to discover what actually happens at a girls' party. Godfrey has also written *There's a Cow in My Swimming Pool* (1991), *Can You Teach Me to Pick My Nose?* (1990), *The Great Science Fair Disaster* (1992), and *Meet You in the Sewer* (1993), all enjoyed by upper elementary readers.

MARTYN GODFREY

Martyn Godfrey moved to Canada from England when he was eight; he currently resides in Alberta. He became a teacher and taught in Ontario and Alberta. His first book, *The Day the Sky Exploded* (1991, originally released as *The Vandarian Incident*, 1982), originated when he was attempting to inspire a student who was a reluctant reader and writer.

Martyn believes it is essential to grab the reader's attention in the first few sentences and claims that the last thing he writes in a novel is the first paragraph. He has written many books, in various genres, and several of his books have won awards. In 1985, Martyn won the Vicky Metcalf Short Story Award for *"Here She Is, Ms Teeny Wonderful!"* published in Crackers Magazine; in 1987, he won the University of Lethbridge Children's Book Award for the full-length book of *Here She Is, Ms Teeny Wonderful.* In 1989, *Mystery in the Frozen Lands* won the Geoffrey Bilson Award for Historical Fiction for Young People; and in 1993, *Can You Teach Me to Pick My Nose?* won the Manitoba Young Readers' Choice Award.

Series Stories: Several series books have already been mentioned (i.e., Nancy Drew, Hardy Boys, Encyclopedia Brown, Stevie Brown). *The Baby-Sitters Club* (Martin) and *Goosebumps* (Stine) books are two series popular with elementary readers. Series books may also be called formula fiction and appear as mysteries, sports stories, fantasies, adventures, and romances. In addition to those discussed here, some other series books are identified in the beginning novel section.

Jon Scieszka has written the *Time Warp Trio* series about three boys, Joe, Sam, and Fred. The books are illustrated and range in length from 55 to 75 pages. Via "The Book," a gift Joe received from his magician uncle, Joe, Sam, and Fred travel to various periods in history. The boys have many adventures involving a variety of other characters including knights, dragons, giants, cowboys, Native Americans, pirates, cavepeople, and humans in the future. Some of the books in this series include *Knights of the Kitchen Table* (1991), *The Not-So-Jolly Roger* (1991), *The Good, the Bad, and the Goofy* (1992), *Your Mother Was a Neanderthal* (1993), *2095* (1995), and *Tut Tut* (1996).

Gary Paulsen is author of the Culpepper Adventures series about Dunc Culpepper and his best friend Amos. In *The Case of the Dirty Bird* (1992), Dunc and Amos are mildly interested in the pet store's scruffy, elderly parrot who can speak four languages and has outlived ten of its owners. When the bird begins to talk about buried treasure, Dunc and Amos become intrigued. The boys engage in some amateur sleuthing in order to find the buried riches. In *Dunc Breaks the Record* (1993), Amos and Dunc try hang-gliding but they crash in the wilderness. Fortunately, in a stroke of comic intertextuality, Amos has read *Hatchet* (Paulsen, 1987), a novel about how a boy survived for 54 days in the wilderness. The problem is, Amos and Dunc do not have a hatchet! To compound the situation, they are captured by a wild man and held captive. Paulsen has written other books about Amos and Dunc including *Dunc and Amos Hit the Big Top* (1993), *Amos Gets Married* (1995), *Dunc and Amos Go to the Dogs* (1996), and *Dunc and Amos on Thin Ice* (1997).

Historical Fiction

Several books address issues associated with culture and race from a historical perspective; they are classified as historical fiction. Some books deal with recent historical periods, events, and people, while others address distant times. When reading historical fiction, students often need some knowledge of the period in which the story is set; in some cases, this knowledge is essential. Historical fiction can create a context for and a deeper understanding of many social studies topics.

British author Rosemary Sutcliff wrote many excellent volumes of historical fiction for children as well as adults. Her books are superbly crafted, well researched, and extremely well written but even teachers can have some difficulty reading her work. *Warrior Scarlet* (1958), for example, is set in the Bronze Age in Great Britain, a period for which there is no written record and which is not connected to the real lives of most Canadians— children or adults. It takes a good reader to savour her descriptive passages, but once into the story, the reader is hooked. The book addresses issues that are as relevant today as they likely were hundreds of years ago, such as living with a physical handicap, being accepted, and being a member of a minority group.

War forms an essential part of many well-researched and well-written historical fiction books. The 1998 Governor's General Award winner, *The Hollow Tree* (1997) by Janet Lunn, is set during the American Revolution in the Thirteen Colonies. Phoebe, the main character, experiences the horrors of war as she embarks on a mission and encounters both Loyalists escaping to British Canada and Rebel soldiers fighting for freedom from Britain. *Journey Home* (Uchida, 1978) is a story about the imprisonment of Japanese-American citizens during World War Two. Other books that involve the clashing of cultures during wars include *Number the Stars* (Lowry, 1990), *The Upstairs Room* (Reiss, 1972), *Letters From Rifka* (Hesse, 1992), *Zlata's Diary: A Child's Life in Sarajevo* (Filipovic, 1994), and *A Place Not Home* (Wiseman, 1996).

Much well-crafted historical fiction focusses on cultural and racial issues. *The Slave Dancer* (Fox, 1973) is told from the point of view of a boy who witnesses the cruel capture and inhumane treatment of some Africans who are being transported to America to be sold as slaves. The books *Sing Down the Moon* (O'Dell, 1970) and *Thunder Rolling in the*

Mountains (O'Dell & Hall, 1992) are told from the point of view of Native American people. Each novel tells a story (based on fact) of the horrendous injustices experienced by Native Americans when they were forced onto reservations. *Sign of the Beaver* (Speare, 1983), a 1984 Newbery Honor book set in 1769, tells the story of twelve-year-old Matt. Matt stays on his own while his father returns to Massachusetts to bring the rest of the family to the homestead. He meets Attean, a Native American boy, and the two become friends and learn about each other's culture.

KIT PEARSON

Before becoming a full-time writer, Kit Pearson was a children's librarian. She was born in Edmonton, Alberta in 1947 and wanted to be a writer after reading *Emily of New Moon* by L.M. Montgomery as a child. She later studied at Simmons College, Boston, and received a Master of Arts in children's literature. Kit's first book, *The Daring Game* (1986), was largely based on her own experiences of moving away from home and attending a boarding school. But it was her second book, *A Handful of Time* (1987), which won the Canadian Library Association Book of the Year Award for Children, that put Kit on centre stage. Since then she has written a number of books, including *The Sky is Falling* (1989), which won the CLA Book of the Year Award for Children and the Geoffrey Bilson Award for Historical Fiction for Young People, and *Awake and Dreaming* (1996), which won the 1997 Governor General's Award.

Kit acknowledges that working on historical fiction requires a great deal of research—about a year's worth for *The Sky is Falling*. For that book, she began by talking with people who had known children evacuated to Canada during World War Two, then went to England to acquire further information. She deliberately did not talk with people who had been "war guests" because she had the character of Noah developing in her mind and did not want to write someone else's story. Kit finds the research a fascinating part of writing and invariably wants to read one more book before sitting down to write.

Kit has always been an avid reader and remembers as a child tearing off the corners of pages and chewing them as she read!

Some well-written pieces of Canadian historical fiction include *Underground to Canada* (Smucker, 1977), *Ticket to Curlew* (Lottridge, 1992), *Wings to Fly* (Lottridge, 1997), sequel to the former, *The Sky Is Falling* (Pearson, 1989), and *Prairie Fire!* (Freeman, 1998). Other selections of historical fiction are included in the list of books for upper elementary students at the end of the chapter.

Fantasy

According to Tomlinson and Lynch-Brown (1996), modern fantasy "refers to the body of literature in which the events, the settings, or the characters are outside the realm of possibility" (p.121). The authors note a lack of distinction between the types of modern fantasy, and indeed there is much overlap between the types of modern fantasy identified by Tomlinson and Lynch-Brown: modern folk tales, animal fantasy, personified toys and objects, unusual characters and strange situations, supernatural events and mystery fantasy, historical fantasy (i.e., time-slip fantasy), quest stories, and science fiction and science fantasy (pp.127-131).

Some popular authors of fantasy include Lloyd Alexander, Lynne Reid Banks, Susan Cooper, Roald Dahl, Monica Hughes, Brian Jacques, Ursula Le Guin, Madeleine L'Engle, C.S. Lewis, J.R.R. Tolkein, and E.B. White. Some of their stories have their roots in ancient myths and legends, particularly in the *Tales from the Mabinogian* (Thomas & Crossley-Holland, 1985), a collection of Welsh myths. Both Susan Cooper and Alan Garner (*The Owl Service*, 1967) refer to the Mabinogian in their writing, and it is useful if readers have at least a nodding acquaintance with this material when reading these authors' books.

ANIMAL FANTASY

E.B. White has written three classic animal fantasies. *Charlotte's Web* (1952) is about the friendship between a pig named Wilbur and a spider named

Charlotte. The plot revolves around Charlotte's efforts to save her friend from becoming pork chops. *Stuart Little* (1945) tells the story of Stuart, a mouse who sets out on an adventure to find his dearest friend. *The Trumpet of the Swan* (1970) is about Louis, a trumpeter swan born without a voice, who is befriended by a boy named Sam Beaver. With Sam's assistance, Louis learns to communicate in a number of ways.

James Howe has written several books about the Monroe family and their pets. Each book includes elements of humour, adventure, and mystery. In *Bunnicula* (Howe & Howe, 1979), Harold the dog tells the story of Bunnicula, a bunny found by the Monroes at a Dracula movie. Chester, a paranoid but well-read cat, believes the bunny is a vampire rabbit and devises several humorous schemes to alert the family and banish the bunny. In *Howliday Inn* (1982), the Monroe family goes on vacation, leaving Harold and Chester at the foreboding Chateau Bow-Bow. Harold tells the story of the mysterious guests and unusual occurrences at Chateau Bow-Bow. Harold narrates further adventures of the Monroe family and their pets in *The Celery Stalks at Midnight* (1983), *Nighty-Nightmare* (1987), and *Return to Howliday Inn* (1992).

Silverwing (Oppel, 1997), winner of both the 1998 Ontario Silver Birch Award and the 1998 Canadian Library Association Book of the Year for Children Award, tells the story of Shade, a young silverwing bat who embarks on a physical and moral quest to rejoin his colony in their winter migration. Shade encounters both friends and foes along his adventure-filled journey. Beverly Cleary has written several books about a mouse named Ralph including *The Mouse and the Motorcycle* (1965), *Runaway Ralph* (1970), and *Ralph S. Mouse* (1982). *I, Houdini* (Banks, 1978) is a book written from the point of view of a hamster who is a great escape artist. *Poppy* (Avi, 1995) is the story of a courageous deer mouse who searches for a new home for her family away from Mr. Ocax, a great horned owl. *Redwall* (Jacques, 1987), one book in the *Redwall* series, is a fantasy about animals with the universal theme of good versus evil. All of the characters in *Redwall* are animals (foxes, weasels, stoats, ferrets, badgers, otters, mice, and moles), and Jacques (1995) has written about how he used the characters of humans he has met for the animal characters in *Redwall*.

PERSONIFIED TOYS AND OBJECTS

Lynne Reid Banks has written a series of books about a character named Omri and his adventures with a magical cupboard that is capable of transforming miniature toy figures into living people. In the first book, *The Indian in the Cupboard* (1980), Omri receives a cupboard as a birthday present and finds a key in his mother's box of keys that fits the keyhole. When Omri puts a plastic toy Indian figure in the cupboard and turns the key, the figure comes to life. Omri must make many decisions that concern the welfare of Little Bear, the Native American; when Omri's friend uses the cupboard to transform a cowboy figure named Boone, the situation becomes further complicated. In the second book, *Return of the Indian* (1986), a year has passed since Omri returned Little Bear to his own time. Omri misses Little Bull (Banks changes the name of Little Bear) and decides to bring him back to the present. However, when Omri opens the cupboard door, Little Bull is injured and Omri must get help for his friend, which means transforming more plastic figures. Little Bull is involved in battles in his own time, and Omri must make some decisions that affect the life and death of people in the past. He travels back to Little Bull's time and experiences a dangerous battle. On his return to the present, Omri has another battle to fight as his parents' house is being burglarized by Skinheads. *The Secret of the Indian* (1989), *The Mystery of the Cupboard* (1993), and *The Key to the Indian* (1998) chronicle the further adventures of Omri and the magic cupboard.

Other books about personified toys include *The Velveteen Rabbit* (Williams, 1922), *Winnie the Pooh* (1926) and other books by A.A. Milne, *The Castle in the Attic* (Winthrop, 1985), *The Battle for the Castle* (Winthrop, 1993), and *Castle Tourmandyne* (Hughes, 1995).

UNUSUAL CHARACTERS AND STRANGE SITUATIONS

In some books included in the category unusual characters and strange situations, the "authors approach fantasy through reality, but take it beyond reality to the ridiculous or exaggerated" (Tomlinson & Lynch-Brown, 1996, p.128). Roald Dahl wrote many books that included both peculiar (at times outlandish) characters and strange situations. *James and the Giant Peach* (1961) is a story about a boy named James who lives with two cruel and greedy aunts. James is given some magical green crystals by a strange little man, but in his hurry, James drops the crystals and they sink into the ground near an old peach tree. A peach as large as a house grows on the tree, and when James crawls inside the peach, he meets a group of large and friendly insects. The peach becomes too heavy for its stem and rolls down away, flattening both aunts. And that is only the beginning of James' marvellous adventures with the peach! In *Charlie and the Chocolate Factory* (1964), Charlie is one of five lucky children to find a golden ticket in a chocolate bar; this good fortune allows him to take a tour through Mr. Wonka's incredible Chocolate Factory. Charlie and his Grandpa are mesmerized by the extraordinary and amazing things in the factory and disgusted by the behaviour of the other four children on the tour. Mr. Wonka is secretly searching for a new owner for his factory, and Charlie's honesty and sincerity are rewarded at the end of the tour. In *Charlie and the Great Glass Elevator* (1972), Charlie has further adventures with Mr. Wonka, including a journey into outer space. In *The BFG* (1982), a young girl named Sophie is snatched from her bed in the middle of the night by a giant. The BFG takes her to his land, where Sophie learns about his occupation and his disgusting giant neighbours. *Matilda* (1988) tells the story of Matilda, an amazing and brilliant child who must endure her insensitive parents and an abominable headmistress who terrorizes the entire school. When Matilda discovers her extraordinary power, she causes problems for the loathsome adults in her life.

Tuck Everlasting (Babbitt, 1975) and *The Wish Giver* (Brittain, 1983) both involve magic. In *Tuck Everlasting*, Winnie discovers that the Tuck family has drunk from a spring that has given them eternal life. An enterprising man overhears the Tuck family explain their situation to Winnie and attempts to capitalize on the fountain of youth. However, Winnie and the Tucks intervene, and the situation becomes complicated. In the beginning of *The Wish Giver*, a mystery fantasy, four individuals at a local church social visit Mr. Blinn, a wish giver. Each individual purchases a card with a red dot; to make a wish, they simply need to press a thumb on the red dot. Mr. Blinn warns the people to be cautious about their wishes as they may get what they wish for. And indeed three wishes are granted—but not in the way the people expected.

Harry Potter and the Philosopher's Stone (Rowling, 1997) is another novel that involves magic. In the first novel about Harry Potter, readers quickly learn that he is no ordinary boy. Harry lives with Mr. and Mrs. Dursley, his abusive uncle and aunt, and their spoiled and unpleasant son, Dudley. Many years ago, Harry was forbidden by the Dursleys to ask questions about his parents: according to his relatives, they were killed in a car accident. Harry's life changes dramatically when he is informed that he is to attend Hogwarts School of Witchcraft and Wizardry because he, Harry Potter, is a wizard! Harry discovers the truth about his identity and learns that he is a celebrity in the witch and wizard community because the evil wizard who killed his parents was unable to destroy Harry. At Hogwarts, Harry makes friends and foes; takes classes on Potions,

Transfigurations, Charms, the History of Magic, and Defence Against the Dark Arts; and learns to play Quidditch. Harry and his friends Ron and Hermione become involved in solving a mystery at Hogwarts, and Harry must ultimately face the evil wizard who tried to destroy him. *Harry Potter and the Chamber of Secrets* (Rowling, 1998) records Harry's adventures during his second year at Hogwarts School of Witchcraft and Wizardry, and *Harry Potter and the Prisoner of Azkaban* (Rowling, 1999) continues the story in Harry's third year.

The Secret World of Og (Berton, 1961) is a wonderful tale about five children who descend into an underground world where they meet the Og people. Ogs are small green people who speak a different language and come up to the world above to catch rabbits and collect human artifacts left lying about. In their attempts to rescue their youngest sibling, the children learn much about the Ogs' culture. Other books that fit the category of unusual characters and strange situations are included in the list of novels for upper elementary readers at the end of the chapter.

Certain individuals or groups have objected to specific books that fit into the supernatural and mystery fantasy category because the selections deal with ghosts and the supernatural (see Chapter 1). John Bellairs is well known for writing fantasy mysteries that include some supernatural elements. He has written several books, including *The Dark Secret of Weatherend* (1984), *The Chessmen of Doom* (1989), *The Secret of the Underground Room* (1990), *House with a Clock in Its Walls* (1992), *The Doom of the Haunted Opera* (1995), and *The Hand of the Necromancer* (1996). *Shivers* (Ioannov & Missen, 1995) is an edited collection of new and old ghost stories including works by authors L.M. Montgomery, Timothy Findley, and Robertson Davies. Janet Lunn has compiled an anthology of 21 ghost stories and poems written by Canadians in *The Unseen* (1994). Three additional Canadian publications—*Strange and Eerie Stories* (Hancock, 1995), *Ghosts and Other Scary Stories* (Gould & Hancock, 1993), and *What If...? Amazing Stories* (Hughes, 1998)—are collections of stories that deal with supernatural elements.

It is imperative for teachers to *read* the books they use in their programs to determine the appropriateness of the content. Although the following suggestions are always important to keep in mind when choosing, recommending, and using literature, they are especially significant when selecting books that deal with supernatural events: know the community and its standards, select materials of good literary quality, weigh the positive features of the work against possible objections, and be prepared to articulate a rationale for using a book should it be challenged.

TIME-SLIP FANTASY

Time-slip fantasy is sometimes referred to as historical, time-warp, or time-travel fantasy. This subgenre of fantasy has its roots in *Tom's Midnight Garden* (Pearce, 1958), a book about a boy who is sent to live in the country for the summer because his brother is ill and needs much rest. While staying with his aunt and uncle, Tom wakes one night and wanders into the garden where he meets a young woman, Hattie. The changes in the garden make Tom realize that he has travelled to the past. Tom and Hattie have many encounters, but eventually Tom meets Hattie in the present time; she is an elderly lady living upstairs in his aunt's and uncle's house. Their bond of friendship is strong, and Tom and Hattie are grateful for their last meeting—an opportunity to say farewell and thank-you.

Time-slip fantasy usually, but not always, begins in the present; through some type of artifact from the past, the protagonist is transported into a different time, usually a specific period in time. By travelling through time, characters generally learn something about themselves or others that assists them in understanding their current circumstances. For example, in *Tom's Midnight Garden*, the time slip is facilitated by an old grandfather clock which strikes an "odd" midnight (the number thirteen). Through his adventures with Hattie, Tom learns more about friendship, sharing, and his own family.

Time-slip fantasy is a powerful vehicle for exploring history and has become an intriguing alternative to pure historical fiction. A well-known Australian time-slip fantasy, *Playing Beatie Bow* (1980) by Ruth Parks, won the 1982 Boston Globe-Horn Book Award for Fiction. This book slips between modern time in Sydney, Australia and the time when The Rocks, the original settlement, was being settled in the 1800s. Readers can develop an appreciation of the living conditions and culture of that period in Australian history.

The Olden Days Coat, written by Margaret Laurence (1979) and illustrated by Muriel Wood, is a picture story book which fits into this category of fantasy. While exploring the shed behind her grandmother's house, Sal discovers photograph albums and an "olden days" coat in a trunk. When Sal dons the coat, she is magically transported into the past where she meets a girl, Sarah, who is Sal's grandmother in present time.

Cora Taylor's *The Doll* (1987) is a time-slip fantasy about Meg's travels to pioneer-era Saskatchewan. Meg, who is ill with rheumatic fever, is staying with her grandmother. When she stares into the eyes of an old-fashioned doll that her grandmother has given to her, Meg becomes Morag. Morag and her family are travelling west across the Canadian prairies in a covered wagon. A tragedy occurs as the pioneer family approaches Fort Carlton, and Meg must cease her time-travelling and choose between being Meg or Morag, a complicated choice because in the past, Morag is part of a close, loving family, while Meg's contemporary nuclear family is in turmoil. There are many intertextual connections between Taylor's *The Doll* and Silverthorne's *The Secret of Sentinel Rock* (1996), another Canadian time-slip fantasy. In Silverthorne's book, Emily, a girl who lives on a prairie farm, is magically transported to 1899, where she meets Emma. Through her time-slip experiences, Emily learns about her family, her heritage, and life and death on the Canadian prairies during pioneer times.

Five other Canadian time-slip fantasies are *Dark of the Moon* (Haworth-Attard, 1995), *Three Against Time* (Taylor, 1997), *Who is Frances Rain?* (Buffie, 1987), *A Handful of Time* (Pearson, 1987), and *Where Have You Been, Billy Boy?* (Hughes, 1995). In *Dark of the Moon*, fourteen-year-old Meaghan's mother remarries, and the family moves from Toronto to the country. An elderly neighbour, Miss Sarah, experiences some discrimination because of her interracial background. Miss Sarah talks to Meaghan about hatred and freedom and shows her a tin money-box that her great-grandmother brought with her from South Carolina when she escaped slavery. When Meaghan opens the box, she is transported back in time to a plantation in South Carolina where she is "seen" as a slave. Meaghan is befriended by a slave named Joshua and learns of his plans to escape to Canada via the Underground Railway. Meaghan returns to the present but is haunted by her experiences. She and her fourteen-year-old stepsister, Laura, return to the past to assist Joshua and his family. Miss Sarah's life is connected to the escape of Joshua's family, and Meaghan and Laura must return to the past on a second occasion to assist both the slave family and Miss Sarah.

Three Against Time takes place in British Columbia. While on vacation in the Cariboo Mountains near Quesnel, three brothers, Mike, Rob, and Grant Smith, ages twelve, eleven, and nine, respectively, stumble across the remains of a prospector's cabin. Once the boys enter the cabin, however, they discover that they have been transported back in time to 1868. The boys meet George Howard, the owner of the cabin, and tell him their story. Initially skeptical, George soon discovers that the boys are telling the truth. The boys assist George with his prospecting and accompany him to Barkerville to stake his claim. The boys experience several adventures, including interactions with a violent claim-jumper and a dramatic escape from the Great

Barkerville fire. Upon their return to the present, the boys use their knowledge of the past to rescue a young girl. They discover that George Howard has taken action to ensure that their parents believe their time-slip adventure story and to show his appreciation for their assistance with the prospecting.

In *Who is Frances Rain?*, fifteen-year-old Lizzie and her family travel to Fish Narrows, north of Lake Winnipeg, for a summer vacation. Lizzie's mother has recently remarried and family relationships are strained. Once at her grandmother's, Lizzie explores Rain Island, a small island located a short canoe ride from Lizzie's grandmother's camp. Lizzie decides to excavate the site of an old cabin on Rain Island and, among other artifacts, she discovers a pair of wire-rimmed spectacles. When she puts the spectacles on, Lizzie is transported 60 years into the past. By time-travelling on several occasions, Lizzie is able to discover information that brings closure to many years of uncertainty for her grandmother.

In *A Handful of Time*, the 1988 Canadian Children's Book of the Year winner, twelve-year-old Patty spends the summer at her cousin's cottage. Patty feels lonely because her parents are separated, her mother has little time for her, and her cousins at the lake are unfriendly. One day, Patty finds an old watch hidden under a floorboard in a guest cabin. The watch transports Patty into the past where she observes her mother, Ruth, as a twelve-year-old girl. Through several time slips to the past, Patty discovers that Ruth was treated unfairly and unkindly by her parents; this knowledge assists Patty in understanding her mother as an adult. Patty and her mother reconcile, and in the end, Patty shows Ruth the watch that she, Ruth, hid 35 years ago.

Where Have You Been, Billy Boy? tells the story of a character moving forward, rather than backward, in time. Billy rides a carousel in 1908 and travels to Colorado in 1993, where he meets Susan. Susan lies to her family about Billy's identity, but her brother, Jim, becomes suspicious and discovers the truth about the time-traveller. Billy is desperate to return to the past but the carousel needs repairing. They work to fix the carousel but other factors prevent Billy's immediate return to 1908. The book has a unique ending: the past and present connect when Billy's great-granddaughter delivers information about the carousel to Susan in 1993.

Canadian author Jan Lister has written the Time-Tripper series (published by Menagerie Publishing), a collection of books about the adventures of two boys who travel back in time through a time machine invented by a mysterious neighbour. Two other humorous books about time-travelling with time machines are *Max and Me and the Time Machine* (Greer & Ruddick, 1983) and *The Bunjee Venture* (McMurty, 1977). One of the characters in *Max and Me and the Time Machine* purchases a time

CORA TAYLOR

Cora Taylor grew up an only child on a farm in the Fort Carlton area of Saskatchewan. She was born in 1936 in Fort Qu'Appelle and moved to Alberta in 1955. Cora went to business college in Saskatoon and worked as a secretary while raising a family. She earned a Bachelor of Arts in English, followed by a one-year teacher education program which led to a teaching position in a combined grades three/four classroom. During her Bachelor of Arts program she took courses from Rudy Wiebe, who encouraged her to begin a Master of Arts in English. It was in this program in 1976 that *Julie* was written. The novel began as a Master's thesis, but grew to become an independent novel, finally published in 1985. *Julie* won the Canada Council Children's Literature Prize in 1985, the CLA Book of the Year Award for Children in 1986, and the Austrian Youth Book Prize in 1991. Cora received the CLA Book of the Year Award for Children a second time with *Summer of the Mad Monk* (1994). *The Doll* (1987), a book based largely on her own family history, won the Ruth Schwartz Children's Book Award in 1988. Cora has served as President of the Canadian Authors' Association and has had many plays, articles, and short stories read on CBC radio and published in *Canadian Living*, *Chatelaine*, and other magazines.

machine at a garage sale, and it transports him and his friend from the twentieth century to medieval England. The characters have many adventures and learn a great deal about medieval life. In *The Bunjee Venture,* characters travel back to a prehistoric world. The Bunjee, a hairy creature with a trunk that can be transformed into a balloon and feet like suction cups, assists the children in escaping danger and finding their father in the mysterious land. Other excellent time-slip fantasy novels are included in the list of novels for upper elementary readers at the end of the chapter.

QUEST STORIES

Quest stories are sometimes called high fantasy. They are "adventure stories with a search motif. The quest may be pursuit for a lofty purpose, such as justice or love, or for a rich reward, such as a magical power or hidden treasure" (Tomlinson & Lynch-Brown, 1996, p.130). The conflict in most of these stories is between good and evil. The characters are sometimes drawn from myth and legend, and the quest often represents a journey of personal growth and self-discovery for the protagonist. Several books already described in this chapter include elements of high fantasy.

Lloyd Alexander has written several quest stories including *The Book of Three* (1964), the first of his five quest Prydain Chronicles. Susan Cooper has also written a five-book quest series. The first book in her Arthurian quest series is *Over Sea, Under Stone* (1965), but the most popular book in the series is *The Dark Is Rising* (1973). Ursula Le Guin has written a series of quest books as well, the first being *A Wizard of Earthsea* (1968). C.S. Lewis wrote the Narnia Chronicles, another quest series, of which *The Lion, the Witch and the Wardrobe* (1950) is the best known. This book describes the adventures of four children who enter the world of Narnia through a magical wardrobe. In Narnia, the children assist the lion king, Aslan, in regaining his kingdom by defeating the evil White Witch.

SCIENCE FICTION AND SCIENCE FANTASY

"Science fiction is a form of imaginative literature that provides a picture of something that could happen based on real scientific facts and principles... story elements in science fiction must have the appearance of scientific plausibility or technical possibility" (Tomlinson & Lynch-Brown, 1996, pp.130-131). Popular topics in science fiction include visitors from outer space, space travel and technologies, mind control, future political and social systems, and genetic engineering. Some individuals refer to science fiction as futuristic fiction.

Tomlinson and Lynch-Brown (1996) note that the distinction between science fiction and science fantasy lacks clarity and acceptance. They describe science fantasy as a type of science fiction and state that science fantasy "presents a world that often mixes elements of mythology and traditional fantasy with scientific or technological concepts, resulting in a setting that has some scientific basis but never has existed or never could exist" (p.131).

Mrs. Frisby and the Rats of NIMH (O'Brien, 1971), the 1972 Newbery Medal winner, tells the story of a group of rats whose former laboratory imprisonment has increased their intelligence and longevity. The rats provide assistance to Mrs. Frisby, a widowed mouse, and her family. The rats get involved in a quest for a better life for themselves and work together to overpower larger adversaries. Jane Conly has written two sequels to O'Brien's original story: *Rasco and the Rats of NIMH* (1986) and *R.T., Margaret, and the Rats of NIMH* (1990).

Madeleine L'Engle and Monica Hughes have both written several science fiction novels. *A Wrinkle in Time* (L'Engle, 1962), winner of the 1963 Newbery Medal, is a story about how three children, Meg, Calvin, and Charles, with the assistance of three very unusual women, travel to another dimension to confront an evil force in order to save their father and themselves. *A Wind in the Door* (1973) and *A Swiftly*

Tilting Planet (1978) recount the further adventures of the three children. Many of the themes of the books by Canadian author Monica Hughes centre on the role of free will. Three of her books are *The Keeper of the Isis Light* (1980), *The Crystal Drop* (1992), and *The Golden Aquarians* (1994). Hughes' novel *The Story Box* (1998) is about a future community, Ariban, that has deliberately isolated itself. The island community members live highly regimented and controlled lives, and dreaming is regarded as an intolerable sin. Dreams are seen as lies, expressions of the imagination that present alternatives to the truth defined by the Ariban community; dreaming is punishable by banishment or death. After a storm, fifteen-year-old Colin discovers a young woman washed up on a beach clutching a locked chest. He takes her home, although foreigners are forbidden to contaminate the community. When it is discovered that the young woman, Jennifer, is a storyteller and that the chest contains books, the community becomes even more suspicious about her presence.

MONICA HUGHES

Monica Hughes was born in Liverpool, England in 1925 but almost immediately moved to Egypt, where her father had accepted a position as a professor of mathematics at the University of Cairo. Monica remained in Cairo until she was of school age. At that time, her father's work took him to London and then on to Edinburgh, where the family made their permanent home. Monica studied design and became a dress designer in London, but comments that "after the war England was cold, grey and sad" and she needed to live where there was sunshine. As a result, she moved to Rhodesia for two years, returning to England only because of the Korean conflict and the perceived threat of another world war. Monica later moved to Canada, still in pursuit of sunshine, and lived in Ottawa for a number of years, working as a lab technician for the National Research Council. After her marriage, she eventually settled in Edmonton, Alberta. She notes that, through all her travels, she "absorbed a lot of atmosphere but not much fact," which as a writer she deeply regrets.

Monica first began writing when she was living in London, England, but although she submitted articles and short stories for publication, she had no success. In Canada, she began to write adult novels. Still not meeting with success, she read literary criticism and contemporary works of literature written for children. Until that time, she had read, and shared with her own children, only the classic adventure novels of the eighteenth and nineteenth centuries. To that point, she had not considered that contemporary writers might write seriously for children. It was a turning point for Monica, and she decided to devote a year to serious writing for children. She disciplined herself to spend each morning at her typewriter. Her first published book was *Gold Fever Trail* (1974), but her first major success developed from a question she formed while watching a short movie about an underwater habitat. Her question, "what would it be like to grow up entirely under water?", led to the writing of *Crisis on Conshelf Ten* (1975). Since that time, Monica Hughes has published almost 30 novels for adolescents. Interestingly, her work was originally published in Britain, where she has been an acclaimed writer of science fiction for more than twenty years. *The Ghost Dance Caper* (1986) was one of the first Canadian children's books to question mainstream attitudes towards Aboriginal people. It was published in Britain and Australia before it was published in Canada. Monica can only say that in Canada, "local writers were ignored."

Monica is internationally known for both her science fiction and realistic fiction, most notably *The Keeper of the Isis Light* (1980) and *Hunter in the Dark* (1982). *The Faces of Fear* (1998), *The Story Box* (1998), and *The Seven Magpies* (1996) are among her other publications. *The Seven Magpies*, set in Scotland during World War Two, is based on her own experience of the remote Scottish coast during her evacuation there. She has also edited a book of Canadian science fiction short stories for young readers (*What If...? Amazing Stories*, 1998). Hughes continues to be one of Canada's most prolific authors.

Monica won the Vicky Metcalf Award (for a body of work) in 1981, the Alberta Culture Juvenile Novel Award in 1981 (for *Hunter in the Dark*), the Canada Council Prize for Children's Literature in 1981 and 1982 (for *The Guardian of Isis* and *Hunter in the Dark* respectively), the Vicky Metcalf Short Story Award in 1983 (for *The Iron-Barred Door*), the R. Ross Annett Award (1983 and 1992), the CLA Young Adult Book Award (1983), the Silver Feather Award (1986) in Germany, and the Boeken Leeuw (Book Lion) Award in Belgium (1987).

I Spent My Summer Vacation Kidnapped into Space (Godfrey, 1990) is a futuristic tale of how Reeann and Jared are kidnapped by Torkan aliens. They are put into an arena to fight giant slime worms to entertain the aliens. Reeann and Jared must generate plans to escape from the worms and from their kidnappers. In *The Mad Queen of Mordra* (Yost, 1982), Billy Brown is taken to a strange planet by a mysterious bubble. He quickly finds himself entangled in a battle with an evil queen in a city under the sea. Billy must win a deadly game of chess against the queen in order to save himself and his friends from a hideous monster. *The Giver* (Lowry, 1993), the 1994 Newbery Medal winner, is also an outstanding science fiction novel that, like *The Story Box*, addresses future political and social systems; the issues addressed in *The Giver* seem to make it more appropriate for junior high-level readers.

We have identified a *brief* selection of the many high-quality novels available for upper elementary students. A list at the end of the chapter contains additional book titles.

Young-Adult Literature

Young-adult literature is most appropriate for more advanced readers in grades five and six (some books already mentioned in this chapter would be classified as young-adult literature). It is important that all readers in our classrooms have access to material that is challenging, yet the material must be appropriate in terms of content as well as reading level. Young-adult novels could be placed on a continuum of difficulty and sophistication. Some books are indeed appropriate for grade five and six students, but many young-adult selections are inappropriate for these students. It is imperative that a teacher know the content, language, and style of books before recommending them to students. Many young-adult books deal with issues and topics that are age-appropriate and of intense interest to students in grades seven to nine, such as romance, sexual orientation, drugs, peer relationships, the search for identity, and establishing independence. *Bad Boy* (Wieler, 1989), *Up to Low* (Doyle, 1982), *The Tuesday Café* (Trembath, 1996), and *The Maestro* (Wynne-Jones 1995) are examples of such books. Competent readers in grades five and six could read these books, and many would enjoy the novels as they are high-quality works of young-adult literature. However, these novels are inappropriate for most upper elementary students because a certain level of maturity is required in order to understand fully the issues raised in these books and to appreciate the situations in which the characters find themselves.

Some young-adult novels, however, are suitable for upper elementary readers. *Rebellion: A Novel of Upper Canada* (Brandis, 1996) is about a boy named Adam who emigrates to Canada from the United Kingdom in 1837. Adam finds work at a Toronto paper mill and becomes involved in the rebellion mounted by William Lyon McKenzie against the Family Compact. Adam takes responsibility for himself and his mother, and risks his life for his friends and for a cause he deeply believes in. In doing so, Adam learns the harsh realities of power and politics. In *Stormbound* (Fairbridge, 1995), a number of factors cause Loren to be locked in the school on a stormy night with his English teacher, Mrs. Duncan, whom he dislikes. An armed robber on the run comes into the school seeking shelter and wanting to use the phone. The suspense builds as Loren and Mrs. Duncan attempt to evade the criminal and survive a night of terror. Their ordeal helps them to overcome their differences and they learn to understand each other, and the criminal, as individuals living through difficult circumstances.

Other selections of young-adult literature that upper elementary teachers may consider using include *A Time to Choose* (Attema, 1996), *The McIntyre Liar* (Bly, 1993), *Bone Dance* (Brooks, 1997), winner of the 1998 CLA Young Adult Book

Award, *Summer of Madness* (Crook, 1995), *Uncle Ronald* (Doyle, 1994), *Summer of My German Soldier* (Greene, 1973), *To Dance at the Palais Royale* (McNaughton, 1996), winner of several awards, including the Geoffrey Bilson Award for Historical Fiction, *Z for Zachariah* (O'Brien, 1974), *Jacob Have I Loved* (Paterson, 1980), *Canyons* (Paulsen, 1990), *Billy and the Bearman* (Poulsen, 1996), and *Homecoming* (Voigt, 1981).

Short Stories

There are many collections of short stories written for children in grades three to eight, among them Tim Wynne-Jones' *Some of the Kinder Planets* (1993) and Sarah Ellis' *The Back of Beyond* (1997). The short story, as a literary form, has existed only since the middle of the nineteenth century. Although it has its roots in ancient tales and narratives, the short story as an art form was developed by the American writers Edgar Allan Poe and Nathaniel Hawthorne, among others. They were followed by writers such as Katherine Mansfield and Somerset Maugham in Britain and then by Ernest Hemingway in the United States. A short story is a brief fictional narrative (from around 500 to 15,000 words) which consists of more than just a mere record of an incident. It has a formal structure with unity of time, place, and action, and a short story generally reveals the true nature of a character. Today, there is a growing number of short story collections consisting of delightful and frequently thought-provoking, well-crafted pieces of writing.

Readers familiar with Tim Wynne-Jones' picture books will be especially appreciative of his three books of short stories. *Some of the Kinder Planets* (1993) won the 1994 Governor General's Award and the 1995 Boston Globe–Horn Book Award for Children's Literature. The second short story in this collection, "Save the Moon for Kerdy Dickus," begins like this:

> *This is Ky's story. It happened to her. It happened at her place in the country. I wasn't there when it happened, but I know what her place in the country looks like, and that's important. In this story, the way things look is really important.*
> *There's more than one version of this story. If Ky's younger brothers, Brad or Tony, told you the story, it would come out different. But not as different as the way the Stranger tells it. We know his name now, but we still call him the Stranger. Perhaps you know his version of the story. It was in the newspapers. Well, the* National Enquirer, *anyway. (p. 15)*

Wynne-Jones has also written *The Book of Changes* (1994) and *Lord of the Fries and Other Stories* (1999).

Kit Pearson has edited an anthology of short stories and excerpts from works of Canadian children's literature entitled *This Land: A Cross Country Anthology of Canadian Fiction for Young Readers* (1998). Jean Little's collection, *Hey World, Here I Am* (1977), is still appreciated by her audience.

Short stories are an oft-neglected genre of literature, as teachers focus increasingly on novels in the classroom. For reading aloud, however, the pleasure provided by a short story is immense. From *Nothing To Be Afraid Of* (Mark, 1980) comes the story "How Anthony Made a Friend," which begins with this unlikely exchange:

> *"We're lucky to get on so well with the people next door," said Mr. and Mrs. Clayton. "Especially after the last lot."*
> *The last lot had pushed their piano against the party wall and played a tune called "Friends and Neighbors" at one o'clock in the morning.*
> *"Do you think they're trying to tell us something?" said Mr. Clayton, on the seventh or eighth occasion.*
> *Mrs. Clayton screamed quietly.*

Canadian children can easily engage and identify with these British short stories. They will similarly enjoy the stories in Allan Ahlberg's collection, *The Better Brown Stories* (1996).

Other collections of short stories suitable for the elementary grades are listed below.

References

Jacques, B. 1995. Describing the fantasy of my own life. In *Battling Dragons: Issues and Controversy in Children's Literature.* S. Lehr, ed. Portsmouth, New Hampshire: Heinemann.

Lukens, R. 1999. *A Critical Handbook of Children's Literature.* Sixth edition. New York: Longman.

MacGregor, R. 1995. *Home Team: Fathers, Sons and Hockey*. Toronto: McClelland & Stewart Inc.

———. 1996. *The Seven A.M. Practice: Stories of Family Life*. Toronto: McClelland & Stewart Inc.

MacGregor, R. and K. Dryden. 1989. *Home Game: Hockey and Life in Canada*. Toronto: McClelland & Stewart Inc.

Moss, B. 1996. Creating classroom encounters through hybrid texts. *Journal of Children's Literature* 22(1), 34-38.

Sipe, L. 1996. The idea of a classic. *Journal of Children's Literature* 22(1), 31-33.

Temple, C., M. Martinez, J. Yokota, and A. Naylor. 1998. *Children's Books in Children's Hands: An Introduction to Their Literature*. Needham Heights, Massachusetts: Allyn and Bacon.

Tomlinson, C. and C. Lynch-Brown. 1996. *Essentials of Children's Literature*. Second edition. Needham Heights, Massachusetts: Allyn and Bacon.

Professional Resources

Temple, C., M. Martinez, J. Yokota, and A. Naylor. (1998). *Children's Books in Children's Hands: An Introduction to Their Literature*. Needham Heights, Massachusetts: Allyn and Bacon. • This textbook, an overview of children's literature, written to introduce and highlight children's books, contains three parts. Part one includes information about the qualities of good books, children's books and childhood development, literary elements of children's literature, reader-response perspectives, and multicultural literature. A large part of the overall text is devoted to part two: an exploration of the various genres of children's literature. Each chapter devoted to a particular genre explains the specific genre and outlines characteristics and/or issues associated with the genre. Information is provided about many authors and/or illustrators and a wealth of books is described and identified in each genre chapter. Part three discusses issues associated with creating literature-based classrooms.

Tomlinson, C. and C. Lynch-Brown. 1996. *Essentials of Children's Literature.* Second edition. Needham Heights, Massachusetts: Allyn and Bacon. • Chapters 1 and 2 of this book discuss many issues related to children and literature, including defining children's literature, identifying the value of children's literature, describing the elements of fiction, and exploring the visual elements, artistic styles, and media of books. The authors devote an entire chapter to each of poetry, picture books, traditional literature, modern fantasy, realistic fiction, historical fiction, biography and informational books, and multicultural and international literature. As well as discussing various issues related to each category, the authors cite extensive references of writers and books for each category of literature. The remaining two chapters of the book describe organizational structures and teaching strategies for literature-based programs. The text also includes an extensive appendix of children's book awards and another appendix of professional resources.

Other Beginning Novels

Avi. 1999. *Abigail Takes the Wheel.* New York: HarperCollins.

Bjornson, H. 1997. *Raymond's Raindance*. Burnaby, British Columbia: Skoal House.

Blume, J. 1981. *The One in the Middle Is the Green Kangaroo*. New York: Bantam Doubleday Dell Publishing Group, Inc.

———. 1971. *Freckle Juice*. New York: Bantam Doubleday Publishing Group, Inc.

Choyce, L. 1998. *Famous at Last*. East Lawrencetown, Nova Scotia: Pottersfield Press.

Cleary, B. 1984. *Ramona Forever*. New York: Bantam Doubleday Dell Publishing Group, Inc.

Corbett, S. 1960. *The Lemonade Trick*. New York: Scholastic, Inc.

Croteau, M. 1996. *Fred and the Stinky Cheese*. Translated by S. Cummins. Halifax: Fromac Publishing.

Dahl, R. 1980. *The Twits*. New York: Bantam Skylark Books.

———. 1981. *George's Marvelous Medicine*. New York: Bantam Skylark Books.

Elste, J. 1996. *True Blue*. New York: Grosset & Dunlap.

Fox, P. 1967. *A Likely Place*. New York: Aladdin Paperbacks.

Garner, A. 1998. *The Well of the Wind*. New York: DK Ink.

Gauthier, G. 1995. *Mooch Forever*. Translated by S. Cummins. Halifax: Formac Publishing.

Gravel, F. 1992. *Mr. Zamboni's Dream Machine*. Translated by S. Cummins. Toronto: James Lorimer and Company.

Hutchins, H. 1997. *Shoot for the Moon, Robyn*. Halifax: Formac Publishing.

Korman, G. 1997. *Liar, Liar, Pants on Fire*. Richmond Hill, Ontario: Scholastic Canada.

MacLachlan, P. 1985. *Sarah, Plain and Tall*. New York: Harper & Row, Publishers.

———. 1994. *Skylark*. New York: Harper Trophy.

Manes, S. 1982. *Be a Perfect Person in Just Three Days*. New York: Bantam Skylark Books.

Manuel, L. 1997. *The Cherry-pit Princess*. Regina: Coteau Books.

Park, B. 1982. *Skinnybones*. New York: Alfred A. Knopf, Inc.

———. 1987. *The Kid in the Red Jacket*. New York: Alfred A. Knopf, Inc.

Paterson, K. 1992. *The King's Equal*. New York: HarperCollins Publishers. (Originally published in picture-book format.)

Richardson, G. 1997. *A Friend for Mr. Granville*. Edmonton: Hodgepog Books.

Roberts, K. 1990. *Crazy Ideas*. Vancouver: Douglas and McIntyre Limited.

———. 1991. *Nothing Wright*. Vancouver: Douglas and McIntyre Limited.

———. 1994. *Past Tense*. Vancouver: Douglas and McIntyre Limited.

Smith, R.K. 1972. *Chocolate Fever*. New York: Bantam Doubleday Dell Publishing Group, Inc.

Smucker, B. 1987. *Jacob's Little Giant*. Toronto: Puffin Books.

Wishinsky, F. 1998. *Crazy for Chocolate*. Richmond Hill, ON: Scholastic Canada.

Novels for Upper Elementary Readers

Alma, A. 1997. *Under Emily's Sky*. Vancouver: Beach Holme Publishing.

Anderson, M. 1978. *Searching for Shona*. New York: Alfred A. Knopf, Inc.

Armstrong, W.H. 1969. *Sounder*. New York: Harper & Row. (1979 Newbery Medal winner)

Avi. 1990. *The True Confessions of Charlotte Doyle*. New York: Orchard Books. (1991 Newbery Honor book)

———. 1992. *Blue Heron*. New York: Avon Books.

———. 1994. *The Barn*. New York: Avon Books.

Bailey, L. 1996. *How Can a Frozen Detective Stay Hot on the Trail?* Toronto: Kids Can Press.

———. 1997. *What's a Daring Detective Like Me Doing in the Doghouse?* Toronto: Kids Can Press.

Bunting, E. 1996. *SOS Titanic*. New York: Harcourt Brace.

Burnford, S. 1961. *The Incredible Journey*. New York: Little, Brown and Company.

Butterworth, O. 1956. *The Enormous Egg*. New York: Bantam Doubleday Dell Publishing Group, Inc.

Byars, B. 1968. *The Midnight Fox*. New York: Scholastic Inc.

———. 1986. *The Blossoms Meet the Vulture Lady*. New York: Bantam Doubleday Dell Publishing Group, Inc.

———. 1986. *The-Not-Just-Anybody Family*. New York: Bantam Doubleday Dell Publishing Group, Inc.

———. 1987. *A Blossom Promise*. New York: Bantam Doubleday Dell Publishing Group, Inc.

———. 1987. *The Blossoms and the Green Phantom*. New York: Bantam Doubleday Dell Publishing Group, Inc.

———. 1991. *Wanted...Mud Blossom*. New York: Bantam Doubleday Dell Publishing Group, Inc.

Callaghan, M. 1948. *Luke Baldwin's Vow*. Toronto: Scholastic Canada Ltd.

Cleary, B. 1975. *Ramona and Her Father*. New York: Dell Publishing Co., Inc.

———. 1977. *Ramona and Her Mother*. New York: Dell Publishing Co., Inc.

———. 1983. *Dear Mr. Henshaw*. New York: Dell Publishing Co., Inc.

Cohen, B. 1997. *Thank You, Jackie Robinson*. New York: Beech Tree.

Coman, C. 1995. *What Jamie Saw*. New York: Puffin Books.

Cushman, K. 1994. *Catherine, Called Birdy*. New York: Clarion. (1995 Newbery Honor book)

————. 1995. *The Midwife's Apprentice*. New York: HarperCollins Publishers. (1996 Newbery Medal winner)

Danakas, J. 1995. *Hockey Night in Transcona*. Toronto: James Lorimer and Company.

Doyle, B. 1979. *You Can Pick Me Up at Peggy's Cove*. Toronto: Groundwood Books/Douglas and McIntyre Limited.

————. 1994. *Uncle Ronald*. Toronto: Groundwood Books.

DeFelice, C. 1990. *Weasel*. New York: Avon Books.

Farmer, N. 1994. *The Ear, the Eye and the Arm*. New York: Puffin Books. (1995 Newbery Honor book)

Fleischman, S. 1995. *The 13th Floor: A Ghost Story*. New York: Greenwillow Books.

Forsyth, C. 1997. *Kate's Midnight Ride*. Toronto: James Lorimer and Co.

Garrigue, S. 1985. *The Eternal Mr. Ito*. Needham, Massachusetts: Silver Burdett Ginn. (Young Adult)

George, J. 1972. *Julie of the Wolves*. New York: Harper & Row. (1973 Newbery Medal winner)

George, J.C. 1994. *Julie*. New York: HarperCollins.

Gipson, E. 1965. *Old Yeller*. New York: Harper & Row.

Hammond, E.B. 1996. *The Secret Under the Whirlpool*. Charlottetown, PEI: Ragweed Press.

————. 1997. *Beyond the Waterfall*. Charlottetown, PEI: Ragweed Press.

————. 1998. *Explosion at Dawson Creek*. Charlottetown, PEI: Ragweed Press.

Harding, L. 1973. *The Fallen Spaceman*. New York: Bantam Skylark Books.

Hesse, K. 1997. *Out of the Dust*. New York: Scholastic Inc. (1998 Newbery Medal winner).

Horne, C. 1995. *Trapped by Coal*. Vancouver: Pacific Educational Press.

Houston, J. 1982. *Black Diamonds: A Search for Arctic Treasure*. Toronto: McClelland & Stewart Inc.

Hughes, T. 1968. *The Iron Man*. London: Faber and Faber Limited.

————. 1993. *The Iron Woman*. London: Faber and Faber Limited.

Hunter, M. 1975. *A Stranger Came Ashore*. New York: Harper & Row, Pubishers.

Hutchins, H. 1994. *Within a Painted Past*. Toronto: Annick Press, Ltd.

Kjelgaard, J. 1948. *Snow Dog*. New York: Bantam Skylark Books.

————. 1950. *Wild Trek*. New York: Bantam Skylark Books.

————. 1959. *Stormy*. New York: Bantam Skylark Books.

Korman, G. 1980. *Who Is Bugs Potter?* New York: Scholastic Inc.

————. 1981. *I Want To Go Home!* Richmond Hill, Ontario: Scholastic-TAB Publications, Ltd.

————. 1983. *Bugs Potter Lives at Nickaninny*. Richmond Hill, Ontario: Scholastic-TAB Publications, Ltd.

————. 1984. *No Coins, Please*. Richmond Hill, ON: Scholastic-TAB Publications, Ltd.

————. 1989. *Radio Fifth Grade*. New York: Scholastic Inc.

————. 1996. *The Chicken Doesn't Skate*. Richmond Hill, Ontario: Scholastic Canada.

————. 1998. *The Sixth Grade Nickname Game*. Markham, Ontario: Scholastic Canada.

Kositsky, L. 1998. *Candles*. Montreal: Roussan Publishers.

Lawson, J. 1993. *White Jade Tiger*. Victoria: Beach Holme Publishing. (Young Adult)

————. 1996. *Cougar Cove*. Victoria: Orca Book Publishers.

————. 1997. *Goldstone*. Toronto: Stoddart Publishing Company Ltd.

————. 1998. *Turns on a Dime*. Toronto: Stoddart Kids.

Lindgren, A. 1950. *Pippi Longstocking*. New York: The Viking Press.

Little, J. 1969. *One to Grow On*. Toronto: Puffin Books.

————. 1972. *From Anna*. New York: HarperCollins Publishers.

————. 1997. *The Belonging Place*. Toronto: Viking Press.

————. 1903. *The Call of the Wild*. New York: The MacMillan Co.

Lottridge, C. 1992. *Ticket to Curlew*. Toronto: Groundwood Books.

———. 1997. *Wings to Fly*. Toronto: Groundwood Books.

Lowry, L. 1993. *The Giver*. New York: Bantam Doubleday Dell Publishing Group. (Young Adult)

Lunn, J. 1981. *The Root Cellar*. New York: Scribner's.

———. 1986. *Shadow in Hawthorn Bay*. New York: Scribner's. (1987 Canadian Children's Book of the Year winner)

MacGregor, R. 1996. *The Screech Owls' Northern Adventure*. Toronto: McClelland & Stewart Inc.

———. 1997. *Terror in Florida*. Toronto: McClelland & Stewart Inc.

———. 1998. *The Quebec City Crisis*. Toronto: McClelland & Stewart Inc.

———. 1998. *Nightmare in Nagano*. Toronto: McClelland & Stewart Inc.

———. 1999. *Danger in Dinosaur Valley*. Toronto: McClelland & Stewart Inc.

Matas, C. 1993. *Daniel's Story*. Richmond Hill, Ontario: Scholastic Canada.

———. 1994. *The Burning Time*. Toronto: HarperCollins Publishers. (Young Adult)

———. 1995. *The Primrose Path*. Winnipeg: Blizzard Publishing. (Young Adult)

———. 1996. *After the War*. Richmond Hill, ON: Scholastic Canada. (Young Adult)

Mazer, H. 1981. *The Island Keeper*. New York: Bantam Doubleday Dell Publishing Group, Inc. (Young Adult)

McLaughlin, F. 1990. *Yukon Journey*. New York: Scholastic, Inc.

McSwigan, M. 1942. *Snow Treasure*. New York: Scholastic Book Services.

Mikaelsen, B. 1991. *Rescue Josh McGuire*. New York: Hyperion Books for Children.

Montero, G. 1982. *Billy Higgins Rides the Freights*. Toronto: James Lorimer and Company.

Morey, W. 1967. *Home is the North*. Hillsboro, Oregon: Blue Heron Publishing, Inc.

———. 1968. *Kavik, the Wolf Dog*. New York: Scholastic.

———. 1969. *Angry Waters*. Hillsboro, Oregon: Blue Heron Publishing, Inc.

———. 1971. *Deep Trouble*. Hillsboro, Oregon: Blue Heron Publishing, Inc.

———. 1971. *Scrub Dog of Alaska*. Hillsboro, Oregon: Heron Publising, Inc.

———. 1974. *Run Far, Run Fast*. Hillsboro, Oregon: Blue Heron Publishing, Inc.

———. 1991. *Death Walk*. Hillsboro, Oregon: Blue Heron Publishing, Inc.

Mowat, F. 1956. *Lost in the Barrens*. Toronto: McClelland & Stewart Inc. (1958 Canadian Children's Book of the Year Award winner)

Norton, M. 1953. *The Borrowers*. New York: Harcourt Brace and Jovanovich.

———. 1959. *The Borrowers Afloat*. New York: Harcourt Brace and Jovanovich.

———. 1961. *The Borrowers Aloft*. New York: Harcourt Brace and Jovanovich.

O'Dell, S. 1960. *Island of the Blue Dolphins*. New York: Bantam Doubleday Dell Publishing Group, Inc. (1961 Newbery Medal winner)

———. 1988. *Black Star, Bright Dawn*. New York: Ballantine Books.

Paterson, K. 1996. *Jip: His Story*. New York: Lodestar Books. (1997 Scott O'Dell Award for Historical Fiction winner)

Paulsen, G. 1971. *The Foxman*. New York: Scholastic Inc.

———. 1983. *Dancing Carl*. Carsdale, New York: Bradbury Press.

———. 1983. *Popcorn Days and Buttermilk Nights*. New York: Puffin Books.

———. 1984. *Tracker*. New York: Scholastic Inc.

———. 1985. *Dogsong*. New York: Scholastic Inc.

———. 1987. *The Crossing*. New York: Orchard Books.

———. 1988. *The Island*. New York: Orchard Books.

———. 1989. *The Winter Room*. New York: Bantam Doubleday Dell Publishing Group, Inc.

———. 1990. *Canyons*. New York: Bantam Doubleday Dell Publishing Group, Inc.

———. 1990. *Woodsong*. New York: Scholastic Inc.

———. 1991. *The Cook Camp*. New York: Orchard Books.

———. 1992. *The Haymeadow*. New York: Bantam Doubleday Dell Publishing Group, Inc.

———. 1993. *Harris and Me*. New York: Bantam Doubleday Dell Publishing Group, Inc.

———. 1993. *Nightjohn*. New York. Bantam Doubleday Dell Publishing Group, Inc.

Pearson, K. 1996. *Awake and Dreaming*. Toronto: Viking.

———. 1989. *The Sky Is Falling*. Markham, Ontario: Viking Kestrel. (1990 Canadian Children's Book of the Year Award winner)

———. 1992. *Looking at the Moon*. Toronto: Viking.

———. 1993. *The Lights Go On Again*. Toronto: Viking.

Peck, R. 1998. *A Long Way from Chicago*. New York: Dial Books For Young Readers.

Poulsen, D. 1996. *Billy and the Bearman*. Toronto: Napoleon Publishing. (Young Adult)

Rawls, W. 1961. *Where the Red Fern Grows*. New York: Bantam Doubleday Publishing Group, Inc.

Rawls, W. 1976. *Summer of the Monkeys*. New York: Bantam Doubleday Dell Publishing Group, Inc.

Sachar, L. 1998. *Holes*. New York: Farrar Straus Giroux. (1999 Newbery Medal winner)

Scrimger, R. 1998. *The Nose from Jupiter*. Montreal: Tundra Books.

———. 1998. *The Way to Schenectady*. Toronto: Tundra Books.

Smith, R. 1995. *Thunder Cave*. New York: Hyperion Books.

Speare, E.G. 1958. *The Witch of Blackbird Pond*. New York: Bantam Doubleday Dell Inc. (1959 Newbery Medal winner)

Sperry, A. 1940. *Call It Courage*. New York: Macmillan. (1941 Newbery Medal winner)

Taylor, C. 1994. *Summer of the Mad Monk*. Vancouver: Greystone Books. (Young Adult)

Taylor, T. 1969. *The Cay*. New York: Avon Books.

———. 1993. *Timothy of the Cay: A Prequel-Sequel*. New York: Avon Books.

Walters, E. 1997. *Trapped in Ice*. Toronto: Viking Press.

Watts, I. 1998. *Good-bye Marianne*. Toronto: Tundra Books.

Winthrop, E. 1985. *The Castle in the Attic*. New York: Bantam Skylark.

———. 1993. *The Battle for the Castle*. New York: Bantam Doubleday Dell Books for Young Readers.

Wood, B. and C. Wood. 1997. *Dogstar*. Victoria: Polestar Book Publishers.

Woodbury, M. 1997. *Jess and the Runaway Grandpa*. Regina: Coteau Books.

Yolen, J. 1988. *The Devil's Arithmetic*. New York: Puffin Books.

Short Story Collections

Alexander, L. 1977. *The Town Cats and Other Tales*. New York: Dutton.

Gould, A. and P. Hancock. 1993. *Ghosts and Other Scary Stories*. New York: Scholastic.

Hancock, P. 1995. *Strange and Eerie Stories*. Toronto: Scholastic.

Pearce, P. 1987. *Who's Afraid? and Other Strange Stories*. New York: Greenwillow Books.

Rylant, C. 1985. *Every Living Thing*. New York: Aladdin Books.

San Souci, R. 1987. *Short and Shivery: Thirty Chilling Tales*. New York: Delacourte Press.

Segel, E., ed. 1986. *Short Takes: A Short Story Collection for Young Readers*. New York: Delacourte Press.

Turner, M.W. 1995. *Instead of Three Wishes*. New York: Greenwillow Books.

Yee, P. 1989. *Tales from Gold Mountain: Stories of the Chinese in the New World*. Vancouver: Douglas & McIntyre.

Yolen, J., M. Greenberg, and C. Waugh. 1986. *Dragons and Dreams: A Collection of New Fantasy and Science Fiction*. New York: Harper & Row.

CHAPTER FIVE

MULTICULTURAL AND TRANSCULTURAL LITERATURE

The objectives of this chapter are

- To know the range of literature available in Canada that is multicultural and transcultural in scope;
- To be able to evaluate multicultural and transcultural literature and select high-quality books for classroom use;
- To understand the role of multicultural and transcultural literature in the elementary classroom;
- To appreciate the rich diversity of Canadian literature for young readers;
- To become aware of available literature in Aboriginal languages.

Multiculturalism

We have devoted a whole chapter of this book to issues of multicultural and transcultural children's literature because Canada is a multicultural society and our Charter of Rights and Freedoms invokes tolerance and understanding of the differences among individuals. Multicultural children's literature provides one vehicle for promoting the acceptance and understanding of difference.

Multicultural education is an important yet controversial area of study, and the concept can be misunderstood and misinterpreted even by well-meaning people. This chapter cannot possibly do justice to the scope of the topic and thus addresses issues only briefly and in the context of the books presented. It is not the purpose of this chapter to delve deeply into issues of multiculturalism, but rather to highlight certain issues in relation to children's literature.

James Banks (1989) defines MULTICULTURALISM as an educational reform movement that seeks to affirm equal opportunity for all students to learn regardless of their background, gender, class, race, ethnicity, or culture. This definition encompasses multiethnic education and global awareness as well as a recognition of racism, prejudice, discrimination, equity, and values. Many educators understand multiculturalism to mean simply an appreciation of ethnic difference, and so they attempt to select literature for use in their classrooms that depicts various ethnic and religious groups—books such as *Something From Nothing* (Gilman, 1992), and *Northern Lights: The Soccer Trails* (Kusugak, 1993). MULTIETHNIC EDUCATION does indeed refer to the study of the ethnic diversity of society, the histories, cultures, and experiences of ethnic groups (Finazzo, 1997), but MULTICULTURAL EDUCATION is an "integrated teaching process which deals with ethnic groups, religious groups, gender, children's issues, handicaps and special needs, giftedness, ageism, and other important issues that influence and enhance the lives of our citizens" (Finazzo, 1997, p.101). Multicultural literature depicts and explores the lives of individuals belonging to a wide range of groups. Many of the children's book titles referred to throughout this book are multicultural in scope.

Some educators argue that we ought not only tolerate each other but embrace each other's cultural ways and diversity. Some teachers have striven to do that by honouring the cultural differences in the children in their own classrooms, by, for example, selecting books that have a Chinese theme because there is a recent immigrant from Hong Kong in the class or choosing a book about a child from a single-parent family because four of the children in the class are from single-parent homes. Others say that such behaviour displays discrimination, not multiculturalism, and that we should use books involving as wide a range of social and cultural groups as possible, regardless of whether these groups are represented in our individual classrooms. Such proponents maintain that children should never be considered as representatives of a culture, but always as individual and unique persons. The topic of multicultural literature and its use in classrooms certainly deserves to be explored thoughtfully.

Canada proclaims itself to be a multicultural society and, at the present time, has the highest rate of population increase in the western world except for New Zealand (Statistics Canada, 1997). This increase is due to immigration rather than to birth rate, and the phenomenon is strongly reflected in Canadian classrooms, especially in large urban areas. Canada's immigration policy can be described as one of "cultural pluralism," where strength is recognized to lie in the acceptance of different races, ethnicities, languages, and cultures. Nieto (1992) describes CULTURAL PLURALISM as "a model based on the premise that all newcomers have a right to maintain their languages and cultures while combining with others to form a new society reflective of all our differences" (p.307). This model is often likened to a salad bowl or mosaic, and contrasts starkly with the "melting pot" policy of immigration and education practised in the United States during the first 60 years of the nineteenth century. Banks (1994) maintains that teachers who apply a multicultural perspective to their teaching honour both the cultural diversity of ethnic groups *and* the shared national culture.

Much of the literature available for children in western countries, and particularly in Canada, has retained a strong British or European flavour and has been dominated by books that depict white, English, Christian, middle-class families and values. James Zarrillo (1994) has suggested three categories of multicultural literature. The first category consists of fiction with characters from underrepresented cultural and ethnic groups (for example, Canadians of Japanese descent, Aboriginal peoples, Afro-Canadians, and people belonging to religions other than Christianity). The second category includes fiction that takes the reader to places and cultures outside North America; this is now often termed transcultural literature and will be dealt with in its own section of this chapter. The third group consists of information books (including biographies) of underrepresented groups. We would add a fourth category, consisting of fiction books that present gender issues and underrepresented social groupings such as gay and lesbian partnerships.

Although the most obvious differences among people are frequently in language, skin tone, and physical features, differences in socio-economic standing, class, and family circumstances can create feelings of difference and alienation among children. In the latter part of the twentieth century, economic and social circumstances have changed family units drastically. The traditional nuclear family with one parent staying at home as a primary caregiver has largely disappeared. Today, most parents must work, many parents choose to work, and many families have only one parent or a mixture of parents and extended family members. Today's family can be defined as a "range from two parents, one male and one female, living together with one or more children (the nuclear family) to any number of people of any age or sex who choose to live together and nurture one another" (Rudman, 1995, p.74). Thus the family unit itself can be a source of discrimination if its legitimacy is disregarded in a classroom context. The affirmation of diverse families is an important aspect of multicultural and transcultural children's literature, as positive models can be presented through the books children read.

Transculturalism

The current expansion in global communication, through the Internet, television broadcasting, and other mass media, has created a global community which calls on people to be knowledgeable about far-distant places and aware of issues facing people living in foreign countries as well as in their own. Pratt and Beaty (1999) write that "citizenship is extending beyond the traditional boundaries of individual countries" (p.1). Part of the task of the classroom teacher is to affirm and celebrate the differences and similarities of the children in Canadian classrooms and throughout the world. It is hoped that through exposure to TRANSCULTURAL LITERATURE (formerly called international literature), children will develop both a strong awareness of themselves as individuals and a sense of the similarities and differences in lifestyles, learning styles, customs, and values of people of varying backgrounds. Its underlying goal is to help children develop an awareness of a more inclusive world and an understanding of how that world relates to those of us living in Canada.

Value Issues and the Understanding of Difference

A common saying about educators is that they don't teach what they know, they teach what they are. Nowhere is this more apparent than in the context of multiculturalism, which is a very value-laden construct. Every time teachers walk into a classroom, they teach values; every time teachers write, speak, or set assignments, they teach values. A teacher's individual awareness of the importance of value issues is part of what that teacher both learns and teaches in the classroom. By our own examples and attitudes, we demonstrate our value systems. Most teachers are unaware of the prejudice and biases they may show in their teaching, and they do not usually display these biases intentionally. However, research shows that teachers treat different groups within classrooms differently. For example, there are clear differences in the ways teachers speak with, question, and interact with boys versus girls. Similar differences may occur when teachers interact with various ethnic groups.

Research about attitudes toward multicultural diversity in elementary school children is sparse. Aboud (1988) suggests that children's attitudes towards diversity tend to stay constant unless altered by life-changing events. More recent research, however, has demonstrated that children who are exposed to multicultural storybook reading in a combination of school and home reading programs in kindergarten, grade two, and grade four develop the most positive attitudes towards differences (Wham, Barnhardt & Cook, 1996). In this study, the largest increases (and decreases) occurred in grade two children, which suggests that this is an important period for modifying attitudes. Wham, Barnhardt, and Cook write, "children cannot be expected to develop a sensitivity towards others

Jennifer reads a French-language book

merely because they are told to do so. Attitudes are difficult to change .... Literature allows individuals to share in the lives of others; it can also provide an avenue for multicultural understanding" (p.2).

Children's literature, then, is one vehicle through which teachers, as well as students, can begin to recognize racism in society and learn the value of keeping an open mind. Teachers can help to heighten awareness of stereotyping and can identify the contributions of various ethic groups and cultures in Canadian society, helping children to become more sensitive to society's biases and more accepting of difference.

At this point, it is necessary to define some of the terms frequently encountered in discussions of multiculturalism. According to Finazzo (1997):

> *BIAS [is] any attitude, belief or feeling that results in, and helps to justify, unfair treatment of an individual because of his/her identity; PREJUDICE [is] an attitude, opinion, or feeling formed without adequate prior knowledge, thought or reason. Prejudice can be prejudgement for or against any person, group or sex. RACISM [is] any attitude, action or institutional practice backed up by institutional power that subordinates people because of their colour. This includes the imposition of one ethnic group's culture in such a way as to withhold respect for, to demean, or to destroy the cultures of other races. (p.236)*

Research (Cross, 1985) illustrates that students can best resist racism when they can see their own minority group represented in books and curricular materials. All students benefit when all groups are represented within the educational system, and are represented in the print materials teachers select for use in their instructional programs.

Multicultural Literature

Any book chosen for inclusion in a program of study should be used because it is a *good book* and not because it is a book about a certain cultural, social, or ethnic group. Problems arise when a book is selected because it is about a certain physical disability, for example, and due regard is not paid to other aspects of the book. Many books about minority groups and people with special needs are, unfortunately, condescending and DIDACTIC. Teachers need to look at all books critically and ensure that they include only good books in their programs. Likewise, books must be accurate and not include stereotypical images. It is generally agreed that in a good multicultural book, the voice of the represented cultural group must be heard throughout. This issue, however, raises important questions about who should write about minorities.

McGuire-Raskin (1996) examined six picture books, three written from an "insider" perspective and three written from an "outsider" perspective. She concluded that there *are* significant differences between children's picture books written and illustrated by people working from within their own culture and those working from without. She suggests that "possibly outsiders employ more stereotyped or generic cultural motifs, adopt a tourist's view of characters and events, and are more careless with the ways culture is portrayed" (p.26). It is important that we heed her word "possibly," for McGuire-Raskin's study involved only six books—a number too small to justify generalization. Clearly, books cannot be selected based only on the fact that they are written by members of a minority group; they must also be good-quality literature, well written and appropriate for the intended age-range. Paul Goble has written extensively and successfully about Aboriginal Americans (see for example, *The Girl Who Loved Wild Horses,* 1978), and women writers, such as Monica Hughes, have written equally successfully about male protagonists (e.g., *Hunter in the Dark,* 1982). Finally, when selecting multicultural books it is important that selections are current and have contemporary settings and characters that children can compare to and contrast with their own lives and situations.

Stereotypical and distorted ethnic images have existed in literature since books were first written, and can be found in many texts, including some of the classics of children's literature published during the nineteenth century. Books such as *The Adventures of Huckleberry Finn* (Twain, 1885), for example, reflect attitudes and beliefs prevalent in society at the time they were written. The central feature of this, and many other American classics, was the presence of "indolent, happy-go-lucky slaves" (Miller-Lachmann, 1992). It is essential, however, that readers accept such books in the historical contexts in which they were written. These books now provide a springboard for discussions of issues such as racism, slavery, social class, and stereotyping.

Many later books purporting to be multicultural have been criticized as "melting-pot books." Such books treat all people the same, focussing on similarities rather than differences. In these books, children of varied ethnicity attend parties and eat pizza, have the same kinds of problems (e.g., a new baby arrives, grandma is blind), but none of this makes any difference to who they are and what they do. It leads to the notion (prevalent in school textbooks for a while) that if a few children in wheelchairs, a few elderly people, and a few people of colour are added to the illustrations, and a few ethnic names are sprinkled throughout a text, then books can be considered multicultural. Little attention was paid to cultural values and diverse ways of life experienced by the various cultures living together in society. The emergence of independent publishing houses—such as Annick, Kids Can Press, Tundra, and others in Canada—has helped to promote the publication of more authentically multicultural, high-quality materials, many of which are written and/or illustrated by people who have rich and varied cultural experiences themselves.

Literature can be considered multicultural today when it contains a central character, plot, theme, setting, or style that is culturally or socially diverse in nature. *Very Last First Time* (1985), written by Jan Andrews and illustrated by Ian Wallace, is multicultural in all of these elements. Probably the most important facet of a multicultural book, however, is that its characters not be stereotyped. This means no flat characters cast in commonplace and predictable images. *Very Last First Time* tells the story of Eva Padlyat, an Inuit child living on Ungava Bay in the far north of Quebec, as she goes alone for the first time collecting mussels from under the ice at the edge of the ocean. Eva is finally old enough to do this job while her mother attends to other tasks. Eva's mother takes her out on the ice, digs a hole through the ice in an appropriate spot, and helps Eva through the ice onto the ocean floor. Here Eva lights candles and begins her job of collecting mussel strings and putting them into a pan. When her pan is full and her mother has not returned for her, Eva begins to explore. Lost in the beauty of the ocean floor, Eva loses track of time, and finally realizes that she has strayed away from her pan and the opening in the ice. She can hear the waves coming closer as the tide comes in again.

Throughout the book, the text and pictures portray Eva as a strong girl, confident in her mother's care, and well suited to the responsibility she has assumed. Eva's clothes are bright and contemporary: a colourful sweater, mitts, parka, and boots. She is determined, unafraid, and competent:

> *Alone — for the first time.*
> *Eva was so happy she started to sing. Her song echoed around, so she sang louder. She hummed far back in her throat to make the echoes rumble. She lifted up long strings of mussels and let them clatter into her pan. (Andrews, 1985, unpaginated).*

When Eva stumbles and her candle sputters out, she experiences a few moments of fear. She is alone in the dark under the ice and cannot locate the spare candle and matches she knows are in her pockets. Eventually, she finds the candle and manages to light it, finding her way back to her pan and the hole in the ice. Although Eva experiences fear, it does not overcome her. It is clear at the end of the story that Eva plans to go back alone many times to collect mussels for her family.

Wallace's illustrations capture the magical light of winter in the Arctic, the ice and snow, and the beauty of the ocean floor. He plays games with the adult reader in the second illustration in the book: a copy of *Odd's End* by Tim Wynne-Jones is sitting on the kitchen table alongside traditional Inuit children's games and a package of Corn Flakes. Wallace successfully shows the meeting of two cultures—the traditional aspects of life in the north (stretched skins from the traplines on frames, dogs, tools, and parkas), and the influence of European settlement and technology (the church, the Hudson's Bay store, a large refrigerator, airplanes, and electrical power). Wallace's illustrations capture the strength and beauty of Inuit life and culture, the reality of a people who weave traditional and modern life together with great skill.

An example of a multicultural book that explores a culturally diverse theme is *Roses Sing on New Snow,* written by Paul Yee and illustrated by Harvey Chan (1991). The main idea of this book originates in traditional Chinese attitudes and values, yet the book is relevant to contemporary children because it is also about gender. The message the reader receives from the book is not an irrelevant historical aspect of a "foreign" culture, but the deeply meaningful message that all people's contributions to society are to be celebrated and respected. *Roses Sing on New Snow* is about a family that runs a restaurant in Vancouver's Chinatown. Since the illustrations depict gravel streets, boardwalks and horse-drawn carts, it is clear, to adult readers at least, that the story is set in the first years of the twentieth century. When the governor of South China comes to town, a banquet is arranged; each restaurant in Chinatown is invited to bring its best dish. The cook in this particular restaurant is Maylin, the daughter, but the father and his two sons take the special dish she has prepared to the banquet and serve it to the governor. The governor tastes the dish, declares it the best, and demands the recipe. When the father claims that the brothers have cooked the dish, they are unable to provide a recipe. Finally, Maylin is brought to meet the governor and she gives directions for cooking the dish. She helps the governor to prepare the dish himself, but to his dismay, he is not able to create exactly the same dish as Maylin created. The governor is perplexed until Maylin explains, "If you and I sat down with paper and brush and black ink, could we bring forth identical paintings?" (unpaginated). Maylin is then honoured as a great cook and a wise person.

A successful multicultural book is Andrea Spalding's *Finders Keepers* (1995). Although the book tells a fictional story designed for children in grades three to six, it is based on real locations and involves issues critical to Canada's future. The book tells the story of the friendship between a fifth-grade Ukrainian child from the town of Fort Macleod and a child from the Peigan Reserve near Head-Smashed-In Buffalo Jump in southern Alberta. Danny Budzynski meets Joshua Brokenhorn on the day Danny runs away from school. Danny has a learning disability, and school is becoming too distressing for him. He runs away to find a quiet place of retreat and

PAUL YEE AND HARVEY CHAN

Paul Yee was born in 1956 in the town of Spalding, Saskatchewan, but he grew up in Vancouver's Chinatown. Paul is a third generation Canadian and says he had "a typical Chinese-Canadian childhood, caught between two worlds and yearning to move away from the neighborhood" (*Something About the Author*, 1996). Paul is a historian, with an M.A. from the University of British Columbia, and has pursued a career as an archivist and policy analyst. As an archivist, he has managed historical documents and papers in library or institutional collections, making them available for study by researchers and writers; as a policy analyst he was required to research and analyze government decision-making. In 1988, Paul moved to Toronto, where he worked as Multicultural Co-ordinator for the Archives of Ontario.

Paul first began writing for children when he was working as director of the Chinese Cultural Centre in Vancouver, organizing festivals and educational programs. A publishing company asked him to develop a children's book that would provide background for the programs. It resulted in his first book, *Teach Me to Fly, Skyfighter!* (1983). Since his writing for children fit perfectly with his work in researching Chinese-Canadian culture, he embarked on a second book, *The Curses of Third Uncle* (1986), which won honourable mention in the Canada Council's Children's Literature Prize (now the Governor General's Awards). Since then, Paul has become well known for his children's books, *Saltwater City* (1988), a history of Vancouver's Chinatown, *Tales from Gold Mountain* (1989), *Roses Sing on New Snow* (1992), *Breakaway* (1994), *Moonlight's Luck* (1995), *Ghost Train* (1996), and *Struggle and Hope: The Story of Chinese Canadians* (1996). Paul explores facets of Chinese-Canadian history, and although his stories are fictitious, they are based on his extensive knowledge of archival records. *Tales From Gold Mountain* is illustrated by Simon Ng, but *Roses Sing on New Snow* and *Ghost Train* are illustrated by Harvey Chan, a partnership that is becoming well known.

Harvey Chan was born in Hong Kong; he moved to Canada in 1976 at the age of nineteen. He studied at the Ontario College of Art and since his graduation in 1982 has been engaged in illustrating children's publications, as well as illustrating for magazines and advertising agencies. Harvey works primarily with chalk pastel, but he continues to explore a wide range of approaches and media to express his personal vision. He has exhibited work at the Guild Inn Outdoor Show in 1993, the Yorkville Public Library in 1991, and numerous group shows throughout North America. His first book, and his first collaboration with Paul (*Roses Sing on New Snow*), won the Ruth Schwartz Children's Book Award for its artwork. Their second collaboration, *Ghost Train*, earned Harvey the Amelia Frances Howard-Gibbon Illustrator's Award in 1997.

meets Joshua, who has the day off school because the teacher has unexpectedly quit. When Danny discovers an object that looks like an arrowhead in a field near his home, he checks out the Fort Macleod Museum but cannot find anything like it. Joshua and his family are able to help find out what the arrowhead is and where it might have come from, but not before Joshua and Danny become good friends and have many adventures together.

Spalding has created an entirely believable book, with strong characters. The plot moves in a natural rhythm, intertwining Danny's problems at school and his feeling of being an outsider with Joshua's pride in his Peigan heritage and traditions. Although the book could be seen as didactic, the information is presented in the context of the characters and plot, and the story remains dynamic and compelling; the book does not preach, but it does have a strong message. At no point is Spalding's writing condescending to the young reader. A Teachers' Guide has been developed by David Spalding for use with *Finders Keepers*. In the introduction to the Guide, he writes, "*Finders Keepers* may be enjoyed as a novel study, but it may also be used as the core of an interdisciplinary unit on geography, history, science, the arts and personal development" (1996, p.1).

In multicultural literature, the style of the writer and illustrator can make a profound difference to the success of the book. How does the book make the reader feel? How are certain techniques used? How is language used? Are there special words with special meanings? How are humour, sadness, and figurative language used? Do the text and illustrations complement each other, thereby adding to the effectiveness of the whole? The answers to questions such as these indicate the connotative meaning of the book. After all, a story is much more than its words. *The Always Prayer Shawl* (1994), written by Sheldon Oberman and illustrated by Ted Lewin, is a stunning example of a successful portrayal of cultural values and beauty. Adam, a young Jewish boy in Tsarist Russia, has to leave his home and his grandfather when the revolution almost completely changes their lives. Adam's grandfather passes on to Adam the prayer shawl he had received from *his* grandfather. He also passes on the message that some things change and some things don't. The young Adam begins a new life with his parents in North America, grows up, marries, has children and grandchildren, and one day has the opportunity to speak to his grandson in the way his grandfather had spoken with him. He passes on the prayer shawl, along with the message "some things change and some things don't." *The Always Prayer Shawl* is a remarkably sensitive book about what it means to belong, and to know that some things are certain, even when the whole of life appears to be changing. Much of the beauty of the book lies in the sparsity of the text:

> *Adam's grandfather kissed him for the last time.*
> *He held out his prayer shawl and he said,*
> *"My grandfather gave me this prayer shawl.*
> *Now I am giving it to you."*
> *Adam held it tightly against his chest.*
> *He could hardly speak for the tears, so he*
> *whispered,*
> *"I am always Adam and this is my always*
> *prayer shawl. That won't change." (unpaginated)*

In this book, the text and illustrations complement each other so well it is hard to imagine that they did not come from the same person—it is a masterful combination of talents. The book presents deeply memorable details, from the prayer shawl to the faces of the characters. The transition from the black-and-white illustrations of Russia and the first half of the twentieth century to the gently coloured illustrations depicting life in the latter part of the century is extremely successful; indeed, it is rare to find a book so appropriately illustrated. Sheldon Oberman grew up and still lives in Winnipeg; Ted Lewin lives and works in New York. The book won the National Jewish Book Award from the Jewish Book Council in the United States.

Red Parka Mary by Peter Eyvindson, illustrated by Rhian Brynjolson

Red Parka Mary (1996), written by Peter Eyvindson and illustrated by Rhian Brynjolson, is a touching story about the friendship and trust that grow between a native elder named Mary and a seven-year-old boy. The setting is an Aboriginal community in northern Manitoba. A young boy passes Mary's house each day on his way to school, but appears to be shy about meeting Mary as she looks "different":

> *It might have been the way Mary dressed. It didn't matter if it was 40 below or 40 above, she always wore big floppy moccasins lined with rabbit fur, thick grey wool socks, three or four sweaters heavily darned at the elbow and a Montreal Canadien hockey toque pulled down over her straggly grey hair. (unpaginated)*

The accompanying illustration of Mary, sitting on an old wooden box outside her home, shows her unfenced yard, with prairie grass and wild flowers reaching across to a small lake beyond her house. The reader is immediately captivated by the story and the character of Mary.

As time passes, the boy, whom Mary calls "Mister," comes to understand that Mary isn't so scary after all, and a strong friendship blossoms. Mary passes down some of the traditions of her people by teaching the boy how to snare a rabbit and showing him how to make a pair of moccasins. At Christmas, the two exchange very special gifts, reflecting the uniqueness of their friendship. *Red Parka Mary* is an affirmation of the value of older members of our society and the special insights they share with the young.

Peter Eyvindson is an "outsider" from an aboriginal perspective, but an "insider" in terms of human relationships. He has spent time living in Canada's north and in rural Saskatchewan, and in *Red Parka Mary* he authentically portrays life in a northern community. Eyvindson has dealt sensitively with the universal theme of friendship and those special relationships that develop between the very young and the very old.

Rhian Brynjolson's illustrations help readers identify with the story. The picture of Mary wiping her glasses as she speaks to the boy is so natural it makes readers forget they are simply reading a story about Mary. The landscape of northern Manitoba is beautifully portrayed. The illustrations gently depict the blending of the old and new, traditional and modern. Mary and the boy are both authentic characters whose special relationship will remind readers of the many similar friendships they have treasured in their own lives.

A list of American books that promote an understanding of difference is given at the end of this chapter.

Testing the Authenticity of Multicultural Literature

When testing the authenticity of children's books with which they are not familiar, teachers *must* seek the advice of people who are knowledgeable about the culture being discussed. Teachers should also select books that depict culturally diverse groups in *active,* rather than passive, roles. Finazzo (1997, p.147) provides some questions to ask about multicultural literature:

- *Does the story include real and authentic characters?*
- *Are the actions of the characters true to life and not stereotypical?*
- *Are different cultures portrayed in a positive fashion?*
- *Within the story, do the characters develop and grow in acceptable ways?*
- *Does the story increase understanding and acceptance?*
- *Does the story help members of the portrayed minority feel greater pride in their own background?*
- *Does the book appropriately reflect the speech of the people featured?*
- *Does the style of the illustrator complement the text and enhance the story?*
- *Do the illustrations reflect an authentic portrayal of physical features and other details?*
- *What experiences have the author and illustrator had to prepare them for the book?*
- *What is the copyright date of the book and does that affect the accuracy and authenticity of the story? (We have to accept that various biases in representing history are common at particular periods in time, as in* The Adventures of Huckleberry Finn *and* Little Black Sambo.*)*
- *Have any reviews of the book been issued by various minority groups representing ethnicity, age, gender, or education?*
- *Does the book encourage children to become more socially conscious?*

There are important warnings to be heeded when working with multicultural literature in classrooms. People from visible minority groups should not be expected to respond to multicultural literature as "representatives" of their culture. Such an expectation is demeaning and detracts from their responses as individual readers with unique histories; it also assumes that the individual is negatively "different" and not fully integrated into Canadian society and culture. Recently, a group of graduate students exploring a selection of multicultural books came across one book with Chinese characters across the front page. One of the students turned to Tammy, who is of Chinese ancestry, and asked her what the characters meant. Tammy laughed (albeit nervously) and said, "I don't know. It was my grandparents who came from China, not me." As the conversation went on, Tammy explained that although she is proud of her Chinese heritage, it is not something she frequently speaks about in public. In the past, her heritage has caused her embarrassment, and she is aware that much of the traditional culture of her family has been lost with her parents' generation. In school, Tammy wanted to be Canadian, not Chinese, and she resisted her parents' and grandparents' attempts to continue their Chinese cultural ways. Tammy now feels more comfortable with her ethnic background, but she still has embarrassing moments when she wishes she did not look different from the white Canadians around her, especially when multiculturalism is being discussed.

A second cautionary point is that mainstream Canadians can easily offend a cultural group by using its literature in a classroom and discussing it without appropriate background knowledge of the culture. Many Aboriginal Canadians have mentioned that they feel their culture is demeaned in schools and universities through a kind of "exploitation." Situations where teachers speak as "experts" on a culture, based almost solely on what they have read, are inappropriate and can undermine the cultural values of a particular group. A third point is that multicultural literature should not be used in a classroom simply because children from a particular cultural or ethnic group are present in that classroom. This is a form of discrimination because it singles out those individuals and categorizes them as representatives of a larger group. (This point relates to Tammy's experiences noted above.) Multicultural literature should be selected on the grounds that all children have a responsibility to learn about a wide range of cultural and social groups; it should be part of the program of studies in every classroom, regardless of the social and cultural composition of each individual room.

Finally, what we deem relevant and appropriate will change through time. We must continue to make room for new materials and be willing to let go of others, and our multicultural selections are part of this dynamic process. One further word of caution: we can continue to value mainstream literature and not fall into the trap of making "white" literature the "bad guy." We do not want children to feel unusual, different, or guilty because they are white, have two parents of different sexes, and live according to more conventionally mainstream values.

Feelings of guilt and anger can be evoked in readers when they encounter such books as *The Eternal Spring of Mr. Ito* (Garrigue, 1985), a book that highlights the injustice of oppressing and incarcerating specific ethnic groups during times of war and unrest. Children may be angry at their parents or grandparents (or at other children in their own classrooms), who may be perceived as racist in light of the new reading experience. Similar emotions can be evoked when children encounter verbal "gay bashing," either in their own home, in the home of a friend, or on the playground. Children who have a friend with a gay parent may find that they hold attitudes quite different from their parents. When multicultural literature (which includes issues of sexual orientation, alternative lifestyles, and gender) is used in classrooms, children must have the opportunity to talk in a safe environment about the literature and how it makes them feel. Children need to feel emotionally and psychologically safe and secure when they share their thoughts and feelings, especially when they encounter reading situations that conflict directly with deeply held family values and attitudes.

Student teachers, immersed in the fairly liberal culture of a university or college, may assume that most people are open-minded and free-thinking. When they work with powerful children's books in classrooms, they need to proceed cautiously and be aware of the deep internal conflict that challenging ideas (especially those that contradict the parents' teachings) can raise for students. Children not only depend on their parents, but are profoundly influenced by family values and attitudes. They often cannot risk their parents' disapproval or anger by voicing thoughts that contradict their family values. At the same time, all children deserve the opportunity to read the best literature and have the best learning experiences possible. If parents or children strongly object to a book being read in the classroom, those particular children have the right *not* to read it and to be provided with an alternative. Offering readers a variety of reading materials and allowing them to choose freely (or with gentle guidance) can help this situation enormously.

It is unfair to insist that all children read the same literature and unreasonable to assume that all children will respond in the same way. This discussion also relates to our earlier comments on censorship and parental expectations (see Chapter 1).

Books by Aboriginal Canadians

Many Aboriginal Canadian authors and illustrators publish material for children. It is important that these books are integrated into school and classroom collections and into our instructional work with children. Heather Blair (1994) maintains that central to addressing the needs of all Canadians is the idea that teachers and students hold knowledge collectively. Through interaction in oral and written modes, further knowledge can be negotiated; from this interaction will come a sharing of knowledge, power, decision-making, and voice. Having one's voice heard is an acknowledgement of one's knowledge, says Blair; thus we must honour the life experiences that Aboriginal people bring to the classroom. We cannot ignore the experiences that Aboriginal children have outside school and outside white culture. Many Canadian Aboriginal children learn stories from their elders, attend sweat ceremonies, and go through other rituals important in their lives and in their identities, yet they do not usually see aspects of *their* culture in school. They do not see their artwork on the walls, their books on the shelves, their leaders' names in the curriculum. Schools can show respect for Aboriginal culture, valuing the earth, the ancestors, and the everyday lives of Aboriginal people; schools can show all students that Aboriginal voices *are* heard. One way to address some of these issues is by having Aboriginal literature present in classrooms.

Harpoon of the Hunter (Markoosie, 1970) was the first piece of Inuit fiction to be published in English. Since then, many excellent Aboriginal writers and illustrators have published their work in both Canada and the United States. Books written and illustrated by Aboriginal people are generally very different from books *about* Aboriginal peoples. Stories by Aboriginal authors generally embody the values of the individual tribes, and they tend to relate their spirituality in subtle, holistic ways. As Blair notes, "Spirituality is an all-encompassing, life-long, private, sacred experience ...not flaunted before the reader" (1982, p.221). A common theme in Aboriginal texts is the need for Aboriginal people to learn more about themselves; non-Aboriginal authors tend to focus on non-Aboriginals learning from Aboriginal people. As a result, some books by non-Aboriginal writers deal awkwardly and insensitively with spirituality.

Aboriginal Canadian authors and illustrators creating works for children include George Littlechild, Leo Yerxa, C.J. Taylor, Michael Arvaarluk Kusugak, Thomas King, and Jordan Wheeler. Wheeler's short stories for elementary-age children are superbly crafted and immensely enjoyable. His work can be found in *Achimoona* (Campbell, 1985) and *Adventure on Thunder Island* (King & Wheeler, 1991). Leo Yerxa's book, *Last Leaf First Snowflake to Fall* (1993), won the Amelia Frances Howard-Gibbon Award from the Canadian Library Association in 1994. The artwork in this book is exceptional.

The visual elements of culturally diverse books are extremely important, especially in a picture book. Michael Arvaarluk Kusugak's *Northern Lights: The Soccer Trails* (1993) is illustrated by Vladyana Krykorka. This book, as with the other books by this writer/illustrator team, embodies the life and spirit of the Inuit people of northern Canada. Each double-page spread consists of a full-page illustration on one side and the text, adorned with beadwork, on the other. The children's toys, the dogs, and the landscapes are lovingly depicted by Krykorka, capturing the tones of the Arctic. The illustrations perfectly complement the text, which recreates the rhythm of the traditional storyteller. Each page is a rich aesthetic experience that captures the unique flavour of Inuit culture. *Hide and Sneak* (1992), by the same pair, also captures the traditional culture and way of life in the Arctic. The book contains illustrations and Inuit script opposite each page of English text. It is a joyful celebration of the mythology of Inuit culture, and the book is a feast for the eyes in its energy and traditional symbolism.

MICHAEL ARVAARLUK KUSUGAK

Michael Arvaarluk Kusugak was born in 1948 at Cape Fullerton, on Hudson Bay, NWT. He spent the first 11 years of his life in Repulse Bay, a small town 500 km north of Cape Fullerton. Michael's family travelled by dogteam, living in igloos in the winter and tents in the summer. He spoke only Inuktitut, and, as there were no print materials available for children in Inuktitut, Michael did little reading. He did, however, hear many stories, for storytelling was a great tradition of the Inuit. It was his grandmother who made the greatest impression on him, telling him stories every night before he fell asleep. It was not until Michael was seven, when he was taken by plane to residential school in Chesterfield Inlet, that he learned English.

Michael found it very hard to be away from his parents, especially at the age of seven, and his memories of that first year are mostly of his tears and unhappiness. The second year the plane came for him, Michael hid in the hills and did not attend school. It was at school, however, that Michael learned to read from the school's reading series and he clearly remembers "Fun with Dick and Jane." He describes the books as "hideous things. I don't think anybody ever fell in love with those." Michael recalls that it was hard to make friends and much easier to sit and write. He later attended schools in Rankin Inlet, Yellowknife, Churchill, and Saskatoon, and was one of the first Inuit from the eastern Arctic to graduate from high school. As an adult, Michael spent fifteen years working for the government of the Northwest Territories in various positions, most recently as Director of Community Programs for Arctic College. He also served on the Library Board in Rankin Inlet.

Although he enjoyed writing, it wasn't until a visit from Robert Munsch during Canadian Children's Book Week that Michael decided he would try his hand at stories for children. Michael found himself telling Munsch many traditional legends, and Munsch suggested that Michael write them down. The result was Michael's first book, written jointly with Robert Munsch, *A Promise is a Promise* (1988). Michael's second book, *Baseball Bats for Christmas* (1990), has become a firm favorite with readers, and *Northern Lights: The Soccer Trails* (1993) won the Ruth Schwartz Children's Book Award. *My Arctic 1 2 3* (1996) is a picture counting book in which beginning readers are introduced to the animals, landscape, and people of the Arctic.

Although Michael likes to write about his Inuit experiences, he writes in English because the Inuktitut audience is very small and he wants to reach a wider Canadian readership. Michael lives with his family in Rankin Inlet, enjoying hunting, fishing, playing string games, and travelling to their cabin high on a hill overlooking Hudson Bay. Michael says, "I want to teach everything I know about how to live here, and write about everything kids like to do."

George Littlechild's book *This Land is My Land* (1993) is a particularly stunning introduction to Cree literature, with personal stories about Littlechild's family members and ancestors. The short narratives are unforgettable in their intensity and poignancy. Littlechild writes and paints about his experiences in boarding school and recalls stories, many of them tragic, of family members. He speaks excitedly about his first visit to New York City and describes the development of his artwork. The book ends optimistically with Littlechild discussing the current revival of Aboriginal culture and traditions, and emphasizes the pride he feels in his Cree ancestry.

Two Pairs of Shoes by Esther Sanderson (1990) is a picture story book about two special gifts Maggie receives for her eighth birthday. Maggie's mother gives her a pair of shiny black patent-leather shoes, a gift Maggie has been hoping for. When Maggie excitedly runs to her *kokum*'s (grandmother's) house to show her the gift, she finds that her *kokum* also has a special gift for her: a pair of hand-made beaded moccasins. As her *kokum* feels the shiny patent-leather shoes with her fingers, Maggie remembers that her *kokum* is blind, and she marvels at the fine beadwork her *kokum* can still create. Grandmother takes Maggie on her lap and tells her, "From now on you must remember when and how to wear each pair." The author has dedicated the book to "all children who walk in two pairs of shoes."

A further selection of fiction by Aboriginal Canadian authors and illustrators can be found at the end of this chapter.

Aboriginal-Language and Bilingual Books

In the past, many Aboriginal children attended boarding schools and were taken away from their homes and families in an effort to promote Christianity, European values, and the English language. For many Aboriginal people, the loss of their first language has equated with the loss of their culture.

In order that Aboriginal languages and cultures be maintained and respected, Aboriginal-language programs have been established in schools and community facilities by cultural and intercultural organizations—for example, programs in Cree and Inuktitut. These programs are flourishing, and it is not uncommon for children to spend part of a school day or part of the weekend learning the language and culture of their parents or grandparents. The programs strive to maintain pride and interest in Aboriginal languages and to promote respect for them, in the hopes of enabling children to feel proud of their ethnic and cultural heritage.

Many Canadian books written in Aboriginal languages and in bilingual editions have been created and published by local school districts and cultural centres. Several independent publishers also produce such materials, most notably Fifth House Publishing in Calgary. In addition, a few works from foreign countries (such as Denmark) have been translated into Aboriginal Canadian languages.

Freda Ahenakew has translated and edited a number of Cree stories that were originally told by Cree-speaking students and elders. Two of them are published as *How the Mouse Got Brown Teeth* (1988) and *How the Birch Tree Got Its Stripes* (1988); Fifth House published separate editions of the stories in English and Cree. Both books retell traditional Cree legends, beautifully illustrated by George Littlechild. *Two Little Girls Lost in the Bush* (1991) is told by Glecia Bear and translated by Freda Ahenakew. This book contains one story, the original text of which is part of a larger collection of women's life experiences (part of the Cree Language Project at the University of Manitoba). The voice of the original storyteller is fully present as she retells the events of one Sunday during her childhood when she and her sister became lost while taking care of a cow and new calf. The compelling story and authentic voice make this a gentle and reassuring reading experience, full of love and demonstrating the community's devotion to the girls. This book, illustrated by Jerry Whitehead, is also published by Fifth House. Rather than separate editions in English and Cree, this book was published in a split-page format, with the top part of the page in Cree and the lower part in English.

Another book with a split-page format (Cree syllabics/English) is *The Legend of Big Bear, Little Bear and the Stars* by Judy Bear (1979), illustrated by Larry Okanee and translated by Ernest Bonaise. It was published by the Saskatchewan Indian Cultural College and is a stunningly illustrated traditional story. Other books in this series include *The Fur Coat* by Rosa Whitstone (1979), *What Is It Like to be an Indian?* by Nellie Sokwaypnace (1979), *Child of Two Worlds* by Pauline Inglehart (1979), and *Our Four Seasons* by Glenda Bird (1979). All of these books are published with Cree syllabics and English in one edition. Other books, such as *Murdo's Story* by Murdo Scribe (1988), are printed in separate English and Cree (roman orthography) editions. One of the Saskatchewan Indian Cultural College's earliest bilingual books was *John Goes Hunting: A Chipewyan Story and Language Lessons* by Margaret Reynolds and Ben Garr (1973).

Byron and His Balloon: An English-Chipewyan Counting Book (La Loche Library Board, 1984), created by "The Children of La Loche and Friends," is a particularly interesting book. Lynn Atkins, who was a grade one teacher in La Loche, Saskatchewan in 1980, invited her students to paint pictures depicting their daily lives. The pictures were eventually put together in the form of a counting book with the help of native artist Gerald McMaster. McMaster painted Byron and his balloon as the page-by-page link for the book. The English text was developed by David May, and the Chipewyan translation was completed by George Montgrand and Mary Jane Kasyon. *Byron Through the Seasons: A Dene-English Story Book* (La Loche Library Board, 1990) is another book in English and Chipewyan produced by the students and teachers of La Loche. The story is narrated by Grandfather Jonas and imagined by his grandson, Byron. As Grandfather tells the story, Byron takes a symbolic journey with his grandfather through the four seasons of the year. The illustrations were completed entirely by the children at the school. Supplementary information at the end of the book provides background details on the illustrations and the dialogue.

In the far north, many books are published in Inuktitut. As with Cree and Chipewyan-language books, however, some are published in syllabics and some in roman orthography. Most books are produced by the Baffin Divisional Board of Education in Iqaluit and are reproduced by other boards of education such as Kitikmeot Board of Education in Coppermine. There are many different dialects of Inuktitut, and this makes the standardization of printed material difficult. Schools frequently tape over the printed text and add their own regional dialect to the books. The Baffin Divisional Board of Education currently lists over 200 books available in Inuktitut; only a few of them are available in Inuktitut/English editions. Two of them are *Someone Smaller than Me* (Cooper, 1993) and *The Killer Whale and the Walrus* (MacDonald, 1994).

Someone Smaller than Me is written by Jane Cooper (1993), a teacher with the Baffin Regional Board of Education, translated by Charlie Lucassie, and illustrated by Annie Padlo. The book is written in Inuktitut syllabics with a translation at the back in both roman orthography and English. *The Killer Whale and the Walrus* (MacDonald, 1994) is a tiny book (about 15 x 10 cm) written in English and Inuktitut syllabics; the text is translated by Amelia Angilirq. One half of the book is the English version; the other half (turned upside down) is the Inuktitut version. Lucy MacDonald wrote and illustrated the fable while she was in grade nine at Ataguttaaluk School in Igloolik. She won the Great Canadian Fable Contest with the story in 1990.

Books published only in Inuktitut include *Rocks Can Have Babies* by Monica Ittusardjuat (1990), a book in syllabics for early readers, and *Tiguyauyuq* by Rosemarie Meyok (1994), written in roman orthography. Other titles include *Poor Old Hungry Polar Bear* by Jeela Aqqiarruq (1990), in syllabics,

Hituaqattaqta! by Annie Ningeok, Enosiq Ejetsiak, and Michael Ipeelee

and *Hituaqattaqta!* by Annie Ningeok, Enosiq Ejetsiak, and Michael Ipeelee (1995), which has a split-page format with syllabics and roman orthography side by side. All of these books are illustrated in full colour with content relevant to children who live in northern Canada. The books can be obtained from the Baffin Divisional Board of Education in Iqaluit, Nunavut.

One early series of books, originally from Denmark, was produced for children in Greenland. A Canadian edition was developed in English in 1981 (translated by Catherine Maggs), and an Inuktitut edition in both syllabic and romanized scripts was produced in 1983 (translated by Sadie Hill). All editions are illustrated in colour by Keld Hansen. The books give a historical depiction of life in the north about three hundred years ago. *Salik and His Father* (Hansen and Maggs, 1981) tells the story of a twelve-year-old boy and his traditional Inuit life, including the hunting and fishing in which he participates. A list of terms is located at the back of the book, along with illustrations to help children understand such things as harpoons, tools, the winter house, and oil lamps.

Transcultural Literature

One of the earliest transcultural books in North America was *The Story of Little Black Sambo* (Bannerman, 1899), set in India but with illustrations depicting black characters. Bannerman's book has received much criticism for its racial stereotyping, for "intentionally or not, Little Black Sambo reinforced the idea of white supremacy through illustrations exaggerating African physiognomy and a name, Sambo, that had been used negatively for blacks since the early seventeenth century" (Lester, 1996, end notes). It is, however, a delightful story that has been retold in more than fifty versions and that essentially transcends its stereotypes. The story must be accepted within its historical context. Bannerman was a British woman living in India who wrote and illustrated the original book for her own daughters. The story has recently been published in two new editions. *The Story of Little Babaji* (Bannerman & Marcellino, 1996) contains the original text, with illustrations by Fred Marcellino, but gives the central characters authentic Indian names. The illustrations place the story clearly in India. *Sam and the Tigers,* written in a southern black storytelling style by Julius Lester and illustrated by Jerry Pinkney (1996), depicts black characters, but the fantasy setting (Sam-sam-samara) removes it from any specific geographic location. In a foreword to the book, Pinkney comments that Sambo is the only picture book depicting a black child that he remembers from his childhood. Research and collaboration with Lester and others enabled Pinkney to find his own interpretation of the story of the young black child who could outwit tigers. *The Five Chinese Brothers* (Bishop, 1938) is another story, frequently retold, that has been accused of promoting the stereotype that all Chinese people look alike. The story is, in fact, a Chinese folktale, and, again, must be accepted within the context of the time in which it was written. A more recent rendition by Margaret Mahy (*The Seven Chinese Brothers*, 1990, illustrated by Jean and Mou-Sien Tseng) reduces the perceived stereotyping and creates a more delightful and racially acceptable interpretation for the turn of the millennium.

Pratt and Beaty (1999, pp.13-15) propose guidelines for selecting appropriate transcultural literature for classroom use. Their guidelines suggest that teachers establish the following information:

- *The book is set in, and the major characters are from, a society and cultural region that differs from that of the readers;*
- *The plot and theme provide insight into another society and culture;*
- *The author/illustrator is well versed in the society and cultural region portrayed in the book;*
- *The physical aspects of the society and culture are presented realistically (not sensationally or stereotypically) and in ways that avoid value judgements;*
- *The story is told from the point of view of a person who is from that region, not a naïve visitor to the region;*
- *Illustrations are used to convey accurate depictions of dwellings, workplaces, outdoor scenes, and events;*
- *The stature, skin colour, and facial features of the people are realistic and typical for that culture;*
- *The main and supporting characters are distinct individuals rather than stereotypical caricatures;*
- *Characters are described in non-pejorative terms;*
- *There is a diverse and authentic repertoire of social relationships, including a variety of economic, social, and behavioral activities;*
- *Positive role models are presented;*
- *Characters solve problems, make decisions, and act successfully without the paternalistic help of someone from another culture;*
- *The reader does not have to be from the culture or society depicted to understand or appreciate the theme;*
- *The reader does not need prior knowledge of the culture or region to benefit from reading the book;*
- *The author uses words that people from the region commonly use;*
- *Words foreign to the reader are defined and accompanied by their pronunciations; and,*
- *The book has been reviewed by others.*

It is imperative that, in transcultural literature, the details of the setting are accurate and authentic. Tololwa Mollel is a Canadian writer and storyteller well known for his retellings of traditional African stories. His best-known book is probably his first, *The Orphan Boy* (1990), illustrated by Paul Morin. In this book, text and illustrations work together to create the atmosphere and setting of Africa. The book is based on a Masai legend about the planet Venus, and tells the story of an orphan boy, Kileken, who comes to live with an old man, bringing him good fortune. The old man cannot resist knowing the secret of the orphan boy's success, and so he follows the boy one morning, discovering the secret and, at the same time, destroying its power. This theme is found all around the world in the folk tales of various regions, but this telling is an exceptionally powerful one, enhanced by Morin's illustrations. Morin went to Africa to prepare to work on this book and, in doing so, captured the vastness of the African sky, the darkness of the African night, and the heat of the African sun. The details found in the faces, clothing, huts, plants, and animals make this book a stunning visual experience. The combination of full-colour illustrations and black-and-white drawings adds to the authenticity of the setting. It is clear that both storyteller and illustrator know their subject well. This thoughtful telling reflects Mollel's Tanzanian heritage and displays his gift and power as a storyteller.

Another book noteworthy for its visual impact is *The Nutmeg Princess* (1992), written by Richardo Keens-Douglas and illustrated by Annouchka Galouchko. This was Keens-Douglas' first book. Born in Grenada, he now lives in Canada where he promotes West Indian culture through his plays and storytelling (sometimes on national radio). Galouchko spent many years in Egypt and Iran as a child, and her artwork, most of it in gouache (a type of water-based paint—a modern "egg tempera"), has

TOLOLWA MOLLEL

Tololwa Mollel was born in Arusha, Tanzania, where he grew up on his grandparents' coffee farm not far from Mount Kilimanjaro. For him, storytelling was a way of life. Tololwa describes his grandfather as a man who "liked to eat words [and so] inevitably stories came out." Tololwa heard many stories and myths from both of his grandparents and so began his own life as a storyteller. He recounts that his grandfather wanted him to have as much schooling as possible because he himself had far less schooling than was available to his grandson. As a result, when Tololwa returned from school each day, he would tell his grandfather much of the day's events. Tololwa went on to study literature and theatre at university in Tanzania, and when he came to Canada in 1976 to earn a Master's degree in drama, he became aware of the richness of his childhood. On returning to Tanzania, he taught theatre at the University of Dar es Salaam, where he also acted, directed, and continued his storytelling. The turning point came for Tololwa when his first child was old enough to be read to. Tololwa saw that through simple, clear language and storytelling techniques, he could increase his son's appreciation of stories. He came to understand the subtleties of writing for young children—the challenge of creating clear prose which children wanted to hear. Tololwa thus began writing stories for children and found that he enjoyed it.

In 1986, Tololwa and his family returned to Edmonton, Alberta, and his writing career began in earnest. He believes that his work in children's theatre, especially as a director, influenced his storytelling; he also feels that his prose should be appropriate for reading aloud. Tololwa travels to schools and libraries across Canada, speaking and reading to both child and adult audiences. His gift as a storyteller is immediately noticeable when Tololwa begins to tell a story. His audience leans forward, listens in rapt attention, and joins in the refrains and responses with him. Children become totally engaged and engrossed in the world of Tololwa's stories. His first book, *The Orphan Boy* (1990), illustrated by Paul Morin, won the Governor General's Award, and *Big Boy* (1995) won the R. Ross Annett Award from the Alberta writing community. Tololwa hopes that through reading and hearing his books, children will understand that although people live differently, they like and dislike the same things, have the same fears (such as a fear of the dark), and experience the same joys.

the flavour of exotic worlds. *The Nutmeg Princess* retells a legend from Grenada (the Isle of Spice) in which two young friends climb a mountain in search of the mythic Nutmeg Princess. After Petal rescues Aglo from drowning in the mountain lake, the Nutmeg Princess tells the children, "Take that gift of caring out into the world. Go now, follow your dreams, and if you believe in yourselves, all things are possible." The children discover that the old lady who first told them the story of the Nutmeg Princess has disappeared, but, knowing the children will tend the fruit and nutmeg trees with care, she has left them her entire estate. The illustrations in the book are in rich hues which emphasize the beauty of the West Indies, including the plant and animal life, as well as the richness of the culture. It is a book of great visual contrast to *Northern Lights: The Soccer Trails* (Kusugak, 1993). When placed side-by-side, the stunning difference in visual impact of the two books is clearly evident; the contrast of the two cultural groups and the geographical locations is felt as much as seen.

Two highly successful and well-written transcultural books, from the US and Britain respectively, are *Morning Girl* by Michael Dorris (1992) and *Amazing Grace* by Mary Hoffman (1991). *Morning Girl,* set in the Bahamas in 1492, tells the story of a twelve-year-old Taino Indian girl and her younger brother, who live on one of the islands in a vibrant community, deeply bound by respect, love, humour, tradition, and shared imagination. The book ends on the day Morning Girl goes for a swim and sees a "fat canoe" packed with oddly dressed strangers rowing towards shore. Morning Girl is polite in spite of the fact that she wants to laugh at the oddity of the canoe's occupants, and she invites the strangers ashore. Michael Dorris, a member of the Modoc tribe, is trained as an anthropologist. He is well known for his adult books, most notably *A Yellow Raft in Blue Water* (1987). In *Morning Girl,* Dorris begins to lift the veil of anonymity that has obscured the fifteenth century Aboriginal Americans who first encountered and welcomed Christopher Columbus. (*Encounter* (1992), a picture book by Jane Yolen, successfully explores this same theme.)

Amazing Grace is set in London, England and involves Grace, her mother, and her grandmother, who grew up in Trinidad. Grace loves stories, whether they are movies, television shows, stories read at school, or stories told by her Nana at home. When her teacher decides the class will perform the play *Peter Pan,* Grace has no doubt which role she wants for herself. But Raj tells her she can't be Peter Pan because she is a girl, and Natalie tells her she can't be Peter Pan because she's black. Grace shares her doubts with her family, so her grandmother takes her to see a ballet in which the leading role is danced by a black ballerina from Trinidad. Nana tells Grace she can be anything she wants to be if she puts her mind to it. This is a beautiful picture story book, with sensitive and gentle illustrations by Caroline Binch to match the text. Binch has travelled widely during her years as an illustrator, photographer, and painter, and spent much time in the Caribbean. Hoffman's other books include *My Grandma Has Black Hair* (1988).

A further selection of transcultural literature worthy of exploration follows at the end of this chapter.

A SELECTION OF AUSTRALIAN ABORIGINAL CHILDREN'S LITERATURE

Although many Australian books are available in Canada, it is difficult to obtain copies of Australian books that depict Aboriginal Australians as central characters. Since the circumstances and histories of Aboriginal Canadians and Aboriginal Australians are somewhat similar, the lack of books in Canada is surprising. However, we would like to mention a few Australian books that might be of interest to Canadian children and their teachers.

One of the first books to depict Aboriginal history in Australia and to have an Aboriginal central character was Nan Chauncy's novel *Tangara* (1960).

Although the book is somewhat dated in its setting and context (the protagonist attends boarding school, and the attitudes and values clearly reflect the 1950s), it remains an appealing story. It is a time-slip novel involving Lexie, a seven-year-old white girl. Merrina, a mysterious Aboriginal girl, appears one day while Lexie is playing at the edge of a hidden valley near a relative's farm in Tasmania. Lexie meets Merrina almost daily and learns some of her ways as well as snatches of her language. Merrina finally takes Lexie through a cleft in the rock and introduces her to the "mothers" of her community, a community that disappeared many years previously. Seven years later, Lexie meets Merrina again, this time when helping to rescue Lexie's brother from a hiking accident in the same valley. Lexie is finally able to make sense of the stories she has heard of the Aboriginal people and the events she witnessed during her time with Merrina, making her uncomfortably aware of the role of white people in the demise of the native population, including her unusual friend. Chauncy's setting allows readers to explore a fragment of Aboriginal history. It is sufficient to create an interest in the topic and to awaken awareness of the current issues surrounding the Aboriginal people; the parallel with Canadian history cannot be ignored.

Ian Abdulla's picture book *Tucker* (1994) is based on his memories of a childhood spent in the Murray River basin of South Australia in the 1950s. Abdulla recalls incidents from his childhood during times of great economic hardship. It was a time when the policy of assimilation in race relations was at its height in Australia, and Aboriginal people found it difficult to gain employment anywhere. The focus of the book is on food, the "tucker" of the title. Abdulla depicts some of the more traditional and delightful foodstuffs his family ate and also the hunting and fishing expeditions that provided the food. He describes looking for *quondongs* (wild peaches), hunting *kungari* (swans), and fishing for *pondi* (Murray cod). Abdulla's stories express a sense of community and the underlying values of sharing and co-operation integral to that community. The style of his paintings can be described as "naïve," in that they reflect his lack of training in traditional Western techniques: all are bold and fresh. The foreword comments that the book is "an inspiring affirmation of the quality of life in the face of material hardship." In 1991, Abdulla was named South Australian Aboriginal Artist of the Year. He has had numerous solo shows and many joint exhibitions, and his work is represented in the National Gallery of Australia.

Stan Breedon and Belinda Wright have created a beautiful photodocumentary in *Growing Up in Kakadu, Australia* (1995). Neither of the duo is Aboriginal, but they have put together an excellent book on Kakadu National Park (in the Northern Territory) and the Gagudju people, the Aboriginal people who live there. The book is intended for primary-school children, but it can be enjoyed by students from kindergarten to grade six.

Aboriginal artist Arone Raymond Meeks has illustrated and retold the traditional story of *Enora and the Black Crane* (1991), a story of creation and the loss of innocence. Meeks' rich cultural heritage is evident in the illustrations, which evoke images of lush rain forest, tropical fruits, and native birds; the illustrations are in a traditional Aboriginal style, using ochre, black, and white as the predominant colours.

Idjhil, by Helen Bell (1996), is a picture book that tells the story of a Western Australian Aboriginal boy who, at age nine, is taken from his family during the 1940s. After British settlement of the Swan valley in the nineteenth century, the Aboriginal Nyungar people were pushed off their land; their lifestyles changed dramatically as a result. The 1905 Aborigines Act made provision for persons of Aboriginal descent to be placed on settlements. Throughout the first half of the twentieth century, families were split up and children removed to mission homes and schools. Family groups were destroyed, and the Nyungar people and their culture almost disappeared. Bell's fictional account is based on the memories of a number of people who became her "informants." The story does not end on a note of sadness, however, as Bell recounts how Idjhil maintained his traditional beliefs and spirituality and eventually became an elder of his clan. Bell's illustrations are poignant and memorable.

The Burnt Stick (1994), a short novel written by Anthony Hill and illustrated by Mark Sofilas, won numerous awards in Australia in 1995 including the Australian Christian Literature Award. Until well into the 1960s, it was the practice of the authorities to take children of mixed parentage away from their mothers and place them in institutions or with foster parents; these children are frequently referred to as "stolen children." *The Burnt Stick* tells the story of one such child, John Jagamarra, who never knew his white stockman father. When his mother hears that the Big White Man from Welfare is coming to take John away, she uses ash from a burnt stick to darken his skin and deceive the Welfare Man about her son's parentage. Although the trick works on two different occasions, the men eventually take John away from his mother and he is raised, from the age of five onwards, by the fathers at a mission. John never sees his mother again. When, in later years, he returns to the sheep station and the Aboriginal camp of his early childhood, accompanied by his own son, he finds the place deserted. There is no one to tell him where the group moved to or where he might find them now. At the end of the book, John vows that he and his son will not rest until they have found his Aboriginal family and he is once again united with his people. As a symbol of this vow, he takes the ash from a burnt stick and darkens the skin of his son.

Pilawuk (1996), a small book by Janeen Brian, is one of a series of three oral histories, a book project designed for use in elementary schools. Pilawuk was born in Darwin in 1955. Because she was from mixed parentage, she was separated from her family and placed in a mission on Melville Island. She was later moved to Adelaide to live with two white families, one after the other. In high school, Pilawuk became a boarder at Cabra College and eventually managed to locate her birth family. She was seventeen when she met her mother and sisters, who still spoke the Ngangiwumerri language. Today, Pilawuk describes herself as a mother, teacher, actor, and writer. This series of books is available in Canada through Vanwell Publishing in St. Catherines, Ontario.

Research has shown that storybook reading, accompanied by discussion, can significantly improve a child's acceptance of difference (Wham, Barnhardt & Cook, 1996). Knowing this, individual teachers must select multicultural books for their students, allowing time to discuss the issues that arise from them. We know that children bring all of their experiences to any reading event; these experiences will frequently include feelings of fear, hostility, and curiosity. At the same time, most children are enormously accepting and trusting of others. The early years in preschool and the elementary grades are important in developing attitudes and values that are compatible with current expectations and circumstances of Canadian society.

The coming years will see rapid changes in Canada's population. Educators have a responsibility to ensure that all children are welcomed and treated with dignity and respect. Multicultural children's books can be used most effectively as avenues for coming to understand individual human stories and the universal emotions and themes they contain.

References

Banks, J. 1989. Integrating the curriculum with ethnic content: Approaches and guidelines. In *Multicultural Education: Issues and Perspectives.* J.A. Banks, ed. Boston: Allyn & Bacon.

———. 1994. *Multiethnic Education: Theory and Practice*. Boston: Allyn & Bacon.

Blair, H. 1994. Voice for indigenous youth: Literature for adolescents. In *If This Is Social Studies, Why Isn't It Boring?* Stephanie Steffey and Wendy Hood, eds. York, Maine: Stenhouse Publishers.

Blair, H. 1982. Canadian native peoples in adolescent literature. *Journal of Reading* 26(3), 217-221.

Cross, W. 1985. Black identity: Rediscovering the distinctions between personal identity and reference group orientations. In *Beginnings: The Social and Affective Development of Black Children.* M.B. Spencer, G.K. Brookins, and W.R. Allen, eds. Hillsdale, New Jersey: Erlbaum.

Dorris, M. 1987. *A Yellow Raft in Blue Water*. New York: Holt.

Finazzo, D. 1997. *All for the Children: Multicultural Essentials of Literature*. Albany: Delmar Publishing (ITP).

McGuire-Raskin, L. 1996. Multiculturalism in children's picture books: An analysis of insider vs. outsider texts. *Journal of Children's Literature* 22(1), 22-27.

Miller-Lachmann, L. 1992. *Our Family, Our Friends, Our World*. New Providence, New Jersey: R.R. Bowker.

Nieto, S. 1992. *Affirming Diversity*. New York: Longman.

Pratt, L. and Beaty, J.J. 1999. *Transcultural Children's Literature*. Columbus: Merrill (Prentice Hall).

Rudman, M. 1995. *Children's Literature: An Issues Approach*. White Plains, NY: Longman.

Spalding, D. 1996. *A Novel Study and Teacher's Guide for* Finders Keepers *by Andrea Spalding*. Pender Island, BC: Brandywine Enterprises Ltd.

Statistics Canada. 1997. *Daily News Report of the 1996 Census*. http://www.statcan.ca

Wham, M.A., J. Barnhardt, and G. Cook. 1996. Enhancing multicultural awareness through storybook reading experience. *Journal of Research and Development in Education* 30(1), 1-9.

Wynne-Jones, T. 1980. *Odd's End*. Toronto: McClelland & Stewart.

Zarrillo, J. 1994. *Multicultural Literature, Multicultural Teaching: Units for the Elementary Grades*. New York: Harcourt Brace College Publishers.

Professional Resources

Finazzo, D. 1997. *All For the Children: Multicultural Essentials of Literature*. Albany: Delmar Publishing (ITP). • This text addresses the most current issues in children's literature, especially cultural diversity and multiculturalism. The book defines, compares, and contrasts various genres of children's literature that can be integrated into the elementary school curriculum. The book includes lesson plans which are activity-based and student-centred. It is an excellent reference for teachers and is built upon a strong theoretical and research framework; unfortunately, most of the books cited are American publications. In spite of this shortcoming, it remains one of the best books available on multicultural children's literature.

Harris, V., ed. 1997. *Using Multiethnic Literature in the K-8 Classroom*. Norwood, Massachusetts: Christopher-Gordon Publishers, Inc. • Along with Finazzo's, this book is one of the best texts available on multiethnic literature. Contributors include Rudine Sims Bishop, Violet Harris, and Daniel Hade. The chapter titles are intriguing and indicative of the range of topics addressed: The Baby-Sitters Club and Cultural Diversity; Creating Good Books for Children: A Black Publisher's Perspective; and Native Americans in Children's Literature, for example. Unfortunately, this book focusses mainly on American titles, with a chapter on Puerto Rican stories as well as Asian Pacific American literature. Only a few Canadian titles are mentioned.

Pratt, L. and Beaty, J.J. 1999. *Transcultural Children's Literature*. Columbus: Merrill (Prentice Hall). • This text surveys children's books that feature culturally and ethnically different peoples living outside the United States. The introductory chapter provides a rationale for exploring transcultural literature in school and describes the relationship among multicultural education, book bonding, and scaffolding children's reading experiences. The authors provide a paradigm for assessing and comparing transcultural children's books in terms of their geographic, social, economic, and political elements. Chapters are included on literature about and from every region of the world, broken down into books from Canada, the Caribbean, Australia and the south Pacific, Eastern Europe, Western Europe, Asia, Africa, Central and South America, and the Middle East. A final chapter explores transcultural literature in the changing classroom.

A Selection of Canadian Multicultural Literature

Andrews, J. 1985. *Very Last First Time*. Toronto: Groundwood Books. (Modern Inuit)

Edmunds, Y. 1993. *Yuit*. Toronto: Napoleon Publishing. (Traditional Inuit)

Eyvindson, P. 1996. *Red Parka Mary*. Winnipeg: Pemmican Publications. (Modern aboriginal, friendships)

Garrigue, S. 1985. *The Eternal Spring of Mr. Ito*. Needham, Massachusetts: Silver Burdett Ginn. (Japanese Canadian internment during World War Two)

Gilman, P. 1992. *Something From Nothing*. Richmond Hill, Ontario: North Winds Press. (Jewish)

Matas, C. 1995. *The Primrose Path*. Winnepeg: Bain & Cox. (Jewish, sexual abuse)

McGugan, J. 1994. *Josepha*. Red Deer, Alberta: Red Deer College Press. (Immigrant to Canada, 1900)

Oberman, S. 1994. *The Always Prayer Shawl*. Honesdale, Pennsylvania: Boyds Mills Press. (Jewish)

Shaw-MacKinnon, M. 1996. *Tiktala*. Toronto: Stoddart Publishing Co. Ltd.

Smucker, B. 1977. *Underground to Canada*. Toronto: Clarke, Irwin. (Black slavery)

Spalding, A. 1995. *Finders Keepers*. Victoria: Beach Holme Publishing. (Aboriginal Canadian)

Takashima, S. 1971. *A Child in Prison Camp*. Montreal: Tundra Books. (Japanese Canadians in prison camps during World War Two)

Trottier, M. 1995. *The Tiny Kite of Eddie Wing*. Toronto: Stoddart. (Chinese Canadian)

Toten, T. 1995. *The Onlyhouse*. Red Deer, Alberta: Northern Lights Young Novels. (Croatian immigrant child in 1960s).

Truss, J. 1977. *A Very Small Rebellion*. Edmonton: J.M. Lebel Enterprises. (Aboriginal Canadian)

Umpherville, T. 1995. *The Spring Celebration*. Winnipeg: Pemmican. (Aboriginal).

Wallace, I. 1984. *Chin Chiang and the Dragon's Dance*. Toronto: Groundwood Books. (Chinese Canadian)

Waterton, B. 1978. *A Salmon for Simon*. Richmond Hill, Ontario: Scholatic-TAB Publications. (Aboriginal Canadian)

Wiseman, E. 1996. *A Place Not Home*. Toronto: Stoddart. (Refugee child from Hungary)

Yee, P. 1989. *Tales from Gold Mountain*. Toronto: Groundwood Books. (Chinese Canadian)

———. 1991. *Roses Sing on New Snow*. Toronto: Groundwood Books. (Chinese Canadian)

———. 1996. *Ghost Train*. Toronto: Groundwood. (Chinese Canadian)

A Selection of Canadian Transcultural Literature

Bell, W. 1997. *The Golden Disk*. Toronto: Doubleday Canada. (China).

Comissiong, K. 1997. *Mind Me Good Now*. Toronto: Annick Press. (Caribbean)

Keens-Douglas, R. 1992. *The Nutmeg Princess*. Toronto: Annick Press. (Traditional story from Grenada, Caribbean)

Little, J. 1972. *From Anna*. New York: Harper Trophy. (Immigrant from Germany).

Matas, C. 1987. *Lisa*. Toronto: Scholastic. (Jews in Denmark during World War Two)

Mollel, T. 1990. *The Orphan Boy*. Toronto: Oxford University Press. (African Maasi folk tale)

———. 1992. *A Promise to the Sun*. Toronto: Little, Brown & Co. (African folk tale)

Sacks, M. 1985. *Themba*. Toronto: Penguin Canada. (South Africa).

Santos, J. 1995. *Jack's New Power*. Toronto: Harper Collins Canada. (Caribbean).

Wolf, G. 1994. *Mala: A Women's Folktale*. Toronto: Annick Press. (Indian folktale)

Ye, T. 1997. *Three Monks, No Water*. Toronto: Annick Press. (Chinese folktale).

Zhang, S.N. 1995. *The Children of China: An Artist's Journey*. Montreal: Tundra Books. (Traditional Chinese)

Fiction by Aboriginal Canadian Authors and Illustrators

Bouchard, D. 1990. *The Elders Are Watching*. Illustrated by R.H. Vickers. Tofino: B.C.: Eagle Dancer Enterprises Ltd.

Campbell, M., ed. 1985. *Achimoona*. Saskatoon: Fifth House.

Clutesi, G. 1990. *Stand Tall, My Son*. Victoria: Newport Bay Publications.

King, E. and J. Wheeler. 1991. *Adventure on Thunder Island*. Toronto: James Lorimer and Co.

King, T. 1992. *A Coyote Columbus Story*. Toronto: Groundwood Books.

———. 1998. *Coyote Sings to the Moon*. Toronto: Groundwood Books.

Kusugak, Michael. 1990. *Baseball Bats for Christmas*. Illustrated by V. Krykorka. Toronto: Annick Press.

———. 1992. *Hide and Sneak*. Illustrated by V. Krykorka. Toronto: Annick Press.

Loewen, I. 1993. *My Kookum Called Today*. Winnipeg: Pemmican Publications.

McLellan, J. 1989. *The Birth of Nanabosho*. Winnipeg: Pemmican Publication.

Pachano, J. 1985. *The Changing Times: Baby William*. Chisabi, Quebec: James Bay Cree Cultural Education Centre.

Paul-Dene, S. 1992. *I Am the Eagle Free (Sky Song)*. Penticton, B.C.: Theytus Books.

Plain, F. 1993. *Amikoonse*. Winnipeg: Pemmican Publications.

Slipperjack, R. 1987. *Honour the Sun*. Winnipeg: Pemmican Publications.

Taylor, C.J. 1994. *Bones in the Basket*. Montreal: Tundra Books.

Waboose, J. 1997. *Morning on the Lake*. Toronto: Kids Can Press.

Weber-Pillwax, C. 1989. *Billy's World*. Edmonton: Reidmore.

American Books That Promote Understanding

Baylor, B. 1986. *I'm in Charge of Celebrations*. Illustrated by Peter Parnall. New York: Charles Scribner's Sons.

Bunting, E. 1992. *Summer Wheels*. San Diego: Voyager Books.

Curtis, C.P. 1996. *The Watsons Go to Birmingham — 1963*. New York: Delacourte.

Hamilton, V. 1993. *Cousins*. New York: Scholastic.

Hazen, B.S. 1997. *Digby*. New York: Harper Trophy.

Lisle, J.T. 1989. *Afternoon of the Elves*. New York: Orchard Books.

Martin, B., Jr. 1987. *Knots on a Counting Rope*. New York: Holt, Rinehart & Winston.

Paterson, K. 1988. *Park's Quest*. New York: Lodestar, Dutton.

Paulsen, G. 1993. *Nightjohn*. New York: Bantam Doubleday Dell Publishing Group, Inc.

Rylant, C. 1992. *Missing May*. New York: Orchard.

Spinelli, J. 1990. *Maniac Magee*. Boston: Little, Brown and Co.

Taylor, M. 1987. *The Friendship*. New York: Puffin Books.

CHAPTER SIX

NONFICTION LITERATURE

The objectives of this chapter are

- To understand children's interests in nonfiction books, both for pleasure and for information;
- To become acquainted with a range of high-quality nonfiction materials;
- To develop a practical understanding of criteria for selecting and assessing quality nonfiction books;
- To become familiar with a range of Canadian nonfiction materials, including award-winning books.

Understanding the Genre of Nonfiction

Nonfiction literature plays a major role in every elementary classroom, because this genre provides the resource material for most teaching across the entire curriculum. By reading about a topic from many sources and from a number of different perspectives, students are able to construct a fuller understanding of that topic. Each piece of information, each point of view, helps to create a broader picture in the mind of the student and provides the fertile ground for new meanings to develop—meaning, after all, resides in the individual learner.

Many children in the primary grades (and earlier) thoroughly enjoy reading nonfiction materials, and this genre caters to students' special interests, providing them with the resources they need to pursue their avocations. However, it is only recently that educators have recognized children's interest and pleasure in reading nonfiction materials and have begun to teach children how to read expository texts as well as narrative texts. A friend recently told Joyce that he rarely reads fiction: to him, it seems frivolous and a waste of time. But he is an avid reader of nonfiction material on a wide range of topics. This admission comes as less of a surprise to us since we began taking note of children's reading preferences in libraries and classrooms. Boys, in particular, express an interest in nonfiction as their first choice in reading material. Although we have tried to avoid gender stereotyping children's reading interests, it is hard to ignore the fact that many boys, even at the age of two and three years, prefer books about cars and trucks, machines, boats, and airplanes.

Jason is standing by the end-table in the living room, ready to go to bed. He is two-and-a-half years old and is intently scrutinizing a brochure that came with a Tonka toy he recently received. Jason examines the pictures of the

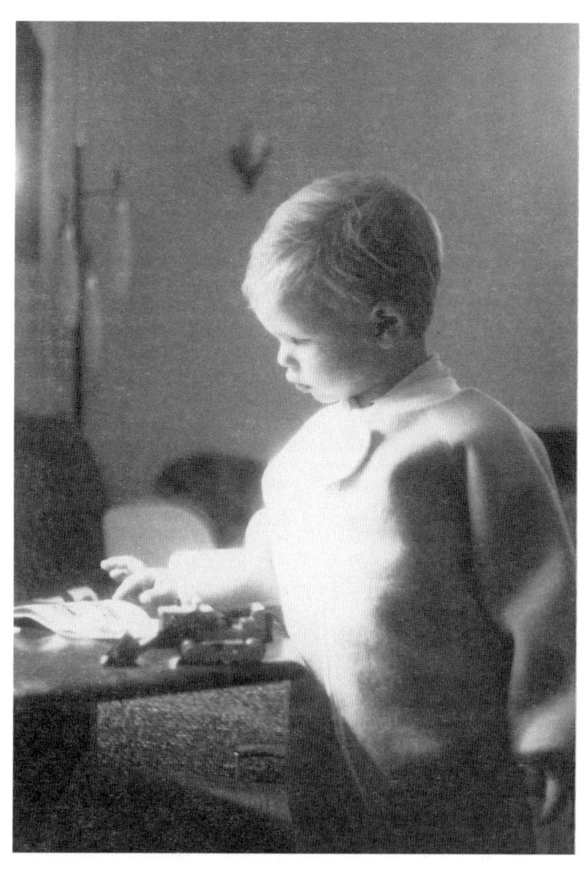

Jason explores one of his books

various toy machines that Tonka makes—a firetruck, digger, and front-end loader. Jason closes the brochure and picks up his Richard Scarry book, *Hop Aboard! Here We Go!* (1972). This is one of his favourite books, along with *Scuffy the Tugboat and His Adventures Down the River* (Crampton, 1955).

Doiron (1994) comments that "the primacy of fiction in our literacy programs" is being challenged, and Pappas (1991) maintains that a lack of exposure to nonfiction text translates into a lack of opportunity to write non-story compositions. Pappas believes that this situation leaves children unprepared for the expository writing requirements of secondary school. Clearly, children need both narrative and non-narrative reading and writing experiences. Today, children in the primary grades are required to write reports and projects using nonfiction resources. Educators must teach youngsters how to use a book's index, glossary, and table of contents, as well as how to browse through a book quickly, to see from the pictures and headings whether the book is going to be helpful or interesting.

NONFICTION BOOK AWARDS

Nonfiction material has greatly improved in quality and presentation over the last ten years. Many of the nonfiction materials still on library shelves from the 1970s and early 1980s look dull and uninviting compared to more recent publications. The explosion in technology—allowing for high-quality reproduction of photographs, maps, and other graphics and offering a more interesting and accessible page layout—has created a new age of nonfiction, especially for young readers. In recent years, a number of nonfiction books have won honours like the prestigious Newbery medal in the United States; in addition, many awards have been created specifically for nonfiction books. These awards include the Information Book Award, sponsored by the Children's Literature Round Tables of Canada; the Orbis Pictus Award for Outstanding Nonfiction for Children, established by the National Council of Teachers of English; the *Times Educational Supplement Information Book Awards;* and the Boston Globe-Horn Book Award, established jointly by the *Boston Globe* and *The Horn Book*. The designation of these awards marks the increasing recognition accorded nonfiction books, as well as a recognition of children's strong interest in informational materials; it also indicates that the quality of nonfiction materials has improved sufficiently to merit awards specifically for the genre.

The Canadian INFORMATION BOOK AWARD, sponsored by the Children's Literature Round Tables of Canada, recognizes an outstanding information book for children and young adults (ages five to fifteen) written by a Canadian citizen or landed immigrant (see Appendix A for a list of award-winners). All original

English-language nonfiction trade books are eligible for the award, with the exclusion of poetry, plays, folklore, and textbooks; at present, there is no French-language award. Criteria for the award include accuracy, clarity, imaginative approach, appropriateness of organization and format, and sensitivity to ethnocentric and gender bias. In 1996, for the first time, the award was given to the *book* rather than to the author alone, and the cash prize of $500 was shared between author and illustrator. A committee based in Vancouver sends out a selective list of about 25 titles that have been judged across Canada as the best in the previous year. The regional round-table organizations consider the list and send back their recommendations for five finalists. The winning book is announced in time for the Canadian Children's Book Week in November each year.

The ORBIS PICTUS AWARD FOR OUTSTANDING NONFICTION FOR CHILDREN was established in 1990 by the National Council of Teachers of English in the United States. The award was named in commemoration of a book published in 1657, *Orbis Pictus, or The World in Pictures* by Johann Comenius (Vardell, 1991), thought to be the first informational book written and published specifically for children. The selection criteria for this award include:

- *Accuracy: facts are current and complete; there is a balance of fact and theory; varying points of view are included; stereotypes are avoided; the author is appropriately qualified; the book offers appropriate scope and authenticity of detail.*
- *Design: attractive, readable; illustrations complement the text; placement of illustrative material is appropriate; complementary media, format, and typeface are appropriate.*
- *Organization: logical development and clear sequence; interrelationships are indicated; patterns are provided (e.g., general-to-specific, simple-to-complex).*
- *Style: interesting, stimulating writing; the author's enthusiasm for the subject is evident; curiosity and wonder are encouraged; appropriate terminology and rich language are used.*

The TIMES EDUCATIONAL SUPPLEMENT INFORMATION BOOK AWARDS were established in 1972 in London, England, by the *Times Educational Supplement*. The award honours distinction in content and presentation in nonfiction trade books originating in the United Kingdom or Commonwealth countries (which makes it open to Canadian nominations). One award is given in the junior category (up to age nine), and one in the senior category (ages ten to sixteen). A list of books that have won this award is presented in Appendix A.

Other nonfiction awards include the BOSTON GLOBE–HORN BOOK AWARD, which originated in 1967 for fictional text and illustration, and in 1976 for outstanding nonfiction. One award-winner and up to three honour books are chosen each year in each category. Nominated books must have been published in the United States. The National Science Teachers Association in the United States presents the OUTSTANDING SCIENCE TRADE BOOKS FOR CHILDREN award. Three criteria are used by the NSTA in judging books: accuracy, readability, and appropriateness of text, format, and illustrations—similar criteria to those used by the NCTE in judging the Orbis Pictus Award.

Criteria for Selecting Nonfiction Materials

A list of evaluation criteria for nonfiction books for children is presented below (based on a list compiled by Frances Smardo Dowd in Freeman & Person, 1992):

- *Format: books should have a clear and unambiguous format, with high-quality construction and a high degree of concreteness through maps, diagrams, charts, and other explanatory illustrations to accompany the print.*
- *Simplification of advanced topics: any simplification must maintain accuracy, but the*

content must be presented in such a way that young children can connect content to their own experiences.

- *Graphics and illustrations: a visual, colourful approach is necessary, with large photographs and clear diagrams that extend the text and clarify size relationships. Pages should be clear and uncluttered, and all photographs and graphics should be clearly labelled.*
- *Evidence of research: facts are not invented. To make this clear to children, data sources should be included in the book, as well as an indication of any current research activity being conducted in the field.*
- *Accuracy and authenticity: this can be satisfied partly through the qualifications and experience of the authors, which should be stated somewhere in the book. Further, the text should demonstrate a lack of omissions in information; avoidance of stereotypes and inclusion of diversity; generalizations supported by facts; clear distinctions made among fact, theory, and opinion; and the omission of both anthropomorphic and teleological explanations.*
- *Content/Perspective: books should contain adequate coverage, present different viewpoints, foster the use of scientific method and inquiry, and discuss the interrelationships among subjects.*
- *Styles: informational books should create a feeling of reader involvement, use vivid and interesting language, and convey a positive tone.*
- *Organization: content should be structured clearly and logically, with appropriate subheadings and reference aids (table of contents, index, bibliography, glossary, and appendix).*

The information available in all subject areas is growing rapidly. Keeping a nonfiction collection up to date is both a major challenge and a major expense. Books published on a topic ten or fifteen years ago are likely to have inaccurate, out-of-date content today. It is therefore important that nonfiction books be purchased for the school or classroom library with discrimination and with the aid of the available library selection tools (such as *Resource Links: Connecting Classrooms, Libraries & Canadian Learning Resources*, *The Canadian Book Review Annual*, *Canadian Children's Literature*, *Language Arts*, *The Reading Teacher* and *The Horn Book)*. Children must have access to current books, ones that have not sat on the library or classroom shelves for years without being reviewed. Since outdated books may spread misinformation, the onus is on teachers and librarians to evaluate the books in their nonfiction collections every few years and discard those books that are no longer of informational value.

The ACCURACY and AUTHENTICITY of material are probably the most difficult criteria for educators to assess. The first thing to look for in any nonfiction book is an indication from the authors that they either have the expertise themselves (as with Beatty and Geiger (1992) in *Buried in Ice: Unlocking the Secrets of a Doomed Arctic Voyage*) or have consulted with experts in the creation of the book, such as the *Starting with Space* series from Kids Can Press. This series contains high-quality illustrations, clear explanations, and activities for readers to complete either at home or at school. The books in the series have a glossary of terms and an index, a table of contents, *and* an acknowledgement of the assistance provided by the scientists at the Royal Ontario Museum (McLaughlin Planetarium). This last piece of information tells the reader that the book contains information from a reliable source. Other than standard checks like these, readers must judge content based on their own background knowledge of the subject.

Diane Swanson's book *Safari Beneath the Sea* (1994) is a prime example of a book that maintains accuracy and authenticity throughout. It won the Orbis Pictus Award in 1995 and was short-listed for the 1995 Children's Literature Round Tables of Canada Information Book Award. The book describes the wildlife seen in the north Pacific Ocean by children who embarked on two adventure trips sponsored by the Friends of the Royal British Columbia Museum in 1992 and 1994. The trips took children from across Canada on an exploration of the Pacific Northwest coast. Museum crews took photographs and also developed a series of television broadcasts from two remote sites on the coast. The children on the trip were able to talk to the divers and researchers at the sites as they conducted their activities. A selection of photographs provided by the Royal British Columbia Museum, taken on the trips, provides a primary focus for the book. The photographs are spectacular; combined with Swanson's well-written text, and the information boxes inserted regularly throughout the book, they create a highly readable, entertaining, and informative work. The book has a table of contents, a comprehensive index, and clear graphics; is well organized; and is written in a tone that invites the reader into the safari adventure.

DIANE SWANSON

The question of who should write nonfiction books for children and what that writer's qualifications should be remains open for discussion. Diane Swanson is an acclaimed nonfiction writer who has written many books on the topic of animals and "backyard nature" for children. Diane was born in Lethbridge, Alberta; she holds an Honors BA from the University of Alberta. Diane began her working life in the West Indies as a teacher for CUSO and later worked as a planner for the federal government. In 1975, she began writing full-time. She has now researched and written more than 20 nature books, 8 education books, and more than 200 magazine articles, as well as various booklets, reports, and manuals. Diane says, "The astonishing natural world is what inspires my writing, and children influence how I approach it: the child I once was, my own children and the children I know today... I'm a nature sleuth, addicted to digging out information... whether I'm writing about eagles, dandelions or avalanches, I want to know how things work and what's really neat about them" (CCBC, 1994).

Some of Diane's many books include *Safari Beneath the Sea* (1994), which won the Orbis Pictus Award in 1995, *Buffalo Sunrise* (1996), *Bug Bites* (1997), and *Animals Eat the Weirdest Things* (1998). Diane currently lives in Vancouver, British Columbia.

A further aid to accuracy and authenticity is the presence of clear statements that help young readers distinguish among fact, theory, and opinion. *Canadian Wild Animals* (Mastin, 1994) is part of the *Nature Canada* series published by Grasshopper Books in Kamloops, British Columbia. This picture book contains a combination of expository text and verse (which is often problematic in a book for young children). This excerpt is from the double-page spread that introduces the mountain goat:

> *Mountain goats in winter,*
> *Have coats of snowy white;*
> *In summer, when their* [sic] *shedding,*
> *They're a most repulsive sight.*

The spelling error is in the book. A second error on the same page (two indented lines of print at the beginning of the paragraph instead of just one) occurs in the expository text below the verse. Such errors are distracting to young readers, who are learning how to distinguish homophones and homonyms and how to create paragraphs. Apart from simple proofreading errors and simplistic verse, the opinion that these animals in their natural state are repulsive is troubling. Most educators would agree that people who find animals repulsive should not be writing about them for young children, who are extremely impressionable and who are developing attitudes that will likely last a lifetime.

Teachers and librarians also need to be particularly watchful for stereotyping and for anthropomorphic or teleological statements or explanations. A TELEOLOGICAL EXPLANATION is one that assigns an intention or purpose to a natural phenomenon that cannot be proven or known. In nonfiction books for children, this usually takes the form of ascribing a human-like purpose to a natural phenomenon, such as explaining that the Grand Canyon has been carved by Mother Nature (capitalized and personified) or that plants turn toward light so that they can bask in the warmth of the sun (Huck, Hepler & Hickman, 1993). Teleological explanations can be particularly pervasive in books for young readers. Similarly, ANTHROPOMORPHIC EXPLANATIONS ascribe human characteristics to animals and natural phenomenon—for example, baby foxes described as lonely or happy. While this does not happen in most wildlife books, it happens frequently enough to be noticeable. It is generally accepted that *nonfiction* books should reflect a scientific attitude, and "since young children are animistic and accepting of personification in fictional stories, nonfiction writers have a responsibility to exclude teleological and anthropomorphic aspects...in order to foster accuracy" (Dowd, in Freeman & Person, 1992, p.39).

One Canadian picture book that refrains from teleological explanations and anthropomorphism is the narrative nonfiction *Wolf Island* by Celia Godkin (1989). The book, which won the Children's Literature Round Tables of Canada Information Book Award in 1990, is based on an event that took place on an island in northern Ontario. The story illustrates what happens when the natural order of the food chain is disturbed. A family of wolves living on the island drifts to the mainland on a raft of logs. The resulting population growth among the island deer creates a food shortage, leading to starvation among the rabbits, mice, owls, and every other member of the food chain. Balance is eventually restored when the wolves cross the ice back to the island in winter. The book, illustrated by Godkin, is a superb example of high-quality nonfiction literature. In *Ladybug Garden* (1995) and *Sea Otter Inlet* (1997), Godkin again explores the cause-and-effect relationships that maintain a stable natural environment. Unfortunately, many information books for children are not as successful as *Wolf Island*. *Canadian Birds* (Mastin, 1994), part of the *Nature Canada* series, attributes human-like characteristics to many of the birds included in the book. Rather than focussing on how birds relate to each other and their role in the natural order, the text suggests that birds possess anthropomorphic qualities like friendliness and shyness.

A further issue to keep in mind when exploring the accuracy and authenticity of a book is INCLUSION. Photographs in most books today include children from various racial backgrounds and children with special needs. Our multicultural classrooms make it imperative that all children see themselves reflected in the photographs and illustrations in nonfiction books (unless there are clear reasons why one ethnic group in particular should be shown—e.g., in a book on a specific country).

There is also a need for authentic and appropriate inclusion of both girls and boys in photographs, especially in books about science. Some authors and illustrators have worked too hard at gender inclusion, resulting in inauthentic representation. For example, *Dirt Movers* by Bobbie Kalman and Petrina Gentile (1994) contains photographs of the large earth-moving equipment used in quarrying, snow removal, building roads and buildings, and similar jobs. They have cleverly included a little girl in some of the pictures (even on the front cover!), as a device to indicate the size of the machines. However, not one woman is depicted working in any capacity with the machines or on a building site in all of the photographs in the book. This is a serious omission, because many women work with large machines and many more are part of the crews that direct traffic around road-construction areas. Thus, the little girl is simply a decoration—a stereotype of women that we are working hard to eliminate.

The FORMAT of nonfiction books is an especially important area to evaluate. The layout of some books is too "busy" for young readers. The visual effect is one of overload, as the reader must attend to too much input at one time. An example of a well-formatted book is *The Disaster of the Hindenburg* (Tanaka, 1993), which provides a moving focus of attention from text to diagram to photograph and back to text. Students will read the book from beginning to end. *Light Magic* (Rising & Williams, 1994) is an excellent book in terms of content, but its layout is busy. Readers will likely pick up and read this book in occasional short bursts rather than as either a reference or a continuous text. The book includes many activities that students can complete by themselves, and the illustrations are generally of a high quality. It is a good book for a classroom collection, as it covers many broad topics related to energy.

Linda Granfield has won the Children's Literature Round Tables of Canada Information Book Award twice: in 1994 for *Cowboy: A Kid's Album* (Granfield, 1993) and in 1996 for *In Flanders Fields: The Story of the Poem by John McCrae* (Granfield, 1995). Both books are exceptionally well formatted, well researched, and creatively presented. Granfield is particularly aware of how both language and format must suit the topic of the book. These two award-winning books are "landscape" size, a horizontal format that fills the laps of one or more readers. The format suits both the vistas of Flanders and the wide-open prairie of the "cowboy" west. *Cowboy* traces the history of the cowboy (and cowgirl) and explores the dress, language, routines, and myths of the cowboy (including those spawned by the movie industry), particularly during the cowboy heyday of 1866–1886. The book ends with a view of contemporary cowboys in the Canadian west. Granfield took pains to search out archival material that would not be readily available elsewhere. The result is an intriguing and unusual book. The photographs, artwork, letters, posters, and drawings are beautifully reproduced; in all, the book is a pleasure to read.

LINDA GRANFIELD

Linda Granfield remembers that as a child growing up in Boston, she loved history. She visited historic sites and museums and enjoyed writing history reports in school, taking pleasure in the research process. History lived on her doorstep, and she took every advantage of it. In 1974, Linda moved to Canada to pursue doctoral studies in Victorian literature at the University of Toronto. She has remained in Canada ever since, marrying a Canadian and making her home in Toronto.

Linda worked in a children's bookstore, eventually writing book reviews and interviewing children's authors for magazine articles, before she tried her hand at writing her own books for children. Her first book was *All About Niagara Falls* (1988); over the next ten years, she produced fifteen more books. Linda usually has three or four books "on the go," and she spends a great deal of time researching the books and thinking about the format and presentation of the material. She generally takes anywhere from two to four years to complete a book.

In writing historical nonfiction, Linda tries to dispel the myths of the topic she is exploring. In *Cowboy: A Kid's Album*, she presented the cowboys of the nineteenth century as working men who lived hard lives, were paid very little, and often squandered what they had in the boomtowns of the west. In *High Flight: A Story of World War II* (1999), illustrated with full-colour paintings by Michael Martchenko, she presented the terrible realities of the often-short lives of the young Second World War flyers, their role in the war, and their training. The book was inspired by the poem "High Flight" by RCAF pilot John Gillespie Magee, Jr. Magee died in England in 1941 at the age of nineteen, just a few months after writing "High Flight." Linda says that when she travels to schools, which she does frequently, children often have their own personal family stories of the war to tell her.

Linda speaks eloquently about the language of nonfiction books, maintaining that nonfiction can carry as much poetry as a picture book or a novel. The language must suit the topic. When writing *Silent Night: The Song from Heaven* (1997), which is exquisitely illustrated in silhouettes by Nelly and Ernst Hofer, she struggled to find the most appropriate diction and sentence structures to tell the story of the famous Christmas hymn. In *Amazing Grace: The Story of the Hymn* (1997), Linda says she spent as much time on the last sentence as she did on the rest of the book: it was hard for her to end this moving story appropriately. Her final words, "from the slave ships echo still," capture both the pain and the serenity of the story.

Children identify with Linda's books and are fascinated by them. Linda calls her books "intergenerational books," designed to be read by a child along with a parent, grandparent, or friend. Her books appeal to all ages and certainly invite dialogue.

Cowboy: A Kid's Album by Linda Granfield

Even in the late 1990s, many nonfiction books were printed without colour photographs or diagrams. The reason was usually an issue of expense, but expense must be balanced against the readability and appeal of the book. A book may contain interesting information and new ideas for children, but if the book is not designed in ways that make the content accessible to elementary readers, it cannot be considered successful. Books containing black-and-white drawings, in combination with the black-and-white text, make it hard for children to sustain their attention on the various units of meaning presented on the page. Young readers need as much help from the printed page as possible. They can be overwhelmed by the amount of information presented, even if that information is in the form of a diagram or drawings, and they usually close the book and move on to something else. Colour photographs and drawings help readers to move their eyes and their focus around the page from one unit of meaning to another more easily.

As we browse through collections of nonfiction books, it becomes clear that it is not easy to find good nonfiction materials for *young* children. Apart from concept books (including counting and ABC books) created for preschoolers, very little is written at an age-appropriate level. Most books require a mediator—parent, teacher, or teaching assistant—to read with the child. The illustrations and headings may be appropriate, but the reading level is usually better suited to middle to upper elementary children. This gap between readability and interest level appears to be a problem in nonfiction materials at almost every level of schooling. Books required by students in, for example, the grade five science curriculum are generally written at a level better suited to junior high students. An exception to this rule is the Crabapples series, written by Bobbie Kalman, which includes *Butterflies and Moths* (1994), *How a Plant Grows* (1997), and *Web Weavers and Other Spiders* (1997). These books are usually written at a level appropriate for the primary grades, but they do not provide the detailed information some readers may require. Some books from Crabtree Publishing may be misleading for young children due to lay-out problems (especially the captions below or next to photographs); however, the Crabapples books (and Crabtree's Science of Living Things series, for upper elementary grades) are among the better nonfiction series available and are age-appropriate most of the time. Scholastic also has a good series for upper elementary grades, including *Life in the Deserts* (Baker, 1990), *Life in the Rainforests* (Baker, 1990), *Ancient Egypt* (Nicholson & Watts, 1991), and *Experiment with Water* (Murphy, 1991).

Classification of Nonfiction Books

Nonfiction includes books about all of the sciences (natural, physical and social), sports, history, biography, drama, art, music, and many other topics. However, children's books are becoming increasingly difficult to classify as fiction or nonfiction, because many present information in a story format. Some books, such as biography, are clearly defined, while others, such as narrative nonfiction, are relative newcomers to the field and are less easy to distinguish from fictional materials. Bamford and Kristo (1998) suggest that one helpful way to categorize nonfiction books is to classify them according to the ways in which they are organized or presented. In this chapter, we have chosen to classify nonfiction books into the following categories: narrative nonfiction, biography, photodocumentaries, how-to books, activity and experiment books, question-and-answer format books, survey books, and field guides or identification books. We have also added the special category of picture song books, as they represent a unique blend of music, pictures, and information.

NARRATIVE NONFICTION

Some of the most fascinating nonfiction materials available are narrative texts that incorporate details and explanations into a story. Successful books manage to be non-didactic while remaining interesting and entertaining as well as informative—they are not easy to come by! For example, David Suzuki sought to use narrative in his *Nature All Around* series. Some of the books in the series work better than others, but all remain blatantly didactic, consisting of what is basically a lecture-tour by a mother or father or other character in the story. One would probably not read these books as an aesthetic experience!

Perhaps the best-known book of narrative nonfiction for young children is the Australian book *Where the Forest Meets the Sea,* by Jeanie Baker (1987). This book won the Friends of the Earthworm Award and was listed as an honour book in the Australian Children's Picture Book of the Year Award. It is an innovative picture book that chronicles the reflections of a young boy exploring with his father in the rainforest of northern Queensland. The illustrations (also created by Baker) consist of relief collage constructed from a mix of natural materials, including lamb's wool, fabric, and leaves. The effect is stunning: a rich, three-dimensional perspective on the rainforest that invites the reader to explore its secrets and discover the majesty of nature. The boy plays, imagines, wonders, and questions: "Will the rainforest still be here when we come back?" No answers are provided—the reader is left to ponder the question. A map of Australia at the back of the book shows the location of the Daintree Rainforest, and a brief paragraph gives information about it. *Where the Forest Meets the Sea* is a lovely reading experience that both teaches and questions through the beauty of its prose and its illustrations.

Theodoric's Rainbow, written by Stephen Kramer (1995) and illustrated by Daniel Mark Duffy, tells the story (largely through pictures) of Theodoric of Freiberg, a German philosopher and theologian who was one of the first people to experiment in science (rather than philosophize). Theodoric discovered how drops of water reflect and refract light, and he developed the first geometrically correct explanation of the rainbow. The illustrations in the book incorporate geometric drawings that Theodoric might have conceptualized and drawn. This book contains far more text than *Where the Forest Meets the Sea*, but the text is straight-forward and well written. Children from grade three onwards (and even earlier) find this book fascinating.

Anno's Medieval World (Anno, 1979) remains a superb example of narrative nonfiction for young readers. Through pictures and text, Anno recreates the slow discovery and acceptance of the sun as the centre of the solar system. From a flat earth to a round earth, Anno takes the reader through a journey of discoveries and controversy beginning in 442 B.C. and ending with yet more questions in the seventeenth century. The illustrations in this book are central to an understanding of the text, and they make the book accessible to a wide range of ages. However, a certain historical perspective and understanding of science is necessary for a full reading of *Anno's Medieval World.*

Thunderstorm! (Tripp, 1994) describes the large and small changes that take place in the atmosphere when weather fronts move. Such changes warn animals and humans to seek shelter from the explosive force of a storm. The book, illustrated by Juan Wijngaard, shows how a thunderstorm builds in intensity, transforming quiet farmland into nature's most spectacular sound and light show. In narrative style, the book traces the events on one farm during a thunderstorm:

> *The sun was shining brightly, but there were lots of anvil clouds coming closer when some of Ben's neighbors began arriving at the farm to help him get the hay in the barn. They knew Ben's crop was in danger and wanted to help out. Now the first rumbles of thunder could be heard deep within the clouds of the cold front. The thunder was a signal from inside each cell that it had stopped growing taller and had become "active." (p.28)*

Two narrative nonfiction books of a more controversial nature are *The Story of the Little Mole Who Knew It Was None of His Business,* by Werner Holzwarth (1996), and *Heather Has Two Mommies,* by Lesléa Newman (1989). *The Story of the Little Mole* is a book on the topic of scatology, or animal droppings, a side of animal life often neglected in urban society. The book can either amuse or disgust its adult readers. (We must admit that the first time we read this book, we wondered what we were reading and why!) Holzwarth has created an amusing story of a little mole who sets out to discover which animal dropped its "business" on his head. The ending of the book may displease some adult readers, but it certainly reflects children's feelings about fair play and revenge!

Heather Has Two Mommies has good intentions but fails to deliver a truly satisfying reading experience. The book cannot steer away from didacticism, although it is lovingly and sensitively written, and it is illustrated in black and white, which is disappointing. *Heather Has Two Mommies* tells the story of a little girl who has two mothers and no "father": the girl was conceived through a surgical procedure involving fertilization from a donor. The story focusses on Heather beginning school and feeling different because of her family composition. The book teaches that there are many different kinds of families, all of them acceptable so long as everyone is loved and respected. The book may disturb some adult readers, and it is not a book teachers will normally share with a class or small group. It is, however, a book that teachers need to know about so they can provide it for a child at an appropriate moment if necessary. Alyson Wonderland Publications produces material intended to teach about minorities, especially same-sex families; the company also published *Daddy's Roommate,* by Michael Willhoite (1990). Another, better-quality book on same-sex parenting is *Asha's Mums* by Rosamund Elwin (1990).

BIOGRAPHIES

Biographies are a form of narrative nonfiction. The information in a biography is true, but the telling often reads like fiction. AUTHENTIC BIOGRAPHY is a well-documented account of a person's life. Only facts supported by solid research are used, and dialogue or statements by the subject are included only if they are known to have been actually made by the subject; consequently, they rely heavily on letters, diaries, and the recollections of reliable persons. Even so, it is possible for a biographer to slant even the most solid evidence by highlighting some facts and downplaying others. FICTIONALIZED BIOGRAPHY may be grounded in thorough research, but the author dramatizes certain events and personalizes the subject rather than presenting a straight-forward report. Books like these are immediately discernible through the amount of dialogue they contain that cannot possibly be historically accurate. BIOGRAPHICAL FICTION is quite a different form altogether, as it consists entirely of imagined conversation and restructured events. It is generally closer to fiction than to biography.

Hugh Brewster is a Canadian editor and writer who compiled *Anastasia's Album* (1996), drawing together letters written by Grand Duchess Anastasia of Russia and photographs taken by members of the royal family. These photographs and letters, along with the accompanying narrative material, provide an intimate look at the last years of the Romanovs. Colour photographs of Russia by Peter Christopher complement the period photographs. The result is a hauntingly beautiful and compelling book that appeals to children and adults alike. Brewster came across the letters and photographs while viewing the imperial family's albums at the State Archives in Moscow, and he realized that Anastasia's story would make a wonderful book of its own.

> *Anastasia's family nickname was* Shvibzik, *which means "imp" in Russian. Years later, her father's sister Grand Duchess Olga recalled Anastasia's hilarious imitations of some of the pompous people who visited the palace. "That is how I remember her," Olga wrote, "brimming with life and mischief and laughing so often." (p.23)*

The book is clearly not a complete biography of Anastasia, but it is a partial and authentic biography, based entirely on historical documents found in Moscow and on the recollections and writings of Anastasia's Aunt Olga.

A good biography for children includes supplementary material such as an index, bibliographies of related material, and sources of photographs and other documents. It also avoids sentimentality, didacticism, and oversimplification, just as any other work of nonfiction does. *Anastasia's Album* contains an epilogue that includes information gleaned from Anastasia's Aunt Olga, who escaped from Russia to Canada during the Russian civil war. Aunt Olga became a reliable source of information after the deaths of the Romanovs. The book also contains a glossary of terms and a map of Russia as it existed during the reign of Nicholas II. There is a detailed list of picture credits, a list of primary works consulted, and acknowledgements of the help provided by individuals from a large number of archives and museums in preparing the book. It is a superb example of an authentic biography for young readers.

This Land Is My Land by George Littlechild (1993) is an autobiography appropriate for readers in grades three and up. It belongs in any Canadian library. In very simple language, Littlechild tells the story of his ancestry within the Plains Cree Nation. The book's illustrations are unique, and Littlechild's use of colour is spectacular. From the birth of his great-great-grandfather in 1858 to the present day, Littlechild relates the story of his people in a moving narrative which attempts to confront bigotry, racism, and poverty and which points to a future in which all people can share the land and its wealth. The book can be accused of being didactic and is certainly biased; however, as Littlechild intimates, the land belongs to the Aboriginal people and Aboriginal people have rights that other Canadians do not have. Littlechild emphasizes that Canada must be a land in which indigenous culture is accepted and celebrated. Because this is an autobiographical book, the reader must accept that it presents one opinion and one person's individual story. The text is brief and simple, with few details:

> *When I was a boy I was taught the song "This land is your land, this land is my land." When I got older I thought it was very strange to be singing about the ownership of the land. Whose land was this? Did it belong to anyone? The first people in this land were the Indians. We prefer to be called First Nations or First Peoples, because this was our homeland first. (p.16)*

PHOTODOCUMENTARIES

Photodocumentaries first appeared in the late 1970s. A good PHOTODOCUMENTARY or PHOTO-ESSAY must have photographs and text in balance. A photodocumentary is not the same as a heavily illustrated book: a photodocumentary conveys much of the information through the photographs so that the text can be compressed and concise. Tight, economical writing is a hallmark of the photodocumentary. *Journey to the Planets,* by Patricia Lauber (1982), was one of the best and earliest photodocumentaries, along with *Small Worlds Close Up,* by Lisa Grillone and Joseph Gennaro (1978), and *The Hospital Book,* by James Howe (1981). The editor of all of these books, Norma Jean Sawicki, insisted on top-quality photographs reproduced on heavy, expensive paper and printed in a handsome format. As a result of the success of these books, published by Crown, other publishers imitated them.

A wide range of quality photodocumentaries is now available, and recent advancements in technology have made the photographs and layout more enticing and exciting. The photodocumentary complements the visual images children encounter through television; in addition, it engages the children's different modes of learning. Visual learners are far more likely to be attracted to a photodocumentary than they are to a typical nonfiction book. Recent work with individuals who have suffered brain injuries has demonstrated that photodocumentaries are the most appropriate vehicle for "book learning" for both youngsters and adults. Many patients recovering from accidents lose the cognitive skills and competencies they had prior to their injury; for them, reading is a slow, laborious task. It takes far less time for patients with brain injuries to read photodocumentaries than a typical nonfiction book, and they can learn a great deal from scrutinizing the photographs that they would not be able to learn as easily from processing text.

A People Apart by Kenna (1995) was an "Our Choice" award selection (Canadian Children's Book Centre) in 1996. The book reveals the lives of Old Order Mennonites in Canada. It describes their style of clothing, services at the meetinghouse, barn raisings, and horse-drawn farm equipment. It also underscores how little life has changed in these communities over the last hundred years. The black-and-white photographs add to the overall effect of this photodocumentary.

HOW-TO BOOKS

How-to books are exactly that: how to make a kite, build a boat, play baseball, cook, or make paper airplanes. They must be clearly laid out so that children can follow the directions. It is too easy, even for adults, to get lost in the middle of directions if they are not logically presented and accompanied by useful pictures and diagrams. (Most of us have experienced the frustration of assembling a piece of furniture, only to "finish" the job and discover one unused section on the floor beside us!) One well-designed Canadian children's how-to book is Camilla Gryski's *Let's Play* (1995). The book contains instructions for playing simple games from leapfrog to sardines and marbles! The playful and humorous illustrations by Dušan Petričić add to the fun of the games. It is an ideal book to use as a springboard for children to develop their own how-to books of other games: games they already know or games their parents and grandparents can teach them. The book makes a sound addition to any classroom collection and is a welcome reminder of the traditional games children played for generations before the computer and television set made an appearance.

For children who have enjoyed Mem Fox's *Possum Magic* (1983), there is *The Grandma Poss Cookbook* (1985), illustrated by Julie Vivas, who also illustrated *Possum Magic*. The *Cookbook* provides recipes for the delicious things Hush ate in order to become visible again—pavlova, lamingtons, Anzac biscuits (cookies), gingernuts, pumpkin scones, and more. For learning how to read informational text and follow printed directions, there is nothing more enjoyable and useful than a recipe book. And to be able to connect fiction and nonfiction and put it into practice is, in this case, literally a treat.

EXPERIMENT AND ACTIVITY BOOKS

Many science books provide children with experiments they can do at home or at school to demonstrate basic scientific concepts. Most of these books are in a picture-book format, designed for interest and enjoyment; they usually include charts and diagrams but rarely an index. It may therefore be difficult to locate specific experiments or activities on particular subjects.

Etta Kaner's *Towers and Tunnels* (1995) is an introduction to design and technology. A volume in the *Structures* series by Kids Can Press, the book includes current and historical information about towers and tunnels around the world. It is intended to be a resource for children interested in exploring the challenges of engineering. Each feat of engineering—such as tunneling through rock or tunneling under water—is accompanied by an activity that demonstrates the principles described. The activities are easily completed, require ordinary household objects (such as cardboard, string, modelling clay, and other materials), and are clearly described.

Valerie Wyatt has created *The Science Book For Girls And Other Intelligent Beings* (1993), a collection of science activities exploring many aspects of science, from the chemistry of toast to the shapes and sizes of snowflakes. Some critics have raised objections to this book, because it places most of the activities in a home environment and may be perceived as perpetuating the stereotyping of girls in regard to the sciences. However, many children will enjoy the book, as it certainly contains some interesting ideas and activities. *The Jumbo Book of Nature Science,* by Pamela Hickman (1996), contains more than a hundred activities and experiments that explore nature indoors and outdoors. Building bird feeders, preserving spider webs, and making a terrarium are just three of the activities described.

QUESTION-AND-ANSWER FORMATS

Some nonfiction books for young readers are presented in the style of questions and answers. Catherine Ripley's *Do the Doors Open By Magic and Other Supermarket Questions* (1995) is intended for children from preschool to grade two. The book asks questions such as, Where do apples come from in winter? What holds jello together? and How does the fizz get into soda pop?. Such books give straight-forward answers to children's frequently asked questions without adding superfluous information. Ripley, a former editor of *Chickadee* magazine, is now the author of a number of science books for children including *Why do the Stars Twinkle? and Other Nighttime Questions* (1996). This book, again aimed for children from preschool to grade two, answers questions such as why we yawn when we are tired, why cats' eyes shine in the dark, and why we dream.

You Asked? (Farris, 1996) contains more than 300 questions and answers about *why* things happen. The book is published by Owl Books, and its questions are derived from the many hundreds of letters children sent to *Owl* magazine over a period of more than twenty years. The book is divided into chapters on the human body, the technology of everyday life, space, and the natural world. This book is exceptionally well formatted, and the illustrations are clear, colourful, and fascinating. Why does it hurt when you laugh really hard? Why do your eyes cry when you're laughing? Why do racing cyclists bend so low over their handlebars? Why do drinking glasses slide across the counter when they're wet? Does the vampire bat suck blood? It is a high-quality information book for children from grades two to six: children love to browse and discuss the questions. The book provides a stimulus to learn about some fascinating topics rather than providing in-depth answers on any one topic. It is the kind of book children begin to read and immediately have to share with a friend—"Hey, did you know that...?"

SURVEY

Bamford and Kristo (1998, p.9) define the survey book as a nonfiction book that provides "an introduction to a topic and includes representative subtopics, but it may not necessarily cover all information." *Cowboy: A Kid's Album* is a fine example of a survey book, as is *A Pioneer Story: The Daily Life of a Canadian Family in 1840* (Greenwood, 1994). Greenwood's book won the Children's Literature Round Tables of Canada Information Book Award in 1995. The book features a fictional pioneer family, the Robertsons, who live in eastern Canada. Sections of the book are devoted to topics such as the log house, the farmyard, making maple sugar, going to school, games the children played, how the land was cleared, making clothing, harvesting, and building roads. Interspersed with these sections are stories about events that might have happened to such a family. One of them, "The Pedlar's Visit," tells of the excitement the whole family felt when a pedlar came by, selling his wares and trading with the family, bringing needles and thread, pieces of lace, scissors, nutmeg, and little tin boxes. *A Pioneer Story* contains a glossary of terms and an index.

The Magic School Bus series and the *Eyewitness Guides* are also survey books. Young readers enjoy both of these internationally popular series. *The Magic School Bus* series, designed for young readers, is produced in the United States. The *Eyewitness Guides* originate in the United Kingdom and are designed for both elementary school children and adults. Like most good literature, the *Eyewitness Guides* appeal to all ages.

The Magic School Bus series, by Joanna Cole, narrates the adventures of a class of children and their teacher, Ms Frizzle; the books are illustrated by Bruce Degan. Each book tells the imaginative story of Ms Frizzle's "field trips" in the magic school bus.

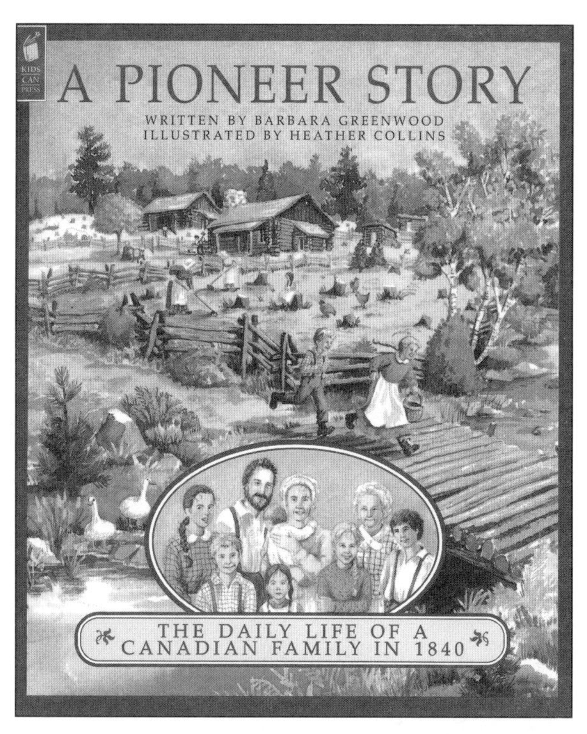

A Pioneer Story by Barbara Greenwood, illustrated by Heather Collins

Topics covered by the series include dinosaurs, the human body, the solar system, waterworks, inside the earth, and the ocean floor. In *The Magic School Bus in the Time of the Dinosaurs* (Cole, 1994), the class is studying dinosaurs; the students are preparing for Visitors' Day when Ms Frizzle announces that she has been invited to take the children to a dinosaur dig. Once at the dig, Ms Frizzle uses the school bus to take the children back in time to see how the area looked in the time of the dinosaurs. Each page is packed with information in an accessible and humorous way. The illustrations capture the details of the animals and plant life in the various periods of time the children visit. On returning to the dig, and then to the classroom, the children are able to provide expert guidance to their visitors as they act as tour-guides for the exhibits they have created. The book presents dinosaurs realistically and dispels many of the "myths" about dinosaurs (for example that humans lived at the same time as did the dinosaurs).

Eyewitness Guides, published in Canada by Dorling Kindersley and Stoddart, are available on every topic from the skeleton, trees, insects, fossils, inventions, knights, cowboys, and castles to writing and Ancient Rome. The books are illustrated with detailed full-colour photographs and drawings. *Car,* written by Richard Sutton (1990), is a guide to the motor car, past and present. It details the story of motoring from the early years of dangers and discomfort, through the 1930s and grand touring, to Formula One racing today. The workings of the car are revealed in detail, yet the explanations are easily understandable when read in conjunction with the illustrations. On the double-page spread devoted to "The Driving Force" (pp.42-43), engine layouts (British) are illustrated and explained thus:

> *The majority of modern car engines have four pistons and cylinders set in line. Yet this is by no means the only possible arrangement. Some alternatives are shown below.*
> *Straight Six: Engines with six cylinders set in line are very long, and costly to make. But they can be very smooth and powerful and are popular in large, expensive saloons.*
> *"V" Six: Big straight engines are too long and tall to fit into low-slung sports cars and their long crankshafts can "whip" under stress. So many sports cars have compact "V" engines with cylinders interlocking in a "V" and a shorter, more rigid crankshaft.*

By the time the reader arrives at this spread, the vocabulary is fully understandable as the terms have been introduced and explained on previous pages. The book includes a thorough list of contents, an index at the back, and a list of credits and acknowledgements that indicates the sources from which the information and the photographs have come (for example, the National Motor Museum at Beaulieu, the Science Museum in London, Renault France, and the Carburettor Centre in London). However, no information is provided on the qualifications and experience of the writer/compiler.

FIELD GUIDES AND IDENTIFICATION BOOKS

In their simplest form, field guides are labelling books, but as children grow in their need for information to help them identify various aspects of the world, so too do field guides. A field guide can help a reader identify trees, plants, animals, birds, tools, houses, seashells, and any other area of life which can be categorized and labelled. *The Kids' Canadian Tree Book* (Hickman, 1995) offers excellent text and illustrations that help a reader understand the various parts of a tree, the difference between coniferous and deciduous trees, leaves, and various species of tree from the Canadian rain forest to fruit trees. The book is suitable for grades one through six and contains many interesting activities and projects for children to complete. In addition to trees, the series features books on birds, bugs, and plants.

Crabapple Books offer a number of field guides for young children. *Horses* (Everts & Kalman, 1995) provides basic information about horses including terminology (e.g., mare, stallion, foal), the horse's body, colours and markings, and information on a number of breeds of horses. These books are designed for children in grades one to four. The books are extremely well illustrated and formatted, and they generally contain age-appropriate material, language, and photo captions.

PICTURE SONG BOOKS

Picture song books present the music and lyrics of songs—sometimes just one song, sometimes a collection of songs. One example of a high-quality Canadian song book is *Silent Night: The Song from Heaven* by Linda Granfield (1997). The book is illustrated in black and gold silhouettes by Nelly and Ernst Hofer. Readers can pore over the intricate illustrations for hours, savouring the details of the unfolding story depicted in the silhouettes.

O Canada by Ted Harrison (1992) is a colourfully illustrated rendition of Canada's national anthem.

Harrison's unique and memorable artwork takes the reader on a spectacular journey across Canada from Newfoundland to the Northwest Territories. Each double-page spread contains a splendid illustration created by Harrison as an accompaniment to a section of the lyrics from the anthem. In addition, Harrison includes footnotes in French and English that describe each painting. For example, on the page pertaining to the Northwest territories:

> *To the north of Yellowknife is a wonderland of vast open spaces filled with myriads of glacial lakes in every shape and size. The arctic wolf trails a barren ground caribou – the life cycle of the north unfolds. In this northern paradise one gains the sense of complete freedom, and a feeling for the greatness of Canada. (unpaginated).*

The music by Calixa LaVallée, along with the French and English lyrics, is located at the back of the book. The very last page contains historical information about the anthem.

Linda Lamme (1979) has classified picture song books into the following categories: lullabies, hymns, and holiday songs, such as *The Twelve Days of Christmas* by Jan Brett (1986); nursery rhymes and animal songs, such as *Oh, A Hunting We Will Go* by John Langstaff (1974); folk songs, such as *Skip to My Lou* (Quackenbush, 1975; Westcott, 1989); and patriotic and historical songs, such as *O Canada* by Ted Harrison and *Pop! Goes the Weasel and Yankee Doodle* by Robert Quackenbush (1976). Picture song books for young children can help literacy development by making a link from the oral to the written through rhyme, rhythm, repetition, and story structure.

Some picture song books do not include the music, a serious omission not only for parents and teachers who might like to accompany the songs, but also for children who lose the opportunity to learn to read music as well as words. The music and lyrics for a song should ideally be on the same page; a good alternative is to include the music at the back of the book. The pairing of language and music is a powerful learning experience for children, and the illustrations accompanying the songs are an added incentive for children to read and sing along. In a successful picture song book, the lyrics and illustrations work together to create an enhanced meaning for the reader.

Periodicals for Young Readers

Periodicals, or magazines, are an essential component of any school library or classroom collection. They frequently supplement thematic studies across the curriculum, and they provide both information and pleasure for young readers. Children frequently select magazines to read during Drop Everything And Read (DEAR) or Uninterrupted Sustained Silent Reading (USSR) periods instead of novels or nonfiction books. Many high-quality periodicals are suitable for the classroom, and many of them have been in print for years.

Magazines were an especially important source of reading pleasure for children in the latter part of the nineteenth century. The first children's magazines grew out of the Sunday School movement, but they quickly developed to include short stories for children and reviews of books such as *Alice's Adventures in Wonderland* (Carroll, 1866). The first magazine planned for children in North America was *The Juvenile Miscellany,* which appeared in 1826. By far the most famous, however, was *St Nicholas Magazine*, first published in 1873, which attracted such writers and illustrators as Arthur Rackham, Frances Hodgson Burnett, Rudyard Kipling, Louisa May Alcott, and Robert Louis Stevenson. Many children's classics were first serialized in *St Nicholas Magazine* before they were published as novels.

Today, the two best-known Canadian magazines for children are *Chickadee* and *Owl Magazine*.

Chickadee: The Canadian Magazine for Young Children is an award-winning periodical designed for younger children (pre-school to grade three). It teaches basic principles of science and nature using a hands-on approach and is filled with games, puzzles, and stories. *Owl Magazine* is designed for readers in grades two to six, and contains intriguing and humorous articles and editorials about nature, science, and technology; again, it is packed with games and puzzles. A relative newcomer to the market is *Yes Mag: Canada's Science Magazine for Kids*. This periodical, aimed at students in grades three to eight, is loaded with science, engineering, and technology news, environmental updates, do-at-home projects, and book and software reviews. *Chirp Magazine* is aimed at preschool children and contains simple puzzles, games, rhymes, crafts, and stories. Every issues offers a "Big Person's Guide" of helpful ideas for adults as they share the magazine with children. More information on periodicals for children in the elementary grades can be found in Katz and Katz, *Magazines for Young People: A Children's Magazine Guide Companion* (1991), and Stoll's *Magazines for Kids and Teens* (1997).

Other popular magazines from outside Canada include *Ranger Rick*, *Boys' Life*, *Cricket: The Magazine for Children*, *Jack and Jill*, *Odyssey*, *Girls' Life*, and *Zoobooks*. *Girls' Life* reinforces the strong role of girls in society: that they are important, have valuable opinions, and can be independent. The magazine (bi-monthly, grades two to nine) includes features on sports, food, crafts, and entertainment, and is published by Monarch Avalon Inc., Baltimore, Maryland, USA. *Zoobooks* focusses on one particular animal in each issue. It is full of colourful illustrations and includes information such as the natural habitat and the anatomy of the specific animal (ten issues per year, kindergarten to grade nine). It is published by Wildlife Education, Ltd., San Diego, California, USA. A further selection of magazines for children can be found at the end of the chapter.

References

Bamford, R. and J. Kristo. 1998. *Making Facts Come Alive: Choosing Quality Nonfiction Literature K-8*. Norwood, Massachusetts: Christopher-Gordon Publishers Inc.

Canadian Children's Book Centre. 1994. *Writing Stories, Making Pictures*. Toronto: CCBC.

Doiron, R. 1994. Using nonfiction in a read-aloud program: Letting the facts speak for themselves. *The Reading Teacher* 47(8), 616-623.

Dowd, F.S. 1992. Trends and evaluative criteria of informational books for children. In *Using Nonfiction Trade Books in the Classroom: From Ants to Zeppelins*. E. Freeman and D. Person, eds. Urbana, Illinois: National Council of Teachers of English.

Freeman, E. and D. Person, eds. 1992. *Using Nonfiction Trade Books in the Classroom: From Ants to Zeppelins*. Urbana, Illinois: National Council of Teachers of English.

Huck, C., S. Hepler, and J. Hickman. 1993. *Children's Literature in the Elementary School.* Fifth edition. New York: Harcourt Brace Jovanovich College Publishers.

Katz, B. and L.S. Katz. 1991. *Magazines for Young People: A Children's Magazine Guide Companion*. Providence, New Jersey: R.R. Bowker Company.

Lamme, L. 1979. Song picture books—A maturing genre of children's literature. *Language Arts* 56(4), 400-407.

Pappas, C. 1991. Fostering full access to literacy by including information books. *Language Arts* 68(6), 449-461.

Stoll, D.R., ed. 1997. *Magazines for Kids and Teens*. Newark, Delaware: International Reading Association.

Vardell, S. 1991. A new "Picture of the World": The NCTE Orbis Pictus Award for Outstanding Nonfiction for Children. *Language Arts* 68(6), 474-479.

Professional Resources

Bamford, R. and J. Kristo, eds. 1998. *Making Facts Come Alive: Choosing Quality Nonfiction Literature K-8*. Norwood, Massachusetts: Christopher-Gordon Publishers Inc. • *Making Facts Come Alive* contains information and discussion on such topics as determining the accuracy and authenticity of nonfiction material; apects of writing styles in nonfiction; accessing visual texts; selecting quality nonfiction for emergent readers; the role of nonfiction literature in social studies, science, and the arts; writing nonfiction; and the role of nonfiction literature in readers' workshop and in drama. The book has a section on well known nonfiction writers for children, incorporating biographical information, photographs, and interviews. The section includes two Canadian writers, Linda Granfield, and Diane Swanson. A list of Orbis Pictus award-winners and honour books is presented, along with bibliographies of children's materials.

Freeman, E. and D. Person, eds. 1992. *Using Nonfiction Trade Books in the Classroom: From Ants to Zeppelins*. Urbana, Illinois: National Council of Teachers of English. • Freeman and Person have compiled a collection of material contributed by classroom teachers, librarians, children's authors, and academics. Topics range from discussions of the genre of nonfiction and the writing of nonfiction, to the elementary curriculum and criteria for selecting nonfiction materials. The authors describe specific books on a particular topic, give numerous suggestions for classroom activities, and include an extensive bibliography. One excellent chapter is devoted to literacy and nonfiction books in science, while another chapter explores social studies materials. Further presentations are made on the reading-writing connection and responding to nonfiction texts.

Canadian Books of Nonfiction for Children

Bateman, R. and R. Archbold. 1998. *Safari*. Toronto: Penguin Books Canada.

Beatty, O. and J. Geiger. 1992. *Buried in Ice: Unlocking the Secrets of a Doomed Arctic Voyage*. Mississauga, Ontario: Random House.

Bondar, B. and R. Bondar. 1993. *On the Shuttle: Eight Days in Space.* Toronto: Greey de Pencier.

Chase, E.N. 1993. *Waters*. Richmond Hill, Ontario: North Winds Press.

Drake, J. and A. Love. 1998. *The Kid's Cottage Games Book*. Toronto: Kids Can Press.

Dudley, K. 1997. *Wolves: The Untamed World*. Calgary: Weigl Educational Publishers Ltd.

Granfield, L. 1995. *In Flanders Fields: The Story of the Poem by John McCrae*. Toronto: Lester Publishing.

Hedge, D. 1996. *Bears: Polar Bears, Black Bears and Grizzly Bears*. Toronto: Kids Can Press.

Hickman, P. 1995. *The Kids' Canadian Tree Book*. Toronto: Kids Can Press.

Kalman, B. 1994. *Homes Around the World*. Niagara-On-the-Lake, Ontario: Crabtree Publishing.

London, J. 1993. *The Eyes of Gray Wolf*. San Francisco: Chronicle Books.

Love, A and J. Drake. 1997. *Fishing (Canada at Work)*. Toronto: Kids Can Press.

MacLeod, E. 1994. *Dinosaurs: The Fastest, The Fiercest, The Most Amazing*. Toronto: Kids Can Press.

MacLeod, E. 1995. *The Phone Book*. Toronto: Kids Can Press.

MacLeod, E. 1996. *Stamp Collecting for Canadian Kids*. Toronto: Kids Can Press.

Newlands, A. 1996. *Emily Carr: An Introduction to Her Life and Art*. Vancouver: Firefly Books.

Owens, A. and J. Yealland. 1996. *Forts of Canada*. Toronto: Kids Can Press.

Raskin, L. and D. Pearson. 1998. *52 Days By Camel*. Toronto: Annick Press.

Reeves, N. and N. Froman. 1992. *Into the Mummy's Tomb: The Real Life Discovery of Tutankhamen's Treasures*. Richmond Hill, Ontario: Scholastic Canada.

Shell, B. 1997. *Great Canadian Scientists*. Vancouver: Polestar Book Publishers.

Shemie, B. 1997. *Houses of China*. Montreal: Tundra Books.

Springer, J. 1997. *Listen to Us: The World's Working Children*. Toronto: Groundwood Books.

Stanford, Q. 1998. *The Canadian Oxford Junior Atlas*. Toronto: Oxford University Press.

Suzuki, D. (1994). *If We Could See the Air*. Toronto: Stoddart.

Tanaka, S. (1998). *The Buried City of Pompeii: What It Was Like When Vesuvius Exploded.* Richmond Hill, Ontario: Scholastic.

Thornhill, J. (1991). *A Tree in a Forest*. Toronto: Greey de Pencier Books.

Webb, J. (1995). *What's a Zoo?* Toronto: Key Porter Books.

Zhang, S. N. (1995). *The Children of China: An Artist's Journey*. Montreal: Tundra Books.

Magazines for and of Interest to Children

The Beaver: Canada and the World, published by the Hudson's Bay Company, Winnipeg, Manitoba; six issues per year, grades three to nine. • *The Beaver* examines the development of commerce and the settlement and expansion of Canada.

Canadian Geographic, published by the Royal Geographical Society, Vanier, Ontario; six issues per year, grades six to twelve. • Featuring high-quality photography, *Canadian Geographic* investigates the significance of geography in Canadian life, well-being, culture, and development. It includes the heritage of Canada, its wilderness, and wildlife, as well as surveys of people and places.

Coulicou, published by Les Éditions Heritage, Saint Lambert, Quebec; monthly, grades preschool to four. • *Coulicou,* the French-language version of *Chickadee* magazine, provides an introduction to the world of nature and animals. Includes games, recipes, and posters.

Equinox, published by Telemedia Publishing, Ontario; six issues per year, grades six to twelve. • *Equinox,* a magazine of Canadian discovery, covers topics as diverse as oceans, stars, and wilderness. It contains excellent photography, which students in grades four to six find especially useful.

Faces, published by Cobblestone Publishing Inc., Peterborough, New Hampshire; nine issues per year, grades three to nine. • *Faces* explores human diversity and encourages understanding and respect for cultures around the world.

Hibou, published by Les Éditions Heritage, Saint Lambert, Quebec; monthly, grades three to eight. • *Hibou,* the French-language version of *Owl Magazine,* explores science, nature, and the world.

National Geographic World, published by the National Geographic Society, Gaithersburg, Maryland; monthly, grades three to nine. • Designed to inspire curiosity within the child's world and beyond, *World* focusses on natural history, science, and outdoor adventure.

Sports Illustrated for Kids, published by Time Magazine Company, Birmingham, Alabama; monthly, grades two to eight. • This magazine highlights amateur and professional athletes, both male and female. Regular features include advice columns for young athletes, art by children, comic strips, and posters.

Stone Soup: The Magazine by Young Writers and Artists, published by the Children's Art Foundation, Santa Cruz, California; five issues per year, grades one to seven. • *Stone Soup* highlights writers and artists from Canada and the United States; the average age of contributors is eleven years. It includes stories, poems, and art work.

CHAPTER SEVEN

RESPONDING TO LITERATURE

The objectives of this chapter are

- To become informed about reader-response theories;
- To understand efferent and aesthetic reading of texts;
- To develop an understanding of responses to literature;
- To understand the role of oral responses in literature-based programs;
- To acquire a repertoire of activities to facilitate and encourage oral, visual, and dramatic responses to literature in the classroom.

CLASSROOM SCENARIO

As Bruce and Craig prepared for their puppet play presentation during recess break, Sylvia discovered that Bruce, one of her grade five students, had beheaded his male Cabbage Patch doll! The original head had been replaced by one constructed from a pair of nylons and stuffed with cotton. For hair, Bruce and Craig had glued white cotton on the sides of the doll's new head. Cotton had been used to form a moustache, and the eyes, mouth, and teeth had been constructed from felt. A nose had been sculptured with a few stitches that pulled the cotton stuffing into a rounded shape. Finally, the boys had made glasses by bending thin wire into a pair of old-fashioned spectacles. The Cabbage Patch doll wore blue jeans, and its brown-and-white-striped top had been stuffed with cotton and paper towels to enlarge its girth. The doll also wore a brown wool sweater that buttoned up the front. Such was the appearance of Farmer Boggis, a character from Roald Dahl's *Fantastic Mr. Fox* (1970). The boys had "reconfigured" the Cabbage Patch doll's appearance in order to complete their puppet play.

Bruce and Craig had also created a Fantastic Mr. Fox puppet. The fox puppet was made from felt and stuffed with cotton; felt was also used to create the fox's facial features. A unique detail of this fox was its detachable tail! The boys had used Velcro to enhance the realism of their depiction of the scene where the farmers shoot off Fantastic Mr. Fox's tail.

Sylvia learned that the boys had spent an entire Saturday constructing the puppets and writing and practising the play script. Bruce's mother informed Sylvia that a continual flow of laughter floated down the stairs one Saturday afternoon. Bruce's mother was aware that the boys were creating puppets but at one point, her curiosity piqued, she ascended the stairs to discover the source of their joviality. To her surprise, the Cabbage Patch doll that Bruce had received several years earlier as a Christmas present had been "altered." Although Bruce's mother supplied the boys with some of the materials, they created the puppets themselves.

Bruce and Craig had read *Fantastic Mr. Fox* during Literature Workshops in Sylvia's classroom. Once every two to four weeks, Sylvia's students engaged in some type of extension activity to a recently read novel (the students selected the activity and the book). Bruce and Craig chose to complete a puppet play depicting the scene in *Fantastic Mr. Fox* where the fox's tail is shot off by the farmers as they wait by the fox's hole to capture him. Bruce and Craig were the first individuals in Sylvia's class that year to present a puppet play, and their highly successful and amusing play inspired many of their peers. Numerous plays were written and presented, and the puppets varied greatly in construction (e.g., sock, paper plate, paper lunch-bag, and scrap-material puppets).

Engaging in puppet plays was one of the many ways that Sylvia's students expressed their responses to the literature they read during Literature Workshops.

REFLECTION

Before you read the next section of this chapter, consider the following questions. What does the phrase "response to literature" mean to you? How would you initiate "response to literature" in your own classroom? Why do you think teachers might provide opportunities for students to engage in response-related activities? What might children learn by engaging in these activities?

Response to Literature

"Response to literature" seems to be a rather ubiquitous phrase used variously by researchers, theorists, and practitioners. Too often the phrase is used as an umbrella term "to refer to any aspect of literature and its teaching" (Squire, 1990, p.13). The phrase is also used in some basal series, but these "response activities" to reading selections are frequently little more than decontextualized skill-based tasks. What do teachers and researchers mean by "response to literature"? Why do teachers want their students to engage in response activities? What are teachers teaching and children learning through response-related activities? These are important questions to explore to gain an understanding of why teachers should—and how they can—implement literature- and response-based reading programs.

Purves and Rippere explain "response to literature" as "mental, emotional, intellectual, sensory, physical. It encompasses the cognitive, affective, perceptual and psychomotor activities that the reader... performs as he reads or after he has read. Yet most teachers know that, in the classroom, a student's response will be like an iceberg: only a small part will become apparent to the teacher or even to the student himself" (1968, p.xiii). Squire (1990) notes that

> *Response to literature does not mean response to just any kind of reading, nor does it mean that 'anything goes' when a child reacts to a particular text. Important as the experiences a child brings to the reading of a book are, the text itself imposes rigorous limits on the nature and direction of his or her response. One cannot give a child a predetermined response. But it does not follow that any response, regardless of stimulus, can be accepted in teaching literature. (pp.13-14)*

Reader-response theories, like theories of reading, attempt to explain the "location of meaning." Is meaning in the text, in the reader's head, or a combination of both? If indeed the reader and text mutually contribute to the construction of meaning, what is the role of each? What is the role of "response" in the construction of meaning? Each of the reader-response theories described in this chapter answers such questions in its own unique way. As you read and reflect on each theory, consider how the adoption of the various theoretical stances would influence the organization of your literature-based program and your instructional practices.

Reader-response Theories

The term READER-RESPONSE is associated with the work of educators who use the words READER, READING PROCESS, RESPONSE, and LITERATURE-BASED READING PROGRAMS to describe a particular approach to teaching reading in the language arts. Reader-response theories arose in direct opposition to NEW CRITICISM, which views a text as an autonomous entity; in other words, New Critics believe that a text has an inherent meaning, regardless of who reads the text, when it is read, where it is read, or why it is read. However, as each New Critic believes his or her interpretation to be the "correct" one, they often disagree about the "right" interpretation of a text. For example, Sylvia's English teacher in grades twelve and thirteen, Mr. Gald, lectured his classes and graded assignments from a New Critical stance. Mr. Gald communicated to his students that each of Shakespeare's texts (e.g., *A Midsummer's Night Dream*, *Romeo and Juliet*, *The Taming of the Shrew*, *King Lear*, *The Merchant of Venice*) had one meaning, that being his interpretation of each text and the work of the scholars he had read and agreed with. Mr. Gald did not consider valid students' ideas about, interpretations of, and responses to Shakespeare's works unless they agreed with him and his accepted critics.

In contrast, reader-response theorists argue that a text does not have one single meaning, but rather that meaning depends on the PARTICULARITY of one's reading (that is, numerous aspects of the reading context). In high school, Sylvia read *The Importance of Being Earnest* (Wilde, 1959) and disliked the play because of the prolonged analysis of its meaning in her English class. However, a recent rereading of the play resulted in an entirely different response as she found the work charming and engaging. The particularity of Sylvia's readings affected her responses. When Sylvia and Joyce each reread *The English Patient* (Ondaatje, 1992), they brought to their second readings both their understandings of how to read Ondaatje's book (based on having learned about the book during their first readings) and their initial affective responses. During their second readings, they experienced some new responses and interpretations, which added to the meanings and understandings created during the initial readings. Thus several factors influenced the particularity of their readings.

Reader-response theorists differ in the emphasis they place on the text or the reader in regard to the creation of meaning, but all believe that readers actively construct meaning as they interact or transact with texts. Louise Rosenblatt (1991a) differentiates among reader-response theories by characterizing them "in terms of the emphases in their treatment of the reader-text relationship" (p.59): i.e., READER-ORIENTED THEORIES (subjective criticism and psychoanalytical theory), TEXT-ORIENTED THEORIES (structuralism), and READER-PLUS-TEXT-ORIENTED THEORIES (reception theory, transactional theory, and interpretive communities). Individuals interested in reading more about these and other reader-response theories may find *A Teacher's Introduction to Reader-response Theories* (Beach, 1993) a useful resource.

READER-ORIENTED THEORIES

Subjective Criticism: David Bleich views reading as a subjective process in that a reader's personality determines what is perceived. As people engage in a perceptual experience, they simultaneously experience an emotional response to that perception. For example, the smell of freshly brewed coffee may arouse a person's appetite or may evoke thoughts and feelings about a lazy weekend morning. The same thing happens when we read: the simultaneous evocation of a cognitive perception and affective response(s). According to Bleich (1980), the study of literature must begin with "response," because a text does not direct or restrain the reader; rather, readers direct their own activities while reading. For example, when Sylvia recently gathered versions of *Little Red Riding Hood* for her children's literature course and reread Trina Schart Hyman's version of the story (1983), she was reminded of Anthony Browne's illustrations in *The Tunnel* (1989) and Browne's talent for embedding many INTERTEXTUAL messages in his illustrations. Whenever Joyce reads *Little Red Riding Hood,* she remembers her childhood and her mother's many warnings not to talk to strangers and admonitions to be a "good girl." Sylvia's response is strongly cognitive, while Joyce's is emotive. As Bleich states, the text is not "directing" Sylvia or Joyce in their responses; rather, as readers, they determine their own responses to the text.

Bleich believes a reader's subjective re-creation of a text can be explored by examining three components of the response: "what the reader perceives in the text; the affective component related to that perception; and the analogies associated with what was perceived" (Schulz, 1991, p.17). After exploring their own responses at the perceptive, affective, and associative levels (i.e., what in our own experiences relates to our reading of the text), Bleich believes that readers are ready to communicate their interpretations of the work to other readers. To Bleich, response acquires meaning only when it is "publicly explained and validated" (Tompkins, 1978, p.1071). Bleich maintains that individuals freely and consciously choose to be members of an interpretive community (i.e., we decide whom to share our responses with). Through negotiation in an interpretive community, readers communicate their responses to group members and, through discussion, decide which responses and interpretations are valid and which are not.

REFLECTION

When Sylvia reread *The English Patient* as part of her adult reading group, she once again found herself caring deeply about the four main characters in the story. Other group members stated that they cared little about the characters and could not empathize or identify with them or their situations. Sylvia was surprised by their responses, disappointed that they did not share similar responses to herself, and wondered why the other readers experienced a lack of emotional bonding with the characters in the book.

Think of a book or a movie that has been significant in your life. Have you shared your feelings and thoughts about this book or movie with anyone else? Did they share your responses or did your responses differ greatly? Did you discuss why your responses were similar or different? The next time you read a book or view a movie, share your responses with a friend and note any differences or similarities in your perceptions and emotional responses. Think about what this tells you about yourself and your friend (i.e., reader/viewer personality, biography, and predilections).

Psychoanalytical Theory: Norman Holland, a psychologist, put forward a reader-response theory that explains how personality affects literary response. Holland states that an individual's "identity theme" (personality, character) could be discerned by identifying patterns and themes in a person's life choices. Holland (1980) contends that a reader shapes a literary work "to give him what he characteristically both wishes and fears" (p.124). As readers take in a literary work, they project characteristic fantasies into it (which are aspects of identity) and "transform these fantasies into themes—meanings—of characteristic concern" (Holland, 1976a, p.338). Holland (1976b) believes there can be many readings for a text as one's identity determines the constructive acts of perception and interpretation; in other words, the reader creates the meaning the reader wants to create. Teachers and parents frequently wonder why children want to read and enjoy scary stories (see Dickson, 1998 and Richards et al., 1999 for discussion on the popularity of scary stories). Holland might suggest that scary stories address the fears of young children, in that children are able to confront their fears through the literature. We need only to look at the popularity of the *Goosebumps* series (Stine) or of many traditional fairy stories to exemplify this concept.

TEXT-ORIENTED THEORIES

Structuralism: Structuralists work from the view that meaning is embedded in the system of signs (i.e., the text) and is constructed literally through the structures of the text. Structuralists want "to find and make explicit the 'grammar' of a literary text, the understanding ideal readers have of how to read literature according to socially determined notions of appropriateness" (Thomson, 1987, p.101). Consistent with New Critics, structuralists ignore the significance of extratextual elements in the reading process—such as the historical background of an author or a reader's values, life experiences, and emotions. However, structuralism differs from New Criticism in that texts are viewed as having meaning as a result of readers actively applying their knowledge of how texts work (i.e., the "grammar" of the text), not because the text itself contains meaning. For example, probably the first literary structure children learn is that of the fairy story. The characteristic opening of "Once upon a time" indicates a particular type of story, characters, and series of events. Older readers are then able to manipulate those structures and enjoy books such as *Once Upon a Golden Apple* (Little, 1991) and *The True Story of the Three Little Pigs* (Scieszka, 1989), which play with traditional structures in facilitating new meanings and experiences for readers.

Jonathan Culler, a structural theorist, labels the understandings and abilities that good readers possess (i.e., those which enable them to create meaning from literary texts) as "literary competences." Culler (1980) describes literary competences as "an implicit understanding of the operations of literary discourse which tells one what to look for....an internalized grammar of literature" which allows readers "to convert linguistic sequences into literary structures and meanings" (p.102). He maintains that this implicit knowledge of publicly accepted conventions is possessed by both readers and authors. For example, when reading a mystery, readers know that the author will have deliberately embedded clues within the story and that these clues will assist them in solving the mystery. Writers know that a good mystery story must have relevant (and sometimes misleading) clues throughout to keep readers entertained and engaged. Thus, both readers and writers possess an internalized grammar of the literary discourse of mysteries.

Roland Barthes, another theorist, discusses the underlying codes that operate in texts (i.e., the codes of action, puzzles, symbols, character discernment, and societies and culture). One example of the code of character discernment is the black-helmeted, masked, and cloaked Darth Vader in the *Star Wars Trilogy* (Lucas, 1977-1983), the enemy of the white-clothed, blond-haired, righteous Luke Skywalker. Anthony Browne uses symbol code in his picture book *The Tunnel* (1989). The symbol of the tunnel is used as an expression of the unknown, a transformational event. The story would be completely different had Browne used a bridge rather than a tunnel in his book. Barthes believes readers learn these codes through both living in society and reading literature (Thomson, 1987). "The codes are the source of the text's meanings and involve the reader in producing those meanings" (Thomson, 1987, p.107). To Barthes, the goal of reading is to "unravel the multiple codes that make meaning possible, thereby freeing as many varied meanings as the text might suggest" (Schulz, 1991, p.18). In other words, there will be several valid interpretations of texts as readers unravel the many codes of texts in numerous ways.

READER-PLUS-TEXT-ORIENTED THEORIES

Reception Theory: Wolfgang Iser believes a reader actively participates in the production of meaning when reading a text. Iser contends that reading is guided by "the text and the personal experience and cultural history of the reader, his or her present representation of the world and the reading conventions s/he has internalized" (Thomson, 1984, p.18). Iser asserts that the literary work is brought into existence by the convergence of reader and text.

Iser (1980) states that reading is always "the process of anticipation and retrospection" (p.50). That is, when reading a book, a reader makes predictions about future events and actions and also reconsiders those predictions (as well as other thoughts and emotions) regarding the characters, the events, and the book as a whole, based on further reading of the text. The text is transformed into an experience for the reader through a continual process of modification of meaning. A reader's wandering viewpoint, travelling inside the text, involves the reader in the processes "of continually forming and modifying both expectations of what is to come and interpretations of what has previously been read" (Thomson, 1984, p.21).

Iser states that OMISSIONS or GAPS or blanks in texts provide invitations for readers to establish their own connections by bringing in past life and literary experiences. As the gaps in text may be filled in various ways, "one text is potentially capable of several different realizations, and no reading can ever exhaust the full potential, for each reader will fill in the gaps in his own way, thereby excluding the various other possibilities" (Iser, 1980, p.55). In the young-adult novel *The Maestro* by Tim Wynne-Jones (1995), Chapter 30 ends with a fire consuming the Maestro's house and igniting a box of cartridges. Chapter 31 begins with Burl, the protagonist, building a fire next to the charred and still smoldering ruins of the house, in order to keep warm. Thus, there is a gap between the ending of Chapter 30 and the beginning of Chapter 31. As readers, we have to fill in the details ourselves, and there are many possible ways to fill in the gap between the two chapters. The INDETERMINACIES found in texts such as *The Maestro* engage readers in the construction of meaning while simultaneously imposing or limiting interpretations. That is, a reader must fill in the gaps with information consistent with what has happened previously in the text—something that makes sense. Browne's book *The Tunnel* has several examples of indeterminacies. Near the end of the picture book, Rose finds Jack turned into stone after his journey through the forest. Browne does not disclose why or how this happened; rather, readers must fill in the gaps, but must do so based on the content of the story and their own literary and life experiences.

Transactional Theory: Louise Rosenblatt adopts Dewey's term "transaction" to describe the reciprocal relationship between reader and text. "Transaction...designates an ongoing process in which the elements or parts are seen as aspects or phases of a total situation" (1985, p.98). In reading, both reader and text act upon each other, each mutually contributing to and defining the relationship. Rosenblatt believes each reader brings a reservoir of life and literary experiences to the text, a set of signs. She states (1981) that the marks or squiggles on a page guide or stimulate elements/memories in readers' minds. Readers selectively choose and organize particular elements/memories according to their interpretations of the text. Rosenblatt asserts that during the transaction between text and reader, a new experience, the POEM, is evoked. The word "poem" is derived from the Latin word *poesis*, which means creation, imaginative power, or creative inspiration. Rosenblatt uses this word to indicate that the new experience evoked by the text is the result of a creative act by the reader (i.e., "the lived-through experience of building up the work under guidance of the text" [1976, p.69]). The poem, an event in the life history of a reader, occurs at a "particular time in a particular environment at a particular moment" (Rosenblatt, 1976, p.20). Rosenblatt explains, "This lived-through 'work,' this 'evocation,' is what the reader 'responds to' as it is being called forth during the transaction, and as it is reflected on, interpreted, evaluated, analyzed, criticized afterward" (1986, p.124). Rosenblatt (1978) believes readers can make various defensible interpretations of their evocations, but emphasizes that some interpretations are more valid than others. For example, an interpretation of *Charlotte's Web* (White, 1952) as a book about friendship is more valid than one focussing on human cruelty to animals.

Rosenblatt distinguishes AESTHETIC from EFFERENT reading and views these two stances as poles of a continuum. In aesthetic reading, the reader "adopts an attitude of readiness to attend to what is being lived through during the reading event" (Rosenblatt, 1988, p.74) and focusses on both the private and public aspects of meaning. Rosenblatt emphasizes that both public and private meanings have cognitive and affective associations; for example, the definition of the word "book" is found in a dictionary (public meaning), yet all readers have their own private meanings for the word "book." Private meanings of the word "book" may include an item that contains information that is too difficult to understand, an item individuals retire to bed with and enjoy as a pleasurable diversion, an item and work of study, or a scholarly tome that is incomprehensible. In efferent reading, "the process of making meaning out of a text involves selective attention to what is to be retained" after the reading as "residue" and focusses mainly on the public referents of meaning (Rosenblatt, 1981, p.6). For example, when assembling a shelving unit, Sylvia concentrated on the written directions and completed each step as instructed (i.e., the "residue"). When she read the word "assembly," she did not reminisce about the assemblies from her elementary school years when various grades performed (i.e., presented a play, sang songs, read chorally) for the rest of the school. "The distinction between aesthetic and non-aesthetic reading, then, derives ultimately from what the reader does, the stance that he adopts and the activities he carries out in relation to the text" (Rosenblatt, 1978, p.27). Rosenblatt believes any text can be read *predominantly* from either an aesthetic or efferent stance, with most reading events falling somewhere along the aesthetic/efferent continuum. She also asserts that there are no purely aesthetic nor purely efferent readings and that readers' stances may fluctuate as they read. For example, although Sylvia's predominant stance when reading the novel *Billy and the Bearman* (Poulsen, 1996) was aesthetic, she also learned about surviving in the wilderness (i.e., residue of efferent reading) as several textual passages described the boys' survival efforts.

Interpretive Communities: Stanley Fish is another literary theorist who rejects the notion that meaning is embedded or encoded in the actual text. Fish denounces the notion of "correct interpretation" of texts and believes that meaning is actively negotiated and constructed by a reader during the reading event. Fish contends that a reader possesses numerous interpretive strategies (e.g., looking for themes, assigning significances), which are learned through experiences with different types of texts and through discussing these texts with other readers. He maintains that interpretive communities are made up of those individuals who share interpretive strategies that "exist prior to the act of reading and therefore determine the shape of what is read" (1980b, p.182). Thus, meaning is not an individual creation but rather the result of readers applying communal strategies or conventions they have assimilated. Alan Purves (1973) conducted an international study to explore the literature instruction of students aged fourteen to eighteen; the findings of his study demonstrated the influence of interpretive communities. Not only did Purves find considerable difference between the responses of educators and students in the various countries he studied, but he also discovered that, between the ages of fourteen and eighteen, students' response preferences became more definite and conformed with the teachers' preferences. Purves argues that response to literature is learned because response is affected by culture, school (which is an aspect of culture), and teaching practices. Other research has demonstrated the salient role of the teacher in the interpretive community (Hickman, 1983, 1984; McMahon, 1992; Pantaleo, 1995, 1998).

When a group of people read common texts and talk with one another about their reading experiences, shared meanings develop among the group members and "they become part of an interpretive community. These meanings they share affect their subsequent interactions and, over time, lead to the development of a thought style, a common approach to viewing the world" (Hanssen, Harste, & Short, 1990, pp.264-265). What is talked about within an interpretive community affects how the members think, and how they think affects what they talk and write about. For example, when Sylvia was in Mr. Gald's English classes, he devoted a large amount of instructional time and energy to symbolism. As a member of that particular interpretive community, Sylvia found herself searching for examples of symbolism when reading. This is an example of how a preferred mode of response is learned. Another example that demonstrates the learning of a particular interpretive strategy is the way many people search for one major subtle and significant meaning of a poem—an approach often encouraged in school. After reading a poem in high school, Sylvia distinctly remembers the dreaded question, "What does this poem mean?" Joyce felt that she never "got it" when reading poetry for high-school English classes and came to believe that she lacked the ability to figure out the meaning the teacher so clearly saw in each poem. Many readers lose interest in poetry (and literature in general) because of such reductive experiences.

Laura Apol (1998) has discussed the need for teachers to understand literary theory and its relationship to ideology and children's literature. Slovan (1997) believes that, among other aspects, literary theory "deals with criticism—approaches to the reading and study of literary works—through analysis, interpretation, and evaluation" and writes that "Knowledge of literary theory...belongs in the teacher's head, where it becomes the basis for a deductive framework" (pp.47-48). Theory and practice are interconnected; each informs and influences the other. It is fundamental for teachers to reflect on and be conscious of their theoretical beliefs and assumptions as the latter shape their practice and drive their teaching of literature; influence their purposes, goals, and expectations of using literature and response; and consequently affect the content of students' responses. McGee and Tompkins (1995) discuss and demonstrate how the adoption of various theoretical approaches influences teachers' literature-based instruction and students' responses. As Fish writes, "not only does one believe what one believes, but one *teaches* what one believes" (1980a, p.364). A teacher's practice is significantly influenced by the adoption of one or more of the theories presented in this section.

The Influence of Reader-response Theories on Language Arts Instruction

CLASSROOM SCENARIO

When Joyce first began teaching in Canada, she taught in a grade three classroom. She was provided with a basal reader for each child and a teacher's guide for herself. There was a language arts textbook as well, but there was no in-class or in-school library. Although she had her own personal collection of children's books, the textbook was the sole resource for teaching language arts, other than the public library some 65 km away. The prevailing thought at the time was that children would learn to read if they were given appropriate direct instruction, read stories together from a basal reader, and completed the relevant skills-based worksheets and workbook exercises. These basic skills included learning the difference between a long (glided) vowel and a short (unglided) vowel sound, learning how to syllabicate words so they could be "sounded out," finding the main idea in a paragraph or story, and creating an alternate title for a story in the basal reader. The children in Joyce's class completed hundreds of pages of exercises, and some of the children read their own books at home, although very few families bought books for their children. Paperback book clubs were new on the scene in Canada, so only one or two children ordered books for themselves. Not one child in Joyce's class visited the public library. However, a consistent part of every school day was the reading aloud of a novel—almost anything Joyce could find in the public library that she thought would interest her students.

What a difference from Sylvia's classrooms in the late 1980s and the 1990s! Sylvia worked mainly with literature (i.e., novels, picture books, and content area books—both fiction and nonfiction) and response to literature. Her students listened to literature read aloud; selected their own books to read; read avidly; talked about the books and poems they read; wrote about their reading; completed author and illustrator studies; created plays, dioramas, and book displays; gave book talks; and engaged in many other activities as they read and responded to their books. Sylvia had an extremely large classroom library as well as many sets of multiple copies (two to seven) of novels. She also provided direct instruction of contextualized skills and strategies in both reading and writing.

What happened in the intervening years that convinced language arts teachers and researchers of the value of programs such as Sylvia's? First of all, they noticed that many children were learning how to read but were not *becoming* readers. They were frequently bored with the exercises, and often with the stories in the basal readers as well. The basals, although attempting to include interesting content material for students, were designed as instructional tools; they were more concerned with presenting age-appropriate vocabulary and syntactic structures, and offering practice for a later time in children's lives when they would eventually read material appealing to their own interests.

James Britton was one of the scholars in English language arts education who helped educators to realize that language is not something children practise, like a juggler practising tricks (Britton calls these worksheet-type activities "dummy runs"). Rather, it is something children practise much as a lawyer practises law and a doctor practises medicine (Britton, 1970, p.130). In other words, children use the skills they possess to help them do the job at hand, and as they do it, they learn more and get better at it.

Round-robin reading was the bane of most children's lives in the 1960s and 1970s, and many people remember engaging in that practice, either as teachers or students. Round-robin reading is an example of a "dummy run," an artificial activity found only in schools—reading for reading's sake, for the purpose of learning how to do it better, not for any appreciation or enjoyment of the text itself. Children follow along in the text silently while someone else reads aloud; at a designated point, they each take their turn to read the next paragraph or section out loud themselves. Children in these circumstances rarely focus on the meaning of the piece or making sense of the whole text; rather, they focus on small parts, often nervous that they will make a "mistake" when it is their turn to read orally. They try to memorize details for the inevitable questions, yet rarely have the opportunity to discuss what they have read or to express an opinion about it.

Another scholar who has had an enormous impact on the teaching of reading through reader-response is Louise Rosenblatt, whose work is described earlier in this chapter. Rosenblatt's work drew attention to the fact that reading is carried out for different purposes by different people at different times; that a reader's response to a reading will profoundly affect the meanings constructed from it; and that reading is frequently taught in schools from an efferent stance. Almost every time a child is required to read, there are teacher-generated questions to be answered and a right answer to be found.

In encouraging students to respond to texts, it is important that teachers understand why they are engaging in this practice and what is being learned through it. Children come to understand how texts work, what constitutes a good book, and how language can be used in different ways to create different meanings and effects. They learn how to create meanings from a text for themselves, explore those meanings, and learn subtle nuances that completing worksheet exercises can never teach. In short, they learn how to become *readers*, not just people able to read. In order to talk about a book, or to write or draw about one, a student must have read the book, understood it, and given some thought to it. Children are more likely to take ownership of the reading process and come to understand that there is no one "right" answer to literature when they are invited to respond to a text—although, as Rosenblatt says, some responses are more valid or appropriate than others.

Children use high-level cognitive abilities when they engage with and respond to a text aesthetically, and they learn to respect and honour their own interpretations. They appear to become more critical in their thinking about texts, more original in their own writing, and much more capable language users and learners when they read and respond from an aesthetic stance. This is not to say that efferent reading is unimportant; indeed, for readers to think in more critical and sophisticated ways about their reading, they must first understand the details, events, and facts of texts. Rosenblatt asserts that students need experience with both efferent and aesthetic reading: "We need to make sure that students are cumulatively developing, in their transactions with texts, the ability to adopt the stance on the continuum appropriate to their particular personal purposes and to the situation—in short, the ability to read both efferently and aesthetically" (Rosenblatt, 1991b, p.448). However, she also emphasizes that if the purpose of the reading is "literary," then students must first experience the work, and recapture and reflect on their lived-through experiences (i.e., aesthetic reading), before they engage in more efferent-type activities (1991b).

A review of some of the research on the student benefits of reader-response approaches to literature (Spiegel, 1998) corroborates our beliefs about and experiences with such programs. According to Spiegel, students who participated in programs with reader-response approaches to literature developed "ownership of what they read and of their response," made personal connections with literature, gained "an appreciation for multiple interpretations along with a tolerance for and even expectation of ambiguity," became "more effective, more critical readers, moving to higher levels of thinking and a richer understanding of literature," and increased their "repertoire of responses to the literature" (1998, pp.43-44). Further, Spiegel's review reveals that students became better strategic readers, viewed themselves as successful readers, and developed metacognitive awareness and other knowledge, strategies, and skills (pp.45-46).

Most reader-response approaches emphasize responding to the literature that has been read. The remainder of this chapter discusses ways to invite children to respond to literature through oral, visual, and dramatic activities.

Facilitating Oral Responses to Literature

REFLECTION

Before reading the next section, consider the following questions.

What is a discussion? What is a dialogue? How are they similar? How are they different? What types of roles can individuals take on during discussions?

Which roles contribute to successful discussions? Which ones detract from successful discussions? What kinds of oral language behaviours are conducive to successful discussions? How can we teach students to participate positively in discussions? What is the teacher's role in teaching about and participating in discussions about literature?

Rosenblatt (1988) maintains that literature should be read from an aesthetic stance, an attitude of readiness to attend to "what is being lived through during the reading event" (p.74). She states that readers respond to the "lived-through work" both during and after the reading event (1986) and believes that initial responses to the reading transaction should be aesthetic in nature (1991b). Although Purves and Rippere (1968) note that, in a classroom, a student's response will be like an iceberg, literature discussion or response groups can facilitate children's appreciation, understanding, and interpretation of literature as they reflect on their evocations of texts. By sharing their thoughts, feelings, images, and memories orally with peers, readers can unravel their reading transactions. Talking can help individuals to "construct ideas and represent experiences" for themselves and others, and is "one of the primary means" through which new learning is incorporated "into existing mental frameworks" (Strickland et al., 1989, p.193).

But how can teachers get children talking about their reading transactions? Where do we start with response? We do not want to make the notion of "response" abstract or uncommon; rather, we want students to realize that, as humans, they are constantly responding in some manner to their environment. It is important to capitalize on students' wealth of experiences with and background knowledge of response. It is also imperative for students and adults to recognize, understand, and acknowledge how personal, social, and cultural factors influence an individual's response.

A teacher can identify a particular topic, event, or circumstance and ask for students' reactions. For example, in Sylvia's grades four and five classroom, she used the topics of siblings, allowance, clothing, music, school lunches, and the closing of the local outdoor swimming pool to demonstrate how individuals naturally "respond" in some fashion to events and topics. The students were asked to visualize a winter's first snowfall, a freshly baked, double-layer chocolate cake with creamy frosting, and a polluted river. The students then shared their mental images and responses to their images. Sylvia also read a poem and showed two illustrations from Chris Van Allsburg's book *The Mysteries of Harris Burdick* (1984), to further demonstrate students' responses. With a grade eight class, the first topic Sylvia had students respond to was school dances—a topic of utmost interest to them. In an undergraduate university class, Sylvia used topics such as country-and-western music, television violence, the Quebec referendum of 1995, cancer, censorship, and physical fitness to make explicit students' knowledge of and experiences with response; she also used an editorial cartoon to elicit response. Response can be made concrete and familiar to students by making explicit to them their tacit knowledge of and experiences with response.

After a discussion of students' experiences with response, a teacher can read a picture book, a chapter from a novel, a poem, or a newspaper article; students can then be asked to articulate what was going through their minds before, during, and after the reading. These personal responses can then be used to connect the initial discussion about response to more specifically responding to literature. It is important to discuss with students that words cannot always accurately communicate or express a reader's responses, and that there may sometimes be issues that people choose not to talk or write about because of their emotional or psychological significance. As teachers, we want to communicate to our students that they "are free to pay attention to what the words call to consciousness" (Rosenblatt, 1991b, p.447). Reading from a predominantly aesthetic stance "happens if students have repeatedly found that in approaching a text called a 'poem' or 'story' they can assume they are free to pay attention to what the words called to their consciousness. They can savour the images, the sounds, the smells, the actions, the associations, and the feelings the words point to" (Rosenblatt, 1991b, p.447). We cannot be

Grade three children at work

sure that what students talk or write about actually was part of their "lived-through experience," but by encouraging students to reflect on, (re)experience, savour, and/or (re)consider their evocations and interpretations of texts, teachers can foster students' thinking about texts, about themselves, and about the human condition in general.

Some students have little or no previous experience with discussing their personal responses to literature. Their reading autobiographies may include a predominance of more efferent reading activities (e.g., oral retellings, written summaries, answering literal level questions about texts, analyzing texts using literary elements) or the belief that there is one correct interpretation of texts—the teacher's. They may have read literature strictly from an efferent stance, with the understanding that readers should not tap their life and literary reservoirs as they read. Such readers may not understand the legitimacy of their interpretations, ideas, thoughts, feelings, wonderings, comparisons, and criticisms. An interesting activity is to ask students what they do in their heads as they read. Some students may be unaware of the active role they should play in the construction of meaning and may not realize that they should pay attention to their aesthetic responses both during and after the reading. As teachers, we must assist students in understanding their active role in reading and the importance of their affective responses.

Prior to having students participate in literature discussion groups, various instructional strategies can be implemented to facilitate their understanding of their role in constructing meaning. These instructional strategies can also provide students with experience in talking about their personal responses to literature.

THINK ALOUD

Although this strategy has generally been employed as a technique to improve the comprehension of poor readers (Baumann, Jones & Seifeert-Kessell, 1993), think alouds also demonstrate the active role of readers in the reading process. This strategy consists of teachers verbalizing their thoughts as they read a piece of text aloud. Teachers model the kinds of strategies that skilled readers use during reading, and specifically point out what they are doing in order to cope with a particular aspect of comprehension.

Five important comprehension techniques may be modelled by the teacher: making predictions; producing mental images (pictures in the head); linking prior knowledge with new topics; monitoring comprehension (e.g., verbalizing confusing parts); and identifying active ways to "fix up" comprehension problems (e.g., maybe I'll reread, I'll read ahead and see if it gets clearer, I'd better change my picture of the story) (Tierney, Readence & Dishner, 1995). The teacher selects a text that includes some points that are unclear, puzzling, difficult, and/or contradictory. The passage may also contain unknown words. A useful idea is to have the text on overhead transparencies; as the teacher reads the passage aloud, the students can follow along silently.

When a think aloud is used as a comprehension strategy, students listen as the teacher thinks through his or her reading of the passage. This articulation of thoughts helps poor readers to realize that they can be actively involved in constructing meaning as they read, that the meaning they construct can make sense, and that there are strategies they can employ to "fix up" comprehension problems. When using this technique as a comprehension strategy, it is useful to focus on only one or two of the aforementioned comprehension techniques, as modelling all five in one think aloud session will tend to overwhelm students.

Think alouds can also be used as a way to illustrate reading from an aesthetic stance and to demonstrate the importance of personal response before, during, and after reading. The comprehension techniques of generating hypotheses before and during reading, producing mental pictures, and making analogies by linking prior knowledge to new information in a text demonstrate the active role of a reader. During a think aloud, teachers also can articulate their general thoughts, feelings, criticisms, comparisons, questions, and wonderings about the piece. One or two specific aspects can be focussed on during a think aloud (e.g., predicting, comparing, questioning). As a whole-class activity, students can engage in a shared think aloud, or they can engage in think alouds with partners. A debriefing session with the class should follow, and students should be encouraged to talk about the kinds of behaviours they engaged in. The goal for students, after listening to and engaging in various think aloud strategies, is to internalize and use these techniques when reading silently.

SAY SOMETHING

Say something (Harste, Short & Burke, 1988) is another strategy that demonstrates the active role of readers when reading, and it encourages expression of personal response. A say something is also a good comprehension activity. The teacher should initially model a say something (on more than one occasion) with the entire class so that students understand the procedure.

The teacher selects a piece of text and divides the passage into sections (e.g., every third paragraph or at the end of each page), or gives students directions about how to divide the passage, or controls the amount to be read by using overhead transparencies of the text. Students work with a partner (either teacher or student choice). Each dyad receives one copy of the text. The selection can be read silently or aloud (if read aloud, the students take turns reading). Through initial modelling of the strategy, the teacher demonstrates that, after reading a certain predetermined portion of the text, each reader then says something to their partner about what they have read; the other person then responds with another remark about the reading. Readers can comment on what was read, make predictions, describe their visualizations, express concerns or criticisms, make intertextual connections, ask questions, relate their own experiences, or comment on their partner's articulations. The second student then reads the next portion of text, and again each individual says something. After the text has been read in this manner, the teacher can engage the students in a debriefing activity, asking them to reflect on the types of comments they made as they read. If students need practice at engaging in one of the strategies that we know active readers employ, the teacher may suggest a particular focus for the say something activity. For example, the teacher may ask the students to make predictions and explain their predictions after each section of text, or the children may be directed to articulate their visualizations, wonderings, or questions after reading each segment of text.

DIRECTED-READING-THINKING ACTIVITY

A directed-reading-thinking activity (DRTA) (Stauffer, 1975) is another worthwhile comprehension strategy to demonstrate the active role of readers. Prior to reading, students are asked to generate predictions of story development based on some limited information, such as the title of the reading selection, the author's name, or a few illustrations. Students are encouraged to explain why they think their predictions will occur. The predictions are recorded on the board, a transparency, or a chart, then the children read a certain portion of the story. (Here again, overhead transparencies of the text assist in controlling the amount of text being read.) Once the students have read a certain amount of text, they return to their predictions to see which have been realized, which seem unlikely to be fulfilled, and which may still possibly occur. The students are encouraged to support their opinions and to make further predictions based on their literary and life experiences. This strategy encourages readers to be actively involved in the construction of meaning.

OTHER STRATEGIES

Picture books are ideal for demonstrating the active role of readers in constructing meaning and the importance of affective responses. After reading *The Tunnel* (Browne, 1989), students can engage in a thoughts-in-the-head activity. The teacher assigns a student to a role (e.g., Jack), then identifies a particular scene (e.g., when he was crawling through the tunnel), and asks "Jack" to describe what was going through his head at that particular point in the story. This type of activity encourages students to think about the thoughts, feelings, and wonderings of characters at various points in books or stories.

Another activity to demonstrate the active role of the reader and the importance of personal responses is hot-seating. Hot-seating is similar to thoughts-in-the-head, as it also involves students taking on roles of various characters. After reading *Piggybook* (Browne, 1986), a student can be assigned the role of the father and then put on the hot-seat. The "father" might be asked to explain his lack of participation in the household chores. The "boys" in the story might be put on the hot-seat to explain their treatment of their mother. Hot-seating requires students to "become" various characters and to use both textual and personal input to explain characters' actions or thoughts.

Songs or poetry can serve as discussion media: once again, students can discuss their interpretations and responses to these types of texts. The piece of literature being read by the teacher or a novel being read by the entire class can also serve as media for discussion. The teacher can generate questions to facilitate discussions about students' thoughts, questions, criticisms, emotions, and intertextual connections.

The kinds of questions that teachers ask communicate explicit information to students about the stance readers should take when reading (and listening). A study by Many and Wiseman (1992) demonstrates how various teaching approaches—including the types of questions and probes asked before, during, and after the reading of a picture book—affected the content of responses of grade three students. Children who received instruction that focussed on their literary experiences—on their reactions and thoughts to stories—wrote responses "indicating more involvement in the story world, described similarities between characters and real people, and treated literature more as an aesthetic experience than a lesson or an object to be studied" (Many &

Wiseman, 1992, p.265). Efferent responses, which focussed on literary analysis, were most frequently written by children who received instruction on identifying and critiquing "literary elements through the analysis of character development, problems and solutions, and themes" (Many & Wiseman, 1992, p.269). Thus, teachers need to reflect on the kinds of questions they pose when working with literature.

Benton and Fox (1985) believe that the "most fruitful questions about stories arise from the sort of mental activities that readers engage in when they are involved in the experience of fiction" (p.18). They suggest posing questions on picturing (e.g., "What pictures do you get in your mind's eye of this character, scene or event?"); "anticipating and retrospecting"; interacting (e.g., "What do you feel about the character, setting or incident?"); and evaluating (e.g., "What do you feel about the way the story is being told?") (p.18). They also note the importance of asking such questions in an open and exploratory manner that encourages reflective response.

All of the aforementioned strategies communicate to students that there is more than one acceptable interpretation of a text; that, as readers, they need to be actively involved in creating meaning as they read (or listen); and that their affective responses are important. These strategies emphasize how both cognition and affect are involved in the construction of meaning. Readers' feelings, thoughts, and experiences are essential aspects of the reading transaction, and readers need not only to explore them but to step back and reflect upon them. Essentially, we want children to see literature as an opportunity to learn more about themselves, texts, and the world around them.

As is evident from this discussion, significant preparation is required before students can be expected to participate successfully in literature discussion groups. Another preparatory activity that is important to the implementation of discussion groups is instruction about discussion questions.

DISCUSSION QUESTIONS

Some teachers require students to bring "issues" to discuss; other teachers require students to bring discussion questions to their discussion groups. Regardless of the requirement, students need to understand what constitutes an "issue" or a "good" discussion question.

Dreher and Yopp (1994) explored how active comprehension instruction affected students' motivation to read. Those grade six students who received instruction about how to generate their own reading questions (versus teacher-generated questions) demonstrated positive attitudes and motivation for reading. Commeyras and Sumner (1996) examined how student-generated questions affected students' discussions of literature. They found that students aged seven and eight became excited, engaged in critical thinking, and assumed more responsibility for their learning when student-generated questions were used in literature discussions (versus teacher-assigned questions).

A strategy by Raphael (1986), called Question Answer Relationships (QARs), can serve as a useful framework for teaching students about "good" (i.e., effective) discussion questions. Raphael's taxonomy consists of Right There, Think and Search, Author and You, and On My Own questions. The answers to Right There questions are in the text: "The words used to make up the question and words used to answer the question are Right There in the same sentence" (Raphael, 1986, p.519). Students quickly learn that Right There questions are not "good" discussion questions, as there is nothing to discuss. The answers to Think and Search (or Putting It Together) questions are in the story or book, but readers need to put together different parts of the text. The answer could be in three sentences, on one page, or in one chapter, or a reader may need to consider the whole book or story. Raphael identifies explanation, compare/contrast, cause/effect, and list/example questions as types of Think and Search questions. Depending on the question, Think and Search questions can make good discussion questions (e.g., How were the characters Billy and the Bearman different and how were they similar?).

The two other types of QARs Raphael identifies, Author and You and On My Own, require readers to access and use their background knowledge. To answer Author and You questions, individuals must use information from the story or book and information from their experiential and literary reservoirs (e.g., What would you have done if you would have been in Jasmin's situation?). It is possible to answer On My Own questions without reading the text. This type of question is typical of the kind that teachers ask in prereading activities to create student interest and curiosity (e.g., Would you like to travel into the past? Why or why not? If you had a dinosaur for a pet, how would you care for it?). Author and You and On My Own questions make good discussion questions as students' opinions and ideas will vary: there is something to discuss.

Raphael's QAR framework must be introduced to students in an instructionally appropriate manner. Raphael (1986) suggests "the value of QAR instruction lies in the way it clarifies how students can approach the task of reading texts and answering questions. It helps them to realize the need to consider both information in the text and information from their own background knowledge" (p.517). We have presented the framework as a method for teaching good discussion questions; but regardless of how QARs are used, students need to understand the reasons for and applicability of learning the framework. Students should not be given several questions for each chapter of a novel and then be required to use Raphael's taxonomy to identify the type of each question. Nor should children be required to generate numerous questions, identify each kind, and then write answers for the questions.

Here are a few examples of "good" discussion questions generated by grade five students who had learned about Raphael's taxonomy of questions.

- *If your mom or dad had cancer, what would you do and why?*
- *What would you do if everyone or everything drank the chemical and became "good"?*
- *What other book does this book remind you of and why?*
- *If you had a dinosaur, what would you do with it?*
- *What would you do if you were being teased like Jacob?*
- *What was your favourite part of* Fantastic Mr. Fox *and why?*
- *If you were to rewrite a part in the book, what would you change and why?*
- *Which book,* Hatchet *or* My Side of the Mountain, *do you think is a more realistic survival story and why?*

Literature Discussions

The following is an excerpt from a student discussion about the book *Underground to Canada* (Smucker, 1977). In the particular classroom in which the discussion was recorded, this type of conference was labelled "independent," as no teacher was present during the conference nor was the conference audio-recorded for the purpose of submitting the tape to the teachers.

Four children, three grade five students and one grade four student, had read approximately two-thirds of Smucker's novel *Underground to Canada*. The novel tells the story of the journey of two slaves, Julilly and Liza, who have escaped from a cotton plantation in the southern United States. Workers on the "underground railway" offer to assist the girls in their flight to freedom in Canada.

According to their teachers, the four students conferencing about the novel were academically "above average" and considered some of the "top" students in the classroom. The following excerpt is taken from the middle of their fifteen-minute conference.

Beth: *I think that if Liza died, Julilly would stop her journey and go back.*

Nick: *I think so.*
Beth: *I don't think she would because her mom told her to go to Canada where she'd be free. She'd stop for a little while because she'd miss her [Liza].*
Simon: *A couple of days.*
Julie: *But, but she's not that kind of person who's going to stop because something got in her way.*
Simon: *No, I think so.*
Nick: *I think that if there weren't all those people from the plantation she could have just jumped off the wagon and just run away and it wouldn't have taken her as long probably.*
Julie: *Well, actually it would have because she needed directions and money and food and stuff and like how they had the barns set up. And she'd probably have got caught because they had special ways of tracking her. Actually she's pretty smart because she told them not to go across the river because she just said, "Don't go. It's not safe," but they didn't listen to her and then they [Lester and Adam] got caught.*
Nick: *Yeah.*
Simon: *I'd be scared. Like when the hounds are right after you and...*
Beth: *I think that she was really kinda big but I didn't think she was that strong. She's carrying Liza all over.*
Simon: *What do you think, Nick?*
Nick: *I think she's actually quite strong if she carries Liza all over the mountain paths and everything. That would be actually quite hard to do.*
Simon: *I don't think she was so strong at first because she was doing all that walking and running away from the hounds. I think she got stronger as she went along. That helps.*
Julie: *I don't think Liza's that heavy either because she's crippled.*
Nick: *Yeah, she got whipped too many times.*
Beth: *I don't know what or how the hounds keep on moving up with them. Wouldn't they search one area first? Like they just follow them?*
Julie: *Because of the scent.*
Beth: *But they went across so many rivers.*
Julie: *Yeah, I know. What's the point of chasing them all over when you could be back at the plantation? There's no point.*
Beth: *There are some others who might have got away and you don't know about it.*
Nick: *Yeah, do you think if a slave ran away that they just wouldn't worry about it because you know they'll run out of food some time or other, and they wouldn't really care about them? The slave drivers, whatever.*
Julie: *But then I suppose if they didn't chase them, then too many would escape and they might like ...*
Nick: *Lose all their slaves.*
Julie: *They might kind of feel scared that Canada would...*
Nick: *Would take over or something.*
Julie: *Canada would get really mad and the U.S. might...Like sometimes the U.S. usually helps other people and I guess Canada didn't think slavery was, well, we still don't think that slavery is right.*
Beth: *Yeah. You never know what could happen.*
Simon: *And the slave drivers paid money for the slaves.*
Nick: *Yeah, just like they were food or something like that or horses.*

The discussion continued.

REFLECTION

In your opinion, what were some of the strengths of the students' discussion of *Underground to Canada*? What types of oral language behaviours were demonstrated during this discussion? Were particular discussion roles fulfilled by group members? If you were talking with this group of children about their discussion, what would you say to them?

FACILITATING LITERATURE DISCUSSIONS

Much has been written about how discussions can be used to facilitate students' reading experiences. Conversational discussion groups (Wiencek & O'Flahavan, 1994) and GRAND CONVERSATIONS (Eeds & Wells, 1989) are two terms used to describe conferences where students talk with peers about the literature they have read. *Lively Discussions! Fostering Engaged Reading* (1996), edited by Gambrell and

Almasi, includes chapters that provide "practical, classroom-based strategies and techniques for using discussion in primary and elementary classrooms to promote interpretation and comprehension of both narrative and informational text" (p.xi). *Book Talk and Beyond: Children and Teachers Respond to Literature* (1995), edited by Roser and Martinez, is composed of chapters that focus on children and teachers talking about literature in elementary classrooms. An entire issue of the *Journal of Reading* (Horowitz, 1994) was devoted to discussion.

Three studies that explored the literature discussions of students in grades four, five, and six found that children need to be taught discussion skills (Eeds & Wells, 1989; Villaume & Worden, 1993; Wiencek & O'Flahavan, 1994). For example, Villaume and Worden (1993) found it necessary for teachers to model, facilitate, and teach the types of conversations they expected in the literature discussion groups of grade four students. In their study, the researchers and teachers demonstrated both initial personal responses and "how to respond to the personal responses of students" by elaborating, probing, and offering "alternative ways of thinking about their responses" (Villaume & Worden, 1993, p.465). Through direct instruction and mini-lessons, the teachers talked about "talk" in order to draw the children's attention to particular aspects of literature discussions (e.g., staying on topic, being respectful, discussing and refining responses). Villaume and Worden discovered that it was necessary for the teachers and researchers to be active participants in the literature discussions, demonstrating "the varied roles of participants: accepting, facilitating, elaborating, and probing" (1993, p.467).

How can students learn about the roles of discussion participants and about the types of talk that contribute to successful discussions? Initially, teachers can access students' understanding of and background experiences with discussions. The questions "What is a discussion?" and "What kinds of behaviours are conducive to successful discussions?" can be posed, and students can brainstorm ideas. A class simulation is useful for demonstrating the various roles of discussion participants. Sylvia and Jenny, a grades four and five teacher, conducted a discussion simulation. After talking about what constitutes a "discussion" as a whole class, the grades four and five students were assigned to a group. Sylvia and Jenny each asked their group of students to identify various roles of discussion participants; through student and teacher input, the behaviours of various roles were discussed. Jenny and Sylvia then assigned each student a discussion role (e.g., leader, interrupter, hitchhiker, non-participant, questioner, supporter) and placed each child in a predetermined group. There were five groups in total, each consisting of various combinations of discussion roles. A fishbowl strategy was used: those students not participating in the discussion sat in chairs around the group that was role-playing its discussion. After each of the five groups had an opportunity to "discuss" the story *Papa's Parrot* (Rylant, 1985), which they had read earlier in the day, a debriefing occurred where the students outside the fishbowl identified the various roles of the participants and judged the contribution of each role to the overall discussion (i.e., Did the role positively contribute to the success of the discussion?). The students recognized and discussed how often the roles and behaviours of discussion participants overlap. But by focussing on singular roles and types of behaviour, the fish-bowl strategy was most successful in illustrating those behaviours that facilitated and enhanced discussions and those that inhibited and deterred successful discussions. It is worthwhile to concentrate on a small number of discussion roles in a simulation and to complete the fishbowl strategy on more than one occasion.

As the types of behaviour we want to promote in small-group discussions are applicable to large-group discussions, teachers can focus on one or two discussion behaviours, then teach and model them to the entire class. A short story, the book being read aloud to the class, a class novel, or content area material can be the discussion medium. For example, a teacher may model how to relate ideas in a discussion through hitchhiking or "piggy-backing." The class focusses on this kind of talk as a group and then has an opportunity to practice this skill in small groups. Each group could then self-evaluate its success at hitchhiking and then as a whole class share suggestions for facilitating this type of "talk."

Another instructional discussion activity involves student modelling. Once children gain experience with discussions, a group of students can model desired discussion behaviours for the class; through a debriefing, the class can identify successful characteristics of the discussion. A group of students from the previous year can come to class and model a discussion, or students' discussions from previous years can be audio-recorded and shared. Again, it would be important to engage in debriefing sessions after both of these activities.

These are only a few suggestions for introducing and facilitating oral response and literature discussions. It is important to remember that it is often necessary to fine-tune and revisit appropriate discussion behaviours and "etiquette" throughout the year. Sylvia has found it useful for students to self-reflect on their discussions. Each student is asked to evaluate his or her group's discussions in writing, commenting on both the successful aspects and areas requiring additional attention (see Chapter 9).

TEACHER INFLUENCE

Not only is it important for teachers to provide instruction about discussion "talk" and "etiquette," but teachers must also be aware of the influence of their own behaviours in literature discussions. Research has shown that teachers influence students' oral and written responses to literature (Eeds & Wells, 1989; Hickman, 1983, 1984; Hynds, 1992; Marshall, 1987; Pantaleo, 1994; Purves, 1973; Villaume & Worden, 1993).

In one upper elementary classroom, when teachers participated in the children's literature discussions, they tended to control the conversations of the response groups. A "gentle inquisition" transpired (Eeds & Wells, 1989) in many conferences as the teachers asked an abundance of questions at a literal level—that is, a recitation rather than a discussion ensued. The teachers' questioning patterns affected the students' behaviours and the types of interactions that occurred during the conferences (Pantaleo, 1994, 1998). Moffett (1973) discusses the process of "expatiation," stating that "the heart of discussion is expatiation, picking up ideas and developing them; corroborating, qualifying, and challenging; building on and varying each other's statements, and images. Questioning is a very important part, but only a part, and should arise out of exchanges among students themselves so that they learn to pose as well as answer questions" (p.46). Both students and teachers need to engage in "expatiation" in order to actually "discuss" the literature.

Eeds and Wells (1989) also found that teachers' behaviours affect the types of interactions that occur during elementary students' literature discussions. The researchers maintained that "grand conversations" about literature were possible when teachers were fellow participants in discussion groups, sharing their own personal transactions with texts and acknowledging that their ideas, interpretations, and opinions were possibilities, not definitive answers (p.28). As teachers, we need to model desired conference behaviours because the "ways students engage in literature discussions with adults and peers set the foundation for the way students think about literature as they read independently" (Villaume & Worden, 1993, p.463).

Beach (1993) states that "responding is a learned social process" (p.104). Through social interactions in a classroom, children learn particular ways of reading, talking, and writing about literature. Teachers must be aware of the implications of the types of social interaction they facilitate or model in their classrooms. Vygotsky (1978) argues that external or socialized speech is turned inward; when children "organize their own activities according to a social form of behaviour," they have internalized social speech (p.27). "Every function in the child's cultural development appears twice: first, on the social level, and later, on the individual level; first, between people (*interpsychological*), and then inside the child (*intrapsychological*)....All the higher functions originate as actual relations between human individuals" (Vygotsky, 1978, p.57). Because social interactions affect how children respond to and think about literature, educators need to be concerned about both the form and content of the interactions that occur in classrooms.

As we said previously, teachers' questioning patterns may tacitly or unconsciously suggest the roles to be assumed by children when they read, listen, and respond to literature (i.e., that there is one correct interpretation of the text, or that the "residue" of reading is more valuable than personal interpretation). Hynds (1992) notes that, when discussing literature, teachers' questions "not only affect students' literary responses and interpretation processes; they affect the stances students take toward texts and toward reading in general" (p.92). As teachers, we need to legitimate and expedite students' aesthetic responses and encourage them to explore the many potentialities of a text. We need to create or facilitate contexts in which students have opportunities to reflect on their literary evocations and their responses to their reading experiences (which, according to Vygotsky, will then lead children to internalize ways of thinking about and responding to literature).

The effects of classroom social interactions demonstrate the influence of the classroom interpretive community. As teachers can acculturate readers into habits of reading and styles or preferences of responding, they "must become more aware of the ways [they]...signal students to conform to preferred modes of behavior and response within the classroom interpretive community" (Hynds, 1992, p.96). What is talked about in an interpretive community affects what is thought and written about, and the teacher is the most influential member in the classroom interpretive community. Students learn to "fit their responses within the accepted conventions of a particular classroom interpretive community" (Hynds, 1992, p.90). The roles and stances teachers adopt invite "students to adopt reciprocal roles" and stances (Beach, 1993, p.109). If teachers adopt the role of "questioner" in conferences, children will react accordingly; however, if teachers adopt the role of "fellow reader and responder," they create classroom contexts where readers are encouraged to extend and elaborate their aesthetic reading experiences. Beach (1993) writes that the "quality of students' response—their willingness to explore and extend their response—depends heavily on teachers' own willingness to themselves engage in thoughtful, engrossing conversations" (p.118). *Therefore, it is imperative for teachers to read the literature they use in their programs in order to genuinely write about and discuss texts.*

Teachers must consider their instructional approaches to and behaviours in literature discussions. Not only do teachers influence students' oral responses to literature, they also affect students' visual and dramatic responses.

Visual and Dramatic Responses to Literature

Children in classrooms are often motivated to respond to a piece of literature, or at least to display their responses to literature, through a visual, auditory, or dramatic medium. A pluralistic approach to response to literature provides students with opportunities to explore literature in several ways, to demonstrate and develop their interpretations of texts in meaningful ways, and to use various thinking processes and functions of language (Halliday, 1969).

Many teachers have found drama strategies effective in eliciting responses and in providing a framework for children to display their responses and reflect on a text at the same time. In this section, we discuss some examples of how teachers have used and can use drama strategies in their literature programs. Many of these strategies overlap with art activities, which will be addressed later in the chapter.

RESPONSE THROUGH DRAMA

Many teachers believe that, in order to work with drama strategies, they must have a gymnasium or hall available for use and be prepared to put in hours of work on a performance or play that will eventually be shared with an audience. The reality is that many drama strategies can be used in a classroom as part of a day's work with literature.

Awake and Dreaming by Kit Pearson (1996) is an appropriate piece of literature to use as a novel study in grades five or six. It tells the story of a young girl named Theo and her "flower child" mother, Rae. Theo dreams of being part of a stable, loving family with her own bedroom and with brothers and sisters to play with. She loves reading and often loses herself in books, the school library being her only source of pleasure. Rae is an immature and irresponsible parent who lives in poverty and moves regularly from one apartment to another. She and Theo live on welfare and supplement their income by begging on the streets of Vancouver. While on the way to Victoria to visit Theo's Aunt Sharon, Theo falls asleep and awakens to find herself in a house in Victoria —part of a family at last. But is it real?

Hot-Seating: Rae has arrived home from panhandling in downtown Vancouver. Theo is exhausted from dancing on the street to recorded music. In groups of three, students take turns hot-seating characters from this chapter of the book (chapter III). The teacher will need to model this strategy first if the children are not familiar with it. In role as Cindy or one of the other characters, the teacher can take questions from the students about Cindy's thoughts and feelings about Rae and her lifestyle. Following this demonstration, the students take turns "being" Theo, Rae, or Cal and entertain questions from the other two students in the group. Students draw on their own experiences and previous knowledge to create answers to the questions which will fit the context of the story.

Tableaux: Theo is sitting in a seat on the ferry, watching the other children in the lounge playing. She notices a woman in a baggy tweed coat watching her. A girl speaks to Theo and invites her to join their group. They go outside on the deck together, playing and "flying" in the wind. Rae reappears, and Theo panics. The next thing Theo hears is a steady dripping of rain as she awakens in a soft warm bed. In groups of four to six, students can create tableaux: "frozen" or "still pictures" of the scene on the ferry. Each group first decides what it wants to include in its tableau and plans who will take the role of each character. Once this is determined, the students take up their positions, perhaps by acting out a brief portion of the story, then freezing the action at a given moment. The children then orchestrate the tableau so that it becomes an artistic and aesthetically pleasing portrayal of the scene. Students can imagine this as either a photograph or an exhibit (diorama) in a museum. Rereading chapter VI will help the students to discover the details of the situation and to portray their interpretations of it. Each group is given the opportunity to show its tableau to the rest of the class.

Thoughts-in-the-Head: While engaged in their tableaux, the teacher touches each character gently on the shoulder. At the touch, the students, *in role*, say what thoughts are going through their heads at that moment. If any students do not wish to speak, they may remain silent; the teacher will move on to the next character.

Puppets: Many different kinds of puppets can be created to perform a play of some part of the story, from paper lunch-bag puppets to sock puppets to paper plates or more elaborate creations. Students generally enjoy this activity. Some groups of students may want to script the play first, while others may simply create the dialogue as they go, ensuring they have the opportunity for rehearsal before sharing their work.

Readers' Theatre: Readers' theatre is a form of presentation where emphasis is placed on the oral reading (rather than memorization) of scripts. Participants read their parts expressively and use their voices, gestures, and facial expressions to communicate images, events, and actions to the minds of audience members. In readers' theatre, the characters may sit on stools or a high bench to read their parts. Participants often wear an item of clothing typical of the character they are reading in order to identify themselves; thus, "Theo" may wear a tattered sweatshirt or jacket. For this dramatic activity, the teacher may need to assist students in rewriting or "scripting" portions of the original text, entering it onto a word processor so that students can read from a clear and well-written manuscript.

Character Profile: Students select a character (e.g., Theo, Sharon, Rae, Ben) and dress as that character. The student enters the classroom wearing appropriate attire and tells the other students, in the first person, about his or her character. Drawing upon the novel, students describe their characters and relay significant events that have happened to them in their (i.e., the characters') lives. Classmates may ask the characters questions.

These activities comprise only a few of the many drama strategies that can be used in a literature or language arts program. Drama activities frequently take longer than planned and should not be rushed. Throughout their drama work, students talk with each other about their interpretations, opinions, likes and dislikes, and personal "pictures" of the characters and settings. This oral processing enhances the students' personal engagement with the text and can help to create a more satisfying and memorable experience with a book. However, only one or two drama activities should be used with any one text. Groups of children in a classroom frequently work on different activities and thus enjoy their sharing sessions all the more. Readers are usually curious about other readers' interpretations of the work under consideration.

RESPONSE THROUGH THE VISUAL ARTS

Visual art activities have the same appeal as drama strategies, because children become actively involved in creating an artifact representative of their responses. Drawing, painting, and making models, dioramas, wall charts, and portraits are just a few activities to allow children the opportunity to display their responses to a text. The following activities might be considered for the book *Awake and Dreaming*.

Photograph album: Students create a photograph album of the Caffrey family during Theo's early life and later when Rae and Theo move to Vancouver. Photographs can consist of pictures taken from magazines or they can be created by the children themselves, either with a camera or with art supplies. A caption can be added beneath each photograph. Students can explain why they chose to include particular photographs in their albums.

Scrapbook: In a similar manner to the photograph album, students can make a scrapbook of mementos of Theo's families—both the Caffrey family and the Kaldors. Students can make notes, menus, paw prints of pets, and other such memorabilia from Theo's life and her encounter with author Cecily Stone.

Mapping: Students create large and colourful maps of the area of Victoria where Theo lives with the Kaldors and where she eventually meets Cecily Stone. The map is not necessarily intended to be a realistic depiction of Victoria, but can be created from the description provided in the text. Alternatively, students could map the journey Theo takes from Vancouver to Victoria. Students can extend their learning by locating a real map of the area and basing their renditions upon it.

The book *Who Is Frances Rain?* (Buffie, 1987) is used as an example to demonstrate the following visual art activities. *Who Is Frances Rain?* tells the story of fourteen-year-old Lizzie, who, while spending the summer at her grandmother's cottage in Manitoba, discovers a pair of spectacles that allow her to see into the past. Through her adventures, Lizzie finds out more about her interesting grandmother and about herself.

Drawings: After reading parts of the book or the entire book, students draw scenes, characters, or various aspects of their own interpretation of the story. Drawing can elicit some insightful responses from students that might not otherwise be captured. Students may also write about their drawings.

Filmstrip: An activity that requires drawing is the creation of a "filmstrip." Students select five or six main events from a book and draw pictures depicting these events. The drawings are taped together to form a "filmstrip" with the first and last pages being blank. The filmstrip should also include a title page citing the book's title and author, and the name of the student creator. A cardboard box and two cardboard rolls from plastic wrap, paper towels, or aluminum foil are used to construct the "film projector." Holes are cut for the rolls on both sides of the cardboard box at the top and bottom and the rolls are inserted through the holes before the filmstrip is attached. The filmstrip is taped to the rolls so that it will roll as students turn the top roll of the projector. The students talk through the filmstrip as they share it with their peers.

Who Is Frances Rain? by Margaret Buffie

If students have knowledge about and access to the appropriate technology, their pictures can be scanned or photographed to create a multi-media presentation. In addition, HyperStudio is an effective software program for elementary school students to use in creating a multimedia presentation in response to a book. Children from grade three and up can work with HyperStudio.

Book covers: Students usually have very definite ideas about the appropriateness of a book cover. Some students may want to design an alternate cover for *Who Is Frances Rain?* They could compare the original Canadian cover to the American cover which Canada has adopted. The graphics used and the positioning of the title and author name, as well as the colours used in the cover, are important elements in determining whether a book will initially appeal to a reader. Book covers can invite a reader into the text or be a factor in dissuading readers from reading a book. An important facet of a reader's response to a book can be found in the alternate cover the reader might design for the book. Covers created by students can be displayed along with other artifacts profiling the novel.

Dioramas: Any setting from a book can be used as the starting point in creating a diorama. There are a number of settings in *Who Is Frances Rain?* that lend themselves to this kind of interpretation, notably Rain Island and the cabin. Dioramas are frequently made from large shoe boxes, and many odds and ends of materials can be put together to create either a single scene or an effective interpretation of the setting and atmosphere of the novel as a whole. Dioramas can provide an enticement for other students to read the book themselves.

Portraits: Strong characters cause readers to create vivid specific images from texts. One reason readers can be disappointed with a movie version of a book is that the characters (or setting) do not match the ones created in the reader's mind. Students may enjoy creating their own portrait gallery to go with the novel. *Who Is Frances Rain?* is a book full of strong characters, from Toothy Tim to Frances Rain herself.

Open-mind Portrait: Students draw a silhouette of a character's head and consider the story events from the character's point of view. Inside the silhouette, students visually represent the character's thoughts through words and/or pictures. Students could draw a silhouette of Lizzie's portrait, trace the outline, and at several pivotal points in the book, fill in an open-mind portrait to convey her feelings and thoughts.

Advertisements: If a reader had to create an enticing poster advertising *Who Is Frances Rain?*, what would it be like? What would a publishing company look for in a poster? What would a prospective reader want to know about the book? What ambiance could be created through a poster? What colours would be most effective in portraying this story? After students have read a novel, an advertising poster can be an exciting way to share their responses to the book with the rest of the class.

Wall charts: Students can develop many kinds of wall charts to help them understand a book. *Who Is Frances Rain?* lends itself to creating a family tree showing family relationships, thus assisting students in understanding the story. Timelines, another type of wall chart, can assist readers in making sense of the story and keeping track of the events.

It is valuable to have students provide a written or oral explanation or description of their visual arts projects. A written accompaniment or oral narration encourages students to be reflective of their processes, understandings, and decisions, and it allows teachers to appreciate the visual art project more fully.

Many other more sophisticated and aesthetic art activities can be used in relation to children's literature, including a study of the art in children's books. Since many illustrators of children's books are also artists who exhibit their work independently of their work as illustrators, teachers may make a point of exploring their work, when appropriate. A wealth of information and resources about Canadian children's book illustrators and illustrations can be found at the following National Library of Canada website [http://www.nlc-bnc.ca/events/illustra/eintro.htm]. *The Potential of Picture Books: From Visual Literacy to Aesthetic Understanding* (Kiefer, 1995), a professional resource recommended in Chapter 2, explores the art of picture books.

When considering various oral, dramatic, visual, and written response activities, Benton and Fox (1985) suggest that teachers ask themselves two basic and fundamental questions: "Will this activity enable the reader to look back on the text and to develop the meanings he has already made? and Does what I plan to do bring reader and text closer together, or does it come between them?" (p.108). Activities must be appropriate, extend students' reading transactions, and avoid a "lengthy" examination of texts that detracts from the overall reading experience.

References

Apol, L. 1998. "But what does this have to do with kids?": Literary theory and children's literature in the teacher education classroom. *Journal of Children's Literature* 24(2), 32-46.

Baumann, J., L. Jones, and N. Seifert-Jones. 1993. Using think alouds to enhance children's comprehension monitoring abilities. *The Reading Teacher* 47(3), 184-193.

Beach, R. 1993. *A Teacher's Introduction to Reader-response Theories*. Urbana, Illinois: National Council of Teachers of English.

Benton, M. and G. Fox. 1985. *Teaching Literature: Nine to Fourteen*. London: Oxford University Press.

Bleich, D. 1980. Epistemological assumptions in the study of response. In *Reader-response Criticism: From Formalism to Post-structuralism*. J. Tompkins, ed. Baltimore, Maryland: The Johns Hopkins University Press.

Britton, J. 1970. *Language and Learning*. Harmondsworth, Middlesex: Penguin Books.

Commeyras, M. and G. Sumner. 1996. Literature discussions based on student-posed questions. *The Reading Teacher* 50(3), 262-265.

Culler, J. 1980. Literary competence. In *Reader-response Criticism: From Formalism to Post-structuralism*. J. Tompkins, ed. Baltimore, Maryland: The Johns Hopkins University Press.

Dickson, R. 1998. Horror: To gratify, not edify. *Language Arts* 76(2), 115-122.

Dreher, M.J. and R.H. Yopp. 1994. Effect of active comprehension instruction on attitudes and motivation in reading. *Reading Horizons* 34(4), 288-302.

Eeds, M. and M. Wells. 1989. Grand conversations: An exploration of meaning construction in literature response groups. *Research in the Teaching of English* 23(1), 4-29.

Fish, S. 1980a. *Is There a Text in This Class?* Cambridge, Massachusetts: Harvard University Press.

——————. 1980b. Interpreting the Variorum. In *Reader-response Criticism: From Formalism to Post-structuralism*. J. Tompkins, ed. Baltimore, Maryland: The Johns Hopkins University Press.

Gambrell, L. and J. Alamsi. 1996. *Lively Discussions!: Fostering Engaged Reading*. Newark, Delaware: International Reading Association.

Halliday, M. 1969. Relevant models of language. *Educational Review* 22(1), 26-37.

Hanssen, E., J. Harste, and K. Short. 1990. In conversation: Theory and instruction. In *Beyond Communication: Reading Comprehension and Criticism*. D. Bodgan and S.B. Straw, eds. London: The Bodley Head Ltd.

Harste, J., K. Short, and C. Burke. 1988. *Creating Classrooms for Authors: The Reading-Writing Connection*. Portsmouth, New Hampshire: Heinemann Educational Books, Inc.

——————. 1983. Everything considered: Response to literature in an elementary school setting. *Journal of Research and Development in Education* 16(3), 8-13.

Hickman, J. 1984. Research currents: Researching children's response to literature. *Language Arts* 61(3), 278-284.

Holland, N. 1976a. The new paradigm: Subjective or transactive? *New Literary History* 7(2), 335-346.

——————. 1976b. Transactive criticism: RE-creation through identity. *Criticism* 18(1), 334-352.

——————. 1980. Unity identity text self. In *Reader-response Criticism: From Formalism to Post-structuralism*. J. Tompkins, ed. Baltimore, Maryland: The Johns Hopkins University Press.

Horowitz, R., ed. 1994. Classroom talk about text: What teenagers and teachers come to know about the world through talk about text. Special issue. *Journal of Reading* 37(7).

Hynds, S. 1992. Challenging questions in the teaching of literature. In *Literature Instruction: A Focus on Student Response*. J.A. Langer, ed. Urbana, Illinois: National Council of Teachers of English.

Iser, W. 1980. The reading process: A phenomenological approach. In *Reader-response Criticism: From Formalism to Post-structuralism*. J. Tompkins, ed. Baltimore, Maryland: The Johns Hopkins University Press.

Kiefer, J. 1995. *The Potential of Picture Books: From Visual Literacy to Aesthetic Understanding*. Englewood Cliffs, New Jersey: Prentice-Hall, Inc.

Lucas, G. 1977-1983. *Star Wars Trilogy*. Hollywood: LucasFilm Ltd.

Many, J. and D. Wiseman. 1992. The effect of teaching approach on third-grade students' response to literature. *Journal of Reading Behavior* 24(3), 265-287.

Marshall, J.D. 1987. The effects of writing on students' understanding of literary texts. *Research in the Teaching of English 21(1), 30-62.*

McGee, L.M. and G.E. Tompkins. 1995. Literature-based instruction: What is guiding the instruction? *Language Arts* 72(6), 405-414.

McMahon, S. 1992. Book club: A case study of a group of fifth graders as they participate in a literature-based reading program. *Reading Research Quarterly* 27(4), 292-294.

Moffett, J. 1973. *A Student Centered Language Arts Curriculum, Grades K-6: A Handbook for Teachers*. Boston: Houghton Mifflin Company.

Ondaatje, M. 1992. *The English Patient*. Toronto: Vintage Books Canada.

Pantaleo, S. 1994. *Teacher Influence on Student Response to Literature*. Unpublished doctoral dissertation, University of Alberta, Edmonton, Alberta.

————. 1995. The influence of teacher practice on student response to literature. *Journal of Children's Literature*, 21(1), 38-47.

————. 1998. Expatiation: Is the heart of literature discussions beating? *Reading: Exploration and Discovery* 19(2), 14-31.

Purves, A. 1973. *Literature Education in Ten Countries: An Empirical Study*. New York: A Halsted Book.

Purves, A. and V. Rippere. 1968. *Elements of Writing About a Literary Work: A Study of Response to Literature*. NCTE Research Report No. 9. Urbana, Illinois: National Council of Teachers of English.

Raphael, T.E. 1986. Teaching question answer relationships, revisited. *The Reading Teacher* 39(6), 516-523.

Richards, P., D. Thatcher, M. Shreeves, P. Timmons, and S. Barker. 1999. Don't let a good scare frighten you: Choosing and using quality chillers to promote reading. *The Reading Teaching* 52(8), 830-840.

Rosenblatt, L. 1976. *Literature as Exploration*. Fourth edition. New York: The Modern Language Association of America.

————. 1978. *The Reader, the Text, the Poem: The Transactional Theory of the Literary Work*. Carbondale, Illinois: Southern Illinois University Press.

————. 1981. The readers' contribution in the literary experience. *The English Quarterly* 14(1), 3-12.

————. 1985. Viewpoints: Transaction versus interaction—A terminological rescue operation. *Research in the Teaching of English* 19(1) 96-107.

————. 1986. The aesthetic transaction. *Journal of Aesthetic Education* 20(4), 122-127.

————. 1988. The literary transaction. In *The Creating Word*. P. Demers, ed. Edmonton: University of Alberta Press.

————. 1991a. Literary theory. In *Handbook of Research on Teaching the English Language Arts*. J. Flood, J. Jensen, D. Lapp, and J. Squire, eds. New York: Macmillan Publishing Company.

————. 1991b. Literature - S.O.S.! *Language Arts* 68(6), 444-448.

Roser, N.L. and M.G. Martinez, eds. 1995. *Book Talk and Beyond: Children and Teachers Respond to Literature*. Newark, Delaware: International Reading Association.

Schulz, R. 1991. Using literary reading theories in the language arts classroom. *Reflections on Canadian Literacy* 9(1), 16-20.

Slovan, G. 1997. Toward literacy through literature: Ten to take along. *Journal of Children's Literature* 23(2), 47-51.

Squire, J.R. 1990. Research on reader-response and the national literature initiative. In *Reading and Response*. M. Hayhoe and S. Parker, eds. Philadelphia: Open University Press.

Stauffer, R.G. 1975. *Directing the Reading-Thinking Process*. New York: Harper & Row.

Strickland, D., R.M. Dillon, L. Funhouser, M. Glick, and C. Rogers. 1989. Research currents: Classroom dialogue during literature response groups. *Language Arts* 66(2), 192-200.

Thomson, J. 1984. Wolfgang Iser's "The act of reading" and the teaching of literature. *English in Australia* 70, 18-30.

————. 1987. *Understanding Teenagers Reading: Reading Processes and the Teaching of Literature*. Norwood, South Australia: Australian Association for the Teaching of English Inc.

Tierney, R., J. Readence, and E. Dishner. 1995. *Reading Strategies and Practices: A Compendium*. Fourth edition. Needham Heights, Massachusetts: Allyn and Bacon.

Tompkins, J. 1978. David Bleich. Subjective criticism. *MLN Comparative Literature* 93(5), 1068-1075.

Villaume, S. and T. Worden. 1993. Developing literate voices: The challenge of whole language. *Language Arts* 70(6), 462-468.

Vygotsky, L. 1978. *Mind in Society*. Cambridge, MA: Harvard University Press.

Wiencek, J. and J. O'Flahavan. 1994. From teacher-led to peer discussions about literature: Suggestions for making the shift. *Language Arts* 71(7), 488-498.

Wilde, O. 1959. *The Importance of Being Earnest*. Woodbury, New York: Barron's Educational Series.

Professional Resources

Gambrell, L. and J. Almasi. 1996. *Lively Discussions!: Fostering Engaged Reading*. Newark, Delaware: International Reading Association. • The four sections of this text speak to creating classroom cultures that foster discussion: examining discussion in action; exploring the teacher's role in discussions; and examining various perspectives on assessment of discussion. The text provides strategies and techniques for using discussion in elementary classrooms to facilitate comprehension and interpretation of both narrative and informational text.

Rosenblatt, L.M. 1978. *The Reader, the Text, the Poem: The Transactional Theory of the Literary Work*. Carbondale, Illinois: Southern Illinois University Press. • In this book, Rosenblatt outlines her transactional theory by describing the two-way process involved in the transaction between reader and text in the construction of a literary work of art. The text includes a detailed discussion of the concepts of aesthetic and efferent reading and describes application of the transactional theory to classroom practice.

Roser, N.L. and M.G. Martinez, eds. 1995. *Book Talk and Beyond: Children and Teachers Respond to Literature*. Newark, Delaware: International Reading Association. • This text includes four sections on using and talking about literature in elementary classrooms. Section one addresses preparatory steps for facilitating aesthetic responses; section two describes the "tools of story talk"; section three discusses teachers' roles and responsibilities in facilitating discussions; and section four describes other ways to encourage response (e.g., drama, writing activities, response journals).

CHAPTER EIGHT

WRITTEN RESPONSES TO LITERATURE

The objectives of this chapter are

- To understand the purposes of written responses in literature-based language arts programs;
- To become aware of the various organizational issues in working with written response;
- To understand the many instructional issues related to using response journals;
- To understand that response journal entries vary in type and quality;
- To become aware that response journals can reveal information about the writer's understandings of literary texts;
- To recognize the influential role of the teacher in structuring and implementing response-based programs.

Why are teachers asking students to write response journal entries about the literature they read? What do they expect to find in their students' written responses? What are students learning by writing responses? Research on students' responses to literature tells us to work toward deepening and extending children's responses—to encourage children to engage in close emotional involvement and in more distanced reflection. If indeed we do

CLASSROOM SCENARIO

Scattered about the room are several groups of children engaged in discussions about the books they are reading. After the groups have discussed the questions that each member has brought, the children return to their desks. Some students open their novels and begin reading, while others take out their response journals and begin writing. Once they have finished writing their responses, students submit their journals to the teacher and begin reading their novels. One grade six student, described as "academically average" by her teacher, has written the following response to the book *Jasmin* by Canadian author Jan Truss (1982).

> *I think the end of this book was excellent because everything wrapped up so well! Jasmin's clay animals were put in a box that had homemade forest surrounding them. She won 2nd grand prize at the Science Fair. Her teachers decided Jasmin could go to Grade 7 as they were giving her another chance. Her parents talked to a family council [sic], advising them [sic] to give Jasmin her own room. Also they advised Leroy to be moved into a special home because he was getting too big for them to be looking after anymore. The good thing was he could visit them on weekends. While Jasmin had run away, her whole family showed love for her again. Jasmin realized that she was pretty (someone had painted a picture of her), and could do useful things with her hands (e.g., clay animals). Best of all, she liked who she was!*

encourage children to deepen and extend their responses, what, in reality, are we asking them to do? What does this require of teachers, both in the development of their personal philosophies and in their pedagogical practices associated with literature and literary response? What does it mean to the children themselves? What differences does it make to children's reading abilities and in their experiences with texts? In this chapter, we will explore answers to such questions.

Reader-response Journals

Journals are a popular medium used by teachers to capture a view of the "iceberg" of students' responses to literature. The written journal response (sometimes referred to as a reading log entry), like the reading process, is a way for readers to work through their understandings and interpretations of texts in personally significant ways, where the uniqueness of their responses is accepted. Writing "about reading is one of the best ways to get students to unravel their transactions so that we can see how they understand and in the process, help them learn to elaborate, clarify, and illustrate their responses by reference to the associations and prior knowledge that inform them" (Petrosky, 1982, p. 24).

Journals provide a pedagogical tool through which children can use personal language (Halliday, 1978) to express their own individuality. As feelings and opinions are part of personal language, children can use personal language to relate their own lives to the books they are reading and discussing. The latter helps children to establish their identities, build self-esteem, and improve confidence. Journals also promote the use of heuristic language (Halliday, 1978) as children wonder, investigate, acquire knowledge, and inquire through their writing. In their journal writing, students can refer to their initial reactions or make autobiographical connections in order to facilitate their insights about the texts, themselves, society, and life in general. Research has demonstrated that autobiographical responses, indicating self-involvement with texts, enhance students' interpretations of those texts (Beach, 1990; Cox & Many, 1992a; Marshall, 1987; Squire, 1964).

Writing literature responses in journals has been shown to have other benefits as well (Cox & Many, 1992a; Fulps & Young, 1991; Kelly, 1990; Wollman-Bonilla, 1989). Through journal writing, students are able to engage and participate personally with text, reflect on evoked emotions and ideas, and imagine the perspectives and experiences of others. Students can take ownership of their reading as they write about their personal interpretations, and connect and associate their prior knowledge and experiences with text. They can express, reflect upon, and clarify their thoughts and understandings, as well as gain self-confidence and motivation as they realize that different interpretations of texts are acceptable. As well as improving their comprehension, discussion, and writing skills, students can become emotionally involved with literature, developing an appreciation of literature. When their attention is directed to the thought processes revealed in the journal entries, students can become aware of how meaning is constructed during reading. Further, response journals facilitate the expression of individual interests, needs, and concerns as students decide on the content of their entries. The content of response journals has allowed teachers to see what children understand, their level of understanding, how they are learning, and their growth in communicating ideas (Crowhurst & Kooy, 1985; Wollman-Bonilla, 1989). The information provided by these insights has further influenced teachers' practices with response journals.

What can response journal entries look like? The responses included below are *examples* of journal entries that demonstrate *some of the possibilities* of written response. As no two readers will have the same experience in reading a text, responses will vary from text to text and from reader to reader. Readers' predilections, abilities, and reading autobiographies (that is, their reading experiences at home and at school), as well as other contextual factors, will affect their responses.

The children who wrote the responses reproduced below were in Sylvia's classroom for two consecutive years (i.e., in combined grades of four/five and five/six); the students wrote these responses during their second year in her classroom. Literature was the central component of Sylvia's reading program. Literature Workshops allowed the students to engage in "real reading" behaviours, as the children selected their own books, set their own reading goals, and talked and wrote about what they read. (See Chapter 9 for an in-depth description of Literature Workshops. Further information about the classroom context and Sylvia's role in facilitating student response to literature is presented later in this chapter.) The spelling has been conventionalized in the following selections. We have also included a discussion about the content of each entry.

Judy's Response: *I am David* (Holm, 1963) is a story about twelve-year-old David, who escapes from a concentration camp toward the end of World War Two. David had been a prisoner in the camp since the age of two. He treks across Europe in search of his identity, always wary that "they" may be in pursuit. Judy, a grade five student who was an avid reader and ranked as "above average" in language arts, wrote the following response to Holm's novel after completing her reading of the text.

> *I think it would be hard for David to be himself because he had lived in the concentration camp so long that he didn't know what it was like to be in a warm bed and he never had seen any colour except black and grey. But when he got out of the camp, his life changed completely. He saw flowers and green countryside and heard music and saw the values of life. When he was in the camp it didn't matter to him if he died because he didn't like life, but when he saw beauty he wanted to keep on living.*

In this response, Judy empathized with the character but also demonstrated an understanding of how David's circumstances affected his perceptions and appreciation of life. Judy's response demonstrates emotional involvement with the character and reflection on the significance of David's experiences. By building on her emotional engagement with the character and reflecting on his situation, Judy developed an interest in and understanding of others and the human condition in general. She went beyond the text to an understanding of what makes life worthwhile and how a lack of love and beauty can affect one's will to survive—profound and mature comments from a grade five student.

Jeremy's Response: *Call it Courage* (Sperry, 1940) tells the story of Mafatu, a Polynesian boy who is afraid of the sea but who decides to prove his courage to himself and other village members. He sets out in a canoe with his dog, Uri, and lands on an island where he must survive and face his fears as well as many physical dangers. The response to this novel was written by Jeremy, an "average" grade five student in language arts.

> *I think Mafatu really showed his courage by going to the island. I think this because he showed his courage by the things that happened to Mafatu. One thing that showed Mafatu's courage was the time when the shark was raiding his bamboo traps. Mafatu dove into the water and killed the shark so it wouldn't take his fish. Another thing that showed Mafatu's courage was when he accidentally dropped his knife into the water and then he dove in and got it. This showed courage because the sea god was angry with him and there was a lot of dangerous animals in the sea that may have hurt Mafatu.*

In his response, Jeremy returned to the text in making his evaluation of Mafatu's courage. He included both personal and textual input in his interpretation of the character's actions. Jeremy demonstrated "interest in other people and the human condition" (Thomson, 1987, p.153) as he recognized how Mafatu had to overcome his fears in order to survive. Jeremy demonstrated his appreciation of Mafatu's growth over the period of the novel and provided specific examples illustrating Mafatu's courage.

Quality Responses

In an effort to understand children's responses to literature, some researchers have investigated how textual factors—such as the genre of a novel; characteristics of readers such as age, interests, and gender; and contextual factors such as assigned purposes for reading and instructional issues—influence students' responses to literature (Beach & Hynds, 1991; Martinez & Roser, 1991). Others have examined qualitative differences among students' responses to literature and have endeavoured to investigate characteristics that constitute a "quality" written response (Blunt, 1977; Hancock, 1993a; Langer 1990; Pantaleo, 1995b; Pantaleo & Bainbridge, 1996; Thomson, 1987).

REFLECTION

Before reading the next section, consider the following questions. What do you think the characteristics of a "quality" written response are? How would you assist your students in deepening or developing their responses?

Read the following response written by an academically "average" (according to her teachers) grade four student near the end of the school year. Do you consider it a "good" response? If so, why? If not, why not? What would you say to the student about the content of the response?

The writing mechanics have been conventionalized in the following journal entry.

> *I am reading* Megan's Island *by Willo Davis Roberts. I am on page 80. I really like this book. The action is a little slow but I like it. The characters are fabulous. In this chapter I liked the part when Megan's friend Ben told that man he was looking for two red heads and claimed to be Megan's and Sandy's Uncle. Megan and Sandy are red heads. But they don't have an Uncle.*

Although many categorization schemes have been generated to analyze the kinds of responses written by students (see Figure 8.1), teachers not only aim to extend the types and frequencies of students' responses, they also want to improve the quality of the responses. But what does it mean to "develop," "extend," or "deepen" responses? What are the meanings of statements such as "the teacher works to elicit the fullest possible response" (Purves, Rogers & Soter, 1990, p.71), or "teachers guide students... toward deeper insights into their individual interpretive processes in order that students will develop fuller interpretations" (Harker, 1990, p.69), or "it is clear that an extended response is also desirable" (Purves, 1992, p.30)? What are teachers' and students' expectations and understandings of a "fullest possible response" or an "extended response," and how do teachers assist students in achieving the latter?

Many scholars and researchers have explored qualitative differences in students' responses to literature. Jean Blunt (1977) wrote "the ultimate requirement of a mature response is the ability to recognize that an author presents an evaluation of possible human experience in his own written style. The book is finally seen as an artifact, a convention to be rejected or applauded by the reader" (p.42). In addressing the notion of assessment of response (and hence qualitative differences), Galda (1982) stated that flexibility might be a criterion to measure response. "Could we say that a 'good' response...is a flexible one which encompasses the interaction of textual demands and a reader's experience...abilities, and predilections?" (p.119). She contended another criterion against which to assess responses "might be the amount of support or documentation provided by the student...Does the responder freely express his or her views but also return to the text for documentation?" (pp.119-120).

Jack Thomson (1987) hypothesized a developmental model of response. Although Thomson's work described reading and responding of teenagers, his ideas are relevant to teachers of all grades who are interested in implementing literature- and response-based programs. Thomson cautioned that he was not "trying to make literary response into a measurable and marketable quantity" (p.149), nor did he view development of response as simple and linear. Thomson wrote "that the development of a mature response to literature involves a progressive movement from close emotional involvement to more distanced reflective detachment, and from an interest in self to an interest in other people and the human condition" (1987, p.153).

Many (1992) conducted a study to investigate the effect of grade level on the stances of children when responding to literature and to examine "the qualitative differences found in responses written from different stances and [to] determine if any differences were related to grade level" (p.170). One of Many's conclusions was that teachers could encourage the development of mature, sophisticated responses by encouraging students to "continually connect the emotions, associations, thoughts and visualizations evoked back to the story world" (p.182). Many also demonstrated that a repertoire of responses—or "variety" alone—does not guarantee "extended" or "quality" responses (e.g., in a one-paragraph response, a student identified her/his favourite parts, made personal associations to characters' actions, articulated judgements about the author's writing style, and formulated predictions). However, quality is also not guaranteed by repetition of the same type of response. If a child repeatedly wrote the same type of response (e.g., "My favourite part was when..." or "If I could speak to the author I would ask..."), the child may be attending to only one aspect of her response to the literature. The student would need to reflect upon her reading transactions and explore, in depth, other aspects of her responses (i.e., the images, thoughts, feelings, and memories) she experienced during and after the reading of the text.

REFLECTION

Return to your own comments about the response to *Megan's Island*. Did your assessment include any of the ideas that were presented by individuals noted above who have investigated quality responses? Has your assessment of the response changed after reading the brief literature review on quality responses? If so, how and why?

STUDENTS' WRITTEN RESPONSES

The written responses included below are examples of journal entries that we believe demonstrate elements of quality responses. They do not define or exhaust the potential of "quality" responses, but rather demonstrate *some of the possibilities*.

Shelia's Response: *Pieces of the Picture* (Joosse, 1991) is a book about a girl named Emily who moves to Wisconsin after the death of her father. Her mother, Agnes, owns an inn, and Emily decides to spy on the guests to relieve her boredom. A sealed-off secret attic and an injured Canada goose provide further diversions for Emily. Shelia, an "above average" language arts student in fifth grade, wrote the following response after reading Joosse's novel.

> *When Agnes was a girl I think her parents deprived her of her childhood. I think this may have happened because she had to hide her true identity. I noticed this when Emily was reading Agnes's diary and she was telling her about her secret world that she was building and how she had to hide it from her parents. Another thing that I noticed was that it seemed like her parents were making Agnes grow up too fast. I found this when Mor said she couldn't read* The Wizard of Oz *because she thought it was a fairy tale that was filling her head with rubbish. I don't think that was helping her to feel better about herself because she was saying that she was too old to read fairy tales when Agnes didn't even want to grow up.*

In this response, Shelia explores the psychological dimensions of the character, Agnes, by examining the influential experiences of her childhood. Shelia's response illustrates both emotional involvement and distanced reflection as she returned to the text to explore her interpretation and understanding of the character by examining the family relationships and the values held by her parents. She used her own experiences of childhood and growing up, and the events related in the story, to form her opinions. Shelia creates intertextual connections through her knowledge of *The Wizard of Oz* (Baum, 1956) and clearly understands the role of fairy tales in childhood.

Kari's Response: *The Crossing* (Paulsen, 1987) tells the story of an orphaned Mexican boy's struggle to live in the streets, his efforts to escape to America, and his friendship with an alcoholic Vietnam war veteran. After reading Paulsen's book, Kari, an "average" language arts student in grade six, wrote the following response.

> *This book has made me realize how lucky I am. I thought I had it hard off because I have to clean my room and do chores in the house and yard. When I read about how Manny has to beg for money, hardly eats and has no parents, I thought and realized that I really actually am very, very lucky to have what I do. I have a house and a bed and blankets. Manny sleeps in a cardboard box. I have food and money to spend. Manny doesn't have either of those. I have several pairs of clothing but Manny has a torn T-shirt and an old pair of jeans. In Manny's country (Mexico) he has hardly any rights. In my country (Canada) we have many rights and privileges. I hardly ever have nothing to eat. Manny hardly ever has something to eat. I do not have to cross a river to a free country for I am in a free country. I do not have to wander the streets although I am conscious nothing happens to me as it would to Manny. Now that I have realized how lucky I am, I think I will have a better attitude about it.*

Kari examined herself, the text, and the human condition in her response. She reflected on her personal state compared to that of the main character. Kari demonstrated an appreciation of her current living conditions and an empathetic understanding of another person's life and culture. She built on her emotional responses, stood back from the text, and explored the effects of social and economic problems on human lives. In other words, as Thomson (1987) has written, Kari showed, "a progressive movement from close emotional involvement to more distanced reflective detachment" (p.153).

Corey's Response: *Tracker* (Paulsen, 1984) is the story of thirteen-year-old John, who must hunt alone for the first time because his hunting companion, his grandfather, is terminally ill. As John tracks a doe, he gains an understanding of the interplay of life and death. *The Foxman* (Paulsen, 1977) is a story about Carl's cousin (a character unnamed by Paulsen), a teenager who is sent to his uncle's farm because his parents are alcoholics. While they are lost in the woods, Carl and his cousin meet the Foxman, an individual who has chosen to live in the wilderness because of his mutilated face. Carl's cousin returns to the Foxman's cabin, and he and the recluse develop a deep friendship. After reading *Tracker*, Corey, a "below average" language arts student in grade six, wrote the following response.

> *Carl's cousin in* The Foxman *and John were very similar. They both had a feeling that they were going to catch something when they were hunting. Carl's cousin had a feeling that he would catch some rabbits in the traps and John had a feeling he would catch the deer. They also both had problems when they were out in the wilderness. John had a problem with killing animals because he was scared. Carl's cousin went too far north with Carl and it was too cold to get back to their farm. Their guardians both had problems. Carl's cousin's parents had drown [sic] themselves with alcohol and tried to kill him. John's grandfather had cancer and that was why John had to hunt for their food. Also*

both Carl's cousin and John liked to be in the wilderness because they felt more alone and there was nobody else there. They both had a reason to hunt. Carl's cousin needed to hunt because they needed the food and he was trying to learn more about the wilderness. John needed to hunt because his grandpa had cancer and they needed the food.

In this entry, Corey created an intertextual understanding by exploring the characters and plot structures of these two books by Gary Paulsen. Although the entry could be viewed as a more efferent response, Corey drew upon his reading experiences to connect the two texts. By picking out similarities in the characters' circumstances and the plot structures of the two books, Corey examined how one author explored themes or "territory" in his writing (Calkins, 1991). Corey's response included both personal interpretation and distanced detachment as he reflected upon Paulsen's two books.

The Teacher's Role in Facilitating Response to Literature

Why were these students (and many others in Sylvia's classrooms) able to generate such high-quality responses? We believe the answer lies in the teacher's role in the "response process" and in the classroom environment that she or he nurtures.

Research has demonstrated that teachers occupy a salient role in facilitating literary response (Hickman, 1983, 1984; Many & Wiseman, 1992a, 1992b; Pantaleo, 1994). Although Sylvia facilitated literary response in a myriad of ways, the most important was that she scheduled *a significant amount of time for students to read* (approximately 350 minutes per week, including time for sustained reading) and provided ample opportunities for *self-selection* of literature. The students had access to more than 100 different novels in the classroom, with multiple copies (2 to 7) of each title. This substantial number of books ranged in quality, reading levels, topics, and genres. Sylvia had read every book from this selection, as she believed that "knowing" the books was integral to her program's success and her approach with the students. This knowledge was important for recommending books, giving book talks, dialoguing with the children about novels, writing literature responses, and being cognizant of the breadth and depth of relevant, related material available to the students.

Sylvia modelled how to have GRAND CONVERSATIONS about literature (i.e., in-depth discussions) (Eeds & Wells, 1989); talked about, modelled, and had her students engage in different kinds of "talk"; taught particular discussion skills; and scheduled time for students to "talk" about their reading in small groups (see the section on Oral Responses in Chapter 7). She also dialogued with the children about books in the role of "fellow reader and responder."

At the beginning of the school year, Sylvia introduced her students to summary writing (an efferent activity). She drew upon her students' background experiences with summaries (e.g., relating to her and/or their peers events of a movie or weekend activities) in order for the children to realize their familiarity and experience with summaries. The students discussed what a summary is, shared strategies to employ when writing a summary, and received some direct instruction in summary writing (demonstration of other strategies and think alouds by Sylvia). Sylvia modelled techniques for writing summaries, provided her students with several opportunities for guided practice (in large and small groups) in summary writing, and had the children engage in independent practice. Summary writing is not only an excellent comprehension activity, but it also clearly illustrates the differences between a written retelling and a response. In some classrooms, teachers find the students summarizing the story rather than writing personal responses. Understanding that a summary is a retelling, an efferent activity, will help students to differentiate between writing a summary and writing a personal response.

Sylvia provided instruction and modelling of the "process" of response writing. She began with the premise that humans are constantly responding to their environment. Working from this foundation, she had the children access their background experiences about responding (i.e., the children were encouraged to talk about their responses to movies, music, clothes, tragic events, surprises, smells, sounds). The students' experiences served as the basis to exemplify and communicate the meaning and "process" of response. There was much talking about responding, and sharing of oral responses to poetry, songs, newspaper articles, picture books, and/or novels before students were asked to write responses. As we say in Chapter 7, we believe a great deal of talking about response is necessary before moving students into writing responses.

Sylvia modelled and encouraged responses of an aesthetic nature and efferent responses based on aesthetic evocation (e.g., sharing opinions of books by comparing two or more texts, discussing opinions of characters in books, and relating these opinions to characters' personalities). Further, she talked directly with the students about the content of their responses, supporting and nurturing the "tender shoots" (Britton, 1968) and inspiring deeper thought through comments, suggestions, and questions. For example, one of the four sentences a "below average" grade five language arts student wrote as his response to a book by Gordon Korman was "I think Gordon Korman is an excellent writer and he opened up reading to me and made it fun." Sylvia talked with the student about what he meant by this sentence. What did he mean by "opened up reading to him"? How had Korman accomplished this? How had Korman been able to do this and yet other authors had not? What was it about Korman's work that made him an excellent writer? The probing was intended to further or deepen the student's reflection on his thoughts and opinions.

Sylvia contends that her responses to the children's journal entries serve as models of response and illustrate how her responses extend her personal evocations of texts. She believes that her role is that of "fellow reader and responder," and feels that the stance she adopts in her responses invites students to adopt reciprocal stances (Beach, 1993). Like Fulps and Young (1991), she believes that "Much of the success (and failure) of reading responses lies with the teacher and the teacher's responses to what the students have written" (p.113). Sylvia wrote the following response after reading Judy's two responses to *I Am David* (Holm, 1963).

> *It is difficult for me to imagine living in a concentration camp where a person was deprived of so many things. In some ways though, I think it would be better to be in the camp from an early age like David was (if a person had to be there at all) because then she/he would not know about a lot of things. The person, if only two years of age, would not know about delicious foods, beautiful sights, scrumptious aromas or the love between children and parents. If a person had been used to all of the wonders of life and then was deprived of them, I think that would be even more difficult to deal with.*

Sylvia wrote the following response to another grade five student's responses to the book *Old Yeller* (Gipson, 1965).

> *The disease that Old Yeller had is a terrible one—it is commonly known as rabies. It is a slow and painful death for an animal. What happens is the animal froths at the mouth and is very thirsty but cannot drink because the disease affects the animal's throat. A rabid skunk got into our barn once and bit one of our cows. The cow became very ill and we did not know what the problem was so my dad had the vet examine it. Then we discovered the poor cow had rabies. It just bawled and bawled and grew very thin. Eventually my dad shot the cow and put it out of its misery. It was an awful thing to see—the cow slowly dying as well as a farmer having to kill one of his own animals.*

Sylvia is aware that the students' responses are indeed icebergs and that what the children write about may not be what "actually transpire[s] during the reading event" (Cox & Many, 1992c, p.119). However, she believes that response writing provides readers with opportunities to savour, reflect upon, or deepen their aesthetic readings of texts. In order to capture a glimpse of the iceberg, both during and after the reading, the children generally wrote responses to the books at the mid-point and completion of the texts. The children decided on the content of their responses, as there was no particular structure or format for the entries. Sylvia encouraged readers to select and write about one or two of the ideas, images, feelings, memories, or thoughts they experienced during or after their reading in order for them to explore, extend, and develop their reading (i.e., she encouraged readers to read and respond aesthetically). Her beliefs about and her experience with response to literature (both written and oral) concur with research, which has demonstrated that aesthetic responses are associated with higher levels of interpretations and understandings of texts (see Beach, 1990; Cox & Many 1992b, 1992c; Many, 1991; Marshall, 1987).

In Sylvia's classroom, the children demonstrated that, when given the opportunity, along with sensitive guidance, they were able to take ownership of the reading transaction and express their thoughts in a mature and sophisticated fashion. By engaging with and distancing themselves from texts, the students explored how the texts worked. They also considered how the texts caused them to ponder their lives, and the experiences and emotions they all share and hold in common (part of what Thomson (1987) refers to as the human condition). Through responding to literature, the children in Sylvia's classroom not only learned how to deepen their responses, but they also read more, and, in our judgement, became more capable, thoughtful, and critical readers.

Categorizing Students' Responses

As well as examining the quality of students' responses, some researchers have analyzed the content of students' literature responses into various categorization schemes (for example, see Cox & Many, 1992a; Hancock, 1992, 1993a, 1993b; Wollman-Bonilla, 1989). By categorizing the content of students' responses, researchers have striven to understand the processes involved in responding to literature. They have also hoped to enable teachers to recognize the influence of teacher practice on student response, to expand students' repertoires of response types, and to improve the quality of students' responses. Indeed, some individuals equate "variety" of response with "quality" of response.

Figure 8.1 outlines several categorization schemes that have been used to analyze students' responses. The findings of a few of these studies are discussed below.

Purves and Rippere (1968) devised a specific scheme for analyzing the content of written literary responses that would apply to a great variety of responses. The four categories they generated described the responses of students aged fourteen and eighteen from four countries. The main categories they identified were engagement-involvement (describing/explaining how the work was experienced); perception (looking at the work as separate from reader); interpretation (connecting the work to the reader's own world); and evaluation (judging the work). Purves and Rippere also identified 24 subcategories to provide sufficient distinction within the four main categories; however, the subcategories within each main category were not arranged hierarchically from simple to complex. This categorization scheme has been used and modified by many other individuals who have explored response to literature.

Another research project that categorized the content of students' literature responses was

FIGURE 8.1: CATEGORIES OF RESPONSE

Purves & Rippere (1968)

1. engagement—involvement (describing/explaining about how the work was experienced)
2. perception (looking at the work as separate from the reader)
3. interpretation (connecting the work to one's own world)
4. evaluation (judging the work)
5. miscellaneous

Odell & Cooper (1976)

1. personal statements–about the reader (an autobiographical digression) or about the work (expression of personal engagement with it)
2. descriptive statements–narrational (retelling part of the work) or aspects of the work (language, characters, setting, etc.)
3. interpretive statements (whole or parts of the work)
4. evaluative statements (evocativeness or construction or meaningfulness of work)

Wollman-Bonilla (1989)

1. opinions about the story events and characters
2. personal involvement
3. discussion of the author's techniques
4. reflections on the reading process and predictions
5. questions about the text (vocabulary, events)

Cox and Many (1992)

1. imaging and picturing the story in the reader's mind
2. extending and hypothesizing about the story
3. relating feelings and associations to the text

Hancock (1992)

1. character interaction (advice and criticism offered to the characters in the text)
2. character empathy (emotional feelings expressed)
3. prediction and validation of events in the text
4. personal experiences related to the experiences and events in the books
5. philosophical reflections (values and personal beliefs shared)

Hancock (1993b)

1. immersion–reader attempts to make sense of the emerging plot and characters
   a) understanding
   b) character introspection
   c) predicting events
   d) questioning
2. self-involvement–reader vicariously becomes the character, becomes part of the setting or plot, and (or) puts him/herself in the place of the character or action
   a) character identification
   b) character assessment
   c) story involvement
3. detachment–reader detaches him/herself from text in order to make a statement regarding evaluation of the literature or to contemplate his/her perspective on reading and writing
   a) literary evaluation
   b) reader/writer digression

conducted by Wollman-Bonilla (1989). In her fourth-grade classroom, the students met regularly in groups to discuss the novels they read, to choose other novels to read, and to share their written assignments. Wollman-Bonilla decided to implement letter-writing (instead of assigned writing tasks) as a component in her program, in order to give students freedom to reflect on the novels they were reading. Wollman-Bonilla organized the content of the students' letters into five categories: opinions about the story events and characters; personal involvement; discussion of the author's techniques; reflections on the reading process and predictions; and questions about the text (vocabulary, events).

Cox and Many (1992a) examined students' responses to literature in order to understand the aesthetic stance of reading and the implications for teaching it. The authors investigated the stances of students in grades four to eight when responding to literature and film. They discovered that the majority of children in the study took on an aesthetic stance as they read and responded to literature. Three main characteristics were discovered in the students' responses: imaging and picturing the story in their minds; extending and hypothesizing about the story; and relating feelings and associations to the text.

Hancock (1993a) categorized the written responses of sixth-grade students into three broad areas of "personal meaning-making, character and plot involvement, and literary criticism" (p.468). She identified various response options within the first two categories. The four personal meaning-making options included monitoring understanding; making inferences; making, validating, or invalidating predictions; and expressing wonder or confusion. Character interaction, character assessment, and story involvement were response patterns in the character and plot involvement category.

Although the categorization schemes outlined above (and those included in Figure 8.1) differ from researcher to researcher, commonalties are apparent regarding the kinds of content identified by research which has examined students' written literature responses: personal engagement; description; discussion of the text at both distanced and personal levels; interpretation; and evaluation.

REFLECTION

Take a moment to reexamine some of the responses included in this chapter. How would you categorize the content of the responses? What type or kind of response is each one? Is each response more than one type or kind? Did any of the categories accurately describe the responses? If not, what kind of categorization scheme could you generate? Do you think categorizing the content of students' responses would be useful to you as a teacher? How would this affect your pedagogical practices?

Cautions and Concerns About Response Journal Writing

It should be evident from our previous discussion that response journals are worthwhile and beneficial pedagogical tools. But caution needs to be exercised with regards to some instructional practices associated with the implementation of response journals.

RESPONSE STARTERS

Some teachers use response starters or mind maps to assist their students in writing or talking about the books they read. Although the formats are often used with the intent of assisting students to respond personally, these devices can constrain students' responses. In one grade five classroom we know of, the teacher requires the students to use eight sentence starters in every response they write (e.g., The part I liked best was... I wonder why... I think the author... If I were ____ [a character from book], I would have...). Thus the children do not choose what they will write about: their responses are structured and formulaic. This teaching practice illustrates Squire's (1990) concern about predetermining children's responses and reflects the belief of equating "variety" of response with "quality" of response.

In another grades four and five classroom, when writing responses in their journals, students are instructed to follow both the content and format guidelines of an initial response entry provided by their teachers. The initial response journal instructs the children to respond in different ways using a mind map and to comment on plot, character, and setting. The students are also instructed to give reasons for their responses. The students receive a teacher-generated mind map (i.e., a semantic web) with headings describing various types of responses (such as feelings, personal connections, predictions, and opinions) and sentence starters under each heading (e.g., What impressed me with this character was... or In my opinion, etc.). The teachers believe the sentence starters under each type of response help students to begin their responses.

In this classroom, the initial response journal entry and mind map affect both the children's understandings of and beliefs about writing responses to literature, and the content of their journal entries. In their discussions with Sylvia, many students of this classroom stressed the necessity of using starters from the mind map in their literature responses. The teachers seemed to have designed the mind map to encourage personal responses. However, when the students attempted to use different ideas from the mind map (as instructed in the initial journal entry), many of the journal entries seemed disjointed because they contained unrelated ideas and there was little, if any, extension or development of the ideas that students chose to write about.

When asked what made a response "good," several children in the classroom identified three main criteria: the inclusion of explanations of ideas and opinions; the use of beginnings from the response mind map; and the discussion of plot, setting, and characters. As these three characteristics were outlined in the initial journal entry, it seemed that the students had learned the teachers' expectations for literature responses. This finding again exemplifies the powerful influence of being a member of a particular interpretive community.

Hynds (1992) cautions that teachers "must become more aware of the ways [they]...signal students to conform to preferred modes of behavior and response within the classroom" (p.96). It appears that what is taught through reader response depends largely on how the responses are structured and handled by teachers. When children are provided with patterns for response, grids, charts, or starters, they are probably learning more about teacher-preferred modes of response than about communicating and examining their own personal responses to literature (Pantaleo, 1994; Pantaleo & Bainbridge, 1996).

Students' responses can be influenced by teachers' oral instructions as well. Near the end of the school year in a grade one classroom, *Charlotte's Web* (White, 1952) was being read aloud to the students. The students were instructed to write responses to the book. In examining the students' response journals, we can see how the teacher's instructions influenced the content of the students' entries. (The writing mechanics have been conventionalized in the following responses; all were written by the same student.)

In response to listening to Chapter 1, the student (judged as "above average" in language arts by her teacher) wrote the following response.

> *What I didn't like about the story was that when Mr. Arable was about to kill Wilbur. What I did like is when Fern's father said he's yours now and when Fern went to school I like it when she was thinking about Wilbur. What bothers me is when she wasn't paying attention.*

In response to Chapter 10, she wrote the following comment.

> *The part that relates to me is actually two parts. One is the egg part. On a T.V. show someone dropped some eggs on the ground and the other one is when Avery was trying to hit Charlotte. Some people do that to me sometimes too.*

After listening to Chapters 17 and 18, the student wrote,

> *What is funny about the story is when there was a larger pig but what I didn't like was when he might win a prize.*

At the end of Chapter 20, this grade one student wrote,

> *I think the best part of the story was when Wilbur won a prize. I think the funniest part was when Templeton bit Wilbur's tail.*

By sharing the above four responses, and the information about the two upper elementary classrooms, our intent is not to criticize the practices of the teachers. Indeed, it seems that all the teachers are trying to provide students with instructional guidance in order to encourage them to examine various aspects of their responses to literature. Rather, we are demonstrating how students' written literature responses are influenced by teachers' oral and written directions. Although some students may require more teacher guidance initially when writing responses, it is essential for teachers to recognize their influence on students' responses and to ensure that students have control of and ownership over the content of their responses.

INTRODUCING "RESPONSE"

Some of the children in the grades four and five classroom referred to above were asked if they believed they had responded to texts prior to coming into this particular classroom. The children answered affirmatively, acknowledging that they had responded in many ways in their heads while reading, but stated that they had been unaware of the specific terminology to label or identify the various responses they had experienced (i.e., they were referring to the terms used on the mind map). When introducing the notion of response to students, we need to be sure that terminology does not confuse them. We must be cautious and avoid making response too abstract or difficult for students. Humans are constantly responding: this should be the starting point with response—capitalizing on students' background experiences to exemplify what we are expecting of them (as discussed in Chapter 7). We know that one effective way of learning is to connect what is already known to what is being learned.

TEACHERS' WRITTEN COMMENTS

As is evident in the classroom descriptions above, teachers play a fundamental role in developing, directing, or constraining their students' responses. Teachers' responses can serve as models of response and illustrate how their responses extend their personal evocations of texts (Pantaleo & Bainbridge, 1996); however, teachers' responses can also inadvertently send negative messages about the purposes and expectations for response writing. In yet another classroom (a grade five team-teaching situation), the teachers stated that when they replied in writing to the students, they tried "to model what a response should look like." However, the content of the teachers' replies indicated that the teachers did not write about their personal evocations of texts—that is, they did not model response writing. Overwhelmingly, the grade five teachers' replies to the students' responses were evaluative and instructional in nature. Many of their comments focussed on the mechanical aspects of writing, including spelling, handwriting, and journal-entry format. The teachers also frequently marked mechanical errors in the students' responses; for example, they corrected spelling errors and/or wrote the correct spellings in the margins, added capitals and punctuation where appropriate, and drew arrows to indicate correct journal format. Thus, it was not surprising that when the students discussed areas for improvement in their responses, a recurring factor was the mechanical aspects of writing. Further, several students in the class stated that the teachers' written comments were helpful as they provided feedback regarding the favourable and less favourable aspects of their work. Thus, the students did not view the teachers' comments as "models" of responses.

The instructional context affects students' opinions and conceptualizations of writing responses to literature, as well as the content of their journal entries. Research examining aesthetic and efferent teaching styles by Many and Wiseman (1992b) clearly illustrates how students learned (and replicated) what teachers *showed* as opposed to what teachers *said*. Unknowingly and unintentionally, practitioners may teach behaviours and strategies that are inconsistent with their beliefs. Therefore, in reading, responding to, and assessing children's responses, teachers need to ask themselves whether they are encouraging, facilitating, or modelling responses that deepen or extend students' reading experiences.

What Journal Responses Reveal About Students' Understandings of Literature

An unexplored area of response is what students' responses reveal about their understandings and knowledge of the workings of literary texts (Pantaleo, 1995a). Meek (1988) discusses the private lessons readers learn from literature without formal instruction (see Chapter 1). She (1988) states that readers become involved with texts, learning to "become both the teller (picking up the author's view and voice) and the told (the recipient of the story, the interpreter)," and that "this symbolic interaction is learned early" (p.10). Among the many lessons texts teach, Meek (1988) writes, "the most important lesson that children learn is the nature and variety of written discourse, the different ways that language lets a writer tell, and the many different ways a reader reads" (p.21). Through interactions with literature, children give themselves lessons about "authorship, audience, illustration, and iconic interpretation," and intertextuality (Meek, 1988, p.10).

As discussed in Chapter 7, structuralists (text-oriented reader-response theorists) view texts as having meaning as a result of readers actively applying socially acceptable, internalized literary conventions. Jonathan Culler (1980) contends that literary works have structure and meaning because they are read "in a particular way, because these potential properties, latent in the object itself, are actualized by the theory of discourse applied in the act of reading" (p.102). Culler labels this internalized grammar of literature as "literary competences." As noted in Chapter 7, the literary competences (i.e., understandings) that good readers possess enable them to create meaning when reading literature. Culler maintains that this implicit knowledge of publicly accepted conventions is possessed by both readers and authors. Application of this internalized grammar determines the construction of meaning; thus, interpretation of text is limited by a reader's literary competence as the structure of text is created by the reader (Mailloux, 1977).

REFLECTION

Read the following response written by Susan, an "above average" language arts student in grade five. What does this response demonstrate about Susan's knowledge and understandings of how literary texts work? What does this response show about the private lessons Susan has learned from literature or about her literary competences?

Susan wrote the following response to *The True Confessions of Charlotte Doyle* (Avi, 1990). Avi's novel chronicles

Charlotte's account of her voyage across the Atlantic in 1832 as a passenger on a ship captained by the nefarious Captain Jaggery and manned by a mutinous crew.

> *I find Captain Jaggery to be hiding his true identity. When he and Charlotte had tea together he always acted so gentlemanly but in fact, he was like a tiger waiting to pounce. The reason I say this is because when Charlotte joined the crew, he worked them even worse and was always on deck for Charlotte's shift to watch her every move. Another happening was when Charlotte told him that when they found land she was going to take him to court, he turned pale and got a look of murder in his eyes. I knew something was wrong with his brain, like he was half crazy or something.*

STUDENTS' WRITTEN RESPONSES

The three written responses below will be examined in terms of what they reveal about the individual writer's knowledge and understandings of how literary texts work. These responses are "windows" into the children's knowledge, as one response provides only a brief glimpse, *not a panoramic view*. One would need to examine many responses over a period of time, as well as consider a student's questions and articulations about literature, to infer a student's understanding of how literary texts work. However, our goal is to heighten teacher awareness that written literature responses can indeed provide insights into a student's knowledge of the workings of literary texts.

The responses below were written by students in Sylvia's classroom during their second year with her (i.e., grades five and six). Only the spelling of the responses has been conventionalized to assist with reading.

Cathy's Response: *The Castle in the Attic* (Winthrop, 1985) is a fantasy about a boy named William who receives, from his nanny, Mrs. Phillips, a wooden model of a castle, complete with a miniature knight guarding the gate. When the knight comes to life in William's hand, a series of adventures follows, including William shrinking Mrs. Phillips. In order to help the knight regain his kingdom, William travels into the past and battles a dragon and a wizard.

This response was written by Cathy, an "average" grade five language arts student.

> *I thought that the crooked old man was Alastor in disguise and there was a spell on him that if he picked the apple he would turn to lead. I am glad it wasn't because if both William and Sir Simon were turned to lead, who would save the land? William was brave to fight the dragon, wizard and mirror by himself. It must have been hard to fight the wizard on his own because he is just a ten year old boy.*

In this response, Cathy shows an understanding of the need to use previous information about characters and actions to make predictions, and that predictions may not always be verified or actualized. She has articulated her awareness that particular events in texts lead to other events, and that the path of the story may be narrowed or widened as a result of specific events. Cathy also indicates her knowledge of the author's crafting of the plot, as she states that one "good" character (i.e., William or Sir Simon) needs to remain unchanged in order to defeat the "evil" wizard (and save the land). She thus makes reference to her knowledge of recurring structures in texts and the universal theme in literature of "good" versus "evil."

Cathy demonstrates an understanding that it is acceptable for readers to become emotionally involved (that is, empathize) with characters in literature. She also communicates her knowledge that authors develop characters through description of their actions and that the latter can serve as a basis for character evaluation.

John's Response: Gary Paulsen's (1983) novel *Popcorn Days and Buttermilk Nights* tells the story of Carley, a teenager who has broken the law and has been sent to his uncle's farm to escape the "negative influences" of the city. Carley learns to respect the values of his relatives and experiences satisfaction and pride in working in his uncle's blacksmith forge.

This response was written by John, an "average" fifth-grade student in language arts.

> *I enjoyed reading this book because Carley is trying to change his life and he eventually does. For example when Carley lived in the city he used to burn things down and throw rocks at windows of churches, laundromats and other places. Now Carley works at a blacksmith shop and is fixing and building things instead of destroying them. Another reason I really enjoyed reading this book was because there were a couple of funny parts too. One of them is when Tinker and Carley are riding calves. When Carley tries, he gets dragged in the pasture behind the barn. I can just imagine being dragged through the manure because Gary Paulsen is very good at describing what is going on and how it is happening.*

In this response, John articulates an understanding of how readers use characters' actions to discern personalities and goals. He recognizes how the character's actions are symptomatic of his inner conflicts as well as how the character's development is revealed through his solving the conflicts.

John expresses enjoyment of the piece of literature, demonstrating an appreciation of the power of literature to entertain. He comments on the author's language style and recognizes that the latter allows him to imagine himself in a character's position. As a reader of literature, John communicates his knowledge that he is to assume an active role when reading and that literature should be read from a predominantly aesthetic stance.

Richard's Response: *The Dragon Children* (1975), written by Canadian author Bryan Buchan, is a story about the attempts of a group of children to catch a thief who is cheating elderly people. The children receive help from a mysterious boy named Steven.

This response was written by Richard, an "above average" language arts student in grade six.

> *I really liked this book because there were two mysteries in the whole book. One of the mysteries was if the crook would make it out of town in time and if John, Scott, Cathy and Steven would get the crook or not. The other mystery was to find out who or what Steven really was. I figured out what Steven was by putting all the clues together. At the end of the book I found out who Steven was. At first I thought that Steven was a ghost (even though he was) that the crook had drowned in the river. I was half right about that. It was a surprise to me when John, Scott and Cathy found out that the crook wasn't who they thought it was. It surprised me because when Steven told John that the crook was driving a green car with licence plate number 5K-206 it wasn't the crook driving it. Instead it was a man who had come with his family for their vacation. The man did seem like a crook though because when he was walking through the woods with his son, it looked like he had kidnapped the child. My favourite part though was when Scott sneaked up behind the real crook and poked the needle in his back end. I liked it because it really made me laugh.*

Richard communicates an understanding that two stories may occur simultaneously within one piece of literature, and that the reader is to follow the individual storylines as well as to relate them. He displays his knowledge that authors provide clues in mysteries and that readers are to connect or unravel the clues in order to solve the puzzles. In this entry, Richard communicates an understanding that readers need to engage in both anticipation and retrospection (Iser, 1980) as hypotheses may be abrogated, validated, or modified (i.e., readers maintain a wandering viewpoint during their reading, [Iser, 1980]). This response also reveals Richard's awareness that events in literature, as in life, are not always as they appear. Further, Richard communicates his understanding that literature provides aesthetic experiences as he describes his enjoyment of solving the mysteries and his amusement with textual events.

The Dragon Children by Bryan Buchan

REFLECTION

After reading the three responses above, return to your comments about Susan's response to *The True Confessions of Charlotte Doyle*. Would you now revise your comments in any way? If so, how and why?

We believe that Susan's response demonstrates an understanding of the techniques authors use to reveal characters. Susan displays an awareness that she must pick up the "clues" and fill in gaps in the text (Iser, 1980). She engages in several "inferential walks" (Eco, 1978) as she puts together pieces of the text in order to make her evaluative statements regarding Captain Jaggery.

The content of children's written responses to literature can be a rich repository of information. In order to discern what children's written responses reveal about their transactions with literature and their understandings of the workings of literary texts, teachers *must* read the literature their students read. Students' written responses to literature can provide invaluable pedagogical information for teachers as they develop their reading programs and as they support and encourage children in their growth as life-long readers.

Other Written Responses to Literature

Written responses to literature allow readers to think about and reflect upon their reading. Some teachers encourage students to write whatever is going through their minds as they read; thus their responses become a stream of consciousness. There may be questions, images, wonderings, confusions, comparisons, and opinions in the students' responses. Students may move quickly from idea to idea, not stopping long to reflect in more depth on one or more thoughts. This type of entry can be used as a starting point for group discussions or to illustrate the processes being activated while reading. The following is an example of a "stream of consciousness" response written to *The Iron Man* (Hughes, 1968) by Mitch, an academically "average" grade five student.

> *I think the Iron Man will be like the machine in the scrap metal yard that gets rid of the metal. The Iron Man will be happy, the farmers will be happy and Hogarth can visit the Iron Man all the time. Who were the people that had the picnic on the hill and will they show up again? If the Iron Man is controlled by something, who or what is it and what will it think about the Iron Man being so happy? If there is more Iron Men does the Iron Man we know about keep in touch with them? If he does, maybe our Iron Man will tell the others and they will come too. I like how the author called all the metal delicacies. I can see how the chain is spaghetti and maybe the knobs on the bed were chocolate covered*

candy. Brass covered iron. I don't understand how different kinds of metals have different kinds of tastes. What do you think the Iron Man's favourite kind of metal is? ... What will happen when the Iron Man runs out of food at the metal scrap yard? Will they bring him food from other towns? Do you think the Iron Man will ever go back to the sea? Maybe if he leaves the scrap yard all the townsfolk will look for him at the sea. Do you know if the farmers filled up the hole? I sure hope so. It would be disastrous if somebody fell down the hole. If somebody did fall down the hole, maybe the Iron Man will help them out and then he might not be hated so much. Is the Iron Man hated? I think it starts out in the story that the Iron Man was hated but now I think maybe he is more liked.

DIALOGUE JOURNALS are sometimes called response journals. In this book, we use the term *response journal* to refer to those occasions where children are responding in writing to their learning—a piece of literature or a social studies activity—not in response to each other. Dialogue journals generally involve one individual writing to a partner (e.g., a classmate, a teacher, a parent, or other peers and adults). Although a journal can be both a dialogue journal and a response journal, the two terms are not synonymous.

In one grade two classroom, the students wrote response journal entries after the teacher read a piece of children's literature to her class. The journals were then given to a partner (a classmate), who wrote back. Below is an example of two students dialoguing after the teacher read *Doctor DeSoto* (Steig, 1984). The entry below was written by Jenny, who then exchanged journals with Jan. (The spelling has been conventionalized to aid reading.)

Jenny: *My dad is a dentist so I have to brush my teeth. I have to brush my teeth every time I eat anything even a little bit of food. I don't brush my teeth when I stay for lunch. Sometimes I go somewhere that I don't need to brush my teeth. I don't have to go and visit the dentist because my dad comes home and sometimes I go to my dad's office and I have my teeth fixed there. I had to take some of my toys there so the kids could play. Sometimes my dad fixed my teeth at home.*
Jan: *I sometimes have to brush my teeth 2 times with the Alligator. He is funny but his antennas don't move. (Walker, 1993)*

Both students have drawn upon their personal experiences in recording their responses in this exchange.

DOUBLE-ENTRY JOURNALS are another form of journal writing. Students divide their journal page into two columns. In the left column, students write quotations from the story, make predictions, or record particular story events; in the right column, students respond to the quotations they wrote, comment on their predictions, or make personal connections to the events they recorded. Another way double-entry journals may be used is to have students write their immediate responses to their reading in the left column, then add discussion notes in the right column after peer discussion of the literature. Younger children may draw pictures rather than write.

Letter-writing to peers, the teacher, the author, or literary characters is another form of written response. Alternatively, students may select a character and write letters from the character's point of view regarding situations in the book. For example, as a character, students may choose to write a letter to the author seeking justification for the events that he or she must endure and making suggestions to alter the plot. Letters may also be written to other characters, responding to actions or verbalizations; to readers, seeking advice or justifying actions; or to the character himself or herself in the form of diary entries. The letters can include the character's feelings, thoughts, concerns, and questions.

Students can choose to write poems that would be appropriate for inclusion in the book itself or in response to their reading. Ted, an "above average" grade four student, wrote the following "five senses" poem after reading the novel *Naya Nuki: Shoshoni Girl Who Ran Away* (Thomasma, 1983).

FREEDOM
Freedom is yellow.
Freedom tastes like an extra large pepperoni pizza.
Freedom smells like a pie fresh out of the oven.
Freedom feels like a silky blanket.
Freedom sounds like the purr of a kitten.
Freedom looks like a bald eagle
soaring through the sky.
This is what I think freedom is.

In their written responses, students may choose to write an alternative ending for a book, a continuation of the work that picks up immediately where it leaves off, or an epilogue for the book. Students may decide to write a story event from another character's point of view. Other written response ideas include composing an interior monologue that captures the unspoken thoughts of a character at a pivotal moment in the text; creating a flashback that illuminates a character and some aspect of her/his personality that assists readers in better understanding the character; or writing a dream that represents a central issue for that character. Meyers (1997) describes several writing tasks, which he calls dependent authorship activities, that encourage students to write from within the world of the text. As well as identifying many of the same writing activities that we have recommended, Meyers suggests that students write a song that could appear in the text, or incorporate a character from another literary work into the current work being read and discussed (1997, p. 21).

There are often gaps in texts where authors do not explain what happened. Students can fill in the gaps in their responses. In the time-slip fantasy *A Handful of Time* (Pearson, 1987), Patty, the main character, finds an old watch hidden under a floorboard in a guest cabin at her cousins' cottage. The watch transports Patty back in time. Chapter 12 ends with Patty in the past, observing her mother (twelve-year-old Ruth) being disciplined for her involvement in a late-night adventure to frighten some young campers. However, Ruth is being disciplined more severely by her father (Patty's grandfather) than the boys who were involved in the incident. The chapter ends with Ruth protesting her father's unfair treatment. Chapter 13 begins with Patty in present time, thinking about all that she has observed in the past. Patty returns to the past once again, where a week has passed. In their journals, students could write about what they think has happened during the week or about Patty's actions, thoughts, or feelings during the time from observing her mother being disciplined to her next visit to the past.

A Handful of Time by Kit Pearson

Many of these written-response suggestions require initial instruction by the teacher. It is also important that all response-writing activities suggested in this section be adapted in ways that are appropriate for the both the students and the texts. A repertoire of written-response options enables students to choose a strategy that most appropriately expresses and extends their responses to a particular piece of literature.

From our experiences with the written responses included in this chapter, and with many other readers in our classrooms, we believe that how children are encouraged to respond to literature, and how this influences their reading behaviour, depends largely on the philosophy or belief system of the teacher. It appears to us that a strong component in how teachers deepen children's responses is the view they hold of children themselves. Facilitating children's honest and thoughtful responses requires that teachers believe in children's abilities and respect their thoughts and opinions. Encouraging children to respond to literature in deep and meaningful ways demands that students be in control of the reading transaction. Readers who take themselves seriously, who believe in their abilities, and who are supported in their interpretations and explorations of texts come to know their own voices. And this, perhaps, is what responding to literature is essentially about: children learn about themselves as readers and about texts and how they work. They learn about the world in which they live and their place in it. But they also learn to speak out, to take control of their thinking, to respect their own critical faculties, and to respect the thoughts of other people.

Teachers are the central members of classroom interpretive communities. As such, teachers' theoretical beliefs and assumptions influence their purposes and goals for and expectations of using literature and response writing, consequently affecting the content of students' responses. As teachers can acculturate students into particular ways of reading and responding, they must examine their reasons for using children's literature and literary response in their classrooms. They must also reflect on and be reflexive about their conceptualizations, expectations, and instruction in response writing; *and determine what their programs are teaching children, either overtly or covertly, about literature and literary response*. Research indicates that "what students know about literature, what books they read, and how they respond to literature are heavily influenced by their literary experiences in elementary school" (Walmsley, 1992, p.508). Finally, teachers must examine the kinds of opportunities they provide for students to learn about themselves, the texts, and human life, by using quality children's literature and personal literary response.

References

Beach, R. 1990. New directions in research on response to literature. In *Transactions with Literature*. E. Favell and J. Squire, eds. Urbana, Illinois: National Council of Teachers of English.

———. 1993. *A Teacher's Introduction to Reader-response Theories*. Urbana, Illinois: National Council of Teachers of English.

Beach, R. and S. Hynds. 1991. Research on response to literature. In *Handbook of Reading Research: Volume II*. R. Barr, M. Kamil, P. Mosenthal, and P.D. Pearson, eds. New York: Longman Publishing Group.

Blunt, J. 1977. Response to reading: How some young readers describe the process. *English in Education* 11(3), 38-47.

Britton, J. 1968. Response to literature. In *Response to Literature: The Dartmouth Seminar Papers*. J.R. Squire, ed. Champaign, Illinois: National Council of Teachers of English.

Calkins, L. 1991. *Living Between the Lines*. Portsmouth, New Hampshire: Heinemann.

Cox, C. and J.E. Many. 1992a. Toward an understanding of the aesthetic response to literature. *Language Arts* 69(1), 28-33.

———. 1992b. Stance towards a literary work: Applying the transactional theory to children's responses. *Reading Psychology* 13(1), 37-72.

———. 1992c. Beyond choosing: Emergent categories of efferent and aesthetic stance. In *Reader Stance and Literary Understanding: Exploring the Theories, Research and Practice*. J. Many and C. Cox, eds. Norwood, New Jersey: Ablex Publishing Corporation.

Crowhurst, M. and M. Kooy. 1985. The use of response journals in teaching the novel. *Reading—Canada—Lecture* 3(3), 256-266.

Culler, J. 1980. Literary competence. In *Reader-response Criticism: From Formalism to Post-structuralism*. J. Tompkins, ed. Baltimore, Maryland: The Johns Hopkins University Press.

Eco, U. 1978. *The Role of the Reader*. Bloomington, Indiana: Indiana University Press.

Eeds, M. and M. Wells. 1989. Grand conversations: An exploration of meaning construction in literature study groups. *Research in the Teaching of English* 23(1), 4-29.

Fulps, J. and T. Young. 1991. The what, why, when and how of reading response journals. *Reading Horizons* 32(2), 109-116.

Galda, L. (1982). Assessment: Responses to literature. In *Secondary School Reading: What Research Reveals for Classroom Practice*. A. Berger and H.A. Robinson, eds. Urbana, Illinois: National Council of Teachers of English.

Halliday, M.A.K. 1978. *Language as Social Semiotic*. Baltimore, Maryland: University Park Press.

Hancock, M.R. 1992. Literature response journals: Insights beyond the printed page. *Language Arts* 69(1), 36-42.

———. 1993a. Exploring and extending personal response through literature journals. *The Reading Teacher* 46(6), 466-474.

———. 1993b. Exploring the meaning-making process through the content of literature response journals: A case study investigation. *Research in the Teaching of English* 27(4), 335-368.

Harker, W. 1990. Reader response and the interpretation of literature: Is there a teacher in the classroom? *Reflections on Canadian Literacy* 8(2&3), 69-73.

Hickman, J. 1983. Everything considered: Response to literature in an elementary school setting. *Journal of Research and Development in Education* 16(3), 8-13.

———. 1984. Research currents: Researching children's response to literature. *Language Arts* 61(3), 278-284.

Hynds, S. 1992. Challenging questions in the teaching of literature. In *Literature Instruction: A Focus on Student Response*. J.A. Langer, ed. Urbana, Illinois: National Council of Teachers of English.

Iser, W. 1980. The reading process: A phenomenological approach. In *Reader-response Criticism: From Formalism to Post-structuralism*. J. Tompkins, ed. Baltimore, Maryland: The Johns Hopkins University Press.

Kelly, P. 1990. Guiding young students' responses to literature. *The Reading Teacher* 43(7), 464-470.

Langer, J.A. 1990. Understanding literature. *Language Arts* 67(8), 812-816.

Mailloux, S. 1977. Reader-response criticism? *Genre* 10(3), 413-431.

Many, J.E. 1991. The effects of stance and age level on children's literary responses. *Journal of Reading Behavior* 23(1), 61-85.

———. 1992. Living through literary experiences versus literary analysis: Examining stance in children's response to literature. *Reading Horizons* 32(3), 169-183.

Many, J.E. and D.L. Wiseman. 1992a. The effect of teaching approach on third-grade students' response to literature. *Journal of Reading Behavior* 24(3), 265-287.

———. 1992b. Analyzing versus experiencing: The effects of teaching approaches on students' responses. In *Reader Stance and Literary Understanding: Exploring the Theories, Research and Practice*. J.E. Many and C. Cox, eds. Norwood, New Jersey: Ablex Publishing Corporation.

Marshall, J.D. 1987. The effects of writing on students' understanding of literary texts. *Research in the Teaching of English* 21(1), 30-62.

Martinez, M.G. and N.L. Roser. 1991. Children's responses to literature. In *Handbook of Research on Teaching the English Language Arts*. J. Flood, J. Jensen, D. Lapp, and J. Squire, eds. New York: Macmillan Publishing Company.

Meek, M. 1988. *How Texts Teach What Readers Learn*. Stroud, UK: The Thimble Press.

Meyers, D. 1997. Dependent authorship: A dependable teaching activity for reading and writing critically and creatively. *Statement* 34(1), 20-22.

Odell, L. and C.R. Cooper. 1976. Describing responses to works of fiction. *Research in the Teaching of English* 10(3), 203-225.

Pantaleo, S. 1994. *Teacher Influence on Student Response to Literature*. Unpublished doctoral dissertation, University of Alberta, Edmonton, Canada.

Pantaleo, S. 1995a. What do response journals reveal about children's understandings of the workings of literary texts? *Reading Horizons* 36(1), 76-93.

————. 1995b. The influence of teacher practice on student response to literature. *Journal of Children's Literature* 21(1), 38-47.

Pantaleo, S. and J. Bainbridge. 1996. Writing responses to literature: What are children learning? *Reading: Exploration and Discovery* 17(2), 14-26.

A.R. Petrosky. 1982. From story to essay: Reading and writing. *College Composition and Communication* 33(1), 19-36.

Purves, A.C. 1992. Testing literature. In *Literature Instruction: A Focus on Student Response*. J.A. Langer, ed. Urbana, Illinois: National Council of Teachers of English.

Purves, A.C. and V. Rippere. 1968. *Elements of Writing About a Literary Work: A Study of Response to Literature*. Research Report No. 9. Urbana, Illinois: National Council of Teachers of English.

Purves, A., T. Rogers, and A. Soter. 1990. *How Porcupines Make Love II: Teaching a Response-centered Curriculum*. New York: Longman.

Squire, J.R. 1964. *The Responses of Adolescents While Reading Four Short Stories*. Urbana, Illinois: National Council of Teachers of English.

————. 1990. Research on reader response and the national literature initiative. In *Reading and Response*. M. Hayhoe and S. Parker, eds. Philadelphia: Open University Press.

Thomson, J. 1987. *Understanding Teenagers' Reading: Reading Processes and the Teaching of Literature*. Norwood, South Australia: Australian Association for the Teaching of English Inc.

Walker, T. 1993. *Peer Dialogue Journals as Response to Literature in Grade Two*. Unpublished M.Ed. project, University of Alberta, Edmonton, Canada.

Walmsley, S. 1992. Reflections on the state of elementary literature instruction. *Language Arts* 69(7), 508-514.

Wollman-Bonilla, J.E. 1989. Reading journals: Invitations to participate in literature. *The Reading Teacher* 43(2), 112-120.

Professional Resources

Benton, M., and Fox, G. (1985). *Teaching Literature: Nine to Fourteen*. Oxford: Oxford University Press. • Benton and Fox explore many facets of working with children and literature in upper elementary and middle-school grades. However, many of their ideas are also applicable for grades one through three. The book provides an overview of teaching the class novel, individual novels, poetry, plays, and nonfiction materials. Many ideas are suggested for classroom work.

Many, J. and C. Cox, eds. 1992. *Reader Stance and Literary Understanding: Exploring the Theories, Research and Practice*. Norwood, New Jersey: Ablex Publishing Corporation. • This book includes chapters that discuss various theoretical perspectives on reader stance and response, students' perspectives when reading and responding, and the interactions of teachers, students, and literature in classrooms.

Thomson, J. 1987. *Understanding Teenagers' Reading: Reading Processes and the Teaching of Literature*. Norwood, South Australia: Australian Association for the Teaching of English Inc. • This text examines many issues surrounding the teaching of literature. It addresses literary theory, reading habits of students, and response to literature. One chapter describes examples of teachers working with students, literature, and response in classrooms. Although the book describes the reading and responding of teenagers, the information in the text is relevant to teachers of all grade levels who are implementing literature- and response-based programs.

CHAPTER NINE

ORGANIZING FOR INSTRUCTION

The objectives of this chapter are

- To become aware of the issues involved in selecting literature for children;
- To become aware of the multiple tools available to assist teachers in selecting literature for children;
- To develop an understanding about children's reading interests and factors associated with reading motivation;
- To develop an understanding of various classroom organizational structures appropriate for literature- and response-based programs.

CLASSROOM SCENARIO

In the school library, Sylvia's grades five and six students are exchanging their library books. The librarian, Mrs. McFarlane, and Sylvia work together to meet the students' needs in selecting books. Michael, James, and Shawn are interested in books about survival. During Literature Workshops, each boy has read *Hatchet* (Paulsen, 1987), *My Side of the Mountain* (George, 1959), *Call it Courage* (Sperry, 1940), *Island of the Blue Dolphins* (O'Dell, 1960), and *The Cay* (Taylor, 1969). Although Sylvia talks with them about other types of survival, for the moment the boys are most interested in books which deal with characters struggling to survive in the "wilderness." She engages in brief book talks about *The Sign of the Beaver* (Speare, 1983), *Julie of the Wolves* (George, 1972), and *The Island Keeper* (Mazer, 1981). Mrs. McFarlane is working with Melanie, Danielle, and Ashley who are interested in reading more "good" mysteries. Jennifer, a grade five student, is assisting Carolyn, a grade six student, in finding books written by Walt Morey. Jennifer has read many of Morey's novels and has gotten her friend interested in his books. Once Sylvia finishes with the "survival" group, she turns her attention to Samson, Russ, Carl, and Danny, who are interested in reading more books by Gary Paulsen. They have been reading Paulsen's works during Literature Workshops. Sylvia engages in brief book talks about *Dancing Carl* (1983), *Canyons* (1990), and *Dogsong* (1985). A few shelves away, Andy is selecting another Gordon Korman novel, as he likes the Bruno and Boots characters and Korman's sense of humour. He then proceeds to another section of the library to search for books dealing with medieval issues, because he is also very interested in knights, castles, and medieval events. Jeff is searching for more books by Marilyn Halvorson, as he has recently read *Bull Rider* (1989) and *Cowboys Don't Cry* (1984) during Literature Workshops. Mrs. McFarlane is assisting Theresa and Gwen in their search for time-slip fantasies, as they have learned about this text structure through their selection of books during Literature Workshops. Brent has self-selected a book about motorcycles and then asks Sylvia about "survival" stories. She directs him to Michael, James, and Shawn. As the library exchange period progresses, Sylvia and Mrs. McFarlane work with other students who require help in locating books to read. Some students assist one other, some students use library reference materials to locate books, but most students seek support in choosing books from Sylvia and Mrs. McFarlane.

Interest in Reading

As teachers, we want our students not only to know how to read, but to *choose* to read. "An enjoyed book provides more than just a few hours of diversion, and is in fact the best vehicle by which youngsters can gain proficiency in reading" (Carter & Harris, 1981, p.57). Cullinan (1989) writes that, in general, children "who read a lot not only read well but become avid readers" (pp.27-28). Taylor, Frye, and Maruyama (1990) discovered that time spent reading silently at school contributed significantly to growth in reading achievement of grades five and six students. Anderson, Wilson, and Fielding (1988) found that reading books was "the out-of-school activity that proved to have the strongest association with reading proficiency" for grade five students and that "time spent reading books was the best predictor of a child's growth as a reader from the second to the fifth grade" (p.297). Further, the 1990 NAEP data (National Assessment of Educational Progress) indicated that students in grades four, eight, and twelve who read more outside of school had higher average reading achievement. Thus, the opportunities individuals have to read positively influence their success in reading.

In literature-based programs, students need to spend *significant* amounts of time reading. Therefore, students need access to a wealth of reading material, representing both a wide range of levels and a variety of genres. Teachers must be aware of children's reading interests and locate high-quality literature to meet children's needs, as well as to broaden their interests.

A positive relationship between reading interest and achievement has been well documented (Guthrie, 1981; Hunt, 1970; Johnson & Greenbaum, 1982; Morrow, 1991). Guthrie (1981) wrote that high-interest "materials are more fully comprehended than low-interest materials" and suggested the latter was a result of the high-interest materials generating knowledge (pp.984-985). Hunt discovered that when individuals chose material to read because of personal interest, they were able to break many comprehension barriers. "Strong interest can frequently cause the reader to transcend not only his independent but also his so-called instructional level. Such is the power of self-motivation" (Hunt, 1970, p.148). Therefore, it is worthwhile to both determine and to disseminate knowledge about reading interests to teachers, parents, authors, publishers, editors, and other stakeholders.

The University of Georgia-University of Maryland consortium conducted a survey to identify issues and/or problems International Reading Association members felt warranted further research. The largest percentage of respondents, 76%, rated "creating interest in reading" as highly important (O'Flahavan, Gambrell, Guthrie, Stahl, Bauman & Alvermann, 1992, p.12). Discovering children's reading interests and subsequently providing books to meet their needs can generate student interest in reading.

Reading Interests

A significant amount of research has examined students' reading interests and reading preferences. Researchers have noted the need to distinguish between the terms "interest" and "preference," as reading preference relates more to reading which *might* be done (Monson & Sebesta, 1991; Summers & Lukasevich, 1983; Weintraub, 1969). Johnson and Greenbaum (1982) contended that in many studies that have examined the reading interests of students, the "children did not actually read the books; often they were reacting only to titles and annotations" (p.36). Although some concerns have been expressed about aspects of research that have explored reading interests and reading preferences, information regarding these topics is pedagogically significant.

The twenty-six students in Sylvia's grades five and six classroom completed a mini-reading survey in mid-year. One survey question asked them to list their favourite books. Unlike much of the previous research examining children's reading interests, the responses of the students were based on books they had actually read, not hypothetical examples. Thus, the book titles the students provided demonstrated reading interest (as opposed to preference), as they self-selected titles from the literature they had actually read.

One of the findings of Sylvia's reading interest survey was that the students were concerned about the topics of the books (Pantaleo, 1995). This finding is consistent with other research, which has noted the relationship between the content (topics) of books and children's interests and selection (Hill, 1984; Johnson & Greenbaum, 1982). In Sylvia's classroom, the topic of survival was cited eleven times as an interest factor. Books dealing with "real life" situations or seeming "like a real story" were of great interest to these grades five and six students. The latter finding was consistent with the discussion of students' reading interests by Martinez and Nash (1992), who state that "realistic fiction, with characters and situations to which these emerging adolescents can relate, is popular" with middle-grade students (p.138).

Other factors students identified as affecting their interest level on Sylvia's reading survey included the writing style of the author ("author described or explained story or events well" and "author told thoughts and feelings of characters"); students' ability to relate to characters in the books ("reader feels like one of the characters" and "liked the characters"); and the characteristics of a "touching story" and the presence of "different emotions in the book" (Pantaleo, 1995).

As a group, Sylvia's students indicated that books that engaged them emotionally were of high interest. Consistent with many other studies (see Figure 9.1), Sylvia's grades five and six students indicated that mystery, excitement, adventure, and humour were important factors that affected their reading interests (Pantaleo, 1995). These elements, along with "grabs reader's attention—wanted to know what happens," indicated students' interest in action and emphasized the importance of texts actively engaging readers.

FIGURE 9.1: RESEARCH ON STUDENTS' READING INTERESTS

Interests	Grade Level	Research
jokes, mystery, adventure, crafts, and animals	British and American students aged seven to ten	Fisher and Ayres (1990)
mystery, humour, adventure, and animal stories	Grade 4	Graham (1986)
mystery, adventure, fantasy, and humour	Grades 4, 5, and 6	Hawkins (1983)
mystery, adventure, fantasy, and humour	Grades 5, 6, and 7	Summers and Lukasevich (1983)
mystery, adventure, ghost stories, comics, science fiction, horse stories, and animal stories (real)	Grades 4, 5, 6, and 7	Ashley (1970)

It seems that several factors affect students' positive responses to or interests in reading materials. The multifaceted nature of reading interests demonstrates the need to provide students with a wide range of reading materials.

CHILDREN AND ADULTS: A DIFFERENCE OF OPINION

In reviewing the literature on reading interests, Pascoe and Gilchrist (1987) "found a serious discrepancy between what children choose to read of their own volition and what adults (librarians and experts) consider suitable for them" (p.55). In two related studies, Pascoe and Gilchrist discovered disagreement between the factors cited by children to determine their likes and dislikes of books and the factors believed by teachers to affect students' enjoyment of books. There appears "to be a general trend for children to respond positively to books which provide them excitement, animal interest, adventure, mystery and humour" (p.59). The teachers in both studies believed that "ability to identify with characters" and "character interest" were the most important factors to children's enjoyment of books; however, both factors were "ranked relatively low by children...[and] teachers s[aw] excitement, suspense, action and mystery as less important than other considerations" (p.62). These findings indicate that the main ingredients of children's reading interests may not be recognized by teachers.

Other research has also documented divergence between student and teacher selection of books. Kellerman (1991) discovered that grade eight students "were rejecting books recommended by teachers for their independent reading" because teachers were ignoring the students' interests (p.2). Carter and Harris (1981) found significant differences between the books favoured by students in grades six, seven, and eight and the books favoured by professionals for those grade levels. Similarly, Nilsen, Peterson, and Searfoss (1980) discovered discrepancies between children and adults in their reactions to books, and maintained that even when "several respected critics and evaluators agree that a particular children's book is distinctive, its popularity with young readers is not guaranteed" (p.530).

DETERMINING AND FACILITATING STUDENTS' READING INTERESTS

Since children's "willingness to read and their comprehension of what they read is affected by the interest level of the material" (Cullinan, Harwood & Galda, 1983, p.30), and since adults and children seem to differ in their opinions about literature, teachers need to be aware of children's reading interests and provide opportunities for students to select their own reading materials. The issue of self-selection is an important component in facilitating student enjoyment of reading.

Teachers can learn about students' reading interests by having them complete a reading survey or inventory at the beginning of the year. A simple questionnaire in mid-year can furnish information about students' changing reading interests. Talking with children about books (both formally and informally) and listening to children converse about books with their peers can provide insights into their opinions and feelings about particular books and authors. Pillar (1992) notes, "We learn from our students when we listen as they speak enthusiastically about books they have read" (p.152). Student booktalks can be a medium for peers and teachers to discover more about the reading interests of classroom community members. As indicated in the classroom scenario at the beginning of this chapter, library exchange is an ideal opportunity for teachers to inquire about students' reading interests. By helping children to locate books of interest and recommending possible titles, teachers demonstrate their commitment to facilitating positive attitudes toward reading.

Students' varying reading interests and levels can be accommodated by classroom libraries that provide a wide variety of books (i.e., genres, level of difficulty). Indeed, research has found that "book-rich" classroom libraries influence student reading motivation (Palmer, Codling & Gambrell, 1994). Norton (1991) notes that if students are to "gain enjoyment, knowledge of their heritage, recognition and appreciation of good literature, and understanding of themselves and others, they need balanced selections of literature" (p.83). As some teachers may be unable to accompany their students to the school library for book exchange, a classroom library allows teachers to monitor their students' reading. In addition, students can keep a record of the titles of the books they read; periodic reviews of these lists can inform teachers of students' reading interests. Further, if desired, the children can appraise the books they have read using some type of rating system.

Providing children with opportunities to self-select literature, other than a daily silent-reading period, can also supply information about students' reading interests. The importance of providing for and respecting student choice in selecting books to read has been emphasized by several individuals (Atwell, 1987, 1998; Fuhler, 1990; Gambell, 1986; Huck, 1987, 1992; Olhausen & Jepsen, 1992). Self-selection empowers students, results in feelings of ownership, develops interest in reading, and enhances motivation. Although children choose books for different reasons, it is important for teachers to model and teach strategies to assist students in making independent and appropriate book choices. As educators, we want to enlarge our students' experiences with and cultivate their tastes of literature. Teachers may therefore need to take a more direct role in children's selection of literature in certain contexts. Olhausen and Jepsen (1992) note that, "While we need to respect children's choices, there are many times when this can be difficult. Sometimes we need to intervene and other times it's best to wait it out" (p.42).

The students in Sylvia's grades five and six class were asked to express their feelings and opinions about the practice of selecting their own reading books (from a large, predetermined collection) (Pantaleo, 1995). The students expressed unanimous pleasure in being able to pick their own novels to read. They stated two main reasons for this preference. First, by making their own choices, they did not have to read books they did not like; second, they viewed self-selection positively because they were aware of individual "reading tastes" and acknowledgement of differing predilections in their literature community. The feelings of "freedom of choice" and "ownership" were two other reasons expressed as contributing to the children's enjoyment of selecting their own books to read.

MOTIVATION FOR READING

As we have stated before, teachers are very concerned about creating student interest in reading. Several individuals have examined the role of motivation in reading. Sweet and Guthrie (1996) determined that children possess various motivational levels for reading and identified four types of intrinsic (internal to the individual) motivation: involvement (getting "lost" in a book); curiosity (interest in learning); social interaction (sharing reading experiences); and challenge (unravelling a complex plot). Sweet and Guthrie also discovered three types of student-extrinsic motivation: compliance (adhering to a teacher's expectations or requirements); recognition (desire to feel publicly acknowledged); and good grades (demonstrating academic superiority). Generally, students who possess intrinsic motivations, such as curiosity and aesthetic involvement, become life-long readers (p.661).

During a year-long study, Palmer, Codling, and Gambrell (1994) asked grades three and five students about their reading habits, preferences, and behaviours. Analysis of questionnaires and personal interviews identified four significant motivational factors. Students mentioned prior experience with books (i.e., some degree of familiarity) most consistently. Another frequent reason for reading particular books was social interaction (i.e., students heard about books from others). A third factor was book access: classroom libraries significantly influenced students' reading habits. The fourth significant factor reported as being motivational was book choice. Self-selection of books facilitated enjoyment and sustained reading experiences.

Gambrell (1996) conducted further research on reading motivation. She distributed a survey to and conducted interviews with grades three and five students to discover their self-concepts as readers and the value they placed on reading. The findings of the Motivation to Read Profile (MRP) confirmed previous research: opportunity to self-select was identified as a major factor in motivating students to read. Students also reported that sharing their reading experiences with others (i.e., book discussions and book recommendations) was an important motivational factor. A third critical component in nurturing and supporting reading was availability of books (i.e., "book-rich environments"). Gambrell's study further emphasized the importance of the teacher as role model: students indicated that teachers were a major influence on their decisions to pursue reading outside of the classroom.

Thus, not surprisingly, there are several commonalities between strategies to determine and facilitate student reading interests and factors which influence motivation to read.

IMPLICATIONS FOR TEACHERS

It is vital for teachers of reading to "remain current with children's books and trends in the field of children's literature....Teachers who effectively use children's literature as the content of their reading programs need to know and love children's books" (Lehman & Crook, 1988, p.240). Selecting and using literature as the content of a reading program "is not an easy way to teach reading. It requires a thorough knowledge of children's literature, an internalization of the reading process, and a thorough understanding of children" (Huck, 1987, p.370). More than ever before, educators must maintain their professional competence by reading books written for children. If teachers are "non-readers" of children's literature, it is unlikely they will be able to create successful literature-based reading programs.

As teachers, we can increase our awareness of children's literature by talking with librarians and colleagues and by attending workshops or courses on children's literature. Various sources can assist teachers in selecting literature for their classroom; some of these sources were mentioned in Chapter 1. *Using Literature in the Middle Grades: A Thematic Approach* (Moss, 1994) contains comprehensive lists of literature appropriate for various units (e.g., friendship, modern fairy tales and traditional literature, dilemmas and decisions in realistic fiction, family stories). In a book edited by Cullinan (1992), *Invitation to Read: More Children's Literature in the Reading Program*, Arlene Pillar outlines a comprehensive list of general, specialized and subject bibliographies, and other professional books to assist teachers in choosing literature for children. *Essentials of Children's Literature* (Tomlinson & Lynch-Brown, 1996), *Discovering Children's Literature* (Hillman, 1999), and *Through the Eyes of a Child: An Introduction to Children's Literature* (Norton, 1995) are three other textbooks that contain comprehensive listings of children's literature. *Research and Professional Resources in Children's Literature: Piecing a Patchwork Quilt* (Short, 1995) describes resources, research, publications, and professional books on using children's literature. *Adventuring with Books: A Booklist for Pre-K–Grade 6* (Sutton, 1997) and *Kaleidoscope: A Multicultural Booklist for Grades K–8* (Barrera, Thompson & Dressman) are excellent publications that provide annotations of selections of children's and young-adult literature. The books in each publication are listed in alphabetical order and organized into topics.

The *Canadian Book Review Annual* publishes an annual issue devoted to reviewing Canadian children's literature. *Resource Links: Connecting Classrooms, Libraries and Canadian Learning Resources* is another valuable source that reviews, among other material, children's and young-adult literature. Lists of young children's and young adults' favourite books are published annually in *The Reading Teacher* ("Children's Choices") and *The Journal of Reading*, now called *The Journal of Adolescent and Adult Literacy* ("Young Adults' Choices"). *The Reading Teacher* also publishes an annual list of "Teachers' Choices" in children's literature. *Canadian Children's Literature, The New Advocate, Language Arts, The Horn Book Magazine, Children's Literature, Children's Literature Association Quarterly, Children's Literature in Education, Journal of Children's Literature, Primary Voices K-6, Book Links, School Library Journal*, and *Young Children* are other professional publications that review children's literature. Many of these journals also publish articles that address various issues surrounding children's literature and its use in elementary classrooms. Further, there are numerous websites on the Internet that explore various issues in children's literature; some site addresses are listed in Appendix B.

As teachers, we must foster a love of reading in our classrooms. Reading to students daily and providing opportunities for self-selection and time to read independently are means to accomplish this. Educators influence the amount of time students spend reading in classrooms (Taylor, Frye & Maruyama, 1990). Anderson, Wilson, and Fielding (1988) found that the children who did the most reading in school, "read 3.6 times as much on the average" during after-school hours as the children who did the least reading in school (p.296). As well as having time to read, students need access to books; as stated previously, classroom libraries play a significant role in motivating students to read. A book-rich classroom library is a vital component of an effective literature-based language arts program. In some classrooms, libraries consist of books purchased by the teachers; in others, in-class libraries are borrowed from the school library.

The significance of teachers as reading models who demonstrate enthusiasm, enjoyment, and respect for reading, and who profit from reading, cannot be overemphasized (Harms & Lettow, 1986; Perez, 1986). If students "do not learn from us [teachers], as models, how much fun reading is—and I mean the excitement, the satisfaction of choosing our own books and settling in for a good read—many of them, maybe most, will never learn" (Donelson, 1990, p.17).

Children are more influenced by what adults do than by what they say. A teacher who reads is the most important educational element in motivating children to read. Teachers' attitudes about reading and reading habits significantly influence children's reading beliefs and behaviours. Students need to observe teachers' genuine interest for and excitement about books. It is fundamental for teachers to read a variety of material in order to expand their knowledge of literature; this breadth and depth of knowledge will assist teachers in their selections of literature to use in their classrooms and in recommending books to their students. Jacobs and Tunnell (1996) outline the following three benefits for teachers who are readers:

> 1. *They gain new knowledge constantly. Teachers who read keep growing intellectually, realizing ever anew how broad and interesting the world is and how little of it is found in the formal curriculum....Teachers who read also discover endless new ways to extend their subject areas....*
> 2. *They better understand education....Only interested learners can become interesting teachers....*
> 3. *They influence students....Teachers who are lifelong readers create students who are lifelong readers. (pp.203-204)*

The multiple issues surrounding reading interests are salient pedagogical concerns. As Lehman (1991) writes, "One of the primary aims of reading instruction is to develop children who value and enjoy reading" (p.18). As educators, we want children to associate reading with pleasure and to develop a life-long habit and love of reading. To accomplish the latter, emphasis must be placed on creating classroom communities where reading is important—where students and teachers behave like "real readers." Children need access to substantial quantities of literature, opportunities to self-select reading material, and substantial time to read independently. In addition, we must recognize the significant relationship between reading interests and interest in reading. Our "greatest hope of raising attitudes toward reading still lies in appraising individuals' interests, meeting them and expanding them" (Monson & Sebesta, 1991, p.670).

As literature is the core resource in literature-based reading programs, it is vital for teachers to understand the many issues surrounding reading interests and motivation for reading, and to continue to increase their knowledge of children's literature.

Organizing for Instruction

Children's literature has become a central component of language arts programs in many elementary and middle school classrooms. The multiple benefits of using children's literature in classrooms have been well documented (Cullinan, 1989; Fuhler, 1990; Galda & Cullinan, 1991; Huck, 1987). Literature can provide children with enjoyable reading experiences, as it has the power to influence readers' lives, to develop compassion, to stretch imaginations, and to "help them to see their world in a new way, or entertain the possibilities of new worlds" (Huck, 1987, p.365). By reading literature, readers can experience "other worlds," feel a wealth of emotions, encounter different beliefs and values, and generate questions and new knowledge. Huck (1987) writes that, "good literature not only entertains, it educates" (p.366). We believe that using literature helps teachers to meet one of the main goals of all language arts programs: to develop a life-long love of reading so that children will choose to read.

Literature- and response-based programs vary in organization and structure (Atwell, 1987, 1998; Hiebert & Colt, 1989; Smith & Bowers, 1989; Tunnel & Jacobs, 1989; Zarrillo, 1989). Regardless of the overall design and structure, there are common objectives of language arts programs that use literature as the core reading material:

a) *To encourage a life-long love of reading*
b) *To provide children with significant amounts of time to read so that they will view reading as an important activity*
c) *To structure a classroom atmosphere where reading is seen as an authentic and enjoyable activity*
d) *To provide children with opportunities to self-select literature to read and to set their own reading goals*
f) *To encourage discussion about texts read by students*
g) *To encourage children to respond and reflect in writing to the literature they read*
h) *To introduce children to a wide variety of authors, illustrators, themes, topics, and genres*
i) *To demonstrate the connections between reading and writing and to have children experience those connections*
j) *To share books with members of the interpretive community through book talks, discussions, dramatic and artistic presentations, and written work.*

In reviewing some of the research on the effectiveness of literature-based programs, Huggins and Roos (1990) concluded that literature-based approaches "produced higher reading achievement and fostered more positive attitudes toward reading" than basal reading methods (p.12). The use of literature in classrooms has been shown to develop student interest in reading, provide language models for students' own writing, foster critical thinking, develop vocabulary, promote awareness and develop social

FIGURE 9.2: THREE CURRICULUM PARADIGMS

Curriculum as fact	Curriculum as activity	Curriculum as inquiry
ROLE OF TEACHERS • use the selections outlined in the anthology • assign tasks from the text or program books • act as technicians	• make decisions about selections and activities • create activities that relate to books (art, speaking, drama, listening, writing, reading) • observe and respond to students' needs	• create an inquiring environment that encourages students to choose literature for themselves • conduct conferences to inquire • respond to issues that are raised in the literature • promote individual and small-group inquiry • facilitate by guiding, encouraging, and providing parameters
ROLE OF STUDENTS • read the same text • complete the same tasks • make few decisions • work individually	• read the same text • complete the same tasks • make some choices regarding activities • work with partners and small groups	• choose their own books • choose how they will respond to literature • inquire about issues, authors, and meanings in literature • develop responsibility for their own learning
LEARNING MATERIALS • basals, commercial reading programs, anthologies • board-prescribed literature studies	• individual trade picture books, novels, nonfiction • activity cards • listening centre • art supplies	• hundreds of different trade book selections • many types of genres • novel sets (6 to 10) • listening centre • art supplies • literature journals
STUDENT ACTIVITIES • focus on factual and literal information • focus on right or wrong answers • are mainly written	• are open-ended • promote high-level thinking • promote interpretation through speaking, drama, listening, writing, and art	• are open-ended • promote high-level thinking • promote interpretation, reflection, and inquiry • involve collaborative problem-solving • explore issues in literature
DECISIONS • are mainly made by outside experts	• are mainly made by teachers • are sometimes made by students	• are made by students and teachers • are frequently made collaboratively
MEANING • resides in the text or with some outside expert	• is constructed by students through interpretive activities	• is derived from the interaction of students with the text • is frequently derived from collaborating with others

and cultural understandings, motivate children to read, promote learning, develop literacy, spark readers' imaginations, and develop a sense of story (Fuhler, 1990; Galda & Cullinan, 1991; Huggins & Roos, 1990; Smith & Bowers, 1989).

Heald-Taylor (1996) developed a framework to assist teachers in identifying the curriculum paradigms with which they may align themselves when using literature in the classroom (see Figure 9.2). She believes that understanding the various curriculum paradigms will help teachers to examine their current practices and reflect on ways to enhance the effectiveness of their literature- and response-based programs. Heald-Taylor's framework demonstrates how the adoption of each of the three curriculum paradigms—"curriculum as fact," "curriculum as activity," and "curriculum as inquiry"—affects the role of teachers, the role of students, the learning materials, the student activities, and the decisions and meaning.

As stated in previous chapters, and as demonstrated by Heald-Taylor's framework, there are explicit connections between teachers' instruction, beliefs, and theoretical stances. An article by McGee and Tompkins (1995) emphasizes how important it is for teachers to understand various theoretical perspectives on reading processes and literary development. They demonstrate how the adoption of four theoretical perspectives (i.e., schema-theoretic, structuralist, reader-response, critical literacy) influenced teachers' use of the novel *Stone Fox* (Gardiner, 1980). McGee and Tompkins note various strengths and concerns associated with each perspective; they also discuss the need for teachers to understand how various theoretical perspectives can be used to guide the organization and implementation of literature- and response-based programs (as discussed in Chapter 7).

A teacher's theoretical stance will influence her or his decisions about the elements listed below. Such decisions will in turn shape the organizational pattern of that teacher's literature- and response-based program:

a) *Who chooses the literature (students and/or teachers)*
b) *Organization of students (one core text for all students; multiple copies of books for small groups of students, who may be grouped by ability [heterogeneously or homogeneously], by the teacher, or by student choice; individual students reading selections either self-selected or teacher assigned; teacher reads aloud)*
c) *How the literature is approached by readers (continuum of aesthetic and efferent stance)*
d) *Who talks about the literature and the classroom interactional patterns (teacher-assigned questions and teacher-led discussions or student-generated questions and small-group student discussions)*
e) *How the literature is responded to (continuum of aesthetic and efferent stance; teacher-assigned or student choice)*
f) *The general media and types of activities used to express readers' responses (oral, visual, written, dramatic; teacher-assigned or student choice)*
g) *The* what *and* how *of instruction experienced by the students (e.g., the characteristics of a "good" discussion, the roles of discussion participants, the notion of response to literature, oral and written responses, literary elements, summary writing)*
h) *How much time is scheduled for student reading (limited to extensive)*
i) *The role of the teacher (evaluator or fellow reader and responder)*
j) *The* how *(tests, teacher observation, anecdotal notes, student self-evaluation) and* what *of assessment (responses, discussion questions, contributions to group discussions, extension activities).*

Each element should be viewed as existing on a continuum, as there are varying ways to implement each element. For example, one teacher may use a balanced approach of teacher and student selection of literature, while another teacher may offer ample opportunities for student choice; a third teacher may dominate the selection of literature and offer few, if any, opportunities for student choice.

Working with readers in response-based programs requires that teachers believe in children's abilities to think critically and analytically—that teachers not provide students with "answers" when they are capable of deriving their own. It requires that teachers recognize children's thoughtfulness and treat their individual literary responses accordingly. In the following sections, we will explore several different organizational approaches for using literature in classrooms. Adopting specific curriculum framework(s) and theoretical perspective(s) will ultimately determine how a teacher structures each approach.

CLASS NOVEL STUDY

One approach to using literature in classrooms is the class novel study (also called the core book model or literature focus unit). Traditionally, when implementing a class novel study, teachers select one novel for all class members to read, and assign common reading goals. In some classrooms, the teacher reads the book aloud to students; in other classrooms, the book is read through a combination of the teacher's oral reading and the students' independent reading. Some teachers also use the technique of round-robin reading to work through a novel. We discourage this method, as it is tedious and boring, and does not generate interest in literature. Further, this method, as with the teacher reading aloud, results in a very slow progression through a novel, causing many students to lose interest in the literature.

When using a class novel approach, many teachers identify vocabulary for students to look up in the dictionary and generate comprehension questions for each chapter. We do not recommend either of these instructional strategies. Literature is not written to be used as a medium for teaching vocabulary words or assessing comprehension solely through teacher-generated questions. There are other strategies teachers can use to address vocabulary and comprehension, such as pizzazz words, word walls, word sorts, student-generated questions, a *limited* number of teacher-generated questions that model "good" questions (see Chapter 7), discussion groups, and written responses. Some individuals teach literary elements through a class novel. Again, caution needs to be exercised in order to avoid a "dissection" of the novel and an extensive literary analysis of the work. Other teachers rely heavily on study guides and activity packets which can accompany core books. These publications frequently "basalize the literature," using it as a teaching tool. The activities in these publications often do not extend students' reading experiences in ways that promote or encourage an appreciation of literature. Rather, they are more efferent and analytical in nature and resemble suggestions found in many basal reading series.

A major concern of selecting one book for an entire class is the varying reading abilities of students. Not all students may be capable of reading the core book independently. Therefore, when introducing a core book, teachers need to develop a variety of methods to ensure that each child has the opportunity to *read* the book. When using a picture book as the core book, a teacher may initially read the book aloud and then have multiple copies of the book for students to read independently, in partners, or in small groups. When using a novel, in addition to providing silent reading time, a teacher may read aloud parts of the book, students may read in pairs, students may read at home with a parent or guardian, students may listen and follow along in their books to audio recordings of the text, or students may read with a teaching aide or another adult. When setting reading goals, teachers may provide students with two or three days to reach a particular goal (e.g., five chapters, five picture books by the same illustrator). Those students who exceed the reading goal can read other books by the same author, read books on the same topic or genre, or read another book of their choosing during reading time.

Some teachers use a class novel as a way to introduce elements of Readers' Workshop. For example,

Sylvia used a class novel to introduce small-group discussion roles and behaviours, discussion questions, and response writing. A core book provided a common context and facilitated discussion and understanding of the elements of Readers' Workshop. Indeed, many of the elements of Readers' Workshop can be incorporated into a class novel study.

When using a core book, some teachers believe it is necessary to integrate the book into all curricular areas. However, Cox and Zarrillo (1993) write, "Children seem to spend more time constructing dioramas, painting murals, cooking meals, making time lines and doing other cross-curricular activities than they spend reading" (p.107). If cross-curricular connections are included in a class novel study, the activities must be authentic and genuine in nature and must truly *extend* students' reading experiences. The children should also have choice in selecting activities. But most importantly, they should spend a significant amount of time each day reading and writing.

There are many ways to use core books in elementary classrooms. In one grade one classroom, the teacher read aloud *Charlotte's Web* (White, 1952) and the students wrote journal entries after each chapter. In a grade two classroom, after listening to the teacher read picture books aloud, the students wrote responses about the books in dialogue journals. Near the end of the year in one grade three classroom, the students independently read *The Magician's Trap* (Piper, 1976). Each student had his/her own copy of the book, and at various points in the book, the children engaged in large-group discussions. At three designated points in the book, the children wrote responses about their reading experiences. In one grade six classroom, the students were assigned the novel *Tuck Everlasting* (Babbitt, 1975). After the teacher read aloud the first chapter and students engaged in a class discussion, the teacher announced that the novel was to be completed in one week's time. During class reading time, the students could read independently, read in pairs, join a group with the teacher, or listen to an audio recording of the book; the students were also expected to read at home every night. The teacher met briefly with each student daily to monitor her or his reading progress and to check the time-line of the story's plot that each student was constructing. These examples are only a few ways of how teachers have used core books in their classrooms.

Many teachers plan a core book unit with several response options. Several response activities were outlined in Chapters 7 and 8 that encouraged the adoption of an aesthetic stance toward literature. Some teachers gather related and supplementary materials to accompany core books: books that have similar themes, style, plot, settings, characters and topics, or books written or illustrated by the same individual. In some classrooms, each student is required to read one supplementary book and then engage in some type of comparison and contrast activity, such as a Venn diagram or a semantic feature analysis chart. Some teachers plan extended projects to accompany core books, requiring students to engage in some type of research (e.g., after reading *Number the Stars* [Lowry, 1989], students choose research topics associated with the Holocaust). Again, it is necessary to consider both the quantity and quality of activities. Extension activities need to be worthwhile, authentic learning opportunities that extend students' aesthetic reading experiences.

READERS' WORKSHOP

Readers' Workshop, Literature Workshops, Community of Readers, Literature Circles, and Book Clubs are some of the terms used to describe programs that use literature as the core reading material. There are numerous interpretations of this type of literature-based program. The basic components of such a program consist of multiple copies of books of varying reading levels and genres; substantial scheduled time for students to read; interactional patterns of small groups of students; student discussion groups; response-based activities; teacher instruction; and teacher- and student-focussed methods of assessment.

The elements described below consist of original ideas and ideas borrowed and modified from several sources. Although there are several fundamental elements of Literature Workshops, there are many ways to implement this type of organizational structure. With teacher adaptation and modification, these elements can be implemented at all elementary and middle school grade levels.

The Literature: One of the central components of Literature Workshops is the literature: multiple copies of books. Plan to have three to five copies of each book and to have reading material for various levels and topics. Many school systems have a central warehouse of resources for teachers, including multiple copies of books. Teachers submit book orders to the central warehouse, identifying the titles they want and indicating the time of year they want the books. Some schools allocate funds to grade-level teams, then each team decides how to spend the money. These funds often consist of money not used to purchase workbooks and other basal support material; money from other school-based funds may also be available. Sylvia was fortunate to work with a principal who thoroughly supported the movement to literature-based programs by providing additional funds to build collections of novels for various grade levels. Some teachers have engaged in grade team or individual classroom fund-raising endeavours in order to purchase literature for their classrooms. Further, *many* of the books available in classrooms have been purchased by teachers themselves. There are book clubs that send out magazines appropriate for various grade levels (e.g., Scholastic Book Club, Troll Book Club). The prices are reasonable, and when students order books from these clubs, there are ways for teachers to obtain free books (i.e., through an accumulation of points or from the total amount of book orders).

What types of books should be made available for students? At the beginning of this chapter we discussed the importance of student interest and factors that influence reading motivation. Being aware of students' reading interests and abilities will enable teachers to gather appropriate literature. We also outlined many resources and references for teachers to consult to remain current about children's literature. A variety of reading material can be used in Literature Workshops—students can read novels, poetry, picture books, or nonfiction material. The number of books required will depend on several factors, including the organizational structure of the program (i.e., the number of children per group).

Organization of Student Groups: There are varying views about the appropriate methods to employ when grouping students for Literature Workshops. Some individuals believe that students should first select a book (from a designated collection); groups are then formed based on student book choice. Others advocate that students should initially form groups, and then each group should choose a book to read. In some classrooms, teachers assign students to groups; the groups may be heterogeneous or homogenous in academic make-up. The students in teacher-assigned groups also select their own books to read (i.e., a common title for the group members). Each initial organizational method has its own particular strengths. It is essential for teachers to consider the composition of their classroom interpretive communities (i.e., the students), their theoretical perspective(s), and the literature itself when choosing methods to organize students. It is also important to remember that various methods of group designation can be used throughout the year, that group membership can change, and that even if students do remain in the same group for an extended period of time (e.g., three months), they frequently interact with other classmates in language arts and other curricular subjects.

Groups should ideally consist of three to five members. Important factors to consider when grouping students include individual personalities and abilities, peer relationships, and group dynamics. If students are first organized into groups (by one of the ways described above) and then required to select a book to read, it is worthwhile to discuss strategies for book selection (e.g., each person writes two or three choices, a vote, turn-taking within the group for choosing a book to read). If students first select a book to read and groups are formed based on book choice, teachers need to consider scaffolding strategies for students who select books that are too difficult for them to read independently (i.e., books at their reading frustration levels). Indeed, some students require instruction on *how* to select appropriate books. Although interest does play an important role in reading achievement, it is important for students to read texts written at their independent and instructional levels.

Some teachers have their students select a book from a collection of books (with multiple copies of each title) that address a particular topic (e.g., survival, dogs, friendship), are written by the same author (e.g., Jean Little, Gordon Korman, Phoebe Gilman), are of the same genre (e.g., historical fiction, fantasy, contemporary realistic fiction), or address the same theme (e.g., "over time, humans have significantly influenced their environment" or "during times of adversity, one must draw upon inner strength"). Other teachers have children choose a book from a collection of "good" literature that includes a variety of reading levels, topics, authors, and genres. In some classrooms, student groups select a book to read from five available titles, some choose a book from ten titles, and others have a choice of twenty to thirty or more titles. Individual teachers must decide what selection methods make the most sense within their overall programming framework (and, of course, with their available resources).

Student Book Selection: Regardless of the method used to group students, teachers should engage in book talks on the various titles available to the children. A book talk should be brief—about two to four minutes in length. It may consist of reading a selection from a book to whet students' appetites or briefly outlining a book's plot without divulging the ending. A book talk can feature a character or a scene around which the story revolves. In some book talks, teachers compare one book to another book already known to the students (e.g., those that share common topics, genres, or authors). Teachers can share information about the author and the book. For example, teachers can explain that Gordon Korman wrote *This Can't Be Happening at Macdonald Hall* (1978) when he was in grade seven or that Cora Taylor, author of *The Doll* (1987), had a doll in her family that was given to provide comfort when a child in the family was ill. Teachers can also share a video recording of students from previous years conducting book talks. When engaging in book talks, it is important to have the books available for the students to examine the cover, illustrations, length, size of print, level of difficulty, and back-cover description.

In order to give authentic book talks, teachers need to read the literature they are sharing with their students. In this book, we have repeatedly emphasized the importance of teachers reading the literature their students are reading. Our assertion does not mean that teachers need to read all of the books in the school and classroom library. However, teachers *must* read the literature their students are reading in Literature Workshops. If teachers are to genuinely talk and write about literature with their students, they need to know the books. There are many other issues associated with teachers reading the literature as well—recommending books, knowing potentially sensitive issues and inappropriate topics or language, knowing reading levels and topics, and modelling reading. A salient message is communicated to students when they know that their teachers believe these books are important enough to read themselves. Some teachers choose to limit the number of books (five to seven) they use when initially trying some variation of Literature

Workshops because they realize the importance of reading the literature. They feel more comfortable working with fewer books and need time to broaden their personal repertoires of literature.

Once the book talks are complete, students can select a book to read. It is useful to provide some "previewing" time, a chance for students to examine the books to assist them in their selection. If student groups have been assigned by the teacher, each group needs to select a book. If groups are determined by book choice, a useful strategy is to have each student submit a list of her or his top three book choices. The teacher will attempt to honour each person's first choice, but this may not always be possible due to the number of available copies, the size of groups, the level of text difficulty, or peer dynamics.

Sylvia purchased book pockets and cards to manage the signing out of books. Some teachers number the books and have students record the title and number of the book on a sign-out sheet. In the back of their response journals, Sylvia's students recorded the date started, the date finished, the title, and the length of each book read. This record provided valuable information to her, the students themselves, the parents, and the school administration.

When Sylvia initially implemented Literature Workshops, she observed that the students began talking and recommending books to each other almost immediately. Certain books were very popular and were read by all groups, while other titles were read by one or two groups. Although Sylvia continued to conduct book talks, the students themselves conducted informal and formal book talks as well.

During the initial stages of the implementation of Literature Workshops in Sylvia's grades four, five, and six classrooms, many of the books that students chose to read were under 100 pages in length (see Chapter 4 for titles). As the students were unaccustomed to literature constituting the core reading material, it seemed that they were choosing book lengths they felt comfortable with. This selection behaviour was absolutely imperative to Sylvia, as she believes students need to experience success in and enjoyment of their reading. Gradually, each group moved on to longer and more challenging material. This trend emphasizes once again the importance of teachers providing students with a wide range of reading material when implementing Literature Workshops.

Time to Read: One essential element of this type of program is that students be provided with substantial time to read during class. It is important for teachers to read as well during this time. In addition to modelling, this reading time gives teachers the opportunity to read other books that they can then use in their programs. Students may also be required to read their books at home (e.g., fifteen to thirty minutes of reading per night). As a group, students need to set appropriate reading goals by considering their own abilities, the amount of scheduled reading time (both during class and at home—and thus consider other commitments), and the book itself (i.e., level of difficulty, length). Some students may require guidance in setting appropriate goals, as they may assign themselves too little or too much reading. Sylvia's students wrote their reading goals on a chart for each day of the week. The physical act of writing the goals on a chart helped Sylvia to monitor each group's goals and seemed to encourage a sense of student obligation and commitment.

Sylvia scheduled 4 45-minute periods and 1 90-minute period a week for Literature Workshops—a significant amount of time for the students to read. At the beginning of the reading periods, time was devoted to small-group discussions. Some students wrote literature responses after their group discussions before they began reading. During the 90-minute block, Sylvia and her students conducted book talks during the last 15 minutes of the period. At the beginning of the year, the students spent approximately ten minutes reading silently during

Natalie and Carol reading

SUSTAINED SILENT READING (SSR); over time, the amount of time scheduled for silent reading was gradually increased, and students were able to stay focussed and read for extended periods of time. In addition to silent reading during Literature Workshops, SSR was scheduled for twenty minutes a day, four days a week. During SSR time, some students read their novel for Literature Workshops, while others read books from Sylvia's classroom library or from the school library.

If students consistently do not reach their group's reading goals, then perhaps the book is too difficult for them, they read more slowly than other group members, or they are choosing not to complete their work. Alternate arrangements will need to be made to deal with these students. In Sylvia's experience, students often exceeded, rather than falling short of, their group's reading goals. When this situation occurs, students must be considerate of other group members and be cautious of their contributions to group discussions in order to avoid inadvertently divulging motivating plot information to their peers.

Small-Group Discussions: The next issue involved in organizing Literature Workshops is deciding the frequency and duration of small-group discussions. A teacher's timetable will be one factor to consider when making this decision. Information and teaching strategies regarding discussions and the role of teachers in facilitating discussions were presented in Chapter 7. It is vital for teachers to provide instruction about discussions and for students to understand the expectations for and responsibilities of group members during discussions.

Students need to come prepared to discuss their book with fellow group members. If all groups are participating in book discussions simultaneously, we recommend assigning each group a location in the room in order to avoid confusion or down-time. In Sylvia's classroom, the groups initially met daily, immediately after morning recess, for fifteen to twenty minutes and discussed some of the questions that each member had generated as a result of reading the book the previous day (during class) and evening (as homework). (Sylvia's students were expected to read approximately twenty to thirty minutes per night). The groups also discussed the "pizzazz" word that each person had recorded (a word encountered while reading that a student found interesting or whose meaning was uncertain). Once the discussion was complete, each group decided on the number of pages or chapters to be read for the following day and recorded the goal on a small chart posted at the front of the classroom. The students then submitted their discussion questions to Sylvia, returned to their desks, read their novels, and/or wrote responses for the remainder of the period. During the discussion time, Sylvia circulated about the room, listening to the ongoing discussions. Sometimes Sylvia joined the discussions, but she was always cautious to enter the conversations as a fellow reader, realizing that her behaviours in the group discussions were communicating messages about the appropriate kinds of talk and questions for group discussions.

In primary classrooms, small-group discussions might be more teacher-directed, as the teacher may assign topics for discussion (e.g., Would you like a friend like Toad? Why or why not?), and might be shorter in duration. After small-group discussions, teachers may assemble the students as a whole class and have them share their responses. At the beginning of implementing group discussions, Sylvia had her students record (in point form) the issues discussed in their groups (one record sheet submitted per group). In addition, she sometimes had the students write reflective accounts of their group's discussion.

When planning the frequency and duration of small-group conferences, it is important to consider the grade level of students and the amount of reading completed by students. Regardless of the age of students, one essential element for engaging in an extended discussion is the requirement of content to discuss (i.e., students need to have read enough text to have something to talk about). When structuring time for small-group discussions, some teachers prefer to schedule several times throughout the day for different groups to meet and talk about their reading. However, it is important to consider management issues associated with this type of rotating schedule.

Sylvia had her students engage in assessment of themselves and other group members. These assessments were confidential and were not shared with other group members. Below are two small-group discussion assessments completed by two different grade five students. Only the initials of students are used to preserve the students' anonymity.

Evaluation by I.S.
[The form was the student's own creation.]

	Listening	*Brings Questions*	*Behaviour*
K.S.	*8.5/10*	*8.5/10*	*9.5/10*
I.S.	*8.0/10*	*6.5/10*	*9.5/10*
A.M.	*9.5/10*	*9.5/10*	*9.5/10*
C.D.	*9.0/10*	*9.5/10*	*9.5/10*
S.J.	*7.5/10*	*8.5/10*	*9.0/10*

K.S. – *Listens most of the time and usually has good questions and doesn't act silly. Always has his reading done.*
I.S. – *Don't always bring my questions but always have my reading done. I behave and don't goof off.*
A.M. – *Listens and follows directions. Reads and brings her questions. Sometimes may act silly.*
C.D. – *She behaves and always has good questions and cooperates. Always has her reading done.*
S.J. – *Doesn't always bring her questions but when she does, they are usually good questions. She behaves right. She always has her book read.*

Evaluation by K.K.
[The form was the student's own creation.]

M.P. – 5/10 – *He does not answer questions and when he does answer, his answers are often silly. He reads a lot but does not bring his questions to the discussion group.*

R.G. – 10/10 – *R. always has questions and almost answers every question. He reads a lot and does not act silly.*

R.B. – 7/10 – *She is quiet and does not talk much about the questions but she almost always brings her questions. She does not act silly and is a good reader. When she comes to our group, she has read to our goal.*

C.W. – 8.5/10 – *C. is a hard worker. She always reads up to the goal and answers a lot of questions. C. does not bring her questions often but she is not silly.*

K.K. – 9/10 *I bring questions but I might not always have three questions. I answer questions and bring pizzazz words. I try not to act silly. I always have my reading done to our goal.*

Group assessments can be shared with members as well. However, it is important for students to know that their evaluations will be shared in a public forum. In Chapter 7, we discussed the strategy of having group members identify and share positive aspects of their discussions, as well as one or two areas requiring additional effort. Some teachers have students engage only in self-assessment. The students report on their positive contributions to the discussions and suggest one or two ways that they themselves could improve their group's discussion.

Some teachers schedule regular times to conference with each group of students (e.g., once during the completion of a novel, once a week, once every two weeks). It is critical for teachers to be cognizant of and reflective about their behaviours and articulations in discussion groups, because teachers are the most influential members of the classroom interpretive community. Some teachers use a checklist with various discussion criteria when participating in small-group conferences; criteria may include such items as: comes prepared to discussions; is courteous to other group members; contributes meaningfully to discussions; and relates personal experiences to the book. Other teachers have students audio-record their conferences and then submit the tape. The conference is then evaluated by the teacher using predetermined criteria that have previously been shared with the students. Whatever conference methods are employed in classrooms, we caution that small-group discussions should not dominate the program time. In literature-based programs, *students need time to read.*

Written Responses: In Sylvia's classroom, once the small group discussions were completed, the students recorded their new reading goal, submitted their discussion questions, and spent the remainder of the period reading their novel and/or writing a response. As discussed in Chapter 8, Sylvia's students generally wrote responses about the literature they read at the mid- and completion-points of the books. Some teachers require three responses per book; others assign one response per book. (If children are reading picture books, then one response per book would be sufficient.) If necessary, Sylvia would provide oral feedback to the students about the content of their responses, such as encouraging students to focus, elaborate, or develop their ideas or discussing the differences between writing a response and a summary. She read the students' mid-point responses but wrote responses about the books after reading the students' final responses. Again, when teachers write literature responses, they can model "good" response writing and show students that teachers are also fellow readers and writers. As the groups in Sylvia's classroom were at different points in their reading, she found the reading and writing of responses very manageable. Sylvia's students also engaged in several other types of written response activities (see Chapter 8).

Extension Activities: One other aspect of Literature Workshops that deserves discussion is the use of literature extension projects, similar to those assigned for core books or class novels. Some teachers have students complete a project for every book they read. Other teachers, like Sylvia, have students complete projects once every two to four weeks. The students select a novel from the list of books they have read during that period. Class members can complete the same activity or project, or they can select an activity from a teacher-generated list of four or five options. As we have said before, it is important that extension projects actually extend students' reading experiences. We remind teachers to reflect on the questions by Benton and Fox (1985) when considering various activities: "Will this activity enable the reader to look back on the text and to develop the meanings he has already made? and Does what I plan to do bring reader and text closer together, or does it come between them?" (p.108).

Several oral, dramatic, visual, and written response activities were described in Chapters 7 and 8. Many of the suggestions in those chapters require instructional support. The activities may be teacher-assigned or may be options from which students choose when responding to literature. Regardless, when generating response activities, it is important for teachers and students to consider the appropriateness of the activity for the book.

Benefits of Participating in Literature Workshops: Evidence from Sylvia's classroom suggests that, by participating in Literature Workshops, many of her students indeed became "better" readers who exhibited more positive attitudes about reading and attained higher levels of understanding of texts. When Jeremy initially came into Sylvia's classroom in grade four, he read little outside of school. Through participating in Literature Workshops, he became an enthusiastic reader with eclectic tastes in literature. Some of his favourite authors included Gary Paulsen, Walt Morey, and Lynne Reid Banks. Shelia was an avid reader in grade five who read and comprehended narrative and expository texts written well above grade five reading level. She was an accomplished writer for her age and experimented with various types of writing during writer's workshop. After reading *The Doll* (Taylor, 1987), *A Handful of Time* (Pearson, 1987), and *Who Is Frances Rain?* (Buffie, 1987), Shelia attempted to write her own time-slip fantasy. The reading Shelia completed during Literature Workshops increased her knowledge about literature and her willingness to take risks in attempting new genres of writing. Kari was another student whose involvement in Literature Workshops strongly affected her reading attitudes. On a questionnaire at the end of grade six, Kari wrote: "Some of the things that I have enjoyed most over the last two years are being able to read and write so much."

At the beginning of the first year in Sylvia's classroom, Corey, a grade five student, was a reluctant reader who experienced difficulties comprehending material written at grade level. As the first year progressed, Corey developed a more positive attitude toward reading, significantly improved his reading abilities, and realized that reading could be an enjoyable and pleasurable activity. On a questionnaire at the end of the first year in Sylvia's classroom, Corey wrote, "My favourite things this year were the reading and basketball in gym." Corey read every book in the classroom written by Gary Paulsen and sought out Paulsen's other works in the school and public libraries.

Other Implementation Aspects: After approximately two and a half months of participating in Literature Workshops in the manner described above, several students in Sylvia's classroom expressed a desire to disband the groups and read novels independently. Over a period of a month, the groups gradually disbanded and students self-selected novels to read during Literature Workshops. Sylvia conferenced with students individually, discussing the questions they prepared. Each student set her or his reading goal with Sylvia, then this information was recorded on a chart. At various times, Sylvia also had students who had read the same novel, the same genre, books by the same author, or books on the same topic meet in small groups to discuss the literature and share their responses. Sylvia's knowledge of children's literature helped her to implement an individualized literature-based reading program.

INDIVIDUALIZED READING

Jeanette Veatch (1959) has long been a strong proponent of individualized reading programs. (Some people call individualized reading the self-selection approach.) Individualized reading involves students self-selecting books and reading at their own pace. Teachers meet with students individually to discuss the literature they are reading. Self-selection programs maximize the amount of time children spend reading, and research has consistently demonstrated that student achievement is significantly related to the amount of time spent reading, both in and out of school. One report, *Patterns of Reading Practice*, stated that "students in the highest-performing states in the NAEP Reading Study engaged in 59% more reading practice than those in states in the bottom quartile" (Paul, 1996, p.2). The report also found that schools in the study allocated very little time to reading, and that by grade nine, "students [we]re only practicing their reading about as much as kindergarteners, 3.6 minutes per day" (p.16).

Willard Olson was historically a proponent of self-selection reading programs. Olson's (1949) work demonstrated how children of the same chronological age differed widely in their rate of reading development. He contended that children should be allowed to self-select reading material and progress at their own rate of development. Although some educators were persuaded by Olson's arguments, self-selection programs comprised a very small percentage of reading programs in the United States at the time (Cox & Zarrillo, 1993). In 1959, Jeanette Veatch edited the book *Individualizing Your Reading Program: Self-Selection in Action*, which contains chapters by teachers and administrators about implementing an individualized reading program. Several articles, presentations, and dissertations also addressed the topic of self-selection reading programs at that time. However, basal readers continued to dominate the field of reading, and by the mid-1970s, the individualized approach was nearly nonexistent. Veatch blamed the domination of basals on publishers, writers, and administrators. However, the individualized reading approach gained renewed interest with the implementation of teaching practices associated with the whole language philosophy.

Some teachers use a self-selection approach throughout the entire school year, while others use individualized reading in combination with other organizational approaches. For example, after completing a class novel study, a grade two teacher moved into Literature Workshops for eight weeks; he subsequently had the students engage in individualized reading for three weeks. At the end of three weeks, the class began a topical unit on friendship, and the teacher used picture books as the core reading material for the unit.

When implementing an individualized reading approach, some teachers spend ten to fifteen minutes each period introducing the students to literature, including informational books and poetry. Some teachers also present readers' theatre scripts and introduce appropriate magazines and reference books during this time. However, the main characteristic of a self-selection model is the scheduling of a significant amount of time for students to read. Once students complete their reading, they may write responses, work on extension activities or projects, conference with the teacher or other students, or select another book. In some classrooms, teachers schedule time at the end of the class period for students to talk about the books they are reading.

Students need access to a large number of books for a self-selection approach to succeed. Discovering students' reading interests will assist teachers in securing appropriate literature for their classes. Further, teachers need an extensive knowledge of children's literature for an individualized reading program to be successful.

THEMATIC INSTRUCTION

In literature, themes refer to a story's underlying significance, central message, or meaning. Lukens describes a theme as "the idea that holds the story together, such as a comment about society, human nature, or the human condition" (1999, p.135). A piece of literature can have several themes, some explicit, others implicit. One reader suggested the theme of *Sarah, Plain and Tall* (MacLachlan, 1985) is that "people need to be flexible and able to change in order to find happiness" (Glazer, 1997, p.53). As Tomlinson and Lynch-Brown (1996) write, "A theme is better expressed by means of a complete sentence than by a single word" (p.30). It is important for teachers to understand the differences between organizing a unit focussed on a theme and one focussed on a topic. For example, "Families come in all shapes and sizes" is a theme, whereas "Families" is a topic. Teachers often say they are implementing a thematic unit when in reality they have organized a unit on a topic (e.g., bears, under the sea, apples, mysteries).

Moss (1994) writes that thematic units can be selected in response to student interests and concerns, current issues, curricular requirements, instructional goals, and students' learning needs and experiences. Thematic units, when done well, promote a discovery of connections and provide depth and breadth in learning. A thematic unit can also provide coherence and a focus for reading, writing, speaking, listening, viewing, and representing activities. Thematic teaching can promote acquisition of an integrated knowledge base and an understanding and appreciation of intertextualities.

Intradisciplinary themes, sometimes referred to as themed literature units or literature focus units, typically use literature as the focus. Activities involving the language arts and related to the theme occur only during language arts and not in any other curricular areas. A variety of materials can be read by the students during a thematic unit. Students may read poetry, novels, picture books, and nonfiction material, and may view visual representations. *Using Literature in the Middle Grades: A Thematic Approach* (Moss, 1994) describes various themes that can be explored through literature. Chapters 2 through 9 in the Moss book are each devoted to particular themes. In each chapter, Moss describes the rationale for the theme and outlines ideas for shared reading experiences, independent reading, literary journals, small dialogue groups, whole-class lessons, independent reading and writing, and extension activities. Each chapter also includes a bibliography of works appropriate for the theme. There are other publications on using themes in language arts programs. Once again, we remind teachers that they, not the manuals or teachers' guides, are in control of their programs. If teachers choose to use study guides or prepared units, they should carefully select ideas that are theoretically and pedagogically sound and appropriate for their students.

Interdisciplinary (also called transdisciplinary or multidisciplinary) thematic units use the communicative arts (i.e., reading, writing, speaking, listening, viewing, and representing) to explore one theme across various curricular areas. For example, students may use the communicative arts in social studies, science, health, math, and language arts to explore the theme of humankind's influence on the environment. A thematic unit may involve two or more curricular areas. Regardless of the number of curricular intersections, it is imperative that the activities be authentic and meaningful to the students.

When planning an interdisciplinary or intradisciplinary thematic unit at any grade level, it is important for teachers to consider several organizational issues. Through examining curricula and considering their students, teachers need to define the topics, subject matter, concepts, goals, and outcomes to be addressed in the unit. Secondly, resources need to be gathered, to include a variety of sources and reading levels (e.g., picture books, novels, plays, poems, newspapers, periodicals, songs, advertisements, nonfiction books, visual representations, software programs). Once the resources are gathered, teachers can brainstorm general learning activities and experiences that address curricular objectives and goals, and that use the gathered resources. Activities and ideas must be organized into a meaningful, coherent, and connected sequence. As well as planning lessons to implement the general activities, teachers need to plan assessment processes and procedures.

The planning issues outlined above need not occur in a linear order. A teacher may initially discover some quality resources and then consult the curricula. However, it is important that all elements in the planning process be addressed in order to prevent thematic units from becoming a collection of activities, lacking structure, and to plan for concept development, objectives, and outcomes.

AUTHOR STUDIES

During an author study, students read and respond to material written by a particular author (e.g., Robert Munsch, Tim Wynne-Jones, Kit Pearson, Martyn Godfrey, Jean Little, Phoebe Gilman). Students can discover personal information about authors as well as information about their writing styles, story preferences, and other idiosyncrasies.

Many authors have websites that students and teachers can visit; however, we need to read the information critically as some information may, in fact, be promotional material. One of the many pages accessed through D.K. Brown's Children's Literature Web Guide (listed in Appendix B) is a list of author and illustrator websites; the list includes authors' and illustrators' personal websites as well as websites maintained by fans, scholars, and readers. In addition, there are audiovisual materials and publications about many authors and illustrators, such as *Something About the Author* (Hile, 1995), *Canadian Books for Children: A Guide to Authors and Illustrators* (Stott & Jones, 1988), *Writing Stories, Making Pictures: Biographies of 150 Canadian Children's Authors and Illustrators* (The Canadian Children's Book Centre, 1994), and *The Storymakers: Illustrating Children's Books* (1999). Journals that publish articles related to children's literature often profile authors in articles. In their textbook *Language Arts: Content and Teaching Strategies*, Tompkins and Hoskisson (1998) include an appendix that identifies books about authors and illustrators, individual articles profiling authors and illustrators, and audiovisual materials featuring authors and illustrators.

In addition to authors of fictional picture books and novels, poets (e.g., sean o huigin, Sheree Fitch, Jack Prelutsky, Eve Merriam, Dennis Lee, Myra Cohn Livingston, Shel Silverstein), illustrators (e.g., Trina Schart Hyman, Ron Lightburn, Anthony Browne, Susan Jeffers, Tomie de Paola, Ian Wallace, Ruth Heller, Ted Harrison, Chris Van Allsburg, Barbara Reid), and nonfiction writers (e.g., Diane Swanson, Patricia Lauber, Shelley Tanaka, Linda Granfield, Joanna Cole, Gail Gibbons, Seymour Simon) can also be explored. Authors and illustrators of picture books can be studied in any elementary grade. Students can examine similarities and differences and can look for common topics or themes in and across the work of authors and illustrators. They can consider various influences on authors' and illustrators' work (e.g., time period, personal events, culture, purpose). Generally, in an author study, students engage in writing, speaking, listening, dramatic, and visual representation activities that extend their reading experiences of the material.

GENRE UNITS

In a genre unit, students concentrate on a particular genre. Nodelman (1996) defines genre as "a category of literary texts defined by their shared characteristics....Within children's literature, there are many subgenres: nonsense poetry, time fantasies, tall tales and so on" (p.291). (As mentioned in Chapters 1 and 4, individuals in the field of children's literature may identify the names and number of genres differently.)

A genre study may focus on contemporary realistic fiction, historical fiction, fantasy, traditional literature, multicultural literature, informational books, or subgenres within the major categories of literary texts. Genre studies can involve both picture books and novels. When participating in a genre study, students read books of a particular genre, and engage in discussions about the literature. As well as sharing their aesthetic responses, students can identify the characteristics of the genre and discuss the value of that category of literature. They may read additional examples of the genre and discuss the presence and treatment of the genre's common characteristics in those books; students can also look for common themes in particular genres. Readers can be encouraged to compare and contrast a variety of elements among several books representative of a particular genre. Students will generally engage in writing activities that facilitate the exploration, application, and extension of the common characteristics of a particular genre under study. Further, similar to other organizational structures of literature-based programs, speaking, listening, writing, dramatic, and visual representational activities of an aesthetic nature should be planned to extend students' reading experiences.

Within a genre unit, students may examine the role of various literary elements (e.g., plot, setting, characters, point of view). For example, in the subgenre of time-slip fantasy, the literary element of setting plays an integral role in understanding the story. The genre unit provides a context for examining literary elements, which can be examined within one book or across several reading selections.

TOPICAL UNITS

As mentioned earlier, some teachers confuse the terms topic and theme when discussing program organizational structures. Teachers can select a topic such as animals, mysteries, adventure, humour, or families and gather reading materials on the topic; again, a variety of reading material can be used in topical units. Some teachers have the topic of study extend across curricular areas; others focus exclusively on language arts. The same planning issues described in the section on thematic instruction are pertinent to planning a topical unit.

Sylvia organized a topical unit on several authors and illustrators of picture books (e.g., Steven Kellogg, Jan Brett, Tomie De Paola, Arnold Lobel, Barbara Reid). Students completed oral, visual, and written activities that encouraged them to reflect on and recapture their reading experiences. In addition, one part of the unit involved students examining versions of various books. Cinderella was one story used in the unit. (At the end of this chapter, there is a book list of different versions of Cinderella.) Students examined various aspects of the different versions. For example, they considered the character depiction and appearance of Cinderella, her stepmother, and her stepsisters in each book; they also examined the plight of Cinderella's stepmother and stepsisters in each selection. There are also many versions of Little Red Riding Hood. Students in Sylvia's class examined various issues in the different versions: how Little Red Riding Hood got her name; what Little Red Riding Hood took to her grandmother's house; why Little Red Riding Hood went to her grandmother's house; the illustrations of Little Red Riding Hood, Grandmother, the hunter, the wolf, and the forest; why Little Red Riding Hood left the road; the advice given to Little Red Riding Hood by her mother; what the wolf did to Little Red Riding Hood; what happened to the wolf at the end; and the ending itself. These aspects can be explored by children (at all grade levels) as a class with teacher guidance, within small student groups, or by individual students. Having students organize their information in a chart aids comparison of the various versions. Sylvia also had her students compare similar issues in the many versions of The Three Little Pigs and Jack and the Beanstalk.

The organizational structures described in this chapter are not exclusive in and of themselves. In many classrooms, teachers combine several structures. For example, students may be participants in Literature Workshops and read books on a particular topic (e.g., survival), theme (e.g., during times of adversity, one must draw upon inner strength), or genre (e.g., historical fiction); in small groups, they may read books that focus on a particular literary element (e.g., stories with integral settings, fully developed main characters, or conflict between a character and society); or they may engage in individualized reading and select multicultural picture books. There are many ways to combine the organizational structures described in this chapter.

Organizing for instruction is a complex and multifaceted endeavour. As we hope we have shown in the nine chapters of this book, teachers must orchestrate many issues when organizing and implementing literature- and response-based programs. But the effort is worthwhile for teachers who want to help students to discover and experience the power and joy of literature.

References

Anderson, R.C., P.T. Wilson, and L.G. Fielding. 1988. Growth in reading and how children spend their time outside of school. *Reading Research Quarterly* 23(3), 285-303.

Ashley, L.F. 1970. Children's reading interests and individualized reading. *Elementary English* 47(8), 1088-1096.

Atwell, N. 1987. *In the Middle: Writing, Reading and Learning with Adolescents*. Portsmouth, New Hampshire: Boynton/Cook Publishers.

———. 1998. *In the Middle: New Understandings about Writing, Reading and Literature*. Second edition. Toronto: Irwin Publishing.

Barrera, R., V. Thompson, and M. Dressman, eds. 1997. *Kaleidoscope: A Multicultural Booklist for Grades K–8*. Second edition. Urbana, Illinois: National Council of Teachers of English.

Benton, M. and G. Fox. 1985. *Teaching Literature: Nine to Fourteen*. Oxford: Oxford University Press.

The Canadian Children's Book Centre. 1994. *Writing Stories, Making Pictures: Biographies of 150 Canadian Children's Authors and Illustrators*. Toronto: The Canadian Children's Book Centre.

———. 1999. *The Storymakers: Illustrating Children's Books*. Markham, Ontario: Pembroke Publishers.

Carter, B. and K. Harris. 1981. The children and the critics: How do their book selections compare? *School Library Media Quarterly* 10(1), 54-58.

Cox, C. and J. Zarrillo. 1993. *Teaching Reading with Children's Literature*. New York: Macmillan Publishing Company.

Cullinan, B.E. 1989. Latching on to literature: Reading initiatives take hold. *School Library Journal 35* (8), 27-31.

———, ed. 1992. *Invitation to Read: More Children's Literature in the Reading Program*. Newark, Delaware: International Reading Association.

Cullinan, B.E., K. Harwood, and L. Galda. 1983. The reader and the story: Comprehension and response. *Journal of Research and Development in Education* 16(3), 29-38.

Donelson, K. 1990. Fifty years of literature for young adults. In *Transactions with Literature: A Fifty-Year Perspective*. E.J. Farrell and J.R. Squire, eds. Urbana, Illinois: National Council of Teachers of English.

Fisher, P. and G. Ayres. 1990. A comparison of the reading interests of children in England and the United States. *Reading Improvement* 27(2), 111-115.

Fuhler, C. (1990). Let's move toward literature-based reading instruction. *The Reading Teacher* 43(4), 312-315.

Galda, L. and B. Cullinan. 1991. Literature for literacy: What research says about the benefits of using trade books in the classroom. In *Handbook of Research on Teaching the English Language Arts*. J. Flood, J. Jensen, D. Lapp, and J. Squire, eds. New York: Macmillan Publishing Company.

Gambell, T.J. 1986. Choosing the literature to teach. *English Quarterly* 19(2), 99-107.

Gambrell, L. 1996. Creating classroom cultures that foster reading motivation. *The Reading Teacher* 58(1), 14-25.

Glazer, J. 1997. *Introduction to Children's Literature.* Second edition. Upper Saddle River, New Jersey: Prentice-Hall, Inc.

Graham, S. 1986. Assessing reading preferences: A new approach. *The New England Reading Association Journal* 21(1), 8-11.

Guthrie, J.T. 1981. Reading interests. *The Reading Teacher* 34(8), 984-986.

Harms, J.M. and L.J. Lettow. 1986. Fostering ownership of the reading experience. *The Reading Teacher* 40(3), 324-330.

Hawkins, S. 1983. Reading interests of gifted children. *Reading Horizons* 24(1), 18-22.

Heald-Taylor, G. 1996. Three paradigms for literature instruction in grades 3 to 6. *The Reading Teacher* 49(6), 456-466.

Hiebert, E. and J. Colt. 1989. Patterns of literature-based reading instruction. *The Reading Teacher* (43)1, 14-20.

Hile, K., ed. 1995. *Something About the Author: Facts and Pictures About Authors and Illustrators of Books for Young People*. New York: ITP.

Hill, S. 1984. What are children reading? *Australian Journal of Reading* 7(4), 196-199.

Hillman, J. 1999. *Discovering Children's Literature.* Second edition. Englewood Cliffs, New Jersey: Prentice-Hall, Inc.

Huggins, L.J. and M.C. Roos. 1990. *The Shared Book Experience: An Alternative to the Basal Reading Approach*. Louisiana: ERIC Document Reproduction Service No. 319 018.

Huck, C.S. 1987. Literature as the content of reading. *Theory into Practice* 26(5), 363-371.

———. 1992. Literacy and literature. *Language Arts* 69(7), 520-526.

Hunt, L.C. 1970. The effect of self-selection, interest, and motivation upon independent, instructional and frustration levels. *The Reading Teacher* 24(2), 146-151.

Jacobs, J. and M. Tunnell. 1996. *Children's Literature, Briefly*. Englewood Cliffs, New Jersey: Prentice-Hall, Inc.

Johnson, C.S. and G.R. Greenbaum. 1982. Girls' and boys' reading interests: A review of the research. In *Sex Stereotypes and Reading: Research and Strategies.* E.M. Sheridan, ed. Newark, Delaware: International Reading Association.

Kellerman, K.K. 1991. *Students' Rejection of Teacher Choice of Free Reading Books*. M.A. thesis, Kean College. New Jersey: ERIC Document Reproduction Service No. ED 329 949.

Lehman, B.A. 1991. Children's choice and critical acclaim: A unified perspective for children's literature. *Reading Research and Instruction* 30(3), 1-20.

Lehman, B.A. and P.R. Crook. 1988. Effective schools research and excellence in reading: A rationale for children's literature in the curriculum. *Childhood Education* 64(4), 235-241.

Lukens, R. 1999. *A Critical Handbook of Children's Literature.* Sixth edition. New York: Longman.

Martinez, M. and M.F. Nash. 1992. Bookalogues: Talking about children's literature. *Language Arts* 69(2), 138-144.

McGee, L. and G. Tompkins. 1995. Literature-based reading instruction: What's guiding the instruction? *Language Arts* 72(6), 405-414.

Monson, D.L. and S. Sebesta. 1991. Reading preferences. In *Handbook of Research on Teaching the English Language Arts*. J. Flood, J. Jensen, D. Lapp, and J.R. Squire, eds. New York: Macmillan Publishing Company.

Morrow, L. M. 1991. Promoting voluntary reading. In *Handbook of Research on Teaching the English Language Arts*. J. Flood, J. Jensen, D. Lapp, and J.R. Squire, eds. New York: Macmillan Publishing Company.

Moss, J. 1994. *Using Literature in the Middle Grades: A Thematic Approach*. Norwood, Massachusetts: Christopher-Gordon Publishers, Inc.

Nilsen, A.P., R. Peterson, and L.W. Searfoss. 1980. The adult as critic vs. the child as reader. *Language Arts* 57(5), 530-539.

Nodelman, P. 1996. *The Pleasures of Children's Literature.* Second edition. New York: Longman Publishers USA.

Norton, D. 1991. *Through the Eyes of a Child: An Introduction to Children's Literature.* Third edition. New York: Macmillan Publishing Company.

———. 1995. *Through the Eyes of a Child: An Introduction to Children's Literature.* Fourth edition. Englewood Cliffs, New Jersey: Prentice-Hall Inc.

O'Flahavan, J., L.B. Gambrell, J. Guthrie, S. Stahl, J.F. Bauman, and D.E. Alvermann. 1992. Poll results guide activities of research center. *Reading Today* 10(1), 12.

Olhausen, M.M. and M. Jepsen. 1992. Lessons from Goldilocks: "Somebody's been choosing my books but I can make my own choices now!" *New Advocate* 5(1), 31-46.

Olson, W. 1949. *Child Development*. Boston: Heath.

Palmer, B.M., R.M. Codling, and L. Gambrell. 1994. In their own words: What elementary students have to say about motivation to read. *The Reading Teacher* 48(2), 176-179.

Pantaleo, S. 1995. Students and teachers selecting literature: Whose choice? *Illinois English Bulletin* 82(2), 33-46.

Pascoe, E. and M. Gilchrist. 1987. Children's responses to literature: Views of children and teachers. *English in Australia* 81, 55-62.

Paul, T. 1996. *Patterns of Reading Practice*. Madison, Wisconsin: Institute for Academic Excellence.

Perez, S.A. 1986. Children see, children do: Teachers as reading models. *The Reading Teacher* 40(1), 8-11.

Pillar, A. 1992. Resources to identify children's books. In *Invitation to Read: More Children's Literature in the Reading Program.* B. Cullinan, ed. Newark, Delaware: International Reading Association.

Short, K. 1995. *Research and Professional Resources in Children's Literature: Piecing a Patchwork Quilt.* Newark, Delaware: International Reading Association.

Smith, J. and P. Bowers. 1989. Approaches to using literature for teaching reading. *Reading Improvement* 26(4), 345-348.

Stott, J. and R. Jones. 1988. *Canadian Books for Children: A Guide to Authors and Illustrators*. Toronto: Harcourt Brace Jovanovich Canada.

Summers, E.G. and A. Lukasevich. 1983. Reading preferences of intermediate-grade children in relation to sex, community, and maturation (grade level): A Canadian perspective. *Reading Research Quarterly* 18(3), 347-360.

Sutton, W., ed. 1997. *Adventuring with Books: A Booklist for Pre-K–Grade 6* (1997 edition). Urbana, Illinois: National Council of Teachers of English.

Sweet, A.P. and J.T. Guthrie. 1996. How children's motivations relate to literacy development and instruction. *The Reading Teacher* 49(8), 660-662.

Taylor, B.M., B.J. Frye, and G.M. Maruyama. 1990. Time spent reading and reading growth. *American Educational Research Journal* 27(2), 351-362.

Tomlinson, C. and C. Lynch-Brown. 1996. *Essentials of Children's Literature.* Second edition. Needham, Massachusetts: Allyn and Bacon.

Tompkins, G. and K. Hoskisson. 1998. *Language Arts: Content and Teaching Strategies.* Fourth edition. Englewood Cliffs, New Jersey: Prentice-Hall, Inc.

Tunnel, M. and J. Jacobs. 1989. Using 'real' books: Research findings on literature-based reading instruction. *The Reading Teacher* 42(7), 470-477.

Veatch, J., ed. 1959. *Individualizing Your Reading Program: Self-Selection in Action*. New York: Putnam.

Weintraub, S. 1969. Children's reading interests. *The Reading Teacher* 22(7), 655-659.

Zarrillo, J. 1989. Teachers' interpretations of literature-based reading. *The Reading Teacher* 43(1), 112-120.

Professional Resources

Atwell, N. 1987. *In the Middle: Writing, Reading and Learning with adolescents*. Portsmouth, New Hampshire: Heinemann Educational Books, Inc. • Although Atwell describes organizational structures and procedures for reading workshop and writing workshop for middle-grade students, her book is also appropriate for elementary teachers. Atwell describes in detail how to prepare for writing workshop, how to get started, how to respond to writers and their writing, and how to conduct writing mini-lessons. She also provides many practical suggestions for organizing and implementing reading workshop, including providing time for reading, selecting books, organizing small-group discussions, implementing dialogue journals, assessing students, and conducting mini-lessons.

———. 1998. *In the Middle: New Understandings about Writing, Reading and Literature.* Second edition. Toronto: Irwin Publishing. • The second edition, like the first, is based on Atwell's extensive teaching experiences in the middle grades. Although Atwell discusses the same topics as in the first book, the new edition reflects her personal professional growth in implementing writing and reading workshops in middle school classrooms. She writes, "my goal is teaching that is based on knowledge—of literature, of young adolescents, of my students' tastes and needs" (p.46). Each chapter includes samples of student writing— writing that demonstrates that reading and writing cannot be separated.

Rothlein, L. and A. Meinbach. 1996. *Legacies: Using Children's Literature in the Classroom.* New York: HarperCollins College Publishers. • In the first chapter of this comprehensive book, Rothlein and Meinbach describe the various genres of children's literature. They then provide background information about and instructional strategies for various components of literature-based programs: reading aloud, shared reading, independent reading, and storytelling. The authors address responding to literature through the language arts, the arts, and other alternatives. One chapter is devoted to describing different types of literature-based programs, and another discusses using themes and literature across the curriculum. The authors also address assessment in literature-based programs. Appendices include children's book awards, resources for teaching literature, publishers and addresses, children's periodicals, and more.

Samway, K. and G. Whang. 1996. *Literature Study Circles in a Multicultural Classroom*. New York: Stenhouse. • This book explains how to organize literature circles in the classroom. Samway and Whang define a literature study circle as "an approach that emphasizes the reading and discussing of unabridged, unexcerpted children's literature in small self selected groups" (p.14). The authors discuss in detail the important components of such a structure, describing instructional strategies and listing many valuable resources.

Cinderella Stories

Brown, M. 1954. *Cinderella*. New York: Scribner.

Burton, E. and L. Offerdahl. 1994. *Cinderfella and the Slamdunk Contest*. Boston: Brandon Publishing Company.

Climo, S. 1989. *The Egyptian Cinderella*. New York: HarperCollins Publishers.

———. 1993. *The Korean Cinderella*. New York: HarperCollins Publishers.

———. 1996. *The Irish Cinderlad*. New York: HarperCollins Publishers.

Cole, B. 1987. *Prince Cinders*. New York: G.P. Putnam's Sons.

de la Touche, G. and P. Storey. 1993. *Cinderella*. London: Grandreams Limited.

Ehrlich, A. 1985. *Cinderella*. New York: Dial Books for Young Readers.

Galdone, P. 1978. *Cinderella*. New York: McGraw-Hill Publishers.

Granowsky, A., B. Kiwak, and R. Childress. 1993. *Cinderella/That Awful Cinderella: A Classic Tale (Point of View)*. Austin, Texas: Raintree/Steck-Vaughn Publishers.

Greaves, M. and M. Chamberlain. 1990. *Tattercoats*. New York: Clarkson N. Potter, Inc.

Han, O. and S. Plunkett. 1996. *Kongi and Potgi: A Cinderella Story from Korea*. New York: Dial.

Hogrogian, N. 1981. *Cinderella*. New York: Greenwillow Books.

Hooks, W.H. 1987. *Moss Gown*. New York: Clarion.

Huck, C. and A. Lobel. 1989. *Princess Furball*. New York: Greenwillow Books.

Karlin, B. 1989. *Cinderella*. Boston: Little, Brown.

Lewis, N. and A. Reed. 1987. *The Stepsister*. New York: Dial Books for Young Readers.

Louie, A.L. 1982. *Yeh-Shen: A Cinderella Story from China*. New York: Philomel.

Martin, R. and D. Shannon. 1992. *The Rough-faced Girl*. New York: G.P. Putman's Sons.

Schroeder, A. 1997. *Smoky Mountain Rose: An Appalachian Cinderella*. New York: Dial Books.

Short, R. 1994. *The Untold Story of Cinderella*. New York: Carol Publishing Group.

Shorto, R. 1990. *Cinderella: The Untold Story*. New York: Birch Lane Press.

Silverman, E. 1999. *Raisel's Riddle*. New York: Farrar, Straus & Giroux.

Steptoe, J. 1987. *Mufaro's Beautiful Daughters: An African Tale*. New York: Lothrop.

Thaler, M. 1997. *Cinderella Bigfoot*. New York: Scholastic Inc.

APPENDIX A

A SELECTION OF CANADIAN CHILDREN'S LITERATURE AWARDS

Governor General's Literary Awards

(GOVERNOR-GENERAL'S AWARDS FOR CHILDREN'S LITERATURE)

This award was established in 1975 as the Canada Council Children's Literature Prize. Up to four prizes are awarded annually by the Canada Council in each of the following categories: text in an English-language book, text in a French-language book, illustrations in an English-language book, illustrations in a French-language book. Recipients are selected by two separate juries, one for English language books, and one for French language books. Awards were initially presented for best writing; awards for illustration were added in 1977/78. The award honours Canadian citizens who create books for young people.

ENGLISH-LANGUAGE AWARDS

1998
Text: Janet Lunn, *The Hollow Tree*
Illustration: Kady MacDonald Denton, *A Child's Treasury of Nursery Rhymes* (selected by Kady MacDonald Denton)

1997
Text: Kit Pearson, *Awake and Dreaming*
Illustration: Barbara Reid, *The Party* (text by Barbara Reid)

1996
Text: Paul Yee, *Ghost Train*
Illustration: Eric Beddows, *The Rooster's Gift* (text by Pam Conrad)

1995
Text: Tim Wynne-Jones, *The Maestro*
Illustration: Ludmila Zeman, *The Last Quest of Gilgamesh* (text by Ludmila Zeman)

1994
Text: Julie Johnston, *Adam and Eve and Pinch-Me*
Illustration: Murray Kimber, *Josepha: A Prairie Boy's Story* (text by Jim McGugan)

1993
Text: Tim Wynne-Jones, *Some of the Kinder Planets*
Illustration: Mireille Levert, *Sleep Tight, Mrs. Ming* (text by Sharon Jennings)

1992
Text: Julie Johnston, *Hero of Lesser Causes*
Illustration: Ron Lightburn, *Waiting for the Whales* (text by Sheryl McFarlane)

1991
Text: Sarah Ellis, *Pick-Up Sticks*
Illustration: Joanne Fitzgerald, *Doctor Kiss Says Yes* (text by Teddy Jam)

1990
Text: Michael Bedard, *Redwork*
Illustration: Paul Morin, *The Orphan Boy* (text by Tololwa M. Mollel)

1989
Text: Diana Wieler, *Bad Boy*
Illustration: Robin Muller, *The Magic Paintbrush* (text by Robin Muller)

1988
Text: Welwyn Wilton Katz, *The Third Magic*
Illustration: Kim LaFave, *Amos's Sweater* (text by Janet Lunn)

1987
Text: Morgan Nyberg, *Galahad Schwartz and the Cockroach Army*
Illustration: Marie-Louise Gay, *Rainy Day Magic* (text by Marie-Louise Gay)

THE CANADA COUNCIL CHILDREN'S LITERATURE PRIZE

This award was renamed the Governor General's Award for Children's Literature in 1986 (see above).

1986
Text: Janet Lunn, *Shadow in Hawthorn Bay*
Illustration: Barbara Reid, *Have You Seen Birds?* (text by Joanne Oppenheim)

1985
Text: Cora Taylor, *Julie*
Illustration: Terry Gallagher, *Murdo's Story* (text by Murdo Scribe)

1984
Text: Jan Hudson, *Sweetgrass*
Illustration: Marie-Louise Gay, *Lizzy's Lion* (text by Dennis Lee)

1983
Text: sean o huigin, *The Ghose Horse of the Mounties*
Illustration: Laszlo Gal, *The Little Mermaid* (text by Margaret Crawford Maloney)

1982
Text: Monica Hughes, *Hunter in the Dark*
Illustration: Vlasta Van Kampen, ABC/123: *The Canadian Alphabet and Counting Book* (text by Vlasta Van Kampen)

1981
Text: Monica Hughes, *The Guardian of Isis*
Illustration: Heather Woodall, *Ytek and the Arctic Orchid: An Inuit Legend* (text by Garnet Hewitt)

1980
Text: Christie Harris, *The Trouble with Princesses*
Illustration: Elizabeth Cleaver, *Petrouchka* (text by Elizabeth Cleaver, adapted from Igor Stravinsky and Alexandre Benois)

1979
Text: Barbara Smucker, *Days of Terror*
Illustration: Laszlo Gal, *The Twelve Dancing Princesses* (text by Janet Lunn)

1978
Text: Kevin Major, *Hold Fast*
Illustration: Ann Blades, *A Salmon for Simon* (text by Betty Waterton)

1977
Text: Jean Little, *Listen for the Singing*

1976
Text: Myra Paperny, *The Wooden People*

1975
Text: Bill Freeman, *Shantymen of Cache Lake*

The Canadian Library Association Book of the Year for Children

Presented by the Canadian Library Association since 1947, this award recognizes the most distinguished children's book published each year by a Canadian citizen. In 1954, an additional award was created for a French-language book. In some years no award may be given.

ENGLISH-LANGUAGE AWARDS

1998: *Silverwing* by Kenneth Oppel, HarperCollins.
1997: *Uncle Ronald* by Brian Doyle, Groundwood.
1996: *The Tiny Kite of Eddie Wing* by Maxine Trottier, Groundwood
1995: *Summer of the Mad Monk* by Cora Taylor, Greystone
1994: *Some of the Kinder Planets* by Tim Wynne-Jones, Groundwood
1993: *Ticket to Curlew* by Celia Barker Lottridge, Groundwood
1992: *Eating Between the Lines* by Kevin Major, Doubleday
1991: *Redwork* by Michael Bedard, Dennys
1990: *The Sky is Falling* by Kit Pearson, Penguin
1989: *Easy Avenue* by Brian Doyle, Groundwood
1988: *A Handful of Time* by Kit Pearson, Viking
1987: *Shadow in Hawthorn Bay* by Janet Lunn, Scribner
1986: *Julie* by Cora Taylor, Western Producer
1985: *Mama's Going to Buy You a Mockingbird* by Jean Little, Penguin
1984: *Sweetgrass* by Jan Hudson, Tree Frog Press
1983: *Up to Low* by Brian Doyle, Groundwood
1982: *The Root Cellar* by Janet Lunn, Lester & Orpen Dennys
1981: *The Violin Maker's Gift* by Donn Kushner, Macmillan of Canada
1980: *River Runners: A Tale of Hardship and Bravery* by James Houston, McClelland & Stewart
1979: *Hold Fast* by Kevin Major, Clarke, Irwin
1978: *Garbage Delight* by Dennis Lee, Macmillan
1977: *Mouse Woman and the Vanished Princess* by Christie Harris, McClelland & Stewart
1976: *Jacob Two-Two Meets the Hooded Fang* by Mordecai Richler, Knopf
1975: *Alligator Pie* by Dennis Lee, Macmillan of Canada
1974: *The Miraculous Hind* by Elizabeth Cleaver, Holt of Canada
1973: *The Marrow of the World* by Ruth Nichols, Macmillan of Canada
1972: *Mary of Mile 18* by Ann Blades, Tundra
1971: *Cartier Discovers the St. Lawrence* by William Toye, Oxford
1970: *Sally Go Round the Sun* by Edith Fowke, McClelland & Stewart
1969: *And Tomorrow the Stars* by Kay Hill, Dodd
1968: *The White Archer* by James Houston, Kestrel
1967: *Raven's Cry* by Christie Harris, McClelland & Stewart
1966: *Tikta'Liktak* by James Houston, Kestrel **and** *The Double Knights* by James McNeal, Walck
1965: *Tales of Nanabozho* by Dorothy Reid, Oxford
1964: *The Whale People* by Roderick Haig-Brown, William Collins of Canada
1963: *The Incredible Journey* by Sheila Burnford, Little, Brown
1962: No English-language award
1961: *The St. Lawrence* by William Toye, Oxford
1960: *The Golden Phoenix* by Marius Barbeau and Michael Hornyansky, Walck
1959: *The Dangerous Cove* by John F. Hayes, Copp Clark

1958: *Lost in the Barrens* by Farley Mowat, Little
1957: *Glooskap's Country* by Cyrus Macmillan, Macmillan of Canada
1956: *Train by Tiger Lily* by Louise Riley, Macmillan of Canada
1955: No English-language award
1954: No English-language award
1953: No award
1952: *The Sun Horse* by Catherine Anthony Clark, Macmillan of Canada
1951: No award
1950: *Franklin of the Arctic* by Richard S. Lambert, McClelland & Stewart
1949: No award
1948: *Kristi's Trees* by Mabel Dunham, Hale
1947: *Starbuck Valley Winter* by Roderick Haig-Brown, Collins

Canadian Library Association Young-Adult Book Award

The award was established in 1980 and is awarded annually by the Canadian Library Association for the best work of creative literature (novel, play, or poetry) for young adults. The author must be a Canadian citizen, and the book must be published in Canada.

1998: *Bone Dance* by Martha Brooks
1997: *Takes: Stories for Young Adults*, edited by R.P. MacIntyre
1996: *The Maestro* by Tim Wynne-Jones
1995: *Adam and Eve and Pinch Me* by Julie Johnson
1994: *Nobody's Son* by Sean Stewart
1993: *There Will Be Wolves* by Karleen Bradford
1992: *Strandia* by Susan Lynn Reynold
1991: *The Leaving* by Budge Wilson
1990: *Bad Boy* by Diana Wieler
1989: *Who Is Frances Rain?* by Margaret Buffie
1988: *January, February, June or July* by Helen Fogwell Porter
1987: *Shadow in Hawthorn Bay* by Janet Lunn
1986: *The Quarter-Pie Window* by Marianne Brandis
1985: *Winners* by Mary-Ellen Lang Collura
1984: *The Druid's Tune* by O.R. Melling
1983: *Hunter in the Dark* by Monica Hughes
1982: *Superbike* by Jamie Brown
1981: *Far from Shore* by Kevin Major

The Amelia Frances Howard-Gibbon Illustrator's Award

Awarded since 1971 by the Canadian Library Association, this medal honours excellence in children's illustration in a book published in Canada. The award must go to a citizen or resident of Canada. (Unless otherwise indicated, the author is also the illustrator.)

1998: *The Party* by Barbara Reid, Scholastic.
1997: *Ghost Train* by Paul Yee, illustrated by Harvey Chan, Groundwood.
1996: *Just Like New* by Ainslie Mason, illustrated by Karen Reczuch, Groundwood
1995: *Gifts* by Jo Ellen Bogart, illustrated by Barbara Reid, Scholastic
1994: *Last Leaf First Snowflake to Fall* by Leo Yerxa, Groundwood
1993: *The Dragon's Pearl* by Julie Lawson, illustrated by Paul Morin, Oxford
1992: *Waiting for the Whales* by Ron Lightburn, illustrated by Sheryl McFarlane, Orca Books
1991: *The Orphan Boy* by Tololwa M. Mollel, illustrated by Paul Morin, Oxford

1990: *Till All the Stars Have Fallen: Canadian Poems for Children* selected by David Booth, illustrated by Kady MacDonald Denton, Kids Can Press
1989: *Amos's Sweater* by Janet Lunn, illustrated by Kim LaFave, Douglas & McIntyre
1988: *Rainy Day Magic* by Marie-Louise Gay, Hodder & Stoughton
1987: *Moonbeam on a Cat's Ear* by Marie-Louise Gay, Stoddard
1986: *Zoom Away* by Tim Wynne-Jones, illustrated by Ken Nutt, Douglas & McIntyre
1985: *Chin Chiang and the Dragon's Dance* by Ian Wallace, Groundwood
1984: *Zoom at Sea* by Tim Wynne-Jones, illustrated by Ken Nutt, Douglas & McIntyre
1983: *Chester's Barn* by Lindee Climo, Tundra
1982: *Ytek and the Arctic Orchid: An Inuit Legend* by Heather Woodall, Douglas & McIntyre
1981: *The Trouble with Princesses* by Douglas Tait, McClelland & Stewart
1980: *The Twelve Dancing Princesses* by Laszlo Gal, Methuen
1979: *A Salmon for Simon* by Betty Waterton, illustrated by Ann Blades, Douglas & McIntyre
1978: *The Loon's Necklace* by William Toye, illustrated by Elizabeth Cleaver, Oxford
1977: *Down by Jim Long's Stage: Rhymes for Children and Young Fish* by Al Pittman, illustrated by Pam Hall, Breakwater
1976: *A Prairie Boy's Summer* by William Kurelek, Tundra
1975: *The Sleighs of My Childhood/Les Traineaux de Mon Enfance* by Carlos Italiano, Tundra
1974: *A Prairie Boy's Winter* by William Kurelek, Tundra
1973: *Au Dela du Soleil/Beyond the Sun* by Jacques de Roussan, Tundra
1972: *A Child in Prison Camp* by Shizuye Takashima, Tundra
1971: *The Wind Has Wings* edited by Mary Alice Downie and Barbara Robertson, illustrated by Elizabeth Cleaver, Oxford

Elizabeth Mrazik-Cleaver Canadian Picture Book Award

This award was established in 1986 by the National Library of Canada and the International Board on Books for Young People in memory of children's book illustrator Elizabeth Mrazik-Cleaver (1932–1985). It is presented annually, unless no book is judged deserving, to a Canadian children's book illustrator whose work on a new book is deemed both original and worthy.

1998: *Rainbow Bay* by Pascal Milleli (text by Stephen Hume)
1997: *Ghost Train* by Harvey Chan (text by Paul Yee)
1996: *Selina and the Bear Paw Quilt* by Janet Wilson (text by Barbara Smucker)
1995: *Josepha: A Prairie Boy's Story* by Murray Kimber (text by Jim McGugan)
1994: *Last Leaf First Snowflake to Fall* by Leo Yerxa (text by Leo Yerxa)
1993: *Two by Two* by Barbara Reid (text by Barbara Reid)
1992: *Waiting for the Whales* by Ron Lightburn (text by Sheryl McFarlane)
1991: *The Orphan Boy* by Paul Morin (text by Tololwa Mollel)
1990: *The Name of the Tree* by Ian Wallace (text by Celia Barker Lottridge)
1989: *Night Cars* by Eric Beddows (text by Teddy Jam)
1988: *Can You Catch Josephine?* by Stéphane Poulin (text by Stéphane Poulin)

1987: *Have You Seen Birds?* by Barbara Reid (text by Joanne Oppenheim)
1986: *By the Sea: An Alphabet Book* by Ann Blades (text by Ann Blades)

The Geoffrey Bilson Award for Historical Fiction for Young People

Established in 1988 in memory of respected historian and children's author Geoffrey Bilson, this annual prize of $1,000 has been made possible by the Canadian children's publishing industry. It is awarded to a Canadian author for an outstanding work of historical fiction for young people by the Canadian Children's Book Centre.

1998: *Goodbye Marianne* by Irene N. Watts
1997: *To Dance at the Palais Royale* by Janet McNaughton
1996: *Rebellion: A Story of Upper Canada* by Marianne Brandis
1995: *The Dream Carvers* by Joan Clark
1994: *The Lights Go on Again* by Kit Pearson
1993: *Ticket to Curlew* by Celia Barker Lottridge
1992: No award given
1991: *The Sign of the Scales* by Marianne Brandis
1990: *The Sky Is Falling* by Kit Pearson
1989: *Mystery in the Frozen Lands* by Martyn Godfrey **and** *Rachel's Revolution* by Dorothy Perkyns
1988: *Lisa* by Carol Matas

Mr. Christie's™ Book Award

Sponsored by Christie Brown & Co., a division of Nabisco Brands Ltd., this award was established in 1990 to encourage the development and publishing of high-quality Canadian children's books and to stimulate children's desire to read. Books must be created by a Canadian author and/or illustrator. At present, there are three categories in both English and French.

ENGLISH-LANGUAGE AWARDS

1998
Ages 7 and under: *Biscuits in the Cupboard* by Barbara Nichol; Philippe Beha, illustrator
Ages 8–11: *The House of Wooden Santas* by Kevin Major, Imelda George, and Ned Pratt
Ages 12 and over: *Silverwing* by Kenneth Oppel

1997
Ages 7 and under: *The Fabulous Song* by Don Gillmor; Marie-Louise Gay, illustrator
Ages 8–11: *Discovering the Iceman* by Shelley Tanaka and Laurie McGaw
Ages 12 and over: *Uncle Ronald* by Brian Doyle

1996
Ages 7 and under: *How Smudge Came* by Nan Gregory; Ron Lightburn, illustrator
Ages 8–11: *Jacob Two-Two's First Spy Case* by Mordecai Richler
Ages 12 and over: *The Dream Carvers* by Joan Clark

1995
Ages 7 and under - *Thor* by W.D. Valgardson; Ange Zhang, illustrator
Ages 8–11: *A Pioneer Story* by Barbara Greenwood; Heather Collins, illustrator
Ages 12 and over: *Out of the Blue* by Sarah Ellis

1994
Ages 7 and under: *Brewster Rooster* by Berny Lucas
Ages 8–11: *A Little Tiger in the Chinese Night* by Song Nan Zhang **and** *Last Leaf First Snowflake to Fall* by Leo Yerxa
Ages 12 and over: *RanVan the Defender* by Diana Wieler

1993
Illustration: *A Prairie Alphabet* by Yvette Moore (text by Joanne Bannatyne-Cugnet)
Text (ages 8 and under): *There Were Monkeys in My Kitchen* by Sheree Fitch
Text (ages 9-14): *The Story of Canada* by Janet Lunn and Christopher Moore

1992
Illustration: *Zoe Board Books (Zoe's Rainy Day, Zoe's Snowy Day, Zoe's Windy Day, Zoe's Sunny Day)* by Barbara Reid
Text: *The Ice Cream Store* by Dennis Lee

1991
Illustration: *The Story of Little Quack* by Kady Macdonald Denton (text by Betty Gibson)
Text: *Covered Bridge* by Brian Doyle

1990
Illustration: *The Name of the Tree* by Ian Wallace (text by Celia Lottridge)
Text: *The Sky Is Falling* by Kit Pearson

Vicky Metcalf Award

Awarded annually by the Canadian Authors Association to a Canadian author who has published at least four books for children ages seven to seventeen. Established in 1963, this award is presented annually to a writer for a body of work "inspirational to Canadian youth."

1998: Kit Pearson
1997: Tim Wynne-Jones
1996: Margaret Buffie
1995: Sarah Ellis
1994: Welwyn Wilton Katz
1993: Phoebe Gilman
1992: Kevin Major
1991: Brian Doyle
1990: Bernice Thurman Hunter
1989: Stéphane Poulin
1988: Barbara Smucker
1987: Robert Munsch
1986: Dennis Lee
1985: Edith Fowke
1984: Bill Freeman
1983: Claire Mackay
1982: Janet Lunn
1981: Monica Hughes
1980: John Craig
1979: Cliff Faulknor
1978: Lyn Cook
1977: James Houston
1976: Suzanne Martel
1975: Lyn Harrington
1974: Jean Little
1973: Christie Harris
1972: William Toye
1971: Kay Hill
1970: Farley Mowat
1969: Audrey McKim
1968: Lorraine McLaughlin
1967: John Patrick Gillese
1966: Fred Savage
1965: Roderick Haig-Brown
1964: John F. Hayes
1963: Kerry Wood

Vicky Metcalf Short Story Award

Established by the Canadian Authors Association in 1979, this award is presented to the Canadian writer (citizen or landed immigrant) of the best children's short story published in Canada in the previous year.

1998: W.D. Valgardson, "Chicken Lady" in *Garbage Creek*
1997: No award
1996: Bernice Friesen for "The Seasons Are Horses" in *The Seasons are Horses*
1995: No award
1994: Tim Wynne-Jones, "The Hope Bakery" in *Some of the Kinder Planets*
1993: Rod McIntyre, "The Rink" in *The Blue Jean Collection*
1992: Edna King, "Adventure on Thunder Island" in *Adventure on Thunder Island*
1991: No award
1990: Patricia G. Armstrong, "Choose Your Grandmother" in *Jumbo Gumbo*
1989: Martha Brooks, "A Boy and His Dog" in *Paradise Cafe & Other Stories*
1988: Claire MacKay, "Marvin and Me and the Files" in *12th Canadian Children's Annual*
1987: Isabel Reimer, "The Viking Dagger" in *Of the Jigsaw*
1986: Diana J. Wieler, "The Boy Who Walked Backwards" in *Prairie Jungle*
1985: Martyn Godfrey, "Here She Is, Ms. Teeny-Wonderful"
1984: Colleen Archer, "The Dog Who Wanted to Die"
1983: Monica Hughes, "The Iron-Barred Door" in *Contexts, Anthology 2*
1982: Barbara Greenwood, "A Major Resolution" in *Contexts, Anthology 1*
1981: James Houston, "Long Claws" in *The Winter Fun Book*
1980: Estelle Salata, "Blind Date" in *Time Enough*

Ruth Schwartz Children's Book Award

Established in memory of Toronto bookstore proprietor Ruth Schwartz in 1976, the award is presented annually to a Canadian children's author by the Canadian Booksellers Association and the Ontario Arts Council. The books are judged by children from a short list compiled by booksellers. The award may be shared by two people. Beginning in 1994, two awards were established: one for a picture book and one for a young adult (fiction or nonfiction) title.

1998
Picture Book: Jo Ellen Bogart (Laura Fernandez and Rick Jacobson, illustrators), *Jeremiah Learns to Read*
Young Adult: Martha Brooks, *Bone Dance*

1997
Picture Book: Paul Yee (Harvey Chan, illustrator) *Ghost Train*
Young Adult: Kit Pearson, *Awake and Dreaming*

1996
Picture Book: Geoff Butler, *The Killick: A Newfoundland Story*
Young Adult: Welwyn Wilton Katz, *Out of the Dark*

1995
Picture Book: Barbara Greenwood (Heather Collins, illustrator) *A Pioneer Story: The Daily Life of a Canadian Family in 1840*
Young Adult: Julie Johnston, *Adam and Eve and Pinch-Me*

1994
Picture Book: Michael Kusugak (Vladyanna Krykorka illustrator), *Northern Lights: The Soccer Trails*
Young Adult: O.R. Melling, *The Hunter's Moon*

1993
Phoebe Gilman, *Something from Nothing*

1992
Paul Yee, *Roses Sing on New Snow*

1991
William Bell, *Forbidden City*

1990
Diana Wieler, *Bad Boy*

1989
Janet Lunn, *Amos's Sweater*

1988
Cora Taylor, *The Doll* (U.S. title: *Yesterday's Doll*)

1987
Barbara Reid, *Have You Seen Birds?* (text by Joanne Oppenheim)

1986
Robert Munsch, *Thomas' Snowsuit*

1985
Jean Little, *Mama's Going To Buy You a Mockingbird*

1984
Tim Wynne-Jones, *Zoom at Sea*

1983
Jan Truss, *Jasmin*

1982
Claire MacKay and Marsha Hewitt, *One Proud Summer*

1981
Suzanne Martel, *The King's Daughter*

1980
Barbara Smucker, *Days of Terror*

1979
Kevin Major, *Hold Fast*

1978
Dennis Lee, *Garbage Delight*

1977
Robert Thomas Allen, *The Violin*

1976
Mordecai Richler, *Jacob Two-Two Meets the Hooded Fang*

I.O.D.E. Violet Downey Children's Book Award

Given annually by the National Chapter of the Canadian International Order of the Daughters of the Empire, this award recognizes the best Canadian English-language book published for children under fourteen years of age. The award may be shared by two people. This award was established in 1985 in memory of Violet Downey, a benefactor of the National Chapter of the IODE. The book must be over 300 words long.

1998: Celia Barker Lottridge, *Wings to Fly*
1997: Janet McNaughton, *To Dance at the Palais Royale.*
1996: Jean Little, *His Banner Over Me*
1995: Sarah Ellis, *Out of the Blue*
1994: Kit Pearson, *The Lights Go On Again*
1993: Julie Johnston, *Hero of Lesser Causes*
1992: Sheryl McFarlane and Ron Lightburn, *Waiting for the Whales*
1991: Barbara Smucker, *Incredible Jumbo*
1990: Paul Yee, *Tales from Gold Mountain*
1989: No award given
1988: Donn Kushner, *A Book Dragon*
1987: Janet Lunn, *Shadow in Hawthorn Bay*
1986: Marianne Brandis, *The Quarter-Pie Window*
1985: Mary-Ellen Lang Collura, *Winners*

Ann Connor-Brimer Award

This award is given annually by the Nova Scotia Library Association to recognize the best book by an Atlantic author.

1998: Kevin Major. *The House of Wooden Santas*. Red Deer: Red Deer College Press, 1997.
1997: Janet McNaughton. *To Dance at the Palais Royale*. St. John's: Tuckamore Books, 1996.
1996: Don Aker. *Of Things Not Seen*. Toronto: Stoddart, 1995.
1995: Sheree Fitch, *Mabel Murple*. Illustrated by Maryann Kovalski. Toronto: Doubleday Canada, 1995.
1994: Lesley Choyce. *Good Idea Gone Bad*. Halifax: Formac Publishing, 1993.
1993: Budge Wilson. *Oliver's Wars*. Toronto: Stoddart, 1992.
1992: Kevin Major. *Eating Between the Lines*. Toronto: Doubleday Canada, 1991.

Manitoba Young Reader's Choice Award

Sponsored by the Manitoba School Library Association, this award is given for the favourite Canadian book of Manitoba's young readers. Winners are selected by Manitoba young people in grades four through eight who have read (or have heard read) at least three titles from the list of nominees.

1998: Roy MacGregor. *Mystery at Lake Placid*. Toronto: McClelland & Stewart, 1995.
1997: Sylvia McNicoll. *Bringing Up Beauty*. Don Mills: Maxwell Macmillan Canada, 1994.
1996: Carol Matas. *Daniel's Story*. New York and Toronto: Scholastic, 1993.
1995: Jeni Mayer. *The Mystery of the Missing Will*. Saskatoon: Thistledown Press, 1992.
1994: Kit Pearson. *Looking at the Moon*. Toronto: Viking, 1991.
1993: Martyn Godfrey. *Can You Teach Me to Pick My Nose*? New York: Avon Books, 1990.
1992: William Bell. *Five Days of the Ghost*. Toronto: Stoddart, 1989.
1991: Gordon Korman. *The Zucchini Warriors*.

Municipal Chapter of Toronto IODE Book Award

This award is presented by the Imperial Order of the Daughters of the Empire – Toronto Chapter for outstanding achievement by a Toronto-area author and/or illustrator in children's literature.

1998: Celia Barker Lottridge (author). *Wings to Fly*. Toronto: Groundwood, 1997.
1997: Ian Wallace (author and illustrator). *A Winter's Tale*. Toronto: Douglas & McIntyre, 1997.
1996: David Booth (author), Karen Reczuch (illustrator). *The Dust Bowl*. Toronto: Kids Can Press, 1996.
1995: Linda Granfield (author), Janet Wilson (illustrator). *In Flanders Fields: The Story of the Poem by John McCrae*. Toronto: Lester Publishing, 1995.
1994: Joanne Findon (author), Ted Nasmith (illustrator). *The Dream of Aengus*. Toronto: Lester Publishing, 1994.
1993: Celia Barker Lottridge. *Ten Small Tales*. Toronto: Douglas & McIntyre, 1993.
1992 Janet Lunn (author), Christopher Moore (author), Alan Daniel (illustrator). *The Story of Canada*. Toronto: Lester Publishing and Key Porter Books, 1992.

R. Ross Annett Children's Award

Established in 1982, the award is presented annually by the Writers Guild of Alberta to recgonize excellence in for children. The award is named after Alberta writer R. Ross Annett and given is for the best book by an Alberta author.

1998: Hazel Hutchins, *The Prince of Tarn*
1997: Don Trembath, *The Tuesday Café*
1996: Tololwa Mollel, *Big Boy*
1994: Beth Goobie, *Mission Impossible*
1993: David Bly, *The McIntyre Liar*
1992: Monica Hughes, *The Crystal Drop*
1991: Hazel Hutchins, *A Cat of Artimus Pride*
1990: Jan Hudson, *Dawn Rider*
1989: Don Meredith, *Dog Runner*
1988: William Pasnak, *Under the Eagle's Claw*
1987: Marilyn Halvorson, *Nobody Said It Would Be Easy*
1986: Monica Hughes, *Blaine's Way*
1985: Cora Taylor, *Julie*
1984: William Pasnak, *In the City of the King*
1983: Monica Hughes, *Space Trap*
1982: Monica Hughes, *Hunter in the Dark*

Sheila A. Egoff Children's Literature Prize

Established in 1987, this award is presented annually by the West Coast Book Prize Society for the best children's book published in the previous year by a writer who has lived in British Columbia for three of the previous five years, published anywhere in the world.

1998 James Heneghan. *Wish Me Luck.*
1997: Sarah Ellis. *Back of Beyond.*
1996: Nan Gregory. *How Smudge Came.*
1995: Lillian Boraks-Nemetz. *The Old Brown Suitcase: A Teenager's Story of War and Peace.*
1994: Julie Lawson. *White Jade Tiger.*
1993: Shirley Sterling. *My Name is Seepeetza.*
1992: Alexandra Morton. *Siwiti: A Whale's Story.*
1991: Nancy Hundal. *I Heard My Mother Call My Name.*
1990: Paul Yee. *Tales From Gold Mountain.*
1989: Mary-Ellen Lang Collura. *Sunny.*
1988: Nicola Morgan. *Pride of Lions.*
1987: Sarah Ellis. *The Baby Project.*

Silver Birch Award

Sponsored by the Ontario Library Association, this award is presented to the best Canadian children's book as chosen by Ontario students in grades four to six. To be eligible to vote for their favourite book in a given list, children must have read a minimum of five of the approximately twelve books identified as Official Selections.

FICTION AWARD

1998: Kenneth Oppel, *Silverwing.*
1997: Eric Walters, *STARS.*
1996: Sylvia McNicholl, *Bringing up Beauty.*
1995: Kit Pearson, *The Lights Go On Again.*
1994: Carol Matas, *Daniel's Story.*

NON-FICTION AWARD

1998: Hugh Brewster, *Anastasia's Album.*
1997: Shelley Tanaka, *On Board the Titanic: What It Was Like When the Great Liner Sank.*
1996: Anouchka Galouchko, *Sho and the Demons of the Deep.*
1995: Daisy Corning Stone Spedden, *Polar, The Titanic Bear.*

Information Book Award

This award was established in 1987 by the Children's Literature Roundtables of Canada and is awarded for an outstanding information book for children ages five to fifteen, written in English by a Canadian citizen and published in Canada during the previous year.

1998: *The Buried City of Pompeii.* Shelley Tanaka, author; Greg Ruhl, illustrator.
1997: *On Board the Titanic.* Shelley Tanaka, author; Ken Marschall, illustrator.
1996: *In Flanders Fields: The Story of the Poem* by John McCrae. Linda Granfield, author; Janet Wilson, illustrator.
1995: *A Pioneer Story: The Daily Life of a Canadian Family in 1840.* Barbara Greenwood, author; Heather Collins, illustrator.
1994: *On the Shuttle: Eight Days in Space.* Barbara Bondar with Dr. Roberta Bondar, authors. **and** *Cowboy: A Kid's Album.* Linda Granfield, author.
1993: *The Story of Canada* by Janet Lunn, Christopher Moore and Alan Daniel.
1992: *A Tree in a Forest* by Jan Thornhill.
1991: *Hands On, Thumbs Up* by Camilla Gryski.
1990: *Wolf Island* by Celia Godkin.
1989: *Exploring the Sky by Day* by Terence Dickinson.
1988: *Let's Celebrate* by Caroline Parry.
1987: *Looking at Insects* by David Suzuki.

Times Educational Supplement Information Book Award

The Times Educational Supplement has sponsored this award program since 1972. In 1973, the program was expanded to include two categories: junior (up to age nine) and senior (ages ten through sixteen). Trade books originally published in the United Kingdom or Commonwealth countries are eligible. Each winning author receives £150 (approximately $CAD330).

JUNIOR AWARDS

1997: *What's Under the Bed?* by Mick Manning and Brita Granstrom; Wonderwise, Watts.
1996: *Children Just Like Me* by Barnabas and Anabel Kindersley; Dorling Kindersley in association with UNICEF.
1995: No Award
1994: No Award
1993: *Read and Wonder: Think of an Eel* by Karen Wallace, illustrated by Mike Bostock; Walker Books.
1992: *My First Book of Time* by Claire Llewellyn; Dorling Kindersley, 1992.
1991: *Ian and Fred's Big Green Book* by Fred Pearce, illustrated by Ian Winton; Kingfisher, 1991.
1990: *The Tree* by Judy Hindley, illustrated by Alison Wisenfeld; Aurum, 1990; Potter, 1990.
1989: *Why Do People Smoke?* by Pete Sanders, illustrated with photos; Gloucester Press, 1989.
1988: *Conker* written and illustrated by Barrie Watts; A&C Black, 1987. **and** *Making a Book* by Ruth Thomson, illustrated by Chris Fairclough; Watts, 1987.

1987: *Being Born* by Sheila Kitzinger, photographs by Lennart Nilsson; Dorling Kindersley, 1986.
1986: *Polar Regions* by Terry Jennings, illustrated; Oxford, 1986.
1985: *KwaZulu South Africa* by Nancy Durrell McKenna, illustrated; A&C Black, 1984.
1984: No Award
1983: *Mum—I Feel Funny!* by Ann McPherson and Aidan Macfarlane, illustrated by Nicholas Garland; Chatto & Windus, 1982.
1982: *A Day with a Miner* by Phillippa Aston, photographs by Chris Fairclough; Wayland, 1981.
1981: No Award
1980: *Earthquakes and Volcanoes* written and illustrated by Robert Updegraff and Imelda Updegraff; Methuen, 1980.
1979: *The Common Frog* by Oxford Scientific Films, Ltd., photographs by George Bernard; Whizzard/Deutsch, 1979.
1978: *Tournaments* by Richard Barber, illustrated by Anne Dalton; Kestrel, 1978.
1977: *Street Flowers* by Richard Mabey, illustrated by Sarah Kensington; Kestrel, 1976.
1976: *Wash and Brush Up* by Eleanor Allen, illustrated with photographs; A&C Black, 1976.
1975: *Spiders* by Ralph Whitlock, illustrated with photographs; Wayland & Priory Press, 1975.
1974: *Frogs, Toads and Newts* by Francis D. Ommanney, illustrated by Deborah Fulfold; Bodley Head, 1973.
1973: No Award
1972: *Introducing Archaeology* by Magnus Magnusson, illustrated by Martin Simmons; Bodley Head, 1972.

APPENDIX B

CHILDREN'S LITERATURE WEBSITES

Below is a *small* sample of the approximately 600,000 websites that focus on some aspect of children's literature. Not only do sites "come and go," but they regularly update their information and revise their offerings. The descriptions of the sites below are accurate as of October 1999.

It is important to remember that once a site is accessed, one can easily link to other sites that provide additional information and references.

I. Getting Started

The following sites are excellent starting points discovering children's literature resources on the Internet. Each site leads to more specific information.

A. The Children's Literature Web Guide

D.K. Brown's site offers the Internet's most comprehensive page on children's literature. The site includes resources for teachers, parents, storytellers, writers, and illustrators; it is very popular, and many other children's literature sites link back to it.
http://www.acs.ucalgary.ca/~dkbrown/

Here are a few examples of the linked sites located on the Children's Literature Web Guide:

- *Web-Traveller's Toolkit: Essential Kid Lit Websites*
- *Conferences Bulletin Board*
- *Children's Literature Organizations on the Internet*
- *Lots of Lists: Recommended Books*
- *Children's Publishers and Booksellers on the Internet*

This site also includes lists of best books, banned books, subject bibliographies, and award-winning books.

B. Carol Hurst's Children's Literature Site

This site contains a collection of reviews of excellent children's books. The books are rated on a three-star system: recommended, highly recommended, and outstanding titles. Hurst's past articles and sections from her professional books offer ideas about themes, curriculum, and other books and services.
http://www.carolhurst.com/

C. Kay Vandergrift's Special Interest Page

The special interest page allows visitors to link to many other sites generated by Dr. Vandergrift. Some of the links include Censorship, the Internet and

Intellectual Freedom; Gender and Culture in Picture Books; Young Adult Literature; Linking Literature with Learning; History of Children's Literature; and more.
http://www.scils.rutgers.edu/special/kay/kayhp2a.html

D. Fairrosa Cyber Library of Children's Literature

This site allows visitors to access several other links, including articles about children's literature, book lists, book reviews, information about authors and illustrators, and other children's literature web sites.
http://www.dalton.org/libraries/fairrosa

2. Resource and Reference Material

The following sites focus on resource, reference and bibliographic materials about children's literature.

A. Internet Resources for Children's Literature

This guide is designed to assist visitors in finding electronic resources in various disciplines. It contains useful starters such as AskERIC, Children's Bookwatch, Fairrosa's Cyberlibrary, and Canadian Children's Literature Service Collection Electronic Products. It also provides connections to discussion lists such as KidLit and Childlit; links to newsgroups; and pointers to electronic journals such as Canadian Review of Materials. http://www.unisa.edu.au/library/internet/pathfind/childlit.htm

B. Children's Literature Reference

This electronic bibliography of children's references guides visitors to basic resources in the area of children's literature. Topics include awards and honours; classics; authors and illustrators; genres; teacher resources; suggested web sites; reviews and criticisms; and electronic journals.
http://mahogany.lib.utexas.edu/Libs/PCL/child/

C. Canadian Children's Literature Service: National Library of Canada

On this site, visitors will find information about award-winning Canadian children's literature, Canadian authors and illustrators, and Internet sites that pertain primarily to Canadian children's literature. The site also identifies suitable books for children and young adults in both English and French. Books date from the nineteenth century to the present.
http://www.nlc-bnc.ca/services/eelec.htm

D. SFU Libraries: Children's Literature

This site lists useful children's literature reference books and explicates the research steps for accessing children's literature resources by discussing a number of frequently asked questions on the topic. Some of the other topics on this page include the on-line catalogue, journal articles, reading lists by age and genre, book reviews, and electronic information.
http://www.lib.sfu.ca/kiosk/finlayso/childlit.htm

E. The IPL Youth Division: Reading Zone

The International Public Library site offers the following categories: Ask the Author, Story Hour, and Writing Contest. The World of Reading link contains book recommendations written by children.
http://www.ipl.org/youth/lapage.html

F. The Canadian Children's Book Centre

This organization was formed to promote and encourage reading, writing and illustrating of Canadian children's books. The web site contains information about the CCBC, Our Choice (book

recommendations), reviews, recommended links, and details of a writing contest.
http://www3.sympatico.ca/ccbc/

3. More Links

The following sites are developed specifically to offer links to other sites that provide information on Children's Literature.

A. Children's Literature: Suggested Web Sites Worth Visiting

This site provides links to children's literature under the following categories: Associations and Discussion Lists; Children's Literature Information Sites; Electronic Books and Serials on the Web; Indexes, Abstracts, and Internet Searching Aids; Libraries; and Sites Especially for Kids.
http://www.lib.utexas.edu/Libs/PCL/child/sites.html

B. Around the Net

The creators of this site claim to have identified the best sites that feature information about Canada, Canadian authors and Canadian literature.
http://www.macabees.ab.ca/net.html

The following are some of the recommended sites:

- *The Canadian Children's Book Centre*
- *Children's Literature Web Guide*
- *CCL: Canadian Children's Literature (periodical)*
- *The National Library of Canada: Forthcoming Books*

4. Issues and Topics

The following sites deal with specific issues or special topics in children's literature.

A. A Guide to Children's Literature and Disability

This site is intended to assist parents/guardians, teachers, and other professionals in identifying books that are written about or include characters who have a disability. Books are categorized by age group or grade-level appropriateness. This site also includes a guide to other children's literature selections about particular disabilities.
http://www.kidsource.com/NICHCY/literature.html

B. Multicultural Book Review Homepage

This site allows visitors to link to reviews of multicultural books and to other multicultural web sites.
http://www.isomedia.com/homes/jmele/homepage.html

C. Dealing With Sensitive Issues Using Children's Literature

This site lists books that identify sensitive issues in regards to inclusion, multiculturalism, and gender. It also provides guidelines and resources to refer to when dealing with sensitive issues in children's literature.
http://www.scils.rutgers.edu/special/kay/issues.html

D. Mathematics Is Elementary: Suggested Children's Literature

This site identifies children's books that focus on various mathematical concepts.
http://www.ait.net/groups/mathematics/booklist.htm

E. Traditional Classics in Children's Literature

This site encourages visitors to read or reread books that have achieved classic status in children's literature. Some books are reproduced in full online. Visitors are invited to consider whether these works appeal to today's children or should be retained only as historical artifacts.
http://www.scils.rutgers.edu/special/kay/classics.html

CHILDREN'S LITERATURE REFERENCES

Note: In the following list, numbers at the end of entries indicate page numbers where the work is discussed in the text.

Aardema, V. 1981. *Bringing Rain to Kapiti Plain*. New York: Dial Books. 29

Abdulla, I. 1994. *Tucker*. Norwood, South Australia: Omnibus Books. 127

Adler, D. 1980. *Cam Jansen and the Mystery of the Stolen Diamonds*. New York: Viking Press.

———. 1989. *Cam Jansen and the Mystery of Flight 54*. New York: Viking Kestrel.

———. 1995. *Cam Jansen and the Triceratops Pops Mystery*. New York: Viking.

———. 1996. *Cam Jansen and the Ghostly Mystery*. New York: Viking.

Ahenakew, F. 1988. *How the Birch Tree Got Its Stripes: A Cree Story for Children*. Illustrated by George Littlechild. Saskatoon: Fifth House Publishers. 122

———. 1988. *How the Mouse Got Brown Teeth: A Cree Story for Children.* Illustrated by George Littlechild. Saskatoon: Fifth House Publishers. 122

Ahlberg, A. 1996. *The Better Brown Stories*. London: Viking. 103

Ahlberg, J. and A. 1978. *Each Peach Pear Plum*. London: Kestrel Books. 8

———. 1982. *The Baby's Catalogue*. Harmondsworth, UK: Puffin.

———. 1986. *The Jolly Postman*. London: Heinemann. 10, 12

———. 1993. *It Was a Dark and Stormy Night*. London: Viking. 10

Alborough, J. 1992. *Where's My Teddy?* Cambridge, Massachusetts: Candlewick Press. 30

Alcott, L. 1992 (1867). *Little Women*. Richmond Hill, Ontario: Scholastic Canada. 75

Alderson, S. 1983. *Comet's Tale*. Edmonton: Tree Frog Press.

Alexander, L. 1964. *The Book of Three*. New York: Holt. 100

———. 1977. *The Town Cats, and Other Tales*. New York: Dutton.

Alma, A. 1993. *Skateway to Freedom*. Victoria: Orca Book Publishers. 87

Andrews, J. 1985. *Very Last First Time*. Illustrated by Ian Wallace. Vancouver: Douglas & McIntyre. 1, 114

Anfousse, G. 1989. *Arthur's Dad*. Halifax: Formac Publishing Company Limited. 80

Anno, M. 1977. *Anno's Counting Book*. New York: Crowell. 28

———. 1979. *Anno's Medieval World*. New York: Philomel Books. 140-41

Aqqiarruq, J. 1990. *Poor Old Hungry Polar Bear*. Coppermine, Northwest Territories: Kitikmeot Board of Education. 123

Asch, F. 1993. *Moonbear's Books*. New York: Simon & Schuster. 30

Attema, M. 1996. *A Time to Choose*. Victoria: Orca Book Publishers. 102

Avi. 1981. *Who Stole the Wizard of Oz?* New York: Alfred A. Knopf, Inc. 80

———. 1990. *The True Confessions of Charlotte Doyle*. New York: Orchard Books. 189-90

———. 1995. *Poppy*. New York: Orchard Books. 95

Babbitt, N. 1975. *Tuck Everlasting*. New York: Farrar, Strauss & Giroux. 84, 96

Baker, J. 1987. *Where the Forest Meets the Sea*. New York: Greenwillow Books. 32, 140

Baker, L. 1990. *Life in the Deserts*. Richmond Hill, Ontario. Scholastic. 139

———. 1990. *Life in the Rainforests*. Richmond Hill, Ontario. Scholastic. 139

Bailey, L. 1992. *How Come the Best Clues Are Always in the Garbage?* Toronto: Kids Can Press. 90

Banks, L.R. 1978. *I, Houdini*. New York: Avon Books. 95

———. 1980. *The Indian in the Cupboard*. New York: Avon Books. 95

———. 1986. *Return of the Indian*. New York: HarperCollins Publishers. 95

———. 1989. *The Secret of the Indian*. New York: HarperCollins Publishers. 95

———. 1993. *The Mystery of the Cupboard*. New York: Avon Books. 95

———. 1998. *The Key to the Indian*. New York: Avon Books. 95

——————— and F. Marcellino. 1996. *The Story of Little Babaji*. New York: Michael di Capua Books (HarperCollins). 124

——————— and F. Marcellino. 1996. *The Story of Little Babaji*. New York: Michael di Capua Books (HarperCollins). 124

Barton, B. 1986. *Trucks*. New York: Crowell. 27

———. 1986. *Trains*. New York: Crowell.

Barwin, S. and G. Tick. 1997. *Roller Hockey Blues*. Toronto: James Lorimer and Company.

———. 1998. *Slam Dunk*. Toronto: James Lorimer and Company.

Bauer, M.D. 1986. *On My Honor*. New York: Bantam Doubleday Dell Publishing Group, Inc. 84

Baum, L.F. 1956 (1900). *The Wizard of Oz*. New York: Reilly Publishing. 3

Baylor, B. 1986. *I'm in Charge of Celebrations*. Illustrated by Peter Parnall. New York: Charles Scribner's Sons.

Bear, G. 1991. *Two Little Girls Lost in the Bush: A Cree Story for Children*. Translated by F. Ahenakew. Saskatoon: Fifth House Publishers. 122

Bear, J. 1979. *The Legend of Big Bear, Little Bear and the Stars*. Translated by Ernest Bonaise. Illustrated by Larry Okanee. Saskatoon: Saskatchewan Indian Cultural College. 122

Beatty, O. and J. Geiger. 1992. *Buried in Ice: Unlocking the Secrets of a Doomed Arctic Voyage*. Mississauga: Random House. 17, 135

Bell, H. 1996. *Idjhil*. Nedlands, Western Australia: University of Western Australia Press. 127-28

Bellairs, J. 1978. *The Treasure of Alpheus Winterborn*. New York: Dial Books for Young Readers. 90

———. 1984. *The Dark Secret of Weatherend*. New York: Dial Books for Young Readers.

———. 1989. *The Chessmen of Doom*. New York: Dial Books for Young Readers.

———. 1990. *The Secret of the Underground Room*. New York: Dial Books for Young Readers.

———. 1992. *House with a Clock in Its Walls*. New York: Dial Books for Young Readers.

———. 1995. *The Doom of the Haunted Opera*. New York: Dial Books for Young Readers.

———. 1996. *The Hand of the Necromancer*. New York: Dial Books for Young Readers.

Bennett, J. 1987. *Noisy Poems*. Don Mills: Oxford University Press. 66

———. 1993. *Machine Poems*. Don Mills: Oxford University Press. 66

Berton, P. 1961. *The Secret World of Og*. Toronto: McClelland and Stewart Limited. 97

Bird, G. 1979. *Our Four Seasons*. Saskatoon: Saskatchewan Indian Cultural College.

Bishop, C. 1938. *The Five Chinese Brothers*. New York: Coward, McCann and Geoghegan. 124

Blake, W. 1993. *The Tyger*. Illustrated by Neil Waldman. New York: Harcourt Brace Jovanovich. 68

Blishen, E., comp. 1963. *The Oxford Book of Poetry for Children*. London: Oxford University Press.

Bly, D. 1993. *The McIntyre Liar*. Edmonton: Tree Frog Press. 102

Bogart, J. 1997. *Jeremiah Learns to Read*. Richmond Hill, Ontario: North Winds Press. 36

Bondar, B. and R. Bondar. 1993. *On the Shuttle: Eight Days in Space*. Toronto: Greey de Pencier.

Booth, D. 1989. *'Til All the Stars Have Fallen*. Toronto: Kids Can Press.

———. 1996. *The Dust Bowl*. Illustrated by Karen Reczuch. Toronto: Kids Can Press. 35

Bouchard, D. and R.H. Vickers. 1990. *The Elders Are Watching*. Tofino, BC: Eagle Dancer Enterprises Ltd.

Bossley, M. 1996. *The Perfect Gymnast*. Toronto: James Lorimer and Co., Publishers.

Brandis, M. 1996. *Rebellion: A Novel of Upper Canada*. Erin, California: The Porcupine's Quill. 17, 102

Breedon, S. and B. Wright. 1995. *Growing Up in Kakadu, Australia*. Fortitude Valley, Queensland: Steve Parish Publishing. 127

Brett, J. 1986. *The Twelve Days of Christmas*. New York: Dodd, Mead and Company. 147

———. 1987. *Goldilocks and the Three Bears*. New York: Dodd, Mead and Company.

———. 1989. *Beauty and the Beast*. New York: Clarion. 55

Brewster, H. 1996. *Anastasia's Album*. Toronto: Penguin Books Canada Ltd. 142

Brian, J. 1996. *Pilawuk*. Flinders Park, South Australia: Era Publications. 128

Briggs, R. 1978. *The Snowman*. New York: Random House. 25

Brittain, B. 1983. *The Wish Giver*. New York: Harper & Row Publishers. 96

Brooks, M. 1997. *Bone Dance*. Toronto: Groundwood Books. 102-103

Brouillet, C. 1996. *The Chinese Puzzle*. Charlottetown: Ragweed Press. 91

Brouwer, S. 1996. *Thunderbird Spirit*. Richmond Hill, Ontario: Nelson Word Canada. 88-89

———. 1996. *Winter Hawk Star*. Richmond Hill, Ontario: Nelson Word Canada. 88

Brown, M. 1947. *Goodnight Moon*. New York: Harper & Row. 75

Brown, R. 1981. *A Dark Dark Tale*. New York: Scholastic Inc. 66

———. 1985. *The Big Sneeze*. New York: Mulberry Books. 29

Brown, S. 1978. *Hey, Chicken Man*. Toronto: Scholastic-TAB Publications Ltd. 83

Browne, A. 1979. *Bear Hunt*. London: Hamish Hamilton. 11, 24

———. 1981. *Hansel and Gretel*. London: Julia MacRae Books. 56-57

———. 1983. *Gorilla*. New York: Alfred A. Knopf, Inc. 11

———. 1986. *Piggybook*. New York: Alfred A. Knopf, Inc. 42, 164

———. 1989. *The Tunnel*. London: Julia MacRae Books. 10–11, 38, 39, 155, 156, **1642**

———. 1998. *Voices in the Park*. New York: DK Publishing Inc. 12

Brownridge, W. 1995. *The Moccasin Goalie*. Victoria: Orca Books. 36

———. 1997. *The Final Game*. Victoria: Orca Books.

Buchan, B. 1975. *The Dragon Children*. Richmond Hill, Ontario: Scholastic-TAB Publications. 90, 193-94

Budbill, D. 1976. *Snowshoe Trek to Otter River*. New York: Bantam Skylark Books. 80

Buffie, M. 1987. *Who Is Frances Rain?* Toronto: Kids Can Press Ltd. 99, 173-74

Bunting, E. 1988. *Is Anybody There?* New York: Harper & Row Publishers. 90

———. 1992. *Summer Wheels*. San Diego: Voyager Books.

———. 1994. *Smoky Night*. San Diego: Harcourt Brace and Company. 32

Burningham, J. 1963. *Borka, the Adventures of a Goose with No Feathers*. New York: Random House. 43

———. 1967. *John Burningham's ABC*. New York: Bobbs-Merrill. 27, 43

———. 1970. *Mr Gumpy's Outing*. London: Cape. 29, 43

———. 1977. *Come Away from the Water, Shirley*. New York: Harper. 6, 13, 43

———. 1984. *Granpa*. London: Jonathan Cape Ltd. 9, 10, 12, 14, 32

———. 1996. *Cloudland*. New York: Crown Publishers. 43-44

Byars, B. 1970. *The Summer of the Swans*. New York: Viking. 82, 86

———. 1977. *The Pinballs*. New York: HarperCollins Publishers. 82

———. 1978. *The Cartoonist*. New York: Viking Press. 82

———. 1985. *Cracker Jackson*. New York: Puffin Books. 82

———. 1995. *Tarot Says Beware*. New York: Viking. 90

———. 1996. *Dead Letter*. New York: Viking. 90

———. 1996. *Tornado*. New York: HarperCollins Publishers. 78

———. 1997. *Death's Door*. New York: Viking. 90

Campbell, M., ed. 1985. *Achimoona*. Saskatoon: Fifth House. 120

Cannon, J. 1993. *Stellaluna*. San Diego: Harcourt Brace and Company. 32

Carle, E. 1968. *The Very Hungry Caterpillar*. New York: World Books. 29

———. 1977. *The Grouchy Ladybug*. New York: HarperCollins Pulishers. 29

———. 1984. *The Very Busy Spider*. New York: Philomel Books.

Carney, M. 1997. *At Grandpa's Sugar Bush*. Illustrated by Janet Wilson. Toronto: Kids Can Press. 33

Carroll, L. 1984 (1866). *Alice's Adventures in Wonderland*. New York: Macmillan.

Cassedy, S. 1993. *Zoomrimes*. New York: HarperCollins Publishers. 66

Catling, P.S. 1952. *The Chocolate Touch*. Toronto: Bantam Skylark Books. 78

Chauncy, N. 1960. *Tangara*. London: Oxford University Press. 126-27

Cherry, L. 1990. *The Great Kapok Tree*. New York: The Trumpet Club. 32-33

Choi, S.N. 1991. *Year of Impossible Goodbyes*. New York: Dell Books for Young Readers.

Christopher, M. 1972. *Face-off*. Toronto: Little, Brown and Company (Canada) Ltd.

———. 1973. *Ice Magic*. Toronto: Little, Brown and Company (Canada) Ltd.

———. 1979. *Dirt Bike Racer*. Boston: Little, Brown and Company. 88

———. 1983. *Dirt Bike Runaway*. Toronto: Little, Brown and Company (Canada) Ltd.

———. 1988. *The Hit-Away Kid*. Boston: Little, Brown and Company.

———. 1991. *Skateboard Tough*. Toronto: Little, Brown and Company (Canada) Ltd.

———. 1992. *Return of the Home Run Kid*. Toronto: Little, Brown and Company (Canada) Ltd.

———. 1992. *Undercover Tailback*. Toronto: Little, Brown and Company (Canada) Ltd.

———. 1993. *Man Out at First*. Boston: Little, Brown and Company.

———. 1996. *Shadow Over Second*. Boston: Little, Brown and Company.

———. 1998. *The Catcher's Mark*. Boston: Little, Brown and Company.

Choyce, L. 1997. *Go For It, Carrie*. Illustrated by Mark Thurman. Halifax: Formac Publishing Limited. 80

Ciardi, J. 1989. *The Hopeful Trout and Other Limericks*. New York: Houghton Mifflin.

Cleary, B. 1965. *The Mouse and the Motorcycle*. New York: Avon Books. 95

———. 1970. *Runaway Ralph*. New York: Avon Books. 95

———. 1982. *Ralph S. Mouse*. New York: Morrow. 95

Clutesi, G. 1990. *Stand Tall, My Son*. Victoria: Newport Bay Publications.

Coerr, E. 1993. *Sadako*. Illustrated by E. Young. New York: Putnam. 41

Coldwell, M. 1995. *Fast Break*. Toronto: James Lorimer and Co., Publishers.

Cole, J. 1994. *The Magic School Bus in the Time of the Dinosaurs*. Illustrated by Bruce Degan. New York: Scholastic. 145

Conly, J. 1986. *Rasco and the Rats of NIMH*. New York: Harper & Row, Publishers. 100

———. 1990. *R. T., Margaret, and the Rats of NIMH*. New York: HarperCollins Publishers. 100

———. 1993. *Crazy Lady!* New York: HarperCollins Publishers. 86

Cooney, B. 1982. *Miss Rumphius*. New York: Viking Penguin Inc. 31

Cooper, J. 1993. *Someone Smaller Than Me*. Translated by Charlie Lucassie. Illustrated by Annie Padlo. Iqaluit, NWT: Baffin Regional Board of Education. 123

Cooper, S. 1965. *Over Sea, Under Stone*. New York: Harcourt. 100

———.1973. *The Dark Is Rising*. New York: Collier Macmillan Company. 100

Crampton, G. 1955. *Scuffy the Tugboat and His Adventures Down the River*. New York: Golden Press.

Creech, S. 1994. *Walk Two Moons*. New York: HarperCollins Publishers. 84

Crew, G. 1991. *Strange Objects*. Melbourne, Australia: Mammoth Australia. 11-12

Crews, D. 1978. *Freight Train*. New York: Greenwillow Books.

———. 1980. *Truck*. New York: Greenwillow Books.

Crook, M. 1995. *Summer of Madness*. Victoria: Orca Book Publishers. 103

———. 1996. *Riding Scared*. Toronto: James Lorimer and Co., Publishers.

Croteau, M.D. 1994. *Fred's Dream Cat*. Halifax: Formac Publishing Company Limited. 80

Cullinan, B., ed. 1996. *A Jar of Tiny Stars*. Honesdale, Pennsylvania: Boyds Mill Press.

Cumming, P. 1993. *Out on the Ice in the Middle of the Bay*. Toronto: Annick Press. 35

Curtis, C. 1995. *The Watsons Go to Birmingham — 1963*. New York: Delacorte. 87

Cushman, D. 1993. *The ABC Mystery*. New York: HarperCollins Publishers. 28

Cushman, K. 1994. *Catherine, Called Birdy*. New York: Clarion.

———. 1995. *The Midwife's Apprentice*. New York: HarperCollins Publishers.

Dahl, R. 1961. *James and the Giant Peach*. New York: Puffin Books. 95

———. 1964. *Charlie and the Chocolate Factory*. New York: Bantam Books.95-96

———. 1970. *Fantastic Mr. Fox*. New York: Alfred A. Knopf, Inc. 78

———. 1972. *Charlie and the Great Glass Elevator*. New York: Puffin Books. 96

———. 1982. *Revolting Rhymes*. London: Jonathan Cape.

———. 1982. *The BFG*. New York: Puffin Books. 96

———. 1983. *The Witches*. New York: Farrar, Straus & Giroux.

———. 1988. *Matilda*. New York: Puffin Books. 96

Davidge, B. and I. Wallace. 1993. *The Mummer's Song*. Toronto: Groundwood Books.

Day, A. 1985. *Good Dog, Carl*. New York: Simon & Schuster. 26

———. 1992. *Carl Goes Shopping*. New York: Farrar, Straus & Giroux.

———. 1995. *Carl Goes to Daycare*. New York: Farrar, Straus & Giroux.

———. 1997. *Carl's Birthday*. New York: Farrar, Straus & Giroux.

Demi. 1993. *Demi's Secret Garden*. New York: Henry Holt and Co. Inc.

dePaola, T. 1980. *The Knight and the Dragon*. New York: G.P. Putnam's Sons. 30

Domanska, J. 1985. *Busy Monday Morning*. New York: Greenwillow Books. 29

Dorris, M. 1992. *Morning Girl*. New York: Hyperion Books for Children. 126

Downie, D. and B. Robertson, comps. 1987. *The New Wind Has Wings: Poems from Canada*. New York: Oxford.

Doyle, B. 1982. *Up to Low*. Toronto: Groundwood Books/Douglas & McIntyre Limited. 102

———. 1984. *Angel Square*. Toronto: Groundwood Books/Douglas & McIntyre Limited.

———. 1994. *Uncle Ronald*. Toronto: Groundwood Books/Douglas & McIntyre Limited. 103

Dueck, A. 1996. *Anywhere But Here*. Red Deer, Alberta: Red Deer College Press. 91

Duke, K. 1992. *Aunt Isabel Tells a Good One*. New York: Penguin Books. 12-13

Dunn, S. 1994. *Gimme a Break, Rattlesnake! Schoolyard Chants and Other Nonsense*. Don Mills: Stoddart Publishing.

Dunph Dunphy, M. 1993. *Here Is the Arctic Winter*. New York: Hyperion Books for Children. 32

———. 1994. *Here Is the Tropical Rain Forest*. New York: Hyperion Books for Children. 32

Eckert, A. 1971. *Incident at Hawk's Hill*. New York: Bantam Books. 91

———. 1998. *Return to Hawk's Hill*. New York: Little, Brown and Company. 91

Edmunds, Y. 1993. *Yuit*. Toronto: Napoleon Publishing. 91

Edwards, P. 1996. *Some Smug Slug*. New York: HarperCollins. 65

Ellis, S. 1997. *Back of Beyond*. Toronto: Groundwood. 102

Elwin, R. and M. Paulse. 1990. *Asha's Mums*. Toronto: Women's Press. 21, 141

Emberley, B. 1967. *Drummer Hoff*. New York: Prentice-Hall. 29

Everts, T. and B. Kalman. 1995. *Horses*. Niagara-on-the-Lake, Ontario: Crabtree Publishing. 146

Eyvindson, P. 1996. *Red Parka Mary*. Winnipeg: Pemmican Publications Inc. 117

Fairbridge, L. 1995. *Stormbound*. Toronto: Doubleday Canada. 102

Farmer, N. 1994. *The Ear, the Eye and the Arm*. New York: Puffin Books.

Farris, K. 1996. *You Asked?* Toronto: Greey de Pencier Books. 144-45

Ferguson, D. 1997. *Kid Carmel Private Investigator*. East Orange, South Africa: Just Books, Inc.

Field, E. 1982. *Wynken, Blynken and Nod*. Illustrated by Susan Jeffers. New York: E. P. Dutton.

Filipovic, Z. 1994. *Zlata's Diary: A Child's Life in Sarajevo*. New York: Penguin. 87

Fisher, L.E. 1987. *Look Around! A Book About Shapes!* New York: Viking.

Fitch, S. 1987. *Toes in My Nose and Other Poems*. Illustrated by Molly Lamb. Toronto: Doubleday. 70

———. 1989. *Sleeping Dragons All Around*. Illustrated by Michelle Nidenoff. Toronto: Doubleday.

———. 1992. *There Were Monkeys in my Kitchen!* Illustrated by Marc Mongeau. Toronto: Doubleday.

———. 1995. *Mable Murple*. Illustrated by Maryann Kovalski. Toronto: Doubleday.

———. 1997. *If You Could Wear My Sneakers!* Illustrated by Darcia Labrosse. Toronto: Doubleday. 70

———. *There's a Mouse in My House*. Illustrated by Leslie Watts. Toronto: Doubleday.

Fleischman, S. 1985. *I Am Phoenix: Poems for Two Voices*. New York: Harper & Row.

———.1986. *The Whipping Boy*. Mahwah, New Jersey: Troll Associates. 78

———.1988. *Joyful Noise: Poems for Two Voices*. New York: Harper & Row.

Fleming, D. 1991. *In the Tall, Tall Grass*. New York: Henry Holt and Company, Inc. 30

Florian, D. 1994. *Beast Feast*. New York: Harcourt Brace.

———. 1996. *On the Wing*. New York: Harcourt Brace.

———. 1997. *In the Swim*. New York: Harcourt Brace.

Fowler, S.G. 1989. *When Summer Ends*. New York: Greenwillow Books.

Fox, M. 1983. *Possum Magic*. Adelaide, Australia: Omnibus Books. 143

Fox, P. 1973. *The Slave Dancer.* New York: Bradbury. 93

Freedman, R. 1987. *Lincoln: A Photobiography*. New York: Clarion Books.

Freeman, B. 1998. *Prairie Fire!* Toronto: James Lorimer and Company Ltd., Publishers. 94

Froman, R. 1971. *Street Poems*. New York: McCall. 67

———.1974. *Seeing Things: A Book of Poems*. New York: Thomas Y. Crowell. 67

Frost, R. 1978. *Stopping by Woods on a Snowy Evening*. Illustrated by Susan Jeffers. New York: Dutton Books.

———. 1988. *Birches*. Illustrated by E. Young. New York: Henry Holt and Company.

Galdone, P. 1974. *Little Red Riding Hood*. New York: McGraw Hill. 55

Galloway, P. 1995. *Aleta and the Queen: A Tale of Ancient Greece*. Toronto: Annick Press.

———. 1995. *Atlanta: The Fastest Runner in the World.* Toronto: Annick Press.

———. 1997. *Daedalus and the Minotaur.* Toronto: Annick Press. 59-60

———. 1999. *My Hero Hercules*. Toronto: Annick Press.

Gardiner, J. 1980. *Stone Fox*. New York: The Trumpet Club. 78

Garner, A. 1967. *The Owl Service*. London: William Collins and Sons. 10, 94

Garrigue, S. 1985. *The Eternal Spring of Mr. Ito*. New York: Bradbury Press. 119

Gavin, J. 1995. *Grandpa's Indian Summer*. London: Methuen Children's Books Ltd.

George, J.C. 1959. *My Side of the Mountain*. New York: Dutton. 85

———. 1972. *Julie of the Wolves*. New York: Harper & Row, Publishers.

———. 1990. *On the Far Side of the Mountain*. New York: Puffin Books. 85

———. 1994. *Julie*. New York: HarperCollins.

Gillham, B. and S. Hulme. 1984. *Let's Look for Shapes*. New York: Coward.

Gilman, P. 1984. *The Balloon Tree.* Toronto: Scholastic.

———. 1985. *Jillian Jiggs.* Richmond Hill, Ontario: Scholastic-TAB.

———. 1988. *The Wonderful Pigs of Jillian Jiggs*. Markham, Ontario: Scholastic Canada Ltd.

———. 1992. *Something From Nothing*. Richmond Hill, Ontario: North Winds Press. 37

———. 1994. *Jillian Jiggs to the Rescue*. Markham, Ontario: Scholastic Canada Ltd.

———. 1998. *Pirate Pearl*. Richmond Hill, Ontario: Scholastic.

Gilmore, R. 1995. *A Friend Like Zilla*. Toronto: Second Story Press. 87

Gipson, F. 1965. *Old Yeller.* New York: Harper & Row. 185

Goble, P. 1978. *The Girl Who Loved Wild Horses*. New York: Bradbury Press. 113

Godfrey, M. 1982. *The Vandarian Indcident*. Richmond Hill, Ontario: Scholastic Canada Ltd. 92

———. 1984. *Here She Is, Ms Teeny-Wonderful.* Richmond Hill, Ontario: Scholastic-TAB Publications, Ltd. 92

———. 1987. *It Isn't Easy Being Ms Teeny-Wonderful.* Richmond Hill, Ontario: Scholastic Canada Ltd. 92

———. 1987. *It Seemed Like a Good Idea at the Time.* Edmonton: Tree Frog Press. 92

———. 1988. *Send in Ms Teeny-Wonderful*. Richmond Hill, Ontario: Scholastic Canada Ltd. 92

———. 1988. *Mystery in the Frozen Lands*. Toronto: James Lorimer and Co., Publishers. 92

———. 1990. *Can You Teach Me to Pick My Nose?* New York: Avon Books. 92

———. 1990. *I Spent My Summer Vacation Kidnapped into Space*. New York: Scholastic Inc. 102

———. 1991. *The Day the Sky Exploded.* (Revised edition of *The Vandarian Incident.*) Richmond Hill, Ontario: Scholastic Canada Ltd. 92

———. 1992. *Wally Stutzgummer, Super Bad Dude.* Richmond Hill, Ontario: Scholastic Canada Ltd. 92

———. 1992. *The Great Science Fair Disaster.* Richmond Hill, Ontario: Scholastic Canada Ltd.

———. 1993. *Meet You in the Sewer*. Richmond Hill, Ontario: Scholastic Canada Ltd.

——————— and F. O'Keeffe. 1991. *There's a Cow in My Swimming Pool*. Richmond Hill, Ontario: Scholastic Canada Ltd.

Godkin, C. 1989. *Wolf Island*. Markham, Ontario: Fitzhenry and Whiteside. 137

———. 1995. *Ladybug Garden*. Markham, Ontario: Fitzhenry and Whiteside. 137

———. 1997. *Sea Otter Inlet*. Markham, Ontario: Fitzhenry and Whiteside.

Goffin, J. 1992. *Who Is the Boss?* New York: Clarion Boooks. 31

Goldsmith, O. 1765. *The History of Little Goody Two Shoes*. London: John Newberry. 76

Gould, A. and P. Hancock. 1993. *Ghosts and Other Scary Stories*. Richmond Hill, Ontario: Scholastic Canada.

Graham, J.B. 1994. *Splish Splash*. Boston: Houghton Mifflin/Ticknor and Fields. 67

Graham, G. 1998. *The Strongest Man This Side of Cremona*. Red Deer, Alberta: Red Deer College Press. 34

Granfield, L. 1988. *All About Niagara Falls*. Toronto: Kids Can Press. 138

———. 1993. *Cowboy: A Kid's Album*. Toronto: Groundwood Books. 138, 145

———. 1995. *In Flanders Fields: The Story of the Poem by John McCrae.* Illustrated by Janet Wilson. Toronto: Lester Publishing. 68, 138

———. 1997. *Amazing Grace : The Story of the Hymn*. Toronto: Tundra Books. 138

———. 1997. *Silent Night*. Toronto: Tundra Books. 138, 146

———. 1999. *High Flight: A Story of World War II.* Toronto: Tundra Books. 138

Greene, B. 1973. *Summer of My German Soldier*. New York: Bantam Doubleday Dell Publishing Group, Inc. 103

———. 1974. *Philip Hall Likes Me. I Reckon Maybe*. New York: Bantam Doubleday Dell Publishing Group, Inc. 83

Greenwood, B. 1994. *A Pioneer Story*. Illustrated by Heather Collins. Toronto: Kids Can Press. 145

Greer, G. and B. Ruddick. 1983. *Max and Me and the Time Machine*. New York: Harper & Row, Publishers. 99

Grillone, L. and J. Gennaro. 1978. *Small Worlds Close Up*. New York: Crown Publishers. 143

Gryski, C. 1995. *Let's Play*. Toronto: Kids Can Press. 143

Halvorson, M. 1984. *Cowboys Don't Cry.* New York: Dell Publishing.

———. 1985. *Let It Go*. Toronto: General Paperbacks.

———. 1987. *Nobody Said It Would Be Easy*. Toronto: Stoddart Publishing.

———. 1988. *Dare*. Toronto: General Paperbacks.

———. 1989. *Bull Rider*. Richmond Hill, Ontario: Collier Macmillan Canada Inc.

———. 1992. *Stranger on the Run*. Toronto: Stoddart Publishing.

———. 1993. *But Cows Don't Fly (and Other Stories).* Toronto: Stoddart Publishing.

———. 1994. *Cowboys Don't Quit.* Toronto: Stoddart Publishing.

———. 1997. *Stranger on the Line*. Toronto: Stoddart Publishing.

Hamilton, V. 1993. *Cousins*. New York: Scholastic.

Hancock, P. 1995. *Strange and Eerie Stories*. Richmond Hill, Ontario: Scholastic Canada.

Hansen, K. and C. Maggs. 1981. *Salik and His Father*. St. John's: Breakwater Books. 123

Hansen, K. and S. Hill. 1983. *Salig og hans far*. St. John's: Breakwater Books.

Harrison, T. 1982. *A Northern Alphabet*. Montreal: Tundra Books. 27

———. 1992. *O Canada*. Toronto: Kids Can Press. 146-47

Harty, N. 1997. *Hold On, McGinty!* Illustrated by Don Kilby. Toronto: Doubleday Canada Limited. 35

Haworth-Attard, B. 1995. *Dark of the Moon*. Montreal, Quebec: Roussan Publishers, Inc. 98

Hazen, B.S. 1997. *Digby*. New York: Harper Trophy.

Heide, F.P. and J.H. Heide 1992. *Sami and the Time of the Troubles*. New York: Clarion Books.

Heller, R. 1987. *A Cache of Jewels and Other Collective Nouns*. New York: Grosset & Dunlap.

———. 1988. *Kites Sail High: A Book About Verbs*. New York: Grosset & Dunlap.

———. 1989. *Many Luscious Lollipops: A Book About Adjectives*. New York: Grosset & Dunlap.

———. 1990. *Merry-go-round. A Book About Nouns*. New York: Grosset & Dunlap.

———. 1991. *Up, Up and Away: A Book About Adverbs*. New York: Grosset & Dunlap.

———. 1995. *Behind the Mask: A Book About Prepositions*. New York: Grosset & Dunlap.

Hepworth, C. 1992. **Ant**ics! An Alphabetical **Ant**hology. New York: G.P. Putnam's Sons. 28

Hesse, K. 1992. *Letters from Rifka*. New York: Puffin Books. 87

Hickman, P. 1995. *The Kids' Canadian Tree Book*. Toronto: Kids Can Press. 146

———. 1996. *The Jumbo Book of Nature Science*. Toronto: Kids Can Press.

Hill, A. 1994. *The Burnt Stick*. Illustrated by Mark Sofilas. Ringwood, Australia: Puffin Books. 128

Hoban, T. 1974. *Circles, Triangles and Squares*. New York: Macmillan.

———. 1986. *Shapes, Shapes, Shapes*. New York: Greenwillow Press.

Hoffman, M. 1988. *My Grandma Has Black Hair*. New York: Dial Books For Young Readers.

———. 1991. *Amazing Grace*. Illustrated by Caroline Binch. New York: Dial Books For Young Readers. 126

Holm, A. 1963. *I Am David*. London: Methuen Children's Books Ltd. 180, 185

Holtzwarth, W. 1996. *The Story of the Little Mole Who Knew It Was None of His Business*. Vancouver: Raincoast Books. 141

Hope, L.L. 1904. *The Bobbsey Twins*. New York: Grosset & Dunlap. 76

Hopkins, L.B. 1987. *Click, Rumble, Roar: Poems About Machines*. New York: Thomas Y. Crowell. 66

Howe, D. and J. Howe. 1979. *Bunnicula*. New York: Avon Books. 95

Howe, J. 1981. *The Hospital Book*. New York: Crown Publishers. 143

———. 1982. *Howliday Inn*. New York: Avon Books. 95

———. 1983. *The Celery Stalks at Midnight*. New York: Avon Books. 95

———. 1987. *Nighty-nightmare*. New York: Avon Books. 95

———. 1992. *Return to Howliday Inn*. New York: Avon Books. 95

Hughes, M. 1974. *Gold Fever Trail*. Edmonton: LeBel Enterprises. 101

———. 1975. *Crisis on Conshelf Ten*. Vancouver: Copp Clark Publishing. 101

———. 1978. *The Ghost Dance Caper*. London: Hamish Hamilton Children's Books Ltd. 101

———. 1980. *The Keeper of the Isis Light*. London: Mammoth.

———. 1982. *Hunter in the Dark*. Toronto: Clarke, Irwin. 113

———. 1983. *My Name Is Paula Popowich!* Toronto: James Lorimer and Co., Publishers. 83

———. 1992. *The Crystal Drop*. Toronto: HarperCollins.

———. 1994. *The Golden Aquarians*. Toronto: HarperCollins.

———. 1995. *Castle Tourmandyne*. Toronto: HarperCollins. 95

———. 1995. *Where Have You Been, Billy Boy?* Toronto: HarperCollins. 99

———. 1996. *The Seven Magpies*. Toronto: HarperCollins. 101

———. 1998. *The Faces of Fear*. Toronto: HarperCollins.

———. 1998. *The Story Box*. Toronto: HarperCollins. 101

———. 1998.*What If...? Amazing Stories*. Montreal: Tundra Books.101

Hughes, S. 1985. *When We Went to the Park*. New York: Lothrop, Lee and Shepard Books. 28

———. 1989. *All Shapes and Sizes*. New York: Lothrop.

———. 1990. *The Big Concrete Lorry*. New York: Lothrop.

Hughes, T. 1968. *The Iron Man*. London: Faber and Faber. 194-95

Hume, S. 1997. *Rainbow Bay*. Illustrated by Pascal Milelli. Vancouver: Raincoast Books. 33-34

Hunt, J. 1989. *Illuminations*. New York: Aladdin Books. 28

Hutchins, H. 1995. *Tess*. Illustrated by Ruth Ohi. Willowdale, Ontario: Firefly Books. 35

Hutchins, P. 1969. *Rosie's Walk*. London: Bodley Head Press. 9

———. 1982. *1 Hunter*. New York: Greenwillow. 28

Hyman, T.S. 1983. *Little Red Riding Hood.* New York: Holiday House. 55-56

Inglehart, P. 1979. *Child of Two Worlds*. Saskatoon: Saskatchewan Indian Cultural College.

Innocenti, R. 1985. *Rose Blanche*. Mankato, Minnesota: Creative Education. 9, 39

Ioannov, G. and L. Missen, editors. 1995. *Shivers*. Toronto: Stoddart Publishing. 97

Ittusardjuat, M. 1990. *Rocks Can Have Babies*. Coppermine, NWT: Kitikmeot Board of Education. 123

Jackson, K.J. 1997. *I Know an Old Lady Who Swallowed a Pie*. New York: E.P. Dutton. 29

Jacques, B. 1987. *Redwall*. New York: Philomel. 95

Jam, T. 1997. *The Fishing Summer*. Illustrated by Ange Zhang. Toronto: Groundwood Books/Douglas & McIntyre. 33

Johnson, A. and E. Johnson. 1964. *The Grizzly*. New York: Harper & Row Publishers, Inc. 82

Joosse, B. 1991. *Pieces of the Picture*. New York: HarperCollins. 182-83

Juster, N. 1989. *As: A Surfeit of Similes*. New York: William Morrow.

Kalan, R. 1981. *Jump, Frog, Jump!* New York: Greenwillow Books. 29

Kalman, B. 1994. *Butterflies and Moths*. Niagara-on-the-Lake, Ontario: Crabtree Publishing. 139

———. 1995. *A...B...Sea*. Niagara-on-the-Lake, Ontario: Crabtree Publishing. 28

———. 1997. *How a Plant Grows*. Niagara-on-the-Lake, Ontario: Crabtree Publishing. 139

———. 1997. *Web Weavers and Other Spiders*. Niagara-on-the-Lake, Ontario: Crabtree Publishing. 139

———. 1998. *What Is a Mammal?* Niagara-on-the-Lake, Ontario: Crabtree Publishing.

———. 1999. *What Is a Bird?* Niagara-on-the-Lake, Ontario: Crabtree Publishing.

——— and P. Gentile. 1994. *Dirt Movers*. Niagara-on-the-Lake, Ontario: Crabtree Publishing. 137

Kandoian, E. 1989. *Is Anybody Up*? New York: Putnam.

Kaner, E. 1995. *Towers and Tunnels*. Toronto: Kids Can Press. 144

Katz, W. 1996. *Out of the Dark*. Toronto: Groundwood Books.

Kellogg, S. 1997. *The Three Little Pigs*. New York: William Morrow and Company, Inc.

Keens-Douglas, R. 1992. *The Nutmeg Princess*. Illustrated by Anna Galouchko. Toronto: Annick Press.125-26

Kenna, K. 1995. *A People Apart*. Toronto: Somerville House Publishing. 143

Kertes, J. 1995. *The Gift*. Toronto: Groundwood Books. 87

Kightley, R. 1986. *Shapes*. New York: Little, Brown and Company.

Kindersley, B. and A. 1996. *Children Just Like Me*. London: Dorling Kindersley in association with UNICEF.

King, E. and J. Wheeler. 1991. *Adventure on Thunder Island*. Toronto: James Lorimer and Co., Publishers. 120

King, T. 1992. *A Coyote Columbus Story*. Toronto: Groundwood Books.

———. 1998. *Coyote Sings to the Moon*. Toronto: Groundwood Books.

Kjelgaard, J. 1945. *Big Red*. New York: Bantam Skylark Books. 91

———. 1951. *Irish Red*. New York: Bantam Skylark Books.91

———. 1953. *Outlaw Red*. New York: Bantam Skylark Books. 91

Knowlton, J. 1988. *Geography from A to Z: A Picture Glossary*. New York: HarperCollins. 28

Kodama, T. 1995. *Shin's Tricycle*. New York: Walker Publishing Company, Inc. 41

Korman, G. 1978. *This Can't Be Happening at Macdonald Hall!* New York: Scholastic Inc. 91, 211

———. 1979. *Go Jump in the Pool!* Richmond Hill, Ontario: Scholastic-TAB Publications, Ltd. 92

———. 1980. *Beware the Fish!* New York: Scholastic Inc. 92

———. 1982. *The War with Mr. Wizzle*. New York: Scholastic Inc. 92

———. 1988. *The Zucchini Warriors*. New York: Scholastic Inc.

———. 1991. *Macdonald Hall Goes Hollywood*. New York: Scholastic Inc.

———. 1995. *Something Fishy at Macdonald Hall*. New York: Scholastic Inc.

Krahn, F. 1970. *How Santa Claus Had a Long and Difficult Journey Delivering His Presents*. New York: Delacourte Press/Seymour Lawrence. 26

———. 1975. *Who's Seen the Scissors?* New York: E.P. Dutton.

———. 1977. *The Mystery of the Giant Footprints*. New York: E.P. Dutton.

———. 1978. *Catch That Cat!* New York: E.P. Dutton.

———. 1981. *Arthur's Adventure in the Abandoned House*. New York: E.P. Dutton.

———. 1981. *Here Comes Alex Pumpernickel!* New York: Little, Brown and Company.

———. 1983. *The Secret in the Dungeon*. New York: Clarion Books.

———. 1985. *Amanda and the Mysterious Carpet*. New York: Clarion Books.

Kramer, S. 1995. *Theodoric's Rainbow*. Illustrated by Daniel Mark Duffy. New York: W. H. Freeman and Co. 140

Kuskin, K. 1980. *Dogs and Dragons, Trees and Dreams*. New York: Harper & Row.

Kusugak, M. 1990. *Baseball Bats for Christmas*. Toronto: Annick Press. 120

———. 1992. *Hide and Sneak*. Illustrated by Vladyana Krykorka. Toronto: Annick Press. 120

———. 1993. *Northern Lights: The Soccer Trails*. Illustrated by Vladyana Krykorka. Toronto: Annick Press. 120, 121, 126

———. 1996. *My Arctic 1, 2,3*. Toronto: Annick Press. 121

———. 1998. *Arctic Stories*. Toronto: Annick Press.

L'Engle, M. 1962. *A Wrinkle in Time*. New York: Farrar, Strauss & Giroux. 100

———. 1973. *A Wind in the Door*. New York: Bantam Doubleday Dell Publishing Group, Inc. 100-101

———. 1978. *A Swiftly Tilting Planet*. New York: Farrar, Strauss & Giroux. 100-101

La Loche Library Board. 1984. *Byron and His Balloon: An English-Chipewyan Counting Book*. Edmonton: Tree Frog Press. 122-23

———. 1990. *Byron Through the Seasons*. Saskatoon: Fifth House Publishers. 122

Lager-Haskell, D. 1990. *Maxine's Tree*. Victoria: Orca Books. 21

Langstaff, J. 1974. *Oh, A Hunting We Will Go*. New York: Athenium. 147

Lauber, P. 1982. *Journey to the Planets*. New York: Crown Publishers. 143

———. 1986. *Volcano: The Eruption and Healing of Mount St. Helens*. New York: Bradbury Press.

Laurence, M. 1979. *The Olden Days Coat*. Illustrated by Muriel Wood. Toronto: McClelland & Stewart. 98

Lawson, J. 1992. *The Dragon's Pearl*. Toronto: Stoddart. 58-59

———. 1997. *Emma and the Silk Train*. Illustrated by Paul Mombourquette. Toronto: Kids Can Press. 35-36

Le Guin, U. 1968. *A Wizard of Earthsea*. New York: Parnassus. 100

———. 1988. *Catwings*. New York: Scholastic Inc. 78

———. 1989. *Catwings Returns*. New York: Scholastic Inc. 78

———. 1994. *Wonderful Alexander and the Catwings*. New York: Scholastic Inc. 78

———. 1999. *Jane on Her Own: A Catwings Tale*. New York: Orchard. 78

Lear, E. 1946 (1846). *The Complete Nonsense Book*. New York: Dodd, Mead. 67

———. 1991. *The Owl and the Pussy Cat*. Illustrated by Jan Brett. New York: Putnam's.

———. 1994. *There Was an Old Man...A Collection of Limericks*. Toronto: Kids Can Press.

Lee, D. 1974. *Alligator Pie*. Toronto: Macmillan Canada.

———. 1974. *Nicholas Knock and Other People*. Toronto: Macmillan Canada.

———. 1977. *Garbage Delight*. Toronto: Macmillan of Canada.

———. 1984. *Lizzie's Lion*. Toronto: Stoddart.

———. 1983. *Jelly Belly*. Toronto: Macmillan.

———. 1991. *The Ice Cream Store*. Toronto: HarperCollins.

Lesser, C. 1997. *Storm on the Desert*. Illustrated by Ted Rand. New York: Harcourt Brace. 68

Lester, J. 1996. *Sam and the Tigers: A New Retelling of Little Black Sambo*. Illustrated by Jerry Pinkney. New York: Dial Books for Young Readers. 124

Levy, E. 1980. *Something Queer on Vacation*. New York: Dell Publishing Co., Inc.

———. 1989. *Something Queer at the Birthday Party*. New York: Delacorte Press.

———. 1993. *Something Queer in Outer Space*. New York: Hyperion Books for Children.

———. 1997. *Something Queer at the Library*. New York: Delacorte Press.

———. 1997. *Something Queer in the Wild West*. New York: Hyperion Books for Children.

Lewis, C.S. 1950. *The Lion, the Witch and the Wardrobe*. New York: Macmillan. 100

Lewis, J.P. 1990. *A Hippopotamustn't*. New York: Dial Books for Young Readers. 67

Lightburn, S. 1998. *Driftwood Cove*. Illustrated by Ron Lightburn. Toronto: Doubleday Canada Ltd. 35

Linden, A.M. 1992. *One Smiling Grandma: A Caribbean Counting Book*. Illustrated by Lynne. Russell. London: William Heinemann Ltd.

Lisle, J.T. 1987. *The Great Dimpole Oak*. New York: Orchard Books.

———. 1989. *Afternoon of the Elves*. New York: Orchard Books.

Little, J. 1962. *Mine for Keeps*. Toronto: Little, Brown and Company (Canada) Ltd. 87

———. 1972. *From Anna*. New York: HarperCollins Publishers. 87

———. 1984. *Mama's Going to Buy You a Mockingbird*. New York: Viking Kestrel. 84

———. 1985. *Lost and Found*. Toronto: Penguin Books Canada Limited. 78

———. 1986. *Different Dragons*. Toronto: Penguin Books Canada Limited. 83

———. 1989. *Hey World, Here I Am!* Toronto: HarperCollins. 103

———. 1991. *Once Upon a Golden Apple*. Markham, Ontario: Viking. 155

Littlechild, G. 1993. *This Land Is My Land*. Emeryville, California: Children's Book Press. 121, 142

Livingston, M., comp.. 1991. *Lots of Limericks*. New York: Viking Kestrel.

Lobel, A. 1970. *Frog and Toad Are Friends*. New York: Harper & Row Publishers.

———. 1972. *Frog and Toad Together*. New York: Harper & Row Publishers.

———. 1976. *Frog and Toad All Year*. New York: Harper & Row Publishers.

———. 1979. *Days with Frog and Toad*. New York: Harper & Row Publishers.

———. 1983. *The Book of Pigericks*. New York: Harper & Row.

Loewen, I. 1993. *My Kokum Called Today*. Winnipeg: Pemmican Publications Inc.

London, J. 1995. *The Sugaring-off Party*. Illustrated by Gilles Pelletier. Toronto: Lester Publishing Limited. 33

Longfellow, H.W. 1990. *Paul Revere's Ride*. Illustrated by Ted Rand. New York: Dutton.

Lottridge, C. 1989. *The Name of the Tree*. Toronto: Groundwood Books. 44

———. 1992. *Ticket to Curlew*. Toronto: Groundwood Books. 94

———. 1997. *Wings to Fly*. Toronto: Groundwood Books. 94

Lowry, L. 1989. *Number the Stars*. New York: Houghton Mifflin. 87

———. 1993. *The Giver*. Boston: Houghton. 102

Luenn, N. 1994. *Squish! A Wetland Walk*. New York: Atheneum Books for Young Readers. 33

Lunn, J. 1979. *The Twelve Dancing Princesses: A Fairy Story*. Illustrated by Lazslo Gal. Toronto: Methuen.

———. 1997. *The Hollow Tree*. Toronto: Alfred A. Knopf Canada. 93

———, comp. 1994. *The Unseen*. Toronto: Lester Publishing. 97

——————— and C. Moore. 1992. *The Story of Canada*. Illustrated by Alan Daniel. Toronto: Lester Publishing.

Macaulay, D. 1973. *Cathedral: The Story of Its Construction*. Boston: Houghton Mifflin. 44

———. 1979. *Motel of the Mysteries*. Boston: Houghton Mifflin. 44

———. 1988. *The Way Things Work*. Boston: Houghton Mifflin. 44

———. 1990. *Black and White*. New York: Houghton Mifflin. 11, 13, 31, 38-39, 44

———. 1995. *Shortcut*. Boston: Houghton Mifflin Company. 12, 44

MacDonald, L. 1994. *The Killer Whale and the Walrus*. Translated by Amelia Angilirq. Iqaluit, NWT: Baffin Divisional Board of Education. 123

MacDonald, S. 1994. *Sea Shapes*. New York: Gulliver. 26

MacGregor, R. 1995. *Mystery at Lake Placid*. Toronto: McClelland & Stewart Inc. 88

———. 1995. *The Night They Stole the Stanley Cup*. Toronto: McClelland & Stewart Inc. 88-89

Mackay, C. 1987. *Exit Barney McGee*. Richmond Hill, Ontario: Scholastic-TAB Publications, Ltd. 82

MacLachlan, P. 1985. *Sarah, Plain and Tall*. New York: Harper & Row. 218

Mahy, M. 1990. *The Seven Chinese Brothers*. New York: Scholastic. 124

Maillet, A. 1945. *Ristonac*. Montreal: Editions Lucien Parizeau.

Manning, M. and B. Granstrom. 1997. *What's Under the Bed?* London: Wonderwise, Watts.

Mark, J. 1981. *Nothing To Be Afraid Of*. New York: Harper & Row Publishers.13, 103

Markoosie. 1970. *Harpoon of the Hunter*. Montreal: McGill-Queen's University Press. 120

Marsden, J. 1991. *Letters from the Inside*. Sydney, Australia: Pan Macmillan Publishers Australia. 11

Martin, A. 1997. *Kristy and the Mystery Train*. New York: Scholastic Inc. 90

Maruki, T. 1980. *Hiroshima No Pika*. New York: Lothrop, Lee and Shepard Books. 41

Mastin, C. 1994. *Canadian Birds*. Kamloops, BC: Grasshopper Books. 137

———. 1994. *Canadian Wild Animals*. Kamloops, BC: Grasshopper Books. 136

Mayer, M. 1989. *The Twleve Dancing Princesses*. Illustrated by Kinuko Craft. New York: Morrow.

———. 1969. *Frog, Where Are You?* New York: Dial Books for Young Readers. 25

———. 1973. *Frog on His Own*. New York: Dial Books for Young Readers. 25

———. 1974. *Frog Goes to Dinner*. New York: Dial Books for Young Readers. 25

Mayer, M. and M. Mayer. 1975. *One Frog Too Many*. New York: Dial Books for Young Readers. 25

Mazer, H. 1981. *The Island Keeper*. New York: Bantam Doubleday Dell Publishing Group, Inc.

———. 1998. *The Wild Kid*. New York: Simon & Schuster. 86

McCloskey, R. 1941. *Make Way for Ducklings*. New York: Viking. 75

McDonald, M. 1990. *Is This a House for Hermit Crab?* New York: Orchard Books. 29

McFarlane, S. 1991. *Waiting for the Whales*. Illustrated by Ron Lightburn. Victoria: Orca Book Publishers. 36

McGovern, A. 1967. *Too Much Noise*. New York: Scholastic Inc. 29

McKee, D. 1980. *Not Now Bernard*. London: Anderson Press.

McLellan, J. 1989. *The Birth of Nanabosho*. Winnipeg: Pemmican Publications Inc. 62

McMurty, S. 1977. *The Bunjee Venture*. New York: Scholastic, Inc. 99-100

McNaughton, J. 1996. *To Dance at the Palais Royale*. Toronto: Tuckamore Books. 103

McNicoll, S. 1988. *Blueberries and Whipped Cream*. Toronto: Gage JeanPac.

———. 1990. *Project Disaster*. Richmond Hill, Ontario: Scholastic Canada.

———. 1994. *Bringing Up Beauty*. Toronto: Maxwell Macmillan. 79, 91

———. 1996. *The Big Race*. Richmond Hill, Ontario: Scholastic Canada. 79

———. 1997. *Walking a Thin Line*. Richmond Hill, Ontario: Scholastic Canada.

Meeks, A.R. 1991. *Enora and the Black Crane*. Gosford, NSW, Australia: Ashton Scolastic. 127

Meyok, R. 1994. *Tiguyauyuq*. Coppermine, NWT: Kitikmeot Board of Education. 123

Miles, B. 1976. *All It Takes Is Practice*. New York: Alfred A. Knopf, Inc. 87

———. 1980. *Maudie and Me and the Dirty Book*. New York: Avon Camelot. 22

Miller, M. and N. Robinson. 1983. *T*A*C*K* into Danger*. New York: Scholastic Inc. 90

Milne, A.A. 1926. *Winnie the Pooh*. New York: Dutton. 95-96

Minarik, E. 1957. *Little Bear*. New York: Harper & Row Publishers.

Mochizuki, K. 1997. *Passage to Freedom: The Sugihara Story*. Illustrated by Dom Lee. New York: Lee and Low Books, Inc. 40

Mollel, T. 1990. *The Orphan Boy*. Illustrated by Paul Morin. Toronto: Oxford University Press. 125

———. 1992. *A Promise to the Sun*. Toronto: Little, Brown and Co.

———. 1995. *Big Boy*. Toronto: Stoddart Publishing.

———. 1997. *Kele's Secret*. Illustrated by Catherine Stock. Toronto: Stoddart Publishing.

Montgomery, L.M. 1995 (1908). *Anne of Green Gables*. Toronto: McClelland-Bantam. 76

Morck, I. 1996. *Tiger's New Cowboy Boots*. Illustrated by Georgia Graham. Red Deer, Alberta: Red Deer College Press. 33, 34

Morey, W. 1965. *Gentle Ben*. New York: Avon Books. 91

———. 1972. *Canyon Winter*. New York: Puffin Books. 84

———. 1973. *Runaway Stallion*. Hillsboro, Oregon: Blue Heron Publishing, Inc.

———. 1976. *Gloomy Gus*. Hillsboro, Oregon: Blue Heron Publising, Inc. 91

———. 1976. *Year of the Black Pony*. Hillsboro, Oregon: Blue Heron Publishing, Inc.

Morimoto, J. 1987. *My Hiroshima*. Sydney, Australia: Collins Publishers. 40-41

Mowat, F. 1961. *Owls in the Family*. Toronto: The Canadian Publishers. 91

Muller, R. 1982, 1995. *Mollie Whuppie and the Giant*. Buffalo: Firefly Books (U.S.) Inc. 56

———. 1985. *The Sorcerer's Apprentice*. Toronto: Kids Can Press.

———. 1989. *The Magic Paintbrush*. Toronto: Doubleday Canada.

———. 1994. *Little Wonder*. Richmond Hill, Ontario: North Winds Press.

Munsch, R. 1980. *The Paper Bag Princess*. Toronto: Annick Press.

———. 1985. *Thomas' Snowsuit*. Willowdale, Ontario: Annick Press.

———. 1989. *Giant: or, Waiting for the Thursday Boat*. Willowdale, Ontario: Annick Press.

——————— and M. Kusugak. 1988. *A Promise Is a Promise*. Toronto: Annick Press.

Murphy, B. 1991. *Experiment with Water*. Richmond Hill, Ontario. Scholastic. 139

Naidoo, B. 1986. *Journey to Jo'burg*. New York: HarperCollins Publishers. 87

Naylor, P. 1991. *Shiloh*. New York: Bantam Doubleday Dell Publishing Group, Inc. 91

———. 1996. *Shiloh Season*. New York: Atheneum.

———. 1997. *Saving Shiloh*. New York: Atheneum.

Neitzel, S. 1989. *The Jacket I Wear in the Snow*. New York: Greenwillow Books.29

Newman, L. 1989. *Heather Has Two Mommies*. Boston: Alyson Wonderland Publications. 21, 141

———. 1998. *Belinda's Bouquet*. Anola, Manitoba: Blue Heron Enterprises. 21

Nicholson, R. and C. Watts. 1991. *Ancient Egypt*. Richmond Hill, Ontario: Scholastic. 139

Ningeok, A., E. Ejetsiak, and M. Ipeelee. 1995. *Hituaqattaqta!* Iqaluit, NWT: Inuit Broadcasting Corporation. 123

Noyes, A. 1981. *The Highwayman*. Illustrated by Charles Mikolaycak. London: Oxford. 68

O'Brien, R. 1971. *Mrs. Frisby and the Rats of NIMH*. New York: Atheneum. 100

———. 1974. *Z for Zachariah*. New York: Aladdin Paperbacks. 103

O'Dell, S. 1960. *Island of the Blue Dolphins*. New York: Bantam Doubleday Dell Publishing Group, Inc.

———. 1970. *Sing Down the Moon*. New York: Bantam Doubleday Dell Publishing Group, Inc. 93

——————— and E. Hall. 1992. *Thunder Rolling in the Mountains*. New York: Bantam Doubleday Dell Publishing Group, Inc.93

o huigin, s. 1983. *The Ghost Horse of the Mounties*. Windsor, Ontario: Black Moss Press. 68

———. 1985. *Atmosfear*. Windsor, Ontario: Black Moss Press.68

———. 1989. *Monsters, He Mumbled*. Windsor, Ontario: Black Moss Press.

———. 1991. *King of the Birds*. Windsor, Ontario: Black Moss Press.

———. 1993. *A Dozen Million Spills (and Other Disasters)*. Windsor, Ontario: Black Moss Press.

Oberman, S. 1994. *The Always Prayer Shawl*. Illustrated by Ted Lewin. Honesdale, Pennsylvania: Boyds Mills Press. 116

Oliviero, J. and B. Morrisseau. 1993. *The Fish Skin*. Winnipeg: Hyperion Press. 58

Oppel, K. 1997. *Silverwing*. Scarborough, Ontario: HarperCollins. 95

Ormerod, J. 1990. *The Frog Prince*. Illustrated by David Lloyd. New York: Lothrop, Lee and Shepard.

Owen, M.B. 1990. *A Caribou Alphabet*. New York: Farrar, Straus & Giroux. 27

Oxenbury, H. 1983. *The ABC of Things*. New York: Delacorte. 27

Pachano, J. 1985. *The Changing Times: Baby William*. (One of a series of four books.) Chisabi, Quebec: James Bay Cree Cultural Education Centre.

Parks, R. 1980. *Playing Beatie Bow*. Ringwood, Australia: Penguin Books Australia, Ltd. 98

Paterson, K. 1977. *Bridge to Terabithia*. New York: HarperCollins. 84

———. 1980. *Jacob Have I Loved*. New York: Crowell. 103

———. 1988. *Park's Quest*. New York: Lodestar, Dutton.

———. 1992. *The King's Equal*. Illustrated by Vladimir Vagin. New York: Harper Collins Publishers. 58

Paul-Dene, S. 1992. *I Am the Eagle Free (Sky Song)*. Penticton, BC: Theytus Books.

Paulsen, G. 1977. *The Foxman*. New York: Scholastic, Inc. 183

———. 1983. *Popcorn Days and Buttermilk Nights*. New York: Puffin Books. 192-93

———. 1984. *Tracker*. New York: Bradbury Press. 183-84

———. 1987. *Hatchet*. New York: Bradbury Press. 85, 92

———. 1987. *The Crossing*. New York: Orchard Books. 83, 183

———. 1990. *Canyons*. New York: Bantam Doubleday Dell Publishing Group, Inc. 12, 103

———. 1991. *The River*. New York: Bantam Doubleday Dell Publishing Group, Inc. 85

———. 1992. *The Case of the Dirty Bird*. New York: Dell Publishing. 92

———. 1993. *Dunc and Amos Hit the Big Top*. New York: Bantam Doubleday Dell Books for Young Readers.

———. 1993. *Dunc Breaks the Record*. New York: Dell Publishing Inc. 92

———. 1995. *Amos Gets Married*. New York: Bantam Doubleday Dell Books for Young Readers.

———. 1996. *Dunc and Amos Go to the Dogs*. New York: Bantam Doubleday Dell Books for Young Readers.

———. 1996. *Brian's Winter*. New York: Delacorte Press. 85

———. 1997. *Dunc and Amos on Thin Ice*. New York: Dell Publishing.

———. 1999. *Brian's Return*. New York: Delacorte Press. 85

Pearce, P. 1958. *Tom's Midnight Garden*. London: Oxford University Press. 97

———. 1987. *Who's Afraid? and Other Strange Stories*. New York: Greenwillow.

Pearson, K. 1986. *The Daring Game*. Markham, Ontario: Puffin Books. 83, 93

———. 1987. *A Handful of Time*. Markham, Ontario: Viking Kestrel. 93, 99, 196

———. 1989. *The Sky Is Falling*. Markham, Ontario: Viking Kestrel. 94

———. 1996. *Awake and Dreaming*. Toronto: Viking. 94, 171-73

———. 1998. *This Land: A Cross Country Anthology of Canadian Fiction for Young Readers*. Toronto: Viking. 103

Phleger, P. 1963. *Pilot Down, Presumed Dead*. New York: Harper & Row, Publishers. 85

Pilon, A. 1972. *Concrete Is Not Always Hard*. New York: Xerox. 67

Piper, E. 1976. *The Magician's Trap*. Richmond Hill, Ontario: Scholastic-TAB Publications, Ltd. 78

Plain, F. 1993. *Amikoonse (Little Beaver)*. Winnipeg: Pemmican Publications Inc.

Potter, B. 1903. *The Tale of Peter Rabbit*. London: Frederick Warne and Co.

Poulsen, D. 1996. *Billy and the Bearman*. Toronto: Napoleon Publishing. 103, 157

Prelutsky, J. 1984. *The New Kid on the Block*. New York: Greenwillow Books.

———, ed. 1983. *The Random House Book of Poetry*. New York: Random House.

Priest, R. 1993. *The Ballad of the Blue Bonnet*. Toronto: Groundwood Books. 67

———. 1993. *Day Songs, Night Songs*. Toronto: Groundwood Books.

———. 1994. *A Terrible Case of the Stars*. Toronto: Penguin Books Canada.

Pullman, P. 1995. *The Golden Compass*. New York: Ballantine Books.

Quackenbush, R. 1975. *Skip to My Lou*. Philadelphia: Lippincott. 147

———. 1976. *Pop! Goes the Weasel and Yankee Doodle*. Philadelphia: Lippincott. 147

Reiss, J. 1972. *The Upstairs Room*. New York: Scholastic, Inc. 87

Reynolds, M. and B. Garr. 1973. *John Goes Hunting: A Chipwyan Story and Language Lessons*. Saskatoon: Saskatchewan Indian Cultural College.

Richler, M. 1975. *Jacob Two-Two Meets the Hooded Fang*. Toronto: Puffin Books. 77

———. 1987. *Jacob Two-Two and the Dinosaur*. Toronto: Puffin Books. 77

———. 1995. *Jacob Two-Two's First Spy Case*. Toronto: McClelland & Stewart, Inc. 77-78

Ripley, C. 1995. *Do the Doors Open by Magic? and Other Supermarket Questions*. Toronto: Owl Books. 144

———. 1996. *Why Do Stars Twinkle at Night? and Other Nightime Questions*. Toronto: Owl Books. 144

Rising, T. and P. Williams. 1994. *Light Magic and Other Science Activities About Energy*. Toronto: Owl (Greey de Pencier Books, Inc). 137-38

Roberts, K. 1987. *Pop Bottles*. Vancouver: Douglas & McIntyre Limited. 78

———. 1988. *Hiccup Champion of the World*. Vancouver: Douglas & McIntyre Limited. 78

Roberts, W.D. 1988. *Megan's Island*. New York: Macmillan Publishing Company. 90, 181

Rounds, G. 1993. *The Three Billy Goats Gruff*. New York: Holiday House.

Rowling, J.K. 1997. *Harry Potter and the Philosopher's Stone*. London: Bloomsbury Publishing Plc. 96

———. 1998. *Harry Potter and the Chamber of Secrets*. London: Bloomsbury Publishing Plc. 97

———. 1999. *Harry Potter and the Prisoner of Azkaban*. Vancouver: Raincoast Books. 97

Roy, R. 1982. *Where's Buddy?* New York: Scholastic Inc. 80

Ruane, J. 1990. *Boats, Boats, Boats*. Chicago: Children's Press.

Ruckman, I. 1984. *Night of the Twisters*. New York: HarperCollins Publishers. 84

Rylant, C. ———. 1985. *Every Living Thing*. New York: Macmillan Publishing Company.

———. 1985. *The Relatives Came*. New York: Aladdin Paperbacks. 32

———. 1986. *Night in the Country*. New York: Bradbury Press.

———. 1990. *Henry and Mudge and the Happy Cat*. New York: Bradbury Press.

———. 1992. *Missing May*. New York: Orchard. 84

Sachar, L. 1987. *There's a Boy in the Girls' Bathroom*. New York: Alfred A. Knopf, Inc. 83

San Souci, D. 1987. *Short and Shivery: Thirty Chilling Tales*. New York: Doubleday.

———. 1990. *North Country Night*. New York: Bantam Doubleday Dell Books for Young Readers. 32

Sandburg, C. 1993. *Arithmetic*. Illustrated by Ted Rand. New York: Harcourt Brace. 68

Sanderson, E. 1990. *Two Pairs of Shoes*. Winnipeg: Pemmican Publications Inc. 121

Sanderson, R. 1990. *The Twleve Dancing Princesses*. New York: Little Brown.

Say, A. 1993. *Grandfather's Journey*. Boston: Houghton Mifflin Company. 32

Scarry, R. 1972. *Hop Aboard! Here We Go!* New York: Golden Books.

Schwartz, A. 1981. *Scary Stories to Tell in the Dark*. New York: HarperCollins.

Scieszka, J. 1989. *The True Story of the Three Little Pigs*. New York: Scholastic. 11, 56, 155

———. 1991. *Knights of the Kitchen Table*. New York: Puffin Books.

———. 1991. *The Not-So-Jolly-Roger*. New York: Puffin Books.

———. 1992. *The Good, the Bad, and the Goofy*. New York: Puffin Books.

———. 1993. *Your Mother Was a Neanderthal*. New York: Puffin Books.

———. 1995. *2095*. New York: Puffin Books.

———. 1996. *Tut Tut*. New York: Viking.

Scribe, M. 1988. *Murdo's Story*. Winnipeg: Pemmican Publications. 122

Segel, E., ed. 1986. *Short Takes: A Short Story Collection for Young Readers*. New York: Lothrop.

Sendak, M. 1963. *Where the Wild Things Are*. New York: Harper & Row, Publishers. 31, 75

———. 1970. *In the Night Kitchen*. New York: Harper & Row.

Service, R.W. 1987. *The Cremation of Sam McGee*. Illustrated by Ted Harrison. New York: Greenwillow. 66-67

Seuss, Dr. (Theodor Geisel). 1957. *The Cat in the Hat*. New York: Random House.

Sewell, A. 1988 (1877). *Black Beauty*. Chicago: World Book Inc.75, 76

Sharmat, M. 1978. *Nate the Great and the Sticky Case*. New York: Coward-McCann.

———. 1985. *Nate the Great and the Fishy Prize*. New York: Dell Publishing Co., Inc.

———. 1992. *Nate the Great and the Stolen Base*. New York: Harcourt and Brace.

———. 1995. *Nate the Great and the Tardy Tortoise*. New York: Delacorte Press.

Shaw, C. 1947. *It Looked Like Spilt Milk*. New York: HarperCollins Publishers. 29

Sherman, G. 1994. *King of the Class*. Richmond Hill, Ontario: Scholastic Canada. 79

Shreve, S. 1987. *Lucy Forever and Miss Rosetree, Shrinks*. New York: Alfred A. Knopf, Inc. 90

Shura, M.F. 1989. *The Mystery at Wolf River*. New York: Scholastic Inc. 90-91

Sidney, M. 1962, 1881. *The Five Little Peppers and How They Grew*. New York: Macmillan. 76

Silverstein, S. 1974. *Where the Sidewalk Ends*. New York: Harper & Row.

———. 1981. *A Light in the Attic*. New York: Harper & Row.

Silverthorne, J. 1996. *The Secret of Sentinel Rock*. Regina: Coteau Books. 98

Simmie, L. 1995. *Mister Got To Go*. Red Deer, Alberta: Red Deer College Press. 17, 32

Smith, D.B. 1973. *A Taste of Blackberries*. New York: Scholastic Inc. 80

Smith, R.K. 1984. *The War with Grandpa*. New York: Bantam Doubleday Dell Publishing Group, Inc. 82

Smucker, B. 1977. *Underground to Canada*. Toronto: Clarke, Irwin. 87, 94, 166-67

Sokwaypnace, N. 1979. *What Is It Like To Be an Indian?* Saskatoon: Saskatchewan Indian Cultural College.

Soto, G. 1990. *Baseball in April, and Other Stories*. New York: Harcourt.

Spalding, A. 1995. *Finders Keepers*. Victoria: Beach Holme Publishing. 82-83, 115-16

———. 1988. *The Most Beautiful Kite in the World*. Red Deer, Alberta: Red Deer College Press.

Speare, E.G. 1983. *Sign of the Beaver*. New York: Bantam Doubleday Dell Publishing Group, Inc. 94

Sperry, A. 1940. *Call It Courage*. New York: Macmillan. 180-81

Spinelli, G. 1990. *Maniac Magee*. Boston: Little, Brown and Co., Inc. 83

Spyri, J. 1962, 1884. *Heidi*. New York: Macmillan. 76

Steig, W. 1976. *The Amazing Bone*. New York: Farrar, Straus & Giroux.

———. 1984. *Doctor DeSoto*. New York: Scholastic. 195

Stevenson, R.L. 1981/1883. *Treasure Island*. New York: Macmillan. 75

———. 1990. *My Shadow*. Illustrated by Ted Rand. New York: Putnam.

Stinson, K. 1997. *One Year Commencing*. Saskatoon: Thistledown Press Ltd. 82

Sutcliff, R. 1958. *Warrior Scarlet*. Harmondsworth, UK: Puffin Books. 93

Sutton, R. 1990. *Car (Eyewitness Guides)*. London: Dorling Kindersley. 146

Suzuki, D. 1994. *Nature All Around Series*. Toronto: Stoddart Publishing. 140

Swanson, D. 1994. *Safari Beneath the Sea*. Vancouver: Whitecap Books. 135-36

———. 1996. *Buffalo Sunrise*. Vancouver: Whitecap Books.

———. 1997. *Bug Bites*. Vancouver: Whitecap Books.

———. 1998. *Animals Eat the Weirdest Things*. Vancouver: Whitecap Books.

Swindells, R. 1993. *Stone Cold*. Toronto: Penguin. 12

Tanaka, S. 1993. *The Disaster of the Hindenburg*. Richmond Hill, Ontario: Scholastic/Time Quest. 9, 137

Tashjian, J. 1997. *Tru Confessions*. New York: Scholastic Inc. 86

Taylor, C. 1985. *Julie*. Saskatoon: Western Producer Prairie Books. 99

———. 1987. *The Doll*. Toronto: Douglas & McIntyre. 17, 98, 99

———. 1994. *Summer of the Mad Monk*. Vancouver: Greystone Books. 99

Taylor, C.J. 1994. *Bones in the Basket*. Montreal: Tundra Books.

Taylor, M. 1976. *Roll of Thunder, Hear My Cry*. New York: Puffin Books. 87

———. 1987. *The Friendship*. New York: Puffin Books.

———. 1997. *Three Against Time*. Victoria: Orca Book Publishers. 98-99

Taylor, T. 1969. *The Cay*. New York: Avon Books.

———. 1981. *The Trouble with Tuck*. New York: Avon Books. 91

———. 1991. *Tuck Triumphant*. New York: Avon Books. 91

Thomas, D. 1997. *Fern Hill*. Red Deer, Alberta: Red Deer College Press.

Thomas, G. and K. Crossley-Holland. 1985. *Tales from the Mabinogian*. New York: Overlook Press. 60, 94

Thomasma, K. 1983. *Naya Nuki: Shoshoni Girl Who Ran Away*. Jackson, Wyoming: Grandview Publishing Company. 195-96

Tolkien, J.R.R. 1937. *The Hobbit*. Boston: Houghton.

Toten, T. 1995. *The Onlyhouse*. Red Deer, Alberta: Red Deer College Press.83

Trembath, D. 1996. *The Tuesday Café*. Victoria: Orca Book Publishers. 102

Tripp, N. 1994. *Thunderstorm!* Illustrated by Juan Wijngaard. New York: Dial Books. 141

Trivizas, E. 1993. *The Three Little Wolves and the Big Bad Pig*. London: William Heinemann Ltd. 11, 56

Trottier, M. 1998. *Prairie Willow*. Illustrated by Laura Fernandez and Rick Jacobson. Toronto: Stoddart Kids. 35

Truss, J. 1982. *Jasmin*. Vancouver: Douglas & MacIntyre (Groundwood). 82, 178

Turkle, B. 1976. *Deep in the Forest*. New York: Dutton Children's Books. 26

Turner, G. 1993. *Opposites*. New York: Viking Press.

Turner, M.W. 1995. *Instead of Three Wishes*. New York: Greenwillow.

Twain, M. 1963, 1885. *The Adventures of Huckleberry Finn*. New York: Washington Square Press. 113

Uchida, Y. 1978. *Journey Home*. New York: Aladdin Paperbacks. 87, 93

Vaage, C. 1995. *Bibi and the Bull*. Edmonton: Dragon Hill Press. 34

Valentine, J. 1994. *One Dad, Two Dads, Brown Dads, Blue Dads*. Boston: Alyson Wonderland Publications. 21

Van Allsburg, C. 1984. *The Mysteries of Harris Burdick*. New York: Houghton Mifflin Company. 161

———. 1987. *The Z Was Zapped*. New York: Houghton Mifflin Company. 65

———. C. 1992. *The Widow's Broom*. New York: Houghton Mifflin.

Vivas, J. 1985. *The Grandma Poss Cookbook*. Adelaide, Australia: Omnibus Books. 143-44

Voigt, C. 1981. *Homecoming*. New York: Atheneum. 103

Waboose, J. 1997. *Morning on the Lake*. Toronto: Kids Can Press Ltd.

Waddell, M. 1986. *The Tough Princess*. Illustrated by Peter Benson. London: Walker Books. 57-58

———. 1992. *Can't You Sleep, Little Bear?* Cambridge: Candlewick Press.

———. 1994. *The Big Big Sea*. Illustrated by Jennifer Eachus. Cambridge: Candlewick Press. 30

Wagner, J. 1978. *John Brown, Rose and the Midnight Cat*. New York: Bradbury.

Wallace. I. 1984. *Chin Chiang and the Dragon's Dance*. Toronto: Groundwood (Douglas & McIntyre. 44

———. 1994. *Hansel and Gretel*. Toronto: Douglas & McIntyre. 57

———. 1997. *A Winter's Tale*. Toronto: Groundwood. 44, 57

———. 1999. *Boy of the Deeps*. Toronto: Groundwood.44, 57

Walsh, A. 1994. *Shabash!* Victoria: Beach Holme Publishing Company. 81, 87

Weber-Pillwax, C. 1989. *Billy's World*. Edmonton: Reidmore.

Westcott, N. 1988. *The Lady with the Alligator Purse*. Boston: Little, Brown and Co.

———. 1989. *Skip to My Lou*. Boston: Joy Street Books. 147

Whatley, B. and R. Smith. 1994. *Whatley's Quest: An Alphabet Adventure*. Sydney, Australia: Angus and Robertson. 28

White, E.B. 1945. *Stuart Little*. New York: Harper & Row, Publishers. 95

———. 1952. *Charlotte's Web*. New York: Harper & Row. 94-95, 157, 189-90

———. 1970. *The Trumpet of the Swan*. New York: Harper & Row, Publishers. 95

Whitstone, R. 1979. *The Fur Coat*. Saskatoon: Saskatchewan Indian Cultural College.

Wieler, D. 1989. *Bad Boy*. Toronto: Douglas & McIntyre. 102

Wiesner, D. 1988. *Free Fall*. New York: Lothrop, Lee and Shepard.

———. 1991. *Tuesday*. New York: Clarion. 25

———. 1992. *June 29, 1999*. Boston: Houghton Mifflin. 39

Wild, M. 1991. *Let the Celebrations Begin!* Illustrated by Julie Vivas. Adelaide, Australia: Omnibus Books. 39-40

Willhoite, M. 1990. *Daddy's Roommate*. Boston: Alyson Wonderland Publications. 21, 141

Williams, L. 1986. *The Little Old Lady Who Was Not Afraid of Anything*. New York: Crowell. 29

Williams, M. 1922. *The Velveteen Rabbit*. New York: Doubleday. 95

Williams, S. 1989. *I Went Walking*. New York: Harcourt Brace and Company. 28-29

Wilson, B. 1995. *Harold and Harold*. Porters Lake, Nova Scotia: Pottersfield Press.78

Wilson, E. 1983. *The Kootenay Kidnapper*. Don Mills: Collins Publishers.

———. 1992. *Lost Treasure of Casa Loma*. Toronto: Stoddart Publishing.

———. 1995. *The Inuk Mountie*. Toronto: HarperCollins Canada Ltd.

———. 1996. *Cold Midnight in Vieux Quebec*. Toronto: HarperCollins Canada Ltd.

Winthrop, E. 1985. *The Castle in the Attic*. New York: Bantam Skylark. 95, 192

———. 1993. *The Battle for the Castle*. New York: Bantam Doubleday Dell Books for Young Readers. 95

Wiseman, E. 1996. *A Place Not Home*. Toronto: Stoddart Publishing Co. Limited.

Wood, A. 1984. *The Napping House*. San Diego: Harcourt Brace and Company. 29

Wood, D. 1985. *King Bidgood's in the Bathtub*. New York: Harcourt Brace and Company. 29

Wood, J. 1992. *The Man Who Loved Clowns*. New York: Putnam. 86

Woods, A. 1982. *As Quick as a Cricket*. New York: Child's Play International Ltd.

Wyatt, V. 1993. *The Science Book for Girls and Other Intelligent Beings*. Toronto: Kids Can Press. 144

Wynne-Jones, T. 1983. *Zoom at Sea*. Toronto: Groundwood (Douglas & McIntyre. 38

———. 1985. *Zoom Away*. Toronto: Groundwood (Douglas & McIntyre). 38

———. 1992. *Zoom Upstream*. Toronto: Groundwood (Douglas & McIntyre). 38

———. 1993. *Some of the Kinder Planets*. Toronto: Groundwood (Douglas & McIntyre). 103

———. 1994. *The Book of Changes*. Toronto: Groundwood.

———. 1995. *The Maestro*. Toronto: Groundwood Books. 102, 156

———. 1998. *Stephen Fair*. Toronto: Groundwood.

———. 1999. *Lord of the Fries and Other Stories*. Toronto: Groundwood.

Yee, P. 1983. *Teach Me to Fly, Skyfighter!* Toronto: Lorimer. 115

———. 1986. *The Curses of Third Uncle*. Toronto: James Lorimer and Co., Publishers. 115

———. 1988. *Saltwater City: An Illustrated History of the Chinese in Vancouver*. Vancouver: Douglas & McIntyre.

———. 1989. *Tales from Gold Mountain*. Illustrated by S. Ng. Toronto: Groundwood Books.

———.1991. *Roses Sing on New Snow*. Illustrated by Harvey Chan. Toronto: Groundwood Books. 114-15, 115

———. 1994. *Breakaway*. Toronto: Groundwood.

———. 1995. *Moonlight Luck*. Toronto: Macmillan.

———. 1996. *The Ghost Train*. Illustrated by Harvey Chan. Toronto: Groundwood Books. 115

Yerxa, L. 1993. *Last Leaf First Snowflake to Fall*. Toronto: Groundwood Books. 120

Yolen, J. 1987. *Owl Moon*. New York: Philomel Books. 32

———. 1992. *Encounter*. New York: Voyager Books (Harcourt Brace). 126

Yolen, Jo, M. Greenberg, and C. Waugh. 1986. *Dragons and Dreams: A Collection of New Fantasy and Science Fiction Stories*. New York: Harper.

York, C. 1986. *Secrets in the Attic*. New York: Scholastic, Inc. 90

Yost, E. 1982. *The Mad Queen of Mordra*. Richmond Hill, Ontario: Scholastic Books Canada. 102

INDEX

Note: The authors and titles of works listed in the Children's Literature References are not included in this index. The page numbers for those works discussed in the text have been added to the individual titles in the References. The names of authors and illustrators are, however, included below when reference is made to their work in general, and not to specific titles.